372.190973
G46c

142469

DATE DUE			

Curriculum Leadership

Curriculum Leadership

Allan A. Glatthorn
Professor of Education
University of Pennsylvania

Scott, Foresman and Company
Glenview, Illinois   London

Library of Congress Cataloging-in-Publication Data

Glatthorn, Allan A., 1924–
  Curriculum leadership.

  Includes bibliographies and indexes.
  1. Education, Elementary—United States—
Curricula.   2. Curriculum planning—United States.
3. Curriculum evaluation.   I. Title.
LB1570.G56   1987   372.19 '0973   86–29761
ISBN 0–673–18267–3

    1 2 3 4 5 6 KPF 91 90 89 88 87

Also Available from
Scott, Foresman and Company
Good Year Books

Good Year Books are reproducible resource and activity
books for teachers and parents of students in preschool
through grade 12. Written by experienced educators, Good
Year Books are filled with class-tested ideas, teaching
strategies and methods, and fun-to-do activities for every
basic curriculum area. They also contain enrichment
materials and activities that help extend a child's learning
experiences beyond the classroom.

Good Year Books address many educational needs in both
formal and informal settings. They have been used widely
in preservice teacher training courses, as a resource for
practicing teachers to enhance their own professional
growth, and by interested adults as a source of sound,
valuable activities for home, summer camp, Scout meetings,
and the like.

Good Year Books are available through your local college or
university bookstore, independent or chain booksellers, and
school supply and educational dealers. For a complete
catalog of Good Year Books, write:

Good Year Books
Department PPG-T
1900 East Lake Avenue
Glenview, Illinois 60025

Preface

This book is intended for those presently functioning as curriculum leaders and those preparing for such roles. Its central intent is to provide such readers with the knowledge and the skills needed to exercise leadership in curriculum at several levels and in many roles.

To that end it begins by exploring the foundations of the field, so that decisions are made from a broad perspective and with a deep knowledge. The first chapter establishes the central concepts used throughout the work, explaining the general concept of curriculum and explicating its essential elements; the goal of this chapter is to provide the reader with a set of conceptual tools. The second chapter reviews the past one hundred years of curriculum history, so that decision makers can see the problems and solutions of the present from an informed historical perspective. The third chapter surveys the several types of curriculum theory, since good theory provides deeper insight about the complex relationships involved in all curriculum work. The final chapter of this "foundations" section examines the politics of curriculum work—the way that power and influence affect curriculum decision making at the federal, state, and local levels.

The second section turns to processes. The general goal of this section is to help the reader acquire the skills needed to bring about major curricular change. The section begins with an overview of the curriculum-planning process. Then separate chapters deal with the more specific processes involved in improving and developing the three levels of curricula—programs of study, fields of study, and courses and units of study.

The third section of the book is concerned with the management of curriculum. If curricula are to be truly effective, they must be managed well. Chapter 9 suggests specific ways in which the leader can supervise both the instructional processes and the selection and use of materials—the "taught" and the "supported" curriculum, to use the constructs employed throughout this work. Chapter 10 surveys what is known about effective curriculum implementation and recommends specific processes for implementing curricula effectively. The next chapter provides a rationale for and explains the processes used in aligning the curriculum—ensuring that the written, the taught, the tested, and the learned curricula are brought into closer alignment. The last chapter of this section reviews several models for evaluating the curriculum and makes specific suggestions for developing and implementing a comprehensive evaluation plan.

The book closes with a section on curricular trends. Chapter 13 examines trends in the subject fields; Chapter 14, trends across the curriculum, including the use of computers. The book ends with an examination of current approaches to individualize and adapt the curriculum for learners with special needs.

Several colleagues and students have assisted me by recommending sources, locating and supplying materials, and reviewing portions of the manuscript. I especially wish to acknowledge the assistance received from the following: Elaine Atkins; Joseph Blass; G. Michael Davis; Helen Felsenthal; Barbara Freed; Frank Finan; Beverly Goodloe-Kaplan; Nancy Hornberger; Eugene Howard; Curtis Howard; Jacqueline Marino; Louise Mayock; Albert Oliver; Tere Pica; Ryda Rose; and Marcia Witlin.

I have also benefited greatly from the assistance and support of my editors at Scott, Foresman, especially Christopher Jennison, who initially encouraged me to undertake the work. I also profited greatly from the constructive reviews of Charles Allen, University of Pittsburgh; Victor Dupuis, Pennsylvania State University; Robert Pinney, Western Washington University; and James Walter, University of Nebraska. Finally, I wish to acknowledge the continuing and supportive help received from my wife and colleague, Barbara, to whom this work is dedicated.

Allan A. Glatthorn

Contents

Part 3   Curriculum Management

Part 1

Foundations of Curriculum

1

The Nature of Curriculum

The intent of this introductory chapter is essentially to provide the reader with a general overview of the curriculum field and a set of concepts for analyzing that field. To accomplish these related goals, the discussion that follows focuses on these outcomes: defining the concept of *curriculum*, examining the several types of curricula, describing the contrasting nature of curriculum components, and analyzing the hidden curriculum. In this manner some fundamental concepts essential for understanding the comprehensive field of curriculum can be established at the outset.

THE CONCEPT OF CURRICULUM

In a sense, the task of defining the concept is perhaps the most difficult of all, for the term *curriculum* has been used with quite different meanings ever since the field took form. To understand the nature and extent of that diversity, it might be useful at this juncture to examine the definitions offered by some of the leaders in the field. The definitions in the list below, which are arranged chronologically, have been chosen simply for their representativeness.

> John Dewey (1902). . . . the child and the curriculum are simply two limits which define a single process. . . . It is a continuous reconstruction, moving from the child's present experience out into that represented by the organized bodies of truth that we call studies. . . . the various studies . . . are themselves experience—they are that of the race. (pp. 11, 12)

1

Franklin Bobbitt (1918). The curriculum may, therefore, be defined in two ways: (1) it is the entire range of experiences, both directed and undirected, concerned in unfolding the abilities of the individual; or (2) it is the series of consciously directed training experiences that the schools use for completing and perfecting the unfoldment. Our profession uses the term usually in the latter sense. But as education is coming more and more to be seen as a thing of experiences . . . the line of demarcation between directed and undirected experience is rapidly disappearing. (p. 43)

National Society for the Study of Education Yearbook Committee (Rugg, 1927). [The curriculum is] a succession of experiences and enterprises having a maximum lifelikeness for the learner . . . giving the learner that development most helpful in meeting and controlling life situations.

Hollis Caswell (Caswell and Campbell, 1935). The curriculum is composed of all the experiences children have under the guidance of teachers. . . . Thus, curriculum considered as a field of study represents no strictly limited body of content, but rather a process or procedure. (pp. 66, 70)

Ralph Tyler (1957). [The curriculum is] all the learning experiences planned and directed by the school to attain its educational goals. (p. 79)

Hilda Taba (1962). All curricula . . . are composed of certain elements. A curriculum usually contains a statement of aims and of specific objectives; it indicates some selection and organization of content; it either implies or manifests certain patterns of learning and teaching. . . . Finally, it includes a program of evaluation of the outcomes. (p. 11)

Robert Gagne (1967). Curriculum is a sequence of content units arranged in such a way that the learning of each unit may be accomplished as a single act, provided the capabilities described by specified prior units (in the sequence) have already been mastered by the learner. (p. 23)

James Popham and Eva Baker (1970). [Curriculum is] all planned learning *outcomes* for which the school is responsible. . . . curriculum refers to the desired *consequences* of instruction. (p. 48)

Michael Schiro (1978). . . . we will use the word curriculum to mean "that output of the curriculum development process that is intended for use in planning instruction." (p. 28)

J. Galen Saylor and William Alexander (Saylor, Alexander, and Lewis, 1981). We define curriculum as a plan for providing sets of learning opportunities for persons to be educated. (p. 8)

Observe that these definitions vary primarily in their breadth and emphasis. Some construe curriculum broadly—all the experiences a learner has in school. Others see it more narrowly—a plan or a set of outcomes. They vary also in emphasis: Dewey emphasizes it as a means of systematically transmitting the cultural experience of the race; Schiro stresses its utilitarian value for curriculum workers, noting in his work that the cultural transmission function is only one of several possible orientations.

It would seem that a useful definition of curriculum should meet two criteria: it should reflect the general understanding of the term as used by educators; and it should be useful to educators in making operational distinctions. With these two criteria in mind, the following definition is offered and will be used in this work:

> The curriculum is the plans made for guiding learning in the schools, usually represented in retrievable documents of several levels of generality, and the actualization of those plans in the classroom, as experienced by the learners and as recorded by an observer; those experiences take place in a learning environment which also influences what is learned.

Several points in this definition perhaps need to be emphasized. First, it suggests that the term *curriculum* includes both the plans made for learning and the actual learning experiences provided. Limiting the term to the plans made for learning is not enough, since, as will be discussed below, those plans are often ignored or modified. Second, the phrase "retrievable documents" is sufficiently broad in its denotation to include curricula stored in computer software, a storage and distribution method which will probably be increasingly used in the future. Also, those documents, as will be more fully explained below, are of several levels of specificity: some, such as curricular policy statements, are very general in their formulation; others, such as daily lesson plans, are quite specific.

Next, the definition notes two key dimensions of the actualized curriculum: the curriculum as experienced by the learner, and that which might be observed by a disinterested observer. The last point serves to remind curriculum workers that the teacher is usually not a reliable source of information about that which was actually taught. As Goodlad (1979) notes, "What teachers perceive the curriculum of their classrooms to be and what they actually are teaching may be quite different things" (p. 62). Finally, the experienced curriculum takes place in an environment which influences and impinges upon learning, constituting what is usually termed the "hidden curriculum."

Although the definition, for the sake of brevity, does not deal explicitly with the relationship between curriculum and instruction, there is an implicit relationship. Instruction is viewed here as an aspect of curriculum, whose function and importance change throughout the several types of curricula. First, in the written curriculum, when the curriculum is a set of documents that guide planning, instruction is only one relatively minor aspect of the curriculum. Those retrievable documents used in planning for learning typically specify five components: a rationale for the curriculum; the aims, the objectives, and the content for achieving those objectives; instructional methods; learning materials and resources; and tests or assessment methods. And instruction as a component of the planned curriculum is usually seen as less important than the aims, objectives, and content.

At the actualized level, when the planned or written curriculum is actually delivered, instruction takes on a new importance. The supervisor or administrator observing the curriculum as the total learning experiences of that classroom seems to focus on instruction—how the teacher is teaching. Often the objectives are subsumed as part of instruction: Does the teacher specify the learning objective, and is that objective appropriate for the learners? And a new component is added now: the learning environment or classroom climate. The learning materials and resources and the tests and assessment methods are usually given only superficial attention. Instruction is now the focus. The other components are seen simply as background factors against which instruction occurs.

THE TYPES OF CURRICULA

The definition stipulated above suggests that there is a major difference between the planned curriculum and the actualized curriculum. Yet even these distinctions are not sufficiently precise to encompass the several different types of curricula. Here Goodlad (1979) was perhaps the first to suggest several key distinctions. As he analyzed curricula, he determined that there were five different forms of curriculum planning. The *ideological* curriculum is the ideal curriculum as construed by scholars and teachers—a curriculum of ideas intended to reflect funded knowledge. Goodlad cites the national curriculum projects of the 1960s (such as PSSC, SMSG, BSCS) as examples of the ideological curriculum. The *formal* curriculum is that officially approved by state and local school boards—the sanctioned curriculum that represents society's interests. The *perceived* curriculum is the "curriculum of the mind"—what teachers, parents, and others think the curriculum to be. The *operational* curriculum is the observed curriculum—what actually goes on hour after hour in the classroom. And the *experiential* curriculum is what the learners actually experience.

While those distinctions in general seem important, the terms are perhaps a bit cumbersome and the classifications are not entirely useful to curriculum workers. It seems to be more useful in the present context to use the following concepts with some slightly different denotations: the recommended curriculum; the written curriculum; the supported curriculum; the taught curriculum; the tested curriculum; and the learned curriculum. Four of these curricula—the written, the supported, the taught, and the tested—are considered components of the intentional curriculum. The intentional curriculum is the set of learnings which the school system consciously intends, in contradistinction to the hidden curriculum, which by and large is not a product of conscious intention.

The Recommended Curriculum   The recommended curriculum is that curriculum which is recommended by individual scholars, professional associations, and reform commissions; it also encompasses the curriculum requirements of policy-making groups, such as federal and state governments. Similar to Goodlad's "ideological curriculum," it is a curriculum that stresses "oughtness," identifying the skills and concepts that ought to be emphasized, according to the perceptions and value systems of the sources. Recommended curricula typically are formulated at a rather high level of generality; they are most often presented as policy recommendations, lists of goals, suggested graduation requirements, and general recommendations about the content and sequence of a field of study, such as mathematics.

Several influences seem to play key roles in the shaping of recommended curricula. First, societal trends seem to have a strong influence on policy makers. The prevailing conservative mood of the 1980s in the United States and the concern about competing with Japan were undoubtedly factors that influenced many of the reform reports of that period. Second, advancements in technology seem to play a role: the widespread use of computers in the school probably influenced several of the professional associations to include some aspect of computer education in their recommendations.

Also, professional associations and individuals seem to have an impact. First, the professional associations representing the several disciplines, such as the National Council of Teachers of Mathematics, and those that represent administrators, such as the National Association for Secondary School Principals, have been active in producing recommended curricula. Also, there seems to be a network of opinion shapers in the profession, who through their writing and consulting have a strong impact on recommended curricula as they attempt to translate the latest research into recommendations for content and methodology. A good example here is the work of McCarthy (1981) on learning styles and the curriculum. Her extensive consulting seems to have reached a large audience of curriculum leaders who used her constructs in recommending curricula that would be responsive to learning-style differences. Such opinion shapers play a key role in translating new knowledge into specific curricular recommendations.

Finally, as will be discussed in Chapter 4, federal and state legislation and court decrees seem to play a part. Public Law 94-142, requiring the "least restrictive environment" for handicapped pupils, had a profound influence on all those developing recommended curricula for this group of learners.

Those recommended curricula serve some useful functions. First, as recommendations about policies and requirements, they identify important boundaries, emphases, and endpoints for curriculum planning: "All high school students should study one semester of computer science." Second, they attempt to synthesize the best that is known about current practice: "Leaders in the field recommend that formal grammar not be emphasized in elementary language arts." (Unfortunately, they are often rather selective and somewhat biased in their use of that research.) Finally, the best of them raise the sights of curriculum workers by suggesting what the curriculum ideally might become. For example, the theories of James Moffett (1968) about the "universe of discourse" seemed to make a significant impact on the thinking of curriculum leaders in English language arts, even though they seemed to have difficulty translating his theories into curricular models.

However, those recommended curricula also have some serious limitations which restrict their usefulness for curriculum workers. Consider, for example, one recommended curriculum published under the aegis of the Commission of the Curriculum of the National Council of Teachers of English. Terming the curriculum a "new heritage model," the author (Evertts, 1980) makes these recommendations as to what the teacher should do in developing the "new heritage model":

1. Choose a suitable number of themes or topics; a first-grade theme might be "animals."
2. Involve the students in locating resources and planning the units.
3. Expand the topics through discussion, to accommodate the special interests of the child.
4. Read to the children many selections from children's literature that relate to the theme.
5. Encourage children to explore literature on their own.
6. Conduct class and small group discussions on the literature.
7. Help the children master the conventions of writing.
8. Encourage children to use the literary selections as models for their own writing.
9. Set up learning centers.
10. Use literature to stimulate the imagination, encouraging improvisation, choral reading, and puppet shows.
11. Use media to expand the topic.
12. Have small groups prepare learning modules for their peers.
13. Have the librarian and other adults visit the class to tell stories.
14. Structure for each unit a culminating activity in which students explain their activities and share their products with each other and with parents.

This particular recommended curriculum has several weaknesses which seem common to many recommended curricula. First, the curriculum suggestions as outlined here seem insensitive to the realities of the classroom world and the ways that teachers conceptualize planning. For example, teachers are advised not to ask questions in a class discussion of literature until the students have ceased to volunteer ideas—a suggestion that most elementary teachers would wisely be very reluctant to adopt. The suggestion given here actually is in conflict with what the research would suggest: teacher questions facilitate the discussion of literature and increase comprehension. (See, for example, the 1985 report of the Commission on Reading.) Second, very little empirical evidence is advanced to support the components of the model; the author notes only that several writers agree with her about the importance of traditional literature in the schools.

Finally, the recommendations are somewhat general; the teacher or curriculum worker searching for guidance on the appropriate placement of units, for example, is given only very general suggestions:

> *First grade themes, for example, could be animals or nature. In the sixth grade, the teacher could consider the Middle Ages, Egyptian art, volcanoes, or conflict. Other topics might be inventions, sports, geographical places, or aspects of the human experience, such as loneliness, fear, death, humor.* (p. 37)

This is not to be unduly critical of this author's effort. She includes some useful suggestions about how to develop teacher-planned units and some helpful recommendations about the use of children's literature. The example is used simply to illustrate some of the limitations of recommended curricula—limitations that have caused most classroom teachers to ignore the recommended curriculum.

The Written Curriculum   The written curriculum, as the term is used here, is the curriculum embodied in approved state and district curriculum guides. Generally similar to Goodlad's "formal curriculum," the written curriculum seems intended primarily to ensure that the educational goals of the system are being accomplished; it is a curriculum of control. Typically, the written curriculum is much more specific and comprehensive than the recommended curriculum, indicating a rationale which supports the curriculum, the general goals to be accomplished, the specific objectives to be mastered, the sequence in which those objectives should be studied, and the kinds of learning activities which should be used. Note, however, that Glatthorn (1980) questions such comprehensiveness; he recommends that the written curriculum should be delivered to teachers as a looseleaf notebook, containing only a scope and sequence chart, a review of the research, a list of course objectives, and a brief list of materials to be used. Such a simpler format, he believes, would make the written curriculum more likely to be used.

Written curricula are both generic and site-specific, to use two concepts proposed by Walker (1979). Generic curricula are those written for use in various educational settings. During the 1960s, numerous generic curricula were produced by federally funded research and development laboratories; now, more typically, they are produced by a state curriculum office and intended for use throughout the state, with some local leeway provided. For example, the Maryland State Department of Education has published for the schools in the state "curricular frameworks" for all the major subjects, which provide a structure for curriculum development at the local level. In social studies the framework specifies the goals for that discipline and suggests four different organizing structures for achieving those goals (Maryland State Department of Education, 1983). Site-specific written curricula are those developed for a specific site, usually for a local school district or even for a particular school.

Site-specific written curricula are influenced by several different sources. First, as will be explained more fully in Chapter 4, federal and state legislation and court directives play a role. The passage of PL 94–142 with its requirement that schools provide the "least restrictive environment" for handicapped learners undoubtedly precipitated much local curriculum work to help teachers work in "mainstreamed" classes. The textbooks and standardized tests in use in the district seem to influence decisions about the inclusion and placement of content. And the expectations of vocal parent and community groups seem to have at least a constraining influence on what can be done.

In general, however, the guides seem to reflect the preferences and practices of a local group of elites: a director of curriculum; a supervisor of that subject area; a principal with a strong interest in curriculum; a small group of experienced teachers used to playing a leadership role. They in turn seem most influenced by the practice of "lighthouse" districts: there is much well-intentioned plagiarizing going on as they meet during the summer to produce the new guide. Recommended curricula seem to play a somewhat unimportant role; the examination of several district curriculum guides indicates that they usually do little more than borrow the rhetoric of the recommenders.

The chief functions of written curricula seem to be three: mediating; standardizing; and controlling. They first mediate between the ideals of the recommended curriculum and the realities of the classroom; in this sense they often represent a useful compromise between what the experts think should be taught and what teachers believe can be taught. They also mediate between the expectations of administrators and the preferences of teachers. The best of them represent a negotiated consensus of administrative and classroom leaders.

They also play an important role in standardizing the curriculum, especially in larger districts. Often they are produced as a result of directives from a superintendent who is unhappy that students in School A are studying a social studies curriculum or using a reading series quite different from that in Schools B and C. In the mid-1980s, for example, the Philadelphia School District, after years of what some termed "curricular anarchy," moved to standardize all major components of the curriculum, including the pacing of learning. Principals and teachers received from the central office "pacing charts," indicating week by week what was to be taught in each subject at each grade level.

Finally, they standardize by controlling. They are often used by district and school administrators as management tools to control what is taught. This control function seems to be perceived differently by administrators and teachers. Administrators believe that controlling the curriculum is an important management responsibility; they point to the research on school effectiveness which seems to indicate that in schools with higher pupil achievement there is a principal actively monitoring the curriculum to ensure that the written curriculum is being delivered. (See, for example, Squires, Huitt, and Segars, 1981.) However, as Walcott (1977) discovered in his ethnographic study of a district monitoring plan, most teachers view such attempts to control the curriculum as intrusive and counterproductive and will work hard at subverting such plans.

Predictably, written curricula, especially site-specific ones, are of uneven quality. The best of them seem to represent a useful synthesis of recommended curricula and local practice; they seem well conceptualized, carefully developed, and easy to use. Too many, however, lack those qualities. Careful reviews of a large number of such guides reveal that they suffer from some common faults: the objectives are not related to the stated goals; instructional activities are not directly related to the objectives; the activities do not reflect the best current knowledge about teaching and learning; and the guides are cumbersome and difficult to use. In his evaluation of twenty-seven guides produced by the curriculum office of a large urban school system, Glatthorn (1981) gave those products an average rating of only fair-to-good, an assessment supported by the teachers surveyed in the study.

The Supported Curriculum   The supported curriculum is the curriculum as reflected in and shaped by the resources allocated to support or deliver the curriculum. Four kinds of resources seem to be most critical here: the time allocated to a given subject at a particular level of schooling (how much time should we allocate to social studies in grade 5?); the time allocated by the classroom teacher within that overall subject allocation to particular aspects of the curriculum (how much time shall I allocate to the first unit on the explorers?); personnel allocations as reflected in and resulting from class-size decisions (how many teachers of physical education do we need in the middle school if we let PE classes increase to an average of 35?); and the texts and other learning materials provided for use in the classroom (can we do with those old basals for one more year?).

The patterns of influence bearing upon the supported curriculum seem rather complex. First, the state seems to exercise a strong influence on the supported curriculum. State curriculum guidelines often specify minimum time allocations, and some state-approved lists of basic texts restrict the choice of textbooks to a relatively small number. In Texas, for example, the practice is to list five basic texts in each subject area at each level. Texts chosen from the approved list are paid for with state funds; texts chosen off the list, with district funds.

The local school board, under the leadership of its superintendent, seems to play a key role. In many districts, boards will adopt curriculum policies specifying minimum time allocations to the several subjects, will approve district-purchased texts, and will make major budget decisions that impact strongly on the personnel and material support provided. At the school level, principals also seem to have a major influence. They usually have some discretion in the allocation of funds for texts and other learning materials. They often are given some latitude in their requests for additional staff. And the school master schedule is the major means for translating school priorities into decisions about curricular support. Such seemingly mundane decisions as class size, length of instructional period, room assignments, and teacher-preparation periods have a subtle but pervasive influence on the curriculum.

And, of course, the teacher plays a crucial role. Elementary teachers exercise a great deal of influence in determining how much time is allocated to particular subjects, despite the attempts of principals to limit such autonomy. And all teachers have much autonomy about how time is allocated to given units or aspects of the curriculum. For example, a middle school science teacher with a special interest in environmental issues will devote a great deal of time to relevant units and slight those that do not seem related.

Obviously the supported curriculum needs to be examined. The data are clear that several aspects of the supported curriculum have a major bearing upon what and how much is learned. First, time seems to be an important factor. In her review of the research, Stallings (1980) concludes as follows:

> *The body of knowledge emanating from the research on teaching in the 1970's suggests that teachers should allocate more time to academic subjects, keeping in mind student ability levels, and students should be kept engaged in the tasks.* (p. 12)

Berliner (1984) cites some examples of the dramatic differences in the way time is allocated in elementary school classrooms. One fifth-grade teacher devoted only 68 minutes a day to reading and language arts; another teacher, 137 minutes. He found similar differences in the way in which that allocated time was used. One fifth-grade teacher devoted more than five thousand minutes during the course of the year to comprehension-type activities in reading; another teacher, only slightly more than nine hundred minutes. Such differences would seem to be significant.

However, Karweit (1983) questions one aspect of this concern for time. In a review of the research on time on task, Karweit notes that, " . . . by a variety of criteria for the importance of an effect, the most outstanding finding relating the effects of time-on-task to learning is that the effects are as small as they are" (p. 46).

Second, class size seems to have an effect—but in a rather special way. In their meta-analysis of the effects of class size on achievement, Glass and Smith (1978) concluded that the greatest gains occurred in classes of fifteen or less; in classes of twenty to forty, the differences were present but were less marked. Their summary was quite direct: "As class size increases, achievement decreases" (p. i).

In trying to understand why such differences occur, Filby (1980) and his colleagues observed four classes which were significantly reduced in size at semester time and found several positive effects in the smaller classes: each child received more attention from the teacher; there were fewer discipline problems; children paid more attention to classroom work; and the curriculum was enriched.

Finally, the quality of the textbook and other learning resources as an aspect of the supported curriculum seems to play a central role. After noting that the text constitutes the basis of many teacher lectures and that seatwork with worksheets represents as much as two-thirds of the time in elementary classrooms, Doyle (1983) notes several deficiencies of texts which researchers have discovered: many texts present information in a confusing manner; the instructional procedures in the teacher's manual are often unnecessarily complicated for students; texts provide little explanation and direct instruction but a great deal of practice and assessment material; and the overlap of texts and standardized tests is very low. The Commission on Reading noted several other flaws in elementary reading series: stories written for use in the primary grades do not give enough insight into characters' goals, motives, and feelings; many of the so-called stories do not actually tell a story; textbooks lack a logical structure, often emphasizing a trivial detail rather than a fundamental principle. A curriculum supported by such flawed textbooks would obviously be less effective than one supported by texts of high quality.

The supported curriculum plays a central role at several stages of the curriculum cycle. First, in developing curricula, educators should give specific attention to the supported curriculum, paying special attention to time allocations and the materials of instruction. Second, in implementing the curriculum, administrators should be sure that adequate support is provided. Next, as Chapter 11 indicates, those involved in aligning the curriculum should assess to what extent there is a good fit between the written, the supported, and the taught curricula. Finally, any comprehensive evaluation of the curriculum should assess the supported curriculum, since deficiencies in support will probably be a major factor in student achievement.

The Taught Curriculum   The taught curriculum, as noted above, is the delivered curriculum—the curriculum that an observer would see in action as the teacher taught. The extent to which there is consonance between the written curriculum and the taught curriculum seems to vary considerably. At one extreme are those school systems—such as Los Angeles (see Niedermeyer and Yelon, 1981) and Pittsburgh (Rifugiato and Wilson, 1983)—which claim to have achieved a high degree of consonance between the two by implementing curriculum-alignment projects. At the other extreme are schools like those studied by Cusick (1983), where a state of curricular anarchy existed: each teacher developed his or her own curriculum, with all sorts of disparate activities going on across the school. And, as Cusick notes, "What was published and advertised gave no hint as to what went on in class" (p. 84).

How does the taught curriculum, regardless of its fit with the written curriculum, become established? The question is a complex and an important one that can best be answered by synthesizing several studies of teachers' thinking, planning, and decision making. The picture that emerges from such a synthesis is something like the sketch that follows.

First, the teacher brings to the classroom what Connelly and Elbaz (1980) call *personal practical knowledge*—a body of knowledge held in a uniquely practical way, structured in terms of the teacher's practical purposes, and derived from the teacher's lived experiences. This personal practical knowledge has five related orientations: to the context of specific situations ("my second-grade class tomorrow"); to various theories of practice ("what does Madeline Hunter suggest?"); to social conditions and constraints ("what do the parents want?"); to self (what kind of teacher do I see myself to be?"); and to experience ("what have I learned about teaching second-graders?").

Next, the teacher uses that personal practical knowledge in a highly complex environment—the classroom—to satisfy certain overriding needs. As Lieberman and Miller (1984) describe it, the elementary classroom especially is a "three-ring circus," with highly different individuals competing for attention in a potentially unstable condition: at any moment there might be rebellion against the teacher's authority or interpersonal conflict among the students. In such an environment the teacher needs to reduce uncertainty and ambiguity so that classroom life can become more predictable and more manageable. To accomplish that goal, the teacher develops schedules that are much influenced by the rhythms of the year ("it's time for Halloween decorations"), routines and instructional rituals ("spelling test on Friday"), and specific rules for regularizing behavior ("no talking while you're writing"). The primary concern here, as Doyle (1979) notes, is to gain and maintain the cooperation of students in activities that fill the available time.

The teacher's personal practical knowledge and the teacher's need for stability and predictability seem to coalesce as the teacher makes decisions about curriculum. The teacher seems to make some tentative decisions about curriculum by drawing from certain significant aspects of personal practical knowledge: the teacher's knowledge of the subject; the teacher's perceptions of the students; the written curriculum; the textbook; administrative pressures; curriculum-based and standardized tests; and perceptions of community concerns. However, those tentative knowledge-based decisions are strongly mediated by the teacher's concern for management: the teacher wants a predictable, smoothly flowing, tension-free environment. To achieve that state, teachers often will exclude topics that they believe are too difficult or will simplify content that they consider too complex. As Doyle (1985) points out cogently, academic work can often be "swamped" by the management function of teaching.

Thus, the teacher's decisions about the curriculum are a product of many interacting variables. Rather than being mindless choices or acts of willful rebellion, those decisions instead seem to represent the teacher's considered judgment about what compromises will be best for that teacher and a particular class.

The Tested Curriculum   The tested curriculum is that set of learnings which are assessed in teacher-made classroom tests, in district-developed curriculum-referenced tests, and in standardized tests. To what extent are these several types of tests related to the taught curriculum? The answers seem to vary. First, teacher-made tests tend not to correspond closely with what was taught. In general, teachers are not highly skilled test developers and tend to be somewhat selective in what they include in unit examinations. For the most part their tests concentrate on assessing students' comprehension and memory of objective information. Even their attempts to measure understanding of concepts result in multiple-choice items that really assess students' guessing ability.

The evidence on the congruence between curriculum-referenced tests and instruction suggests a somewhat different picture. In districts using curriculum-referenced tests as a means of monitoring teacher compliance, the test seems to drive instruction. The result is a closer fit. Yet here the congruence is not reassuring to those who value higher-order learnings. An examination of a curriculum-referenced test used in a large district's alignment project indicated that the test items were concerned almost exclusively with such low-level objectives as punctuating sentences correctly, spelling words correctly, and identifying the parts of speech.

Finally, the research on standardized tests suggests that there is not a good fit between widely used standardized tests and what most teachers teach. One study (Freeman et al., 1980) in examining the fit between three widely used mathematics textbooks (a proxy for the taught curriculum) and five widely used standardized tests indicated that in the best case about 30 percent of what was tested had never been taught and in the worst case about 47 percent of the topics had not been covered.

The consequences of such mismatches are serious. First, the research suggests that achievement is lower in schools where there is not a close fit between what is taught and what is tested. (See Berliner, 1984, for example.) Second, students are put at a disadvantage when the teaching and testing do not match. Their grades and scores would probably not be a valid measure of what they had learned. Finally, there may be serious legal consequences when poorly fitting tests are used to make decisions about promotion and graduation. The courts have ruled that when tests are used for purposes which may deny constitutional guarantees of equal protection or due process (as in retention or denial of graduation), schools must provide evidence that those tests assess skills and concepts actually taught in the classroom.

It might be useful at this juncture to note again that the four curricula discussed above—the written, the supported, the taught, and the tested—might be seen as constituting the intentional curriculum—that set of learning experiences which the school system consciously intends for its students.

The Learned Curriculum   This term is used here to denote all the changes in values, perceptions, and behavior that occur as a result of school experiences. As such, it includes what the student understands, learns, and retains from both the intentional curriculum and the hidden curriculum. The discussion here focuses on what is learned from the intentional curriculum; the last part of the chapter analyzes what is learned from the hidden curriculum.

What then do students learn and retain from the intentional curriculum? Obviously, the answer varies with the student, the teacher, and the curriculum. However, there are some subtle transformations, especially between the taught curriculum and the learned curriculum, that occur in most classrooms, regardless of the specific conditions. (The discussion that follows draws primarily from Doyle's 1983 review of the research on academic work.)

To begin with, the students seem especially sensitive to the accountability system at work in the classroom and take seriously only what they are held accountable for. Regardless of what objectives the teacher announces or what the teacher emphasizes, the students seem to assess the importance of classroom transactions in relation to their value in that accountability system: "Will this be on the test?"

In order to achieve success in that accountability-oriented classroom, the students invent strategies for managing ambiguity and reducing risk. They will restrict the output they provide teachers, giving vague and limited answers to minimize the risk of making public mistakes. They also attempt to increase the explicitness of a teacher's instructions, asking the teacher for more examples, hints, or rephrasings of the question. And they pressure teachers to simplify curriculum complexity, strongly resisting any curriculum which forces them to think, inquire, and discover.

These risk-reduction strategies derive from the students' view of the classroom. Students perceive the classroom as a place where the answering of teacher questions is the primary academic task. Thus, they focus on the answering event itself, rather than the academic context in which the question is embedded. They rely primarily on memory to answer those questions. As a consequence, they do not develop the knowledge structures which will facilitate transferability.

In sum, then, students learn what is assessed and remember those learnings as discrete answers to questions; their learning is somewhat disorganized and unconnected.

COMPONENTS OF THE CURRICULUM

Although several texts in the field seem to treat curriculum development as if it were one undifferentiated process, the realities are quite different. The concept subsumes several distinct entities which might best be described as components of the curriculum: curricular policies; curricular goals; fields of study; programs of study; courses of study; units of study; and lessons. Each of these will be analyzed briefly below and then discussed more fully in the chapters that follow.

Curricular Policies The term *curricular policies*, as used here, designates the set of rules, criteria, and guidelines intended to control curriculum development and implementation. As Kirst (1983) notes, there are macropolicies, such as a board policy on courses required in high school, and micropolicies, such as a set of recommendations for a curriculum unit in mathematics. And policy making, as he notes, is essentially the "authoritative allocation of competing values" (p. 282). Thus, as a board makes a policy requiring three years of science in the high school curriculum but does not require any study of art, it is perhaps unwittingly according a higher value to science as a way of knowing than it does to aesthetics. And Saylor, Alexander, and Lewis (1981) make a useful distinction between *de jure* policy making (as implemented in court decisions, state legislative acts, and local agency regulations) and *de facto* policy making (as carried out by community networks, testing bureaus, accrediting associations, and advisory boards).

Curricular Goals Curricular goals are the general, long-term educational outcomes which the school system expects to achieve through its curriculum. There are three critical elements in this definition. First, goals are stated much more generally than objectives. Thus, one goal for English language arts might be this: "Learn to communicate ideas through writing and speaking." One objective for fifth-grade language arts would be much more specific: "Write a letter, with appropriate business-letter form, suggesting a community improvement." Second, goals are long-term, not short-term, outcomes. The school system hopes that after twelve years of formal schooling, its students will have achieved the goals that the system has set for itself.

Finally, curricular goals are those outcomes which the school system hopes to achieve through its curriculum. Here it is important to make a distinction between educational goals and curricular goals. Educational goals are the long-term outcomes which the school system expects to accomplish through the entire educational process over which it has control. Thus, one of the goals recommended by Goodlad (1984) is this one: "Learn to assess realistically and live with one's limitations and strengths" (p. 56). A school sytem might decide that it would attempt to achieve that goal primarily through its counseling and guidance services, not through its curriculum. In this sense, then, curricular goals are a subset of educational goals, even though many leaders in the field seem to ignore this important distinction.

How do curricular policies and curricular goals interrelate? In a sense, the policies establish the rules of the game ("take three years of health education") and the goals set the targets ("at the end of those three years, you will adopt constructive health habits"). In this sense they should determine in a rational system the form and content of all the other components that follow. However, as will be evident throughout this work, educational organizations are usually not very rational. And, typically, policies are not related to goals, and goals are not related to fields and programs of study.

Fields of Study   A field of study is an organized and clearly demarcated set of learning experiences typically offered over a multiyear period. In most school curricula, such fields of study are equivalent to the standard school subjects: English language arts, mathematics, social studies, science, and so on. At the college level, fields are more narrowly defined: thus, students pursue majors in history, or anthropology, or sociology—not "social studies." It should also be noted, as Chapter 7 explains, that there have been several attempts to reconceptualize fields of study in order to minimize what some consider to be the dysfunctional and arbitrary divisions of knowledge represented by the standard disciplines. Thus, a middle school might offer a four-year field of study called "Humans and Their Environment," which would bring together concepts from the social sciences, the natural sciences, and English language arts.

Programs of Study   A program of study is the total set of learning experiences offered by a school for a particular group of learners, usually over a multiyear period and typically encompassing several fields of study. The program of studies is often described in a policy statement which delineates which subjects are required and which are electives, with corresponding time allocations and credits. Here, for example, is a typical program of studies for an elementary school:

Reading and language arts: eight hours a week

Social studies: three hours
Mathematics: four hours
Art: one hour
Music: one hour
Health and physical education: one hour

At the college level, a student's program of studies includes all the courses he or she will take or has taken.

Courses of Study　A course of study is a subset of both a program of study and a field of study. It is a set of organized learning experiences, within a field of study, offered over a specified period of time (such as a year, a semester, or a quarter) for which the student ordinarily receives academic credit. The course of study is usually given a title and a grade-level or numerical designation. Thus, "third-grade science" and "English II" are courses of study. At the college level, courses of study seem to be the most salient component for both students and faculty: "I'm taking Economics I this term"; "I'm offering Elizabethan Literature this quarter."

Units of Study　A unit of study is a subset of a course of study. It is an organized set of related learning experiences offered as part of a course of study, usually lasting from one to three weeks. Many units are organized around a single overarching concept, such as "Mythical Creatures" or "The Nature of Conflict." Not all teachers think about units as they plan. Many high school teachers simply aggregate lessons: "I'll have a spelling lesson tomorrow and a grammar lesson on the next day." And college instructors as they conceptualize their courses often seem to think about a sequence of lectures, rather than a unit of study.

Lessons　A lesson is a set of related learning experiences typically lasting for twenty to sixty minutes, focusing on a relatively small number of objectives. Ordinarily a lesson is a subset of a unit, although, as noted above, the unit level is sometimes omitted by teachers planning for instruction.

These distinctions among the several components of curriculum have an importance that transcends the need for conceptual clarity. Each seems to involve some rather different planning processes. Thus, to speak generally about "curriculum planning," without differentiating between planning a program of studies and planning a course of studies, is to make a rather serious mistake.

THE MASTERY, THE ORGANIC, AND THE ENRICHMENT CURRICULA

One additional classification system first proposed by Glatthorn (1980) has proved useful especially in developing and improving fields of study. Glatthorn argues that better curriculum work will result if developers in each field of study distinguish between these three types of learning: mastery, organic, and enrichment.

These three types of learnings result from the following analytical steps. First, divide the learnings in that field between those that are *basic* and those that are *enrichment*. Basic learnings are those that, in the views of knowledgeable educators, are essential for all students. (*All*, in this use, refers to the top 90 percent of learners, excluding the least able and those with serious learning disabilities.) Enrichment learnings are the knowledge and skills which are interesting and enriching, but are not considered essential: they are simply "nice to know." Thus, in fifth-grade social studies, curriculum workers might decide that the early settling of the Vikings in Iceland would be interesting enrichment content.

Once the first division between basic and enrichment is made, then further divide the basic learnings into those that require structure and those that do not require structure. Structured learning, as the term is used here, has four characteristics:

1. It requires careful sequencing.
2. It is best facilitated through careful planning.
3. It results in measurable outcomes and is easily tested.
4. It is best mastered when its content is clearly delineated into discrete units, lessons, and parts of lessons.

Nonstructured learning, on the other hand, includes all those skills, knowledge, and attitudes which can be mastered without such careful sequencing, planning, testing, and delineation.

These two analytical steps yield the three types of curricula depicted in Figure 1-1: mastery, organic, and enrichment. Mastery learnings are those that are both basic and structured. Here is an example of a mastery objective for language arts, grade 2:

Use a capital letter for the first word in a sentence.

On the other hand, organic learnings are those that are basic but do not require structuring. They are the learnings that develop day by day, rather naturally, as the result of numerous interactions and exchanges. They tend not to be the focus of specific learnings. They are just as important as the mastery outcomes (if not more so), but they do not require sequencing, pacing, and articulation. Here is an organic learning for language arts, grade 2:

Listen courteously as others speak.

The teacher would emphasize that learning on every occasion, not devote a specific lesson to it. And enrichment learnings, as noted above, are those learnings that simply extend the curriculum; they are not considered basic.

FIGURE 1–1. The Three Types
of Curricula

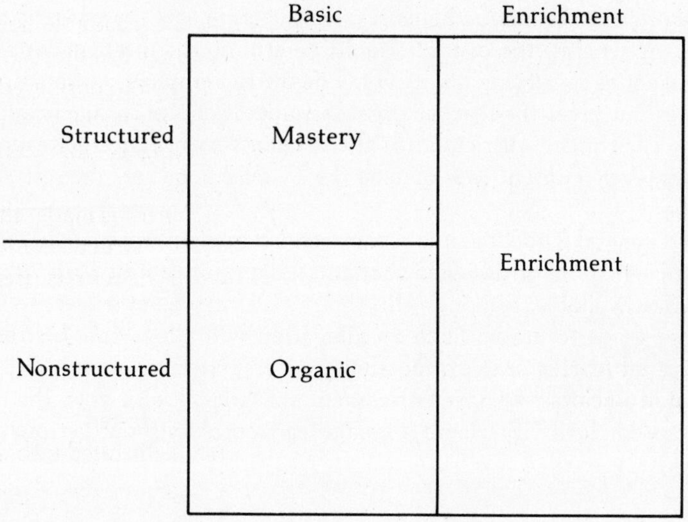

	Basic	Enrichment
Structured	Mastery	Enrichment
Nonstructured	Organic	

This tripartite division is more than an interesting intellectual exercise. It has significant implications for curriculum development. In general, district curriculum guides and scope-and-sequence charts should focus solely on the mastery elements. The nurturing of organic components can be enhanced through effective staff development; such outcomes do not need to be explicated fully and carefully in guides. And the enrichment components can be included in a supplement for those teachers who want to share enrichment activities. This division effects a kind of curricular parsimony: attention is focused on mastery elements; guides and charts are not cluttered with organic outcomes. Note the folly of attempting to sequence organic learnings: in one district's scope-and-sequence chart, "the pupil will enjoy reading poetry" was specified as an objective for third-grade language arts. Obviously, this is an organic outcome, one that should be emphasized in every grade, in every appropriate unit, every time a poem is read.

The division also has clear implications for testing. Curriculum-referenced tests should focus only on mastery elements; organic elements should not be tested. One district that ignored this important distinction wasted a great deal of time trying to develop a test for courteous listening before it was forced to give up in frustration. The distinction also has implications for the purchase of texts: textbooks should focus on the mastery objectives; the teacher can nurture the organic without the aid of textbooks.

Finally, the distinction helps resolve the issue of district versus teacher control. In general, the district should determine the mastery curriculum, to the extent of specifying objectives. The district emphasizes the important outcomes but gives the teacher great latitude of choice in nurturing them. And the enrichment curriculum is the teacher's own: here the teacher can add whatever content he or she feels might be of interest to the students.

As a general guideline, it is recommended in planning curricula that the mastery curriculum be designed so that it will require about 60 to 75 percent of the time available, although this figure will vary from subject to subject and from grade to grade. Such an allocation will allow time for remediation, give the teacher ample opportunity for emphasizing organic outcomes, and enable all classes to have enrichment activities. It also gives the teacher some needed flexibility; some slippage can occur without serious consequences.

THE HIDDEN CURRICULUM

The hidden curriculum, which is sometimes called the "unstudied curriculum" or the "implicit curriculum," might best be defined in this following manner:

> Those aspects of schooling, other than the intentional curriculum, that seem to produce changes in student values, perceptions, and behaviors.

As the definition suggests, students learn a great deal in school from sources other than the intentional curriculum; thus, the hidden curriculum might be seen as those aspects of the learned curriculum that lie outside the boundaries of the school's intentional efforts. And, although the term *hidden curriculum* is often used with negative connotations, those learnings can be both desirable and undesirable from the viewpoint of one desiring optimal human development. In examining the specific nature of the hidden curriculum, it seems useful at this point to distinguish between what might be termed the constants—those aspects of schooling that seem more or less impervious to change—and the variables—those aspects that seem susceptible to reform.

The Constants of the Hidden Curriculum

There are certain important aspects of the hidden curriculum so intrinsic to the nature of schools as a cultural institution that they might be seen as constants. The depiction of those constants presented below has been influenced by a close reading of several authors: curricular reconceptualists such as Apple (1979), Pinar (1978), and Giroux (1979); sociologists such as Dreeben (1968); and educational researchers such as Jackson (1968) and Goodlad (1984). However, the synthesis that follows is the author's own and should not be ascribed to any of the sources cited. The following general picture emerges of the constants in the hidden curriculum.

As one of the important cultural institutions in complex societies, schools and the personnel who operate them share in and are profoundly influenced by the values and belief systems of that larger society; thus, they are closely linked to the principles and processes that govern the workplace. As a cultural institution, they inevitably reproduce the cultural beliefs and the economic relationships that support the larger social order, regardless of the particular nature of the larger social order. Thus, one of the constants of the hidden curriculum is the ideology of the larger society, which permeates every aspect of schooling. Thus, schools in the United States inevitably reflect the ideology of democratic capitalism.

In the process of reproducing those cultural beliefs and economic relationships, certain kinds of knowledge are selected as being worthy of transmission, and other types of knowledge are judged unworthy of knowing. Thus, knowledge becomes a kind of cultural capital which serves to reflect the belief system of the larger society. In imparting this selected knowledge, school administrators and teachers impose upon children certain commonly accepted definitions of such key constructs as *work, play, achievement, intelligence, success,* and *failure;* thus, meanings are imposed, rather than discovered. In this sense, then, a second constant in the hidden curriculum is the way in which educators construe legitimate knowledge and define its operative concepts.

A key component of the school as an organization is the classroom, where the most salient aspects of the hidden curriculum come into play. The classroom is a crowded place, where issues of control often become dominant. And control is achieved through the differential use of power; the teacher uses several kinds of power to control the selection of content, the methods of learning, movement in the classroom, and the flow of classroom discourse. Control also is achieved by the skillful use of accountability measures; teachers spend much time evaluating and giving evaluative feedback. In such a classroom, students unconsciously learn the skills and traits required by the larger society; they learn how to be punctual, clean, docile, and conforming. They learn how to stand in line, take their turns, and wait.

Even though the above features of the hidden curriculum are presented here as constants relatively impervious to change, it is important for curriculum leaders to be aware of their subtle and pervasive influence.

The Variables of the Hidden Curriculum

There are several other important aspects of the hidden curriculum which can be more readily changed by educators. The most significant of these can be classified into three categories: organizational variables, social-system variables, and culture variables.

Organizational Variables The term *organizational variables* is used here to designate all those decisions about how teachers will be assigned and students grouped for instruction. Here there are four issues that seem worthy of attention: team teaching; promotion and retention policies; ability grouping; and curriculum tracking. The evidence on the effects of team teaching on student achievement is somewhat inconclusive. As Bolvin (1982) notes, summaries of the research on the outcomes for both elementary and secondary schools indicate no superiority of one organizational pattern over another.

On the other hand, the evidence is both clear and conclusive that social promotion is a more desirable policy than promotion-by-achievement, at least during the first eight grades of school. Even though many school systems during the 1980s were implementing "promotional gates" policies that promoted students solely on the basis of achievement, several syntheses of the research indicate that social promotion results in better attitudes toward school, better self-image, and improved achievement. (See, for example, the 1986 review by Hall and Wallace.)

Grouping practices in the schools have often been attacked by critics as one of the most baleful aspects of the hidden curriculum. Here the indictment of Giroux and Penna (1979) is perhaps typical:

> The pedagogical foundation for democratic processes in the classroom can be established by eliminating the pernicious practice of "tracking" students. This tradition in schools of grouping students according to "abilities" and perceived performance is of dubious instructional value. (p. 223)

There are two problems with such an indictment. The first is that the authors seem to ignore a rather important distinction made by Rosenbaum (1980) between *ability grouping*—sorting students into ability-based groups for instruction (such as high, average, and low ability)—and *curriculum grouping*—sorting students into such curricular tracks as vocational, general, and college preparatory. The other, more serious problem is that the empirical evidence available does not support their assertions.

What is the evidence on ability grouping? Here a meta-analysis by Kulik and Kulik (1982) of fifty-two objective, comparative studies is most instructive. These are the highlights of their findings.

1. In more than 70 percent of the studies, students from grouped classes outperformed ungrouped students by a small amount. The effects were largest in special classes for the gifted and talented.
2. Ability grouping seemed to have a positive effect on student attitudes towards the subject taught.
3. Students who were grouped by ability tended to have a better attitude towards school and a higher self-concept, although these effects were smaller and less consistent.

In addition, Sanford's (1980) study of more than one hundred junior high classes concluded that increased heterogeneity of classes was associated with these drawbacks: teachers were less able to respond to individual learning needs; teachers were less able to respond to students' affective needs; there was less task engagement; and achievement gains of lower-ability students tended to be lower.

The practice of curriculum grouping or tracking, in which students follow a predetermined career-oriented program, such as college preparatory or vocational, seems to be a more complex matter. Here Rosenbaum's (1980) review of the research seems most enlightening. He first notes that there is no clear finding from the research on whether ability or social class is the primary determiner of track placement. According to several studies, the guidance counselor plays a key role in track selections. And many students, according to Rosenbaum, are in curricular tracks that are inconsistent with career choices. The lack of congruence is complicated by the fact that curricular tracking is relatively stable, and there is more movement from college preparatory to general and vocational than the other way around.

The chief problem with curriculum tracking, according to researchers, is the lack of challenge in the general curriculum. Goodlad's (1984) comprehensive study of high- and low-track classes led him to conclude that high-track classes had better content, pedagogy, and class climate. And teachers in low-track classes conveyed lower expectations and spent more time in enforcing the rules.

The weight of the research evidence would suggest in general, then, that educational leaders interested in improving the organizational variables of the hidden curriculum might focus their attention on promotion policies and curriculum tracking as the key variables. They perhaps should take special pains to ensure that the general curriculum is neither dull nor trivial.

Social-System Variables The term *social system* as an aspect of school climate was first used by Tagiuri (1968) to refer to the social dimension concerned with the patterned relationships of persons and groups in the school. Anderson's (1982) review of the research on school climate indicated that there were several social-system factors associated with positive student attitude and achievement. Several of these had to do with administrator-teacher relationships: the principal was actively involved in instruction; there was good rapport and communication between administrators and teachers; teachers shared in the decision-making process; and there were good relationships between teachers. Others were related to teacher-student relationships: teacher-student interactions in general were positive and constructive; students shared in decision making; and there were extensive opportunities for student participation in activities. Obviously all these factors can be influenced through effective leadership by both administrators and teachers.

Culture Variables   Tagiuri defined culture variables as the social dimension concerned with belief systems, values, cognitive structures, and meaning. According to Anderson's review, several key factors play an important role here in the hidden curriculum. All of the following are associated with either improved achievement or improved attitude.

1. The school has clear goals that are understood by all; and those goals are supported by a strong consensus among administrators and teachers.
2. Administrators and teachers have high expectations for each other, and both groups are strongly committed to the importance of student achievement.
3. Administrators and teachers have high expectations for students, and these high expectations are translated into an emphasis on academics.
4. Rewards and praise are publicly given for student achievement; rewards and punishments are administered in a fair and consistent manner.
5. There is an emphasis on cooperation and group competition, rather than on individual competition.
6. Students value academic achievement; peer norms support the value of such achievement.

These aspects of the hidden curriculum also can be influenced by administrators and teachers working together.

To summarize, then, the hidden curriculum is seen here as both constant and variable aspects of schooling (other than the intentional curriculum) that produce changes in the student. The constants—the ideology of the larger society, the way in which certain knowledge is deemed important or unimportant, and the power relationships that seem necessary in large bureaucratic institutions—seem unlikely to change. However, the variables—those aspects of the organizational structure, the social systems, and the culture of the school that can be influenced—require the systematic attention of curriculum leaders.

APPLICATIONS

1. By reviewing the definitions given here and by reflecting about your own use of the term, write your own definition of *curriculum*.

2. Some educators have suggested that the profession should use simpler definitions for *curriculum* and *instruction:* curriculum is what is taught; instruction is how it is taught. Do these definitions seem to suffice, from your perspective?

3. Some leaders have argued for a very close fit between the written and the taught curriculum, suggesting that teachers should teach only what is in the prescribed curriculum. Others have suggested that some slippage is desirable—that teachers should have some autonomy and latitude, as long as they cover the essentials. What is your own position on this issue?

4. Although most curriculum texts do not make the distinctions noted here between programs of study, fields of study, and courses of study, those distinctions do seem to matter. To test this hypothesis, do the following: (1) List the steps you would follow in designing a program of studies for one level of schooling, such as elementary or middle school. (2) List the steps you would follow in designing a field of studies, such as social studies, K–12.

5. It has been suggested here that the "constants" of the hidden curriculum are not easily changed. Others would argue that they should be changed if we truly desire democratic and humanistic schools. As a school leader, would you attempt to change any of those "constants," or would you give more attention to the "variables"?

6. Outline a change strategy you would use in attempting to improve the "culture" variables that seem to be associated with improved attitude and achievement.

REFERENCES

Anderson, C. S. (1982). The search for school climate: A review of the research. *Review of Educational Research, 52,* 368-420.

Apple, M. W. (Winter, 1979). On analyzing hegemony. *The Journal of Curriculum Theorizing, 1,* 10-43.

Berliner, D. C. (1984). The half-full glass: A review of research on teaching. In P. L. Hosford (ed.), *Using What We Know about Teaching.* Alexandria, VA: ASCD.

Bobbitt, F. (1918). *The curriculum.* Boston: Houghton Mifflin.

Bolvin, J. O. (1982). Classroom organization. In H. E. Mitzel (ed.), *Encyclopedia of Educational Research* (5th Ed.), pp. 265-274. New York: Macmillan.

Caswell, H. L., and Campbell, D. S. (1935). *Curriculum development.* New York: American Book Co.

Commission on Reading. (1985). Becoming a nation of readers: The report of the commission on reading. Washington, DC: The National Institute of Education.

Connelly, F. M., and Elbaz, F. (1980). Conceptual bases for curriculum thought: A teacher's perspective. In A. W. Foshay (ed.), *Considered action for curriculum improvement*, pp. 95–119. Alexandria, VA: ASCD.

Cusick, P. A. (1983). *The egalitarian ideal and the American high school: Studies of three schools*. New York: Longman.

Dewey, J. (1902). *The child and the curriculum*. Chicago: University of Chicago Press.

Doyle, W. (1979). Making managerial decisions in classrooms. In D. L. Duke (ed.), *Classroom management*, 78th Yearbook of the National Society for the Study of Education (Part II). Chicago: University of Chicago Press.

_____. (1983). Academic work. *Review of Educational Research, 53,* 159–199.

_____. (1985). *Classroom management and the curriculum: A strategic research site.* Austin, TX: Research and Development Center for Teacher Education, University of Texas.

Dreeben, R. (1968). *On what is learned in schools.* Reading, MA: Addison-Wesley.

Evertts, E. L. (1980). A new heritage approach for teaching the language arts. In B. J. Mandel (ed.), *Three language arts curriculum models: Pre-kindergarten through college,* pp. 35–46. Urbana, IL: NCTE.

Filby, N. N. (February 1980). Evidence of class size effects. Paper presented at annual convention of American Association of School Administrators, Anaheim, CA.

Freeman, D., Kuhs, T., Porter, A., Knappen, L., Floden, R., Schmidt, W., and Schwille, J. (1980). *The fourth grade mathematics curriculum as inferred from textbooks and tests.* East Lansing, MI: Michigan State University, Institute for Research on Teaching.

Gagne, R. W. (1967). Curriculum research and the promotion of learning. In R. W. Tyler, R. M. Gagne, and M. Scriven, (eds.), *Perspectives of curricular evaluation.* Chicago: Rand McNally.

Giroux, H. A. (1979). Toward a new sociology of curriculum. *Educational Leadership, 37,* 248–253.

Giroux, H. A., and Penna, A. N. (1979). Social education in the classroom: The dynamics of the hidden curriculum. In H. A. Giroux, A. N. Penna, and W. F. Pinar (eds.), *Curriculum and instruction,* pp. 209–230. Berkeley, CA: McCutchan.

Glass, G. V., and Smith, M. L. (1978). *Meta-analysis of research on the relationship of class size and achievement.* San Francisco: Far West Laboratory for Educational Research and Development.

Glatthorn, A. A. (1980). *A guide for developing an English curriculum for the eighties.* Urbana, IL: NCTE.

_____. (1981). An analysis and evaluation of the office of curriculum and instruction in the School District of Philadelphia. Philadelphia: University of Pennsylvania.

Goodlad, J. I., and associates. (1979). *Curriculum inquiry: The study of curriculum practice.* New York: McGraw-Hill.

Goodlad, J. I. (1984). *A place called school: Prospects for the future.* New York: McGraw-Hill.

Hall, F., and Wallace, S. (1986). Promotion vs. retention: What are the implications for policy development? *NASSP Bulletin, 70* (248), 72–77.

Jackson, P. (1968). *Life in classrooms.* New York: Holt, Rinehart and Winston.

Karweit, N. C. (1983). *Time-on-task: A research review.* Baltimore: Center for

Social Organization of Schools, Johns Hopkins University.

Kirst, M. W. (1983). Policy implications of individual differences and the common curriculum. In G. D. Fenstermacher and J. I. Goodlad (eds.), *Individual differences and the common curriculum,* pp. 282–299. Eighty-Second Yearbook of the National Society for the Study of Education (Part I). Chicago: University of Chicago Press.

Kulik, C. C., and Kulik, J. A. (1982). Research synthesis on ability grouping. *Educational Leadership, 39,* 619–621.

Lieberman, A., and Miller, L. (1984). *Teachers, their world, and their work.* Alexandria, VA: ASCD.

Maryland State Department of Education (1983). *Social studies: A Maryland curricular framework.* Baltimore, MD: The author.

McCarthy, B. (1981). *The 4MAT system: Teaching to learning styles with right/left mode techniques* (2nd Ed.). Oak Brook, IL: EXCEL.

Moffett, J. (1968). *Teaching the universe of discourse.* Boston: Houghton Mifflin.

Niedermeyer, F. C., and Yelon, S. (1981). Los Angeles aligns curriculum with essential skills. *Educational Leadership, 38,* 618–620.

Pinar, W. F. (1978). The reconceptualization of curriculum studies. *Journal of Curriculum Studies, 10,* (3), 205–214.

Popham, W. J., and Baker, E. I. (1970). *Systematic instruction.* Englewood Cliffs, NJ: Prentice-Hall.

Rifugiato, F. J., and Wilson, H. A. (1983). *A guide to the MAP Project.* Pittsburgh: School District of Pittsburgh.

Rosenbaum, J. E. (1980). Social implications of educational grouping. In D. C. Berliner (ed.), *Review of research in education,* Vol. 8, pp. 361–404. Washington, DC: AERA.

Rugg, H. (ed.). (1927). *The foundations of curriculum making.* Twenty-sixth yearbook of the National Society for the Study of Education, Part II. Bloomington, IL: Public School Publishing.

Sanford, J. P. (1980). *Comparison of heterogeneous and homogeneous junior high classes.* Austin, TX: Research and Development Center for Teacher Education, University of Texas.

Saylor, J. G., Alexander, W. M., and Lewis, A. J. (1981). *Curriculum planning for better teaching and learning* (4th Ed.). New York: Holt, Rinehart and Winston.

Schiro, M. (1978). *Curriculum for better schools: The great ideological debate.* Englewood Cliffs, NJ: Educational Technology Publications.

Squires, D. A., Huitt, W. G., and Segars, J. K. (1981). Improving classrooms and schools: What's important. *Educational Leadership, 39,* 174–179.

Stallings, J. (December 1980). Allocated learning time revisited or beyond time on task. *Educational Researcher, 9,* (4), 11–16.

Taba, H. (1962). *Curriculum development: Theory and practice.* New York: Harcourt Brace Jovanovich.

Tagiuri, R. (1968). The concept of organizational climate. In R. Tagiuri and G. H. Litwin (eds.), *Organizational climate: Exploration of a concept.* Boston: Harvard University, Graduate School of Business Administration.

Tyler, R. W. (1957). The curriculum then and now. In *Proceedings of the 1956 Invitational Conference on Testing Problems.* Princeton, NJ: Educational Testing Service.

Walcott, H. F. (1977). *Teacher vs. technocrats.* Eugene, OR: Center for Educational Policy and Management, University of Oregon.

Walker, D. (1979). Approaches to curriculum development. In J. Schaffarzick and G. Sykes (eds.), *Value conflicts and curriculum issues: Lessons from research and experience,* pp. 263–290. Berkeley, CA: McCutchan.

2

Curriculum History: The Perspective of the Past

Understanding the history of curriculum development is useful for both scholars and practitioners. It results in a deeper awareness of the extent to which curricular changes are often influenced by and are a manifestation of larger social forces. And it offers a broader perspective from which to view so-called innovations and reforms, which often seem to reverberate with echoes of the past.

This understanding seems especially facilitated by a careful analysis of the last one hundred years of that history. Such a demarcation results in a closer focus on the major developments affecting American schools, while still providing the broader perspective that is so essential. And those developments perhaps can be better grasped if analyzed as parts of specific periods of history. There is, of course, an obvious fallacy in delineating such periods. Historical periods are an artifact of the historian's analysis: people do not live and events do not occur in neat chronological packages called "periods." Given that caution, an analysis of that century of curriculum history seems to suggest that there were six distinct eras each with its own distinguishing features. This framework is therefore suggested as a way of examining the past century of curriculum theory and practice:

Dates	Period
1890–1916	Academic scientism
1917–1940	Progressive functionalism
1941–1956	Developmental conformism
1957–1967	Scholarly structuralism
1968–1974	Romantic radicalism
1975–	Privatistic conservatism

ACADEMIC SCIENTISM

The term used here to identify the period from 1890 to 1916—*academic scientism*—derives from the two influences that seemed to predominate: the academic and the scientific. The academic influence was the result of systematic and somewhat effective efforts of the colleges to shape the curriculum for basic education; the scientific influence resulted from the attempts of educational theorists to use newly developed scientific knowledge in making decisions about the mission of the school and the content of the curriculum.

The Temper of the Times

The educational trends of this period can perhaps best be discerned if viewed against the backdrop of societal changes. The turn of the century was characterized, first of all, by the post-Civil War growth of industry and the development of urban areas, both stimulated primarily by the rapid growth of railroads. As Kliebard (1985) notes, by 1883 the railroad magnates had standardized track gauge, facilitating a dramatic increase in the use of rail. Thus, by 1889, the United States had 125,000 miles of railroad operation, compared with the 20,000 miles operating in Great Britain. And turn-of-the-century railroad magnates and industrialists took an active interest in schools. Cuban (1979) points out that these business leaders put pressure on local school boards to open separate schools and offer distinct programs in manual training. J. P. Morgan was even more direct, endowing the New York Trades School with a gift of $500,000. Cuban notes that many labor unions initially distrusted such schools as "breeding schools for scabs," but the National Association of Manufacturers endorsed them as essential in an industrialized nation.

The second distinguishing feature of the era was the impact of popular journalism. The linotype machine was introduced in 1890; the price of newspapers dropped to one cent; and the number of newspapers doubled. Magazines were also reaching larger audiences. Kliebard notes that by 1892 the circulation of the *Ladies Home Journal* had reached 700,000. Together these two media were exerting a considerable force on the national consciousness, linking the regions and influencing the people.

Finally, it was a time when new immigrant waves were reaching these shores. The volume of immigrants increased, and their places of origin changed markedly. Whereas prior to the 1890s, immigrants came chiefly from the Western European countries, during the turn-of-the-century decades, they were more likely to come from the Eastern European countries. Those Eastern Europeans posed a problem for many Americans, for whom Cubberly probably spoke when, in 1909, he wrote that the responsibility of the school was to "amalgamate these people as part of our American race. . . . "

Thus, it was a sprawling and rapidly growing nation, changing in its complexion. And, as Tyack and Hansot (1982) point out, it was a nation whose business and educational leaders were first realizing that the schools could serve as an agency of social reform.

The Predominant Trends

As noted above, the major educational influences of the period were both academic and scientific. The man who most clearly represented the academic influence of the colleges was Charles W. Eliot, president of Harvard University. In perhaps immodest fashion Eliot saw the entire curriculum as his purview, making specific recommendations for elementary, secondary, and higher education. His recommendations for elementary education, most clearly articulated in an address to the Department of Superintendence of the National Educational Association in 1892, included the following: the amount of arithmetic taught should be reduced, in order to provide time for the earlier introduction of algebra and geometry; foreign language should be introduced in fourth or fifth grade as part of general language study; geography should not be taught as a "memory study," but should emphasize general principles; the amount of time devoted to the study of grammar should be reduced, and grammar should be taught for application; natural science should be taught in the primary grades, and elementary physics in the upper elementary grades—both taught through the laboratory method. His influence on the secondary curriculum was exerted most strongly through his leadership of the Committee of Ten, whose recommendations are discussed below.

Kliebard (1979) characterizes Eliot as an optimistic mental disciplinarian. He was optimistic about human capacities, especially the capacities of the young. "It is a curious fact that we Americans habitually underestimate the capacity of pupils at almost every stage of education from the primary school through the university," he argued in one of his many articles. And he was one of the most influential mental disciplinarians, firmly committed to the belief that the development of the powers of the mind was the main function of schooling. Such development was to be accomplished through the study of the formal aspects of school subjects: to use a more recent formulation, process was more important than content.

Thus, for Eliot and his colleagues, it was the academic function of the schools that was paramount. Yet it is simplistic to assert that Eliot and others of similar persuasion were trying to limit the purpose of the high school to preparation for college. In essence, Eliot's position was that a sound academic curriculum was best for all students, regardless of their college aspirations.

The scientific influence was perhaps even stronger, even though less direct. One interesting sign of this scientific influence was the change of name of one of the major educational organizations: what had once been the Herbart Society changed its name in 1900 to the National Society for the Scientific Study of Education.

The scientific perspective seemed to influence educational thinkers in three important ways, perhaps. First, science provided intellectual support for a rational and meliorist world view, a view widely held by the educational thinkers of the period. Problems could be solved by the rational application of scientific processes: all that was needed was more knowledge and the ability to apply that knowledge. And the application of that knowledge would result in a gradually improving world: societies were evolving, just as the human species had evolved. Educational popularizers of Darwin's theory of evolution, such as Francis W. Parker (see page 34), argued that the schools could play an important role in this gradual improvement of society, especially if they would emphasize the study of science.

Second, science provided a content focus for the curriculum. Flexner (1916) was one of several theoreticians who argued for the primacy of science. In his view the central purpose of the school was to prepare children to cope in the real world—and that preparation would best be accomplished through a study of the physical and social world. Thus, in the "Modern School" he proposed, the curriculum would focus on four major fields—science, industry, aesthetics, and civics—and science would provide the organizing structure. His views were echoed by others, although they were not universally shared.

Finally, science provided a means for improving the schools. Scientific knowledge about the child yielded insights, proponents argued, about the desired nature of the curriculum—about what children could learn. Scientific knowledge also offered a rationale for the optimal methods of teaching. Throughout the era under examination, the methods formalized by Johann Friedrich Herbart, a German philosopher, became almost a formula for teachers and teacher trainers. His *five formal steps* seem perhaps strangely familiar even today:

1. Preparation: the teacher calls the learner's attention to previous learning experiences.
2. Presentation: the new materials are summarized or outlined.
3. Association: the new ideas are compared with the old.
4. Generalization: rules and general principles are derived from new materials.
5. Application: the new generalizations are applied to specific instances.

And science yielded insights about how schools were to be managed. Tyack and Hansot (1982) note that four of the founders of programs for the systematic training of school administrators (Strayer at Columbia Teachers College, Hanus at Harvard, Elliott at Wisconsin, and Cubberly at Stanford) had been teachers of natural science before entering education as a profession. One of their central concerns, he points out, was to develop a scientific technology for decision making in the schools.

The Exemplary Leaders

The major thrusts of this period were probably best represented by the careers and contributions of two educational leaders: G. Stanley Hall and Francis W. Parker.

   G. Stanley Hall   G. Stanley Hall was an eminent psychologist who provided scientific support to the child-centered educators of the day. While earlier developmentalists had argued for the study of the child as the basis for curricular decision making, it was Hall who provided the charismatic leadership for the movement, announcing at the 1894 annual meeting of the National Education Association, "Unto you is born this day a new Department of Child Study." His seminal work, *Adolescence*, published first in 1904 and reprinted in 1969, seemed to convince many educators of the need to understand the mental, physical, and emotional development of adolescence when they made educational decisions about curriculum content and pedagogical methods.

   However, as Kliebard (1985) astutely points out, Hall's curriculum ideas were drawn primarily from his "metaphysical, even mystical, assumptions about the alleged relationship between the stages in individual development and the history of the human race" (p. 10)—not from empirical studies of child development. Hall was perhaps the most ardent advocate of what came to be known as the "culture epoch" doctrine. The culture epoch doctrine, as formulated in the writings of Hall and his followers, argued that the child recapitulates in his or her development the developmental history of the human race. In Hall's words, "The principle that the child and the early history of the human race are each a key to unlock the nature of the other applies to almost everything in feeling, will, and intellect. . . . Thus in seeking the true principle of most education we must not only study the plays, games, and interests of the child today, but also compare these with the characteristic activities of early man . . . " (Hall, 1904, pp. 443–444).

   Although Hall's curricular theories were radical, Tanner and Tanner (1980) are probably correct in assessing his influence as more conservative than reformist. They point out, quite accurately, that Hall in his writings and speeches consistently defended existing institutions and the existing social order. As a social Darwinian, he believed in evolutionary social change, not radical transformation. The essential task of the school was to support this gradual change through the nurturing of the gifted, providing the gifted child with the opportunity to grow through individualized activities.

Francis W. Parker   Francis W. Parker seemed to have had even more influence than G. Stanley Hall; in fact, John Dewey himself called Parker "the father of progressive education." Parker is significant for his contributions to both pedagogy and curriculum development. Appointed superintendent of the Quincy (Massachusetts) school system in 1875 and given a mandate by the Quincy School Committee to improve achievement, he brought to the task some ideas about teaching which he had developed while studying Pestalozzi and Froebel in Germany. The pedagogical methods he advocated could perhaps best be described as natural, child-centered methods. Conversation was emphasized, as a way of facilitating the natural mastery of language. Writing was used as a means of helping the child communicate about experience, and spelling taught in relation to this experience-centered writing, rather than taught in isolation through long lists of "demons." Children studied geography by taking field trips around Quincy. And they learned to read by learning words, not letters and syllables. In addition to these specific methods, he offered also a unifying theory of methodology. All learning took place through two essential processes: attention and expression. Attention included observing, hearing language, and reading; expression included nine modes: gesture, voice, music, speech, making, modeling, painting, drawing, and writing.

His contributions to curriculum theory were similarly comprehensive. In his *Talks on Pedagogics* (1894), he argued for a child-centered curriculum which builds upon what the child instinctively knows. But this curriculum would not be fragmented; it would instead be unified by what Parker called "concentration." Instead of the sixteen "branches" of the elementary school curriculum recommended by some prestigious committees (see below for a fuller discussion), Parker advocated a concentrated curriculum of central subjects—the inorganic sciences, the life sciences, history, anthropology, and geography. And even this smaller number of central subjects could be viewed as one unified study of human nature in the natural environment.

In contrast to Hall's essentially conservative orientation, Parker was in almost every respect a progressive who believed that the common school was the key to human advancement. And in a chapter in his *Pedagogics* work, he anticipated at least the rhetoric of more current social reformers: "This mingling, fusing, and blending [of children from all social classes] give personal power, and make the public school a tremendous force for the upbuilding of democracy" (p. 421).

The Major Publications

The major publications of the academic scientism period were perhaps the reports of two committees established by the NEA: the Committee of Ten, appointed to make recommendations for the high school curriculum; and the Committee of Fifteen, for the elementary curriculum.

The Committee of Ten   Although many educators cite the work of the Committee of Ten as an example of the attempt of colleges to dominate the curriculum, the committee was appointed by the NEA at the request of members. There was so much variation in college preparatory curricula in schools across the country that school administrators themselves desired more uniformity. One of the pressing issues, for example, was whether high schools should continue to teach Greek. Although many colleges required Greek, school administrators were experiencing great difficulty in finding both students and teachers for the subject.

As noted above, Charles Eliot was appointed chairman of the committee and seemed to play a controlling role in setting the agenda, preparing materials, influencing positions, and preparing the final publication. He organized the committee into nine conferences—three focusing on the traditional subjects (Latin, Greek, mathematics); and six on the modern subjects (English, natural history, geography, physical science, modern foreign languages, and social studies). Several critics have noted that the identification of those subjects at the outset as the foci of deliberation determined the outcome: it simply was not possible for the committee to recommend the study of such subjects as art and music, since such subjects had not been included in the nine proposed for examination.

The major recommendation of the committee report (National Education Association, 1893) was that four separate programs of study be offered to high school students: classical, Latin-scientific, modern languages, and English. As the names of the programs indicated, the major difference among the several programs was the nature of the language requirement:

Classical: two years of Greek, four years of Latin
Latin-scientific: four years of Latin
Modern languages: four years of French and German
English: four years of Latin, French, or German

Even though the recommendations of the committee strongly supported an academic orientation for the curriculum, the committee made it clear that they did not view the function of the high school as solely college preparatory. As the report noted, "The secondary schools of the United States, taken as a whole, do not exist for the purpose of preparing boys and girls for colleges. Only an insignificant percentage of the graduates of these schools go to colleges or scientific schools" (p. 51). The committee also recommended that the subjects be taught to all students in the same way, regardless of their program. This view seemed to reflect Eliot's strong bias against the European tracking system and his unshakeable belief in the capacities of all students. In essence, the Committee of Ten said to the profession and to the public, "A sound academic curriculum is the best preparation for life—for all students."

The report generated considerable controversy. Chief among the critics was G. Stanley Hall, who first attacked the report at the meeting where it was presented and then expanded that attack in his book *Adolescence* (1904). In both instances he focused his criticism on the recommendations that all students be offered an academic program and be taught in the same way. He accused the committee of ignoring the "great army of incapables," who in his view needed very different programs and methods of instruction. Eliot responded vehemently. He pointed out that the essential function of the school was to develop the intellect of all students, not to sort them and train them for predetermined positions in adult life.

The Committee of Fifteen   The other committee appointed by the NEA almost at the same time was given the charge of making recommendations for elementary curriculum and instruction. Eliot had some influence with this committee, which accepted two of his recommendations: that the number of elementary grades be reduced from ten to eight; and that algebra be substituted for arithmetic in grades seven and eight. However, it rejected his recommendation that the time devoted to grammar and arithmetic be reduced so that the program could be diversified and enriched. (The committee's recommendations were reported in the NEA's 1895 report.)

In making recommendations about teaching method, the committee seemed to espouse a moderate position. In somewhat liberal tones, the committee recommended that the child's interests should be considered as a means of increasing the motivation to learn. However, the committee protested strongly against the use of the scientific method in teaching elementary science: science should be taught through teacher lecture, since in the view of the committee, elementary pupils lacked the mental capacity to benefit from discovery approaches.

In its curriculum recommendations, the committee advocated a rather conservative approach. Grammar, literature, arithmetic, geography, and history were seen as the central subjects for training the mind—and clear separation of those subjects was essential. The following subjects were to be taught every year, from first to eighth: reading; English grammar (except in the eighth year); geography; natural science and hygiene; general history; physical culture; vocal music; and drawing. Handwriting was to be taught in the first six years; and spelling lists, in the fourth, fifth, and sixth. Latin was to be introduced in the eighth year, and manual training (for boys) and sewing and cooking (for girls) in the seventh and eighth. In mathematics, arithmetic was to be studied in the first through the sixth years, followed by algebra in the seventh and eighth.

In addition to the required oral lessons in general history for all grades, U.S. history was to be taught in the seventh year and the first half of the eighth; the Constitution was to be taught in the second half of the eighth year. Thus, a pupil in the fourth year would be studying eleven separate "branches" or subjects: reading, handwriting, spelling lists, English grammar, arithmetic, geography, natural science and hygiene, general history, physical culture, vocal music, and drawing.

The ultimate impact of the Committee of Fifteen report was to sustain a somewhat fragmented and subject-centered curriculum.

PROGRESSIVE FUNCTIONALISM

The era of *progressive functionalism*, which lasted approximately from 1917 to 1940, was characterized by the confluence of two seemingly disparate views: the progressive, child-centered orientation of the followers of John Dewey and the functional orientation of curriculum scientists.

The Temper of the Times

The historian Paul Johnson, in his recent (1983) history of *Modern Times*, asserts, "The modern world began on 29 May 1919 when photographs of a solar eclipse, taken on the island of Principe off West Africa and at Sobral in Brazil, confirmed the truth of a new theory of the universe" (p. 1). In Johnson's view—and in the eyes of many other historians—this confirmation of Einstein's theory of relativity marked the beginning of a modern era that Johnson characterizes as "relativistic." Although Einstein himself believed in God and held firm beliefs about the necessity of moral absolutes, the uninformed public, misled by some sensational journalists, misinterpreted the scientific theory of relativity as moral relativism. And such a rejection of absolutes was, of course, also supported by the works of Sigmund Freud, whose ideas were beginning to reach a large public audience.

The decade of the Twenties was a time of seemingly unbridled optimism and growth in this country. Houses were being built at a record-making pace. By 1929, there were more than twenty-six million cars registered—one car for every five people. Funding for education increased four-fold: between 1910 and 1930, it rose from $426 million to $2.3 billion—and illiteracy fell from 7.7 to 4.3 percent. The mass appeal of the radio and the movies effected what Johnson terms "the Americanization of immigrant communities and a new classlessness in dress, speech, and attitudes . . ." (p. 224). In his view, the Twenties was the most fortunate decade in American history.

All that optimism and growth were tragically destroyed in the Depression and the very slow recovery that followed. The human suffering of that period is difficult to exaggerate. At one point it was estimated that 28 percent of the population were without any income at all. Many school systems simply shut down because there was no money to pay teachers: at one point Chicago owed its teachers $20 million. And the Health Department estimated that 20 percent of the children attending school were suffering from malnutrition. According to figures from the U.S. Office of Education, some 1,500 colleges had closed.

The international picture was no less depressing, for the Thirties was the decade marking the rise of Hitler in Germany and Stalin in the Soviet Union, both of whom were ultimately responsible for the mass genocide carried out in both nations. And confronted with the global rapacity of the dictators in Germany, Italy, the Soviet Union, and Japan, the Western democratic governments seemed for many years to be confused and impotent.

The Predominant Trends

As noted above, the term given this era derives from two forces—progressivism and functionalism—that, while seemingly antithetical in principle, often combined to influence both curriculum and instruction.

Progressivism in Education It is obviously difficult in the brief space available to summarize a movement so complex and so often misunderstood as progressive education; readers interested in a deeper analysis of the movement should turn to Lawrence Cremin's basic work, *The Transformation of the School* (1961). The intent here instead is to discuss briefly two key ideas of the movement that seemed to persist, even among educators who would not call themselves "progressive": the child-centered curriculum; and the project method of instruction.

Whereas in the prior decade the dominating influence of the curriculum was the academic subject, for progressive educators it was the child. The child-centered curriculum was based upon a somewhat romantic and perhaps even naive view of child development: the child is innately curious and creative, with a thirst for learning and a need for self-expression. Such a view has clear implications for both the process and the content of the curriculum. In using a curriculum-development process, child-centered curriculum workers begin by determining the child's interests, assured that any desired content can be linked with those interests. In an extreme version of this process, there is no predetermined curriculum: all curriculum decisions emerge day by day from the ephemeral interests of the child. In more moderate forms, general decisions are made in advance about content and outcomes, with the child's interests influencing lower-level decisions regarding learning activities, sequence, and resources.

The content of the curriculum is similarly influenced. The arts are emphasized, since the nurturing of creativity is paramount. Subjects that have little immediate appeal to the child, such as mathematics and grammar, tend to be slighted. Topics that are perceived as "relevant" are emphasized; thus, there is much attention to the close-at-hand and the immediate. And divisions between the several subjects are minimized or ignored completely: a child's interests cannot be compartmentalized into the neat packages called the disciplines.

Perhaps this quotation from the Committee on Curriculum Making of the National Society for the Study of Education (1927) best summarizes the then current view of the child-centered curriculum:

> *In times past, and too much in the present, school practice has imposed adult forms of thought, feeling, and behavior upon children. . . . much more vigorously than has been true in the past, it must be recognized that the steps necessary in moving towards these [educational] goals are dictated by the character of the child's interests, needs, capacities for learning, and experiences, as well as by the larger demands of society.* (p. 1)

The project method was perhaps first systematically described in an article by William Kilpatrick (1918) that Kliebard (1985) calls "the single most dramatic event in the revival of the child-centered method" (p. 12). The article made such an impact on educators at that time that more than sixty thousand reprints were requested. Although projects had been used previously by teachers of science and agriculture, Kilpatrick, a professor at Teachers College of Columbia University, was the first to provide the method with a theoretical underpinning and to urge its use across the curriculum. The theory was a result of Kilpatrick's attempt to wed Dewey's educational philosophy and Thorndike's "stimulus-response bond psychology."

According to Kilpatrick, any meaningful experience—intellectual, physical, or aesthetic—could serve as the organizing center of the project, as long as it was characterized by purpose. And for every project, there were four steps: purposing, planning, executing, and judging. While it might be necessary from time to time for the teacher to make suggestions about each of these four stages, it was preferable, from Kilpatrick's viewpoint, for the child to initiate and determine each stage. And these projects, strung together, became the curriculum.

While the Kilpatrick article was obviously influencing a wide audience of educational leaders, critics were quick to point out its limitations: it focused too much on "instrumental" learning—learning that was useful only in solving problems; it minimized the importance of higher-level thinking; and it ran the risk of overemphasizing the individual inquiry at the expense of social learning. To Kilpatrick, however, these dangers were surmountable; in a 1921 article in the *Teachers College Record,* he attempted to show how each of these curricular problems could be solved.

Functionalism   Functionalism is the term given here to the educational theory of those whom Kliebard (1985) calls "the social efficiency educators," who argued essentially that the curriculum should be derived from an analysis of the important functions or activities of adult life. As a curriculum theory, it was clearly influenced by two significant ideas current at the time. It first of all reflected the concern for efficiency that was at the heart of the "scientific management" of Frederick Taylor and his followers. Taylor argued that any task could be analyzed for optimal efficiency by observing skilled workers, studying the operations they carried out, determining the time required, and eliminating wasted motion. Similarly, education could be made more efficient by analyzing learning tasks. And it was avowedly influenced by the stimulus-response learning theory of Edward Thorndike that supported the importance of successful practice.

An example of functionalism as an approach to curriculum making is perhaps best provided by Charters' (1923) *Curriculum Construction.* Obviously influenced by his experience as director of the Research Bureau for Retail Training at the Carnegie Institute of Technology, Charters proposed the following seven-step process for developing curriculum:

1. Determine the major objectives by studying the life of man in its social setting. Such major objectives as citizenship and morality were suggested.
2. Analyze those objectives into ideals and activities, continuing the analysis of the level of working units. The ideals should be identified by the faculty; the activities should be derived from objective studies of the activities of men in society. This analysis of activities should result in a series of discrete and highly detailed steps.
3. Arrange these ideals and activities in their order of importance.
4. Place in a higher order in this list those ideals and activities which are high in value for children but low in value for adults—such as the activity of games and the ideal of obedience.
5. Determine the number of most-important items which can be handled in the time provided for schooling, deducting those which are better learned outside of school.
6. Collect the best practices of the race in handling those ideals and activities.
7. Arrange the resulting materials in the appropriate instructional order, being sensitive to the psychological nature of children.

And he made clear his own view of the project method:

> School projects cannot be selected haphazard. They are controlled by two factors: on the one hand they must parallel life activities, and on the other hand they must include the items of the subjects in their proper proportions. (p. 151)

The Exemplary Leaders

Two figures seem to stand out in retrospect: John Dewey and Franklin Bobbitt. Although they espoused diametrically contrary views of the curriculum in particular, they both seemed to exert a strong influence on their contemporaries.

John Dewey   In a sense, of course, it is fallacious to identify Dewey as a leader of this period alone, since his career as a philosopher and an educator spanned the eras both of academic scientism and progressive functionalism. However, his thinking seems to have been much more influential during the latter period. Rather than attempting to present in detail all his significant works, it seems more appropriate to examine here three closely related contributions: his beliefs about the relationship of school and society; his theories about curriculum; and his implementation of those theories in the curriculum of the University of Chicago Laboratory School.

His beliefs about the relationship of school and society are, of course, fundamental to his theories of the curriculum and are best understood at the outset. For Dewey, democracy was the ideal society, and he believed that the society can prevail only as it enables diverse groups to form common interests, to interact freely, and to achieve a mutual adaptation. In such a society, as Broudy (1971) notes, sharing is the key concept—the sharing of resources, the sharing of ideas. And, as Broudy goes on to note quite insightfully, the Deweyan conception of democracy rejected a laissez-faire philosophy of government and espoused instead an activist stance that would deliver concrete benefits to all. As Broudy puts it, " . . . the Dewey concept of shareability was a vigorous endorsement of equalitarianism and socialism in both the political and economic domains" (p. 130).

And Dewey pointed out in his *Democracy and Education* (1916) that such a society needed schools for more than the superficial reason of producing an educated electorate:

> *A democracy is more than a form of government; it is primarily a mode of associated living, of conjoint communicated experience . . . These more numerous and more varied points of contact denote a greater diversity of stimuli to which an individual has to respond; they consequently put a premium on variation in his action. . . . A society which is mobile, which is full of channels for the distribution of change occurring anywhere must see to it that its members are educated to personal initiative and adaptability. Otherwise, they will be overwhelmed by the changes in which they are caught and whose significance or connections they do not perceive.* (pp. 101–102)

How did the schools relate to such a society? The school, he noted in *The School and Society* (1900), should become an embryonic community, "active with types of occupations that reflect the life of the larger society and permeated through with the spirit of art, history, and science. . . . When the school introduces and trains each child of society into membership within such a little community, saturating him with the spirit of service, and providing him with the instruments of effective self-direction, we shall have the deepest and best guarantee of a larger society which is worthy, lovely, and harmonious" (pp. 43–44).

Thus, as Cremin (1961) observes, Dewey espoused a reformist role for the schools, one which would make the schools less isolated and more central in the struggle for a better society. With the right kind of schools, individuals would understand issues better, would be better equipped to solve social problems, and would be able to control their surroundings. In accomplishing such goals, the schools would not attempt to indoctrinate citizens but would instead develop means by which all could live life to the fullest and become self-directing individuals.

Such a concern with self-directing individuals who could transform their society was manifested, in Dewey's view, in a curriculum that was essentially social in its emphasis. This social emphasis was expressed in both a perspective about curriculum and a view of the classroom environment. His social perspective about the curriculum was expressed this way in *Democracy and Education* (1916):

> The scheme of a curriculum must take account of the adaptation of studies to the needs of existing community life; it must select with the intention of improving the life we live in common so that the future shall be better than the past. Moreover, the curriculum must be planned with reference to placing essentials first, and refinements second. The things which are socially most fundamental, that is, which have to do with the experiences in which the widest groups share, are the essentials. (p. 191)

And the classroom environment should be one, he observed, which was essentially a social environment. In such a social environment, the school would become a genuine community, with open sharing of common experiences. In such a community, the emphasis is on social interaction, cooperation, and communication. Such an emphasis was so important to him that he believed strongly that the true measure of excellence in schooling was the extent to which this sense of community had been achieved: " . . . the measure of the worth of the administration, curriculum, and methods of instruction of the school is the extent to which they are animated by a social spirit" *(Democracy and Education,* p. 358).

It was this concern for the social nature of schooling and learning, of course, that led him to place so much emphasis upon experience. Yet he did not advocate a mindless activity-centered curriculum in which any activity is considered worthwhile as long as it is perceived by the learners as interesting and relevant. In *Experience and Education* (1938), he noted that experience and education cannot be directly equated; some experiences are mis-educative, to use his term. Desirable learning experiences had to meet certain stringent criteria: they had to be democratic and humane; they had to be growth-enhancing; they had to arouse curiosity and strengthen initiative; and they must enable the individual to create meaning.

Two of the essential attributes of experience, from Dewey's perspective, were continuity and interaction. Continuity should inform all genuine learning experiences: " . . . the principle of continuity of experience means that every experience both takes up something from those which have gone before and modifies in some way the quality of those which have come after" *(Experience and Education,* p. 35). Interaction, as he used the term, designated a quality of a learning experience which gave equal attention to the internal conditions of the learner and the objective reality of the external environment. Traditional education, in his view, had given too much attention to the external environment and some misguided progressives were giving too much attention to the internal perceptions of the learner. Desirable learning experiences kept the two in a state of dynamic tension, with the learner interacting with the environment and creating meaning through those interactions.

In Dewey's view of the ideal curriculum, play and work would constitute the main types of such desirable learning experiences, especially for the younger learner. He made the point that play and work, which he saw as closely related, not antithetical, are essential learning experiences because they typify the social situation: " . . . they tap instincts at a deep level; they are saturated with facts and principles having a social quality" *(Democracy and Education,* p. 200). This use of play and work as an organizing principle, he reminded his readers, was not intended primarily to prepare the young for future occupations or to entertain them. Instead it was intended to provide a meaningful basis for present learning. He used gardening as an example:

> *Gardening, for example, need not be taught either for the sake of preparing future gardeners, or as an agreeable way of passing time. It affords an avenue of approach to knowledge of the place farming and horticulture have had in the history of the race and which they occupy in present social organization. Carried on in an environment educationally controlled, they are means for making a study of the facts of growth, the chemistry of soil, the role of light, air, and moisture, injurious and helpful animal life, etc. There is nothing in the elementary study of botany which cannot be introduced in a vital way in connection with caring for the growth of seeds.* (p. 200)

By examining the curriculum of the laboratory school he established at the University of Chicago, we have an excellent opportunity to examine how these theories might work out in practice. He began by constructing a curriculum which would correspond with the growth of the school. He identified three major steps of child growth, with each stage accompanied by a special emphasis in subject matter.

In Stage 1, lasting approximately from age 4 to age 8, the child has a strong need to express himself or herself in manipulation, investigation, and oral communication. Play, games, occupations, storytelling, and informal conversations thus played a central role. More formal studies were grouped around these kinds of familiar activities and evolved from them. Children were grouped so that each learning group included an age range of two to three years; in this way, older children could read to and help the younger ones.

In Stage 2, from age 8 to age 11, the child is able to think about clearer, long-range goals and is ready to master more complex skills. Subject matter was organized to help the child understand how people had developed more effective social institutions in response to more complex challenges. Thus, instead of studying history chronologically, children studied units that exemplified the technical advances that gave people more control over their environment. The same principle was emphasized in the study of science at this stage: science was studied in relation to social studies, and the emphasis was on people using science to exercise increasing control over their environment. Reading, writing, and arithmetic were to be taught at this stage. However, they were not taught through trivial drill; instead, they were presented as learning skills required for increased understanding.

In Stage 3, from age 11 to age 14, interests take on adult form. The child is ready for systematic study of such disciplines as geography, chemistry, history, mathematics, and literature. Such classified and organized knowledge is now seen as essential in more complex inquiries.

Consonant with Dewey's emphasis on work and play, the study of occupations played an important role in the curriculum at all three stages. The study of occupations was important in the curriculum of the laboratory school for several reasons. First, it provided a bridge between community and school. Second, it enabled teachers to capitalize upon the natural instincts of children—to make, to investigate, to interrelate socially, and to express. Next, it helped the child develop a positive attitude toward school and learning: the study of occupations built upon the child's natural interests and enabled the child to engage in activities that were important in both school and community. Finally, the study of occupations readily became a means for moving toward more complex educational experiences.

Franklin Bobbitt   Franklin Bobbitt was the other curriculum theorist who seemed to exert a profound influence on the schools of his time, and who still seems to affect indirectly even those who are not familiar with his work. Early in his educational career, Bobbitt had an opportunity to develop a complete curriculum for schools in the Philippines, an experience which he viewed as having mixed success. He then took graduate studies at Clark University, which under the leadership of its president, G. Stanley Hall, had become a leading center of educational thinking. After his studies at Clark had been completed, he joined the faculty at the University of Chicago in their department of educational administration. While at Chicago, he began to study the Gary schools, where William Wirt had tried to reconstruct both the organization and the curriculum in line with Dewey's theories.

While Bobbitt seemed initially attracted to the innovations at Gary, he became sharply aware of the waste and inefficiency in this experimental institution. It was about this time that he read Taylor's popular work, *The Principles of Scientific Management* (1911). In Taylor's exciting new ideas about efficiency in industry, Bobbitt saw a model for curriculum work. He was quite clear about the direct relationship between industrial production and schooling. The curriculum, in his view, was whatever was needed to process the raw material (the child) into the finished product (the model adult). He summarized in this early work the curriculum process as he saw it in the following manner:

1. . . . we need first to draw up in detail for each social or vocational class of students in our charge a list of all of the abilities and aspects of personality for the training of which the school is responsible.

2. Next we need to determine scales of measurement in terms of which these many different aspects of the personality can be measured.

3. We must determine the amount of training that is socially desirable for each of these different abilities and state these amounts in terms of the scales of measurement.

4. We must have progressive standards of attainment for each stage of advance in the normal development of each ability in question. When these four sets of things are at hand for each differentiated social or vocational class, then we shall have for the first time a scientific curriculum for education worthy of our present age of science. (p. 49)

This earlier view, which in some ways seems rather simplistic and insensitive to the societal context, was refined in a later (1918) publication. According to Seguel (1966), in the intervening years Bobbitt had become more aware of the need to know the particular culture in which the adult lived and also had become more aware of the problems emerging in the society of which he was a part. The technological developments in that society had created a social interdependence which required social cooperation for human welfare. Consequently, he now saw a need to examine that ideal man in the context of the social environment of which he was a part.

And that social environment which would be analyzed should not represent the status quo, in Bobbitt's view; instead, it should represent a desired future, a better society which would provide the greatest good to the greatest number. By using the scientific method, educators would gather representative knowledge about that social behavior which would permit control of the future. He put it this way in that later publication:

> *Scientific management demands* prevision—accurate prevision. [Emphasis in original.] *It demands understanding that sees all factors in true and balanced relation without any distortion due to claims or oppositions of special interests. This means that scientific survey and analysis of human needs must be the method of discovering the objectives of the training that is demanded not by individuals, but by the conditions of society.* (pp. 69-70)

Thus, while both Dewey and Bobbitt espoused a social meliorist view of the purpose of schooling, they differed sharply in their conception of the curriculum. From Dewey's perspective, the developing child was the beginning point for curriculum development; from Bobbitt's, the model adult was the starting point. And, while Dewey embraced an experience-centered program in which learnings emerged somewhat organically and informally from social interactions, Bobbitt seemed more concerned with a precise scientific matching of activity with outcome.

The Major Publications

Obviously, the writings of both Dewey and Bobbitt had an important influence on educational leaders of the times. However, two other works might be seen to have had a more direct impact: the *Cardinal Principles of Secondary Education* and *The Foundations of Curriculum Making*, the Twenty-Sixth Yearbook of the National Society for the Study of Education. While quite different in both their genesis and their intended audience, the two publications were surprisingly similar in their major emphases.

The Cardinal Principles of Secondary Education   In 1913 the National Education Association, perceiving a need to reconcile some important differences about the nature of secondary education, appointed the Commission on the Reorganization of Secondary Education. After five years of deliberation, the Commission (1918) published its recommendations. In its rationale, the commission argued that secondary education should be determined by "the needs of the society to be served, the character of the individuals to be educated, and the knowledge of educational theory and practice available" (p. 7); all three had undergone significant changes. And the overriding goal of the secondary schools was to provide a democratic education.

The seven cardinal principles therefore emerged from this rationale: health; command of fundamental processes (reading, writing, arithmetic, oral and written expression); worthy home membership; vocation; citizenship; worthy use of leisure time; and ethical character. These principles were seen as closely interrelated, not as separate goals. In achieving those goals, schools were encouraged to construct programs of study around three elements: *constants* (required courses); *curriculum variables* (specialized subjects chosen in relation to the student's goals); and *free electives* (subjects chosen to develop the special interests of the student).

While recommending a 6-3-3 organization of the twelve years of schooling, the commission was also strong in advocating a closely coordinated program of studies throughout the twelve years. The junior high school, in the commission's view, should serve as an opportunity for the young adolescent to explore developing interests; thus, seventh graders should have an opportunity to explore a variety of vocations and foreign languages. And, in a position that was radical for those times, the commission recommended that overage elementary pupils should be promoted to the secondary school, where their needs could be better served.

In addition to providing a useful framework for the secondary school curriculum, the commission accomplished two other important goals. It attempted somewhat successfully to free the secondary schools from the domination of the colleges, and it articulated forcefully a rationale for the comprehensive high school. In the commission's view, the American high school should serve the needs of all youth, not just the college-bound. How important were these accomplishments? Cremin (1955) expresses it this way: " . . . most of the important and influential movements in the field since 1918 have simply been footnotes to the classic itself" (p. 307).

The Twenty-Sixth Yearbook   In the midst of all the ferment resulting from the attempts to reshape the schools, the National Society of Education (Rugg, 1927) decided to bring together in two volumes the thinking of all the major experts in the field—as the preface noted, " . . . making a special effort to bring together, and as far as possible to unify or to reconcile, the varying and often seemingly divergent or even antagonistic philosophies of the curriculum that were being espoused by leading authorities . . . " (p. 6). It is obviously difficult to summarize adequately these two volumes produced by men whom Tyler (1971) calls "pioneering leaders in curriculum development" (p. 28). Only certain major contributions will be noted here.

First, Rugg, the editor of both volumes, clearly articulated a simple process of curriculum making:

> *First: The determination of fundamental objectives; the great purposes of the curriculum as a whole of its several departments.*
> *Second: The selection of activities and other materials of instruction; choice of content, readings, exercises, topics for open-forum discussions, manual activities; health and recreational programs.*
> *Third: The discovery of the most effective organization of materials and their experimental placement in the grades of the public schools.* (Part I, p. 51)

As Tyler (1971) points out, Rugg's outline was very similar to the one Tyler developed; Rugg's formulation, however, omitted the task of evaluating the curriculum.

Next, in their chapter, Rugg and Counts delineated an organizational procedure by which districts could accomplish this job. First, develop a research attitude toward the problem. Second, provide adequate funds for continuous and comprehensive development. Third, employ trained specialists in curriculum making. Fourth, give them adequate facilities. Fifth, organize committees of workers under the direction of the specialists. Sixth, secure the assistance of external consultants. As Tyler notes, a major weakness in the Rugg and Counts system was its failure to recognize the importance of the classroom teacher.

Perhaps the major contribution of the Twenty-Sixth Yearbook, as Tyler points out, was its achievement of a consensus on two of the major issues that seemingly had divided the profession. First, the committee articulated a balanced position on whether studies of the child or the adult should provide the grounding of the curriculum: "We would stress the principle that in the selection and validation of curriculum materials expert analysis must be made both of the activities of adults and interests of children" (Part I, pp. 12–13). The committee also recognized the importance of both individual and societal needs: "The individual becomes an individual in the best sense only through participation in society. . . . The curriculum can prepare for effective participation in social life by providing a present life of experiences which increasingly identifies the child with the aims and activities derived from an analysis of social life as a whole" (p. 14).

DEVELOPMENTAL CONFORMISM

The next period of educational history—the era of *developmental conformism* (1941–1956)—might be seen as a transition period, with the nation first embroiled in a catyclysmic war and then recovering from it to find a "cold war" on its hands.

The Temper of the Times

This period, of course, was in many ways a turbulent time. It was first of all a time of international conflict and tension. The United States entered World War II in 1941, and by 1945 the Allies had defeated the Axis nations. However, only three years after the war ended, tensions between the United States and the Soviet Union became critical with the Soviet blockade of Western Berlin—tensions that were to affect the nation for the next four decades. Those tensions and the concomitant distrust of the USSR provided a fertile bed for Joseph McCarthy's "witchhunts" of the 1950s. The Korean war began in 1950, ending finally in 1953. And only two years later, in 1955, the country took the first step in involving itself in the war in Vietnam: in 1955, the United States began to train the South Vietnamese army.

It was also a time of racial unrest. For most of the period, this was a strongly segregated society, with deep-seated racial and ethnic biases. In 1942 the government interned 110,000 Japanese-American citizens in detention camps. In 1943 there were major race riots in Detroit and New York. And until 1947, major league baseball maintained a strong color barrier: only whites were welcome. But slowly the barriers began to crumble. During World War II, war contractors were barred from racial discrimination. Jackie Robinson joined the Brooklyn Dodgers and became the first of a long line of black baseball stars. The Supreme Court outlawed school segregation in 1954, and in 1955 Rosa Parks refused to give her seat to a white man on a bus in Montgomery, Alabama.

Finally, it was the dawning of the atomic age. The first nuclear chain reaction was produced at the University of Chicago in 1942. The atom bomb was dropped on Hiroshima and Nagasaki in 1945. The first hydrogen device was exploded in 1953, and the *Nautilus*, the first atomic-powered submarine, was launched in 1954. As several observers noted, the atom bomb profoundly changed the way the average person felt and thought about the world.

Most of the American people seemed to react to this societal turbulence by attempting to live lives of quiet conformity. As Presidents, both Truman and Eisenhower seemed able to assure the American people that, despite these signs of unrest, the nation was essentially sound and its future was bright.

The Predominant Trends

Here again two trends are singled out as shaping educational efforts: the interest in the developmental abilities and needs of youth, and a concern with conformity as an educational goal.

The Developmental Theorists It was, first of all, a period marked by rather intensive interest in the educational implications of child and adolescent development. As noted above, Dewey had long been concerned with delineating and responding to the stages of growth in children and youth. Dewey (1964) put the concern for development rather clearly and forcefully:

> . . . the aim of education is growth or development, both intellectual and moral. Ethical and psychological principles can aid the school in the greatest of all constructions: the building of a free and powerful character. Only knowledge of the order and connection of the stages in psychological development can insure this. Education is the work of supplying the conditions which will enable the psychological functions to mature in the freest and fullest manner. (p. 213)

As will be discussed below, Piaget's work was just becoming known by educators who perhaps sensed its importance but could not yet discern fully its implications. However, it was the theories and research of Havighurst that during this period seemed to make the most immediate difference to educators. Havighurst (1972) conceptualized *need* as a "developmental task," which he defined as "a task which arises at or about a certain period in the life of the individual, successful achievement of which leads to his happiness and to success with later tasks, while failure leads to unhappiness in the individual, disapproval by society, and difficulty with later tasks" (p. 2). These tasks emerge from the confluence of several factors: the nature of the biological organism, which sets the conditions for learning social tasks; the social and cultural patterns which produce a set of expectations for learning; and the sequential pattern of preferences and dislikes which emerge in the individual.

The importance of these developmental tasks for curriculum can be

seen at once by examining just a few of the tasks which Havighurst identified for childhood and adolescence. Consider these examples:

Early Childhood
1. Getting ready to read.
2. Learning to distinguish right from wrong.
3. Learning sex differences and sexual modesty.
4. Learning to talk.

Middle Childhood
1. Learning physical skills necessary for games.
2. Learning to get along with age-mates.
3. Learning an appropriate masculine or feminine social role.
4. Developing fundamental skills in reading, writing, and calculating.

Adolescence
1. Accepting one's physique and using the body effectively.
2. Preparing for marriage and family life.
3. Preparing for an economic career.
4. Desiring and achieving socially responsible behavior.
5. Developing intellectual skills and concepts necessary for civic
   competence.

As Havighurst pointed out, the concept of developmental tasks is
educationally useful for two reasons. First, in his view, it helps in discovering and stating the purposes of education. From his perspective the primary
purpose of education is to help the individual achieve certain of his
developmental tasks. The second use is to find the right time for certain
educational efforts. Havighurst (1972) put the matter this way:

> When the body is ripe, and society requires, and the self is ready to
> achieve a certain task, the teachable moment has come. Efforts at teaching,
> which would have been largely wasted if they had come earlier, give gratifying
> results when they come at the teachable moment. (p. 5)

Once Havighurst had delineated these needs and had articulated a
rather cogent rationale for their importance, educational leaders of the time
attempted to translate those tasks into curricular outcomes and appropriate
learning activities. If, for example, "learning to get along with age-mates" is
a task of middle childhood, then that became a curricular goal for the intermediate grades and learning experiences were selected accordingly. Thus,
there would be class discussions of the importance of age-mate relationships, stories about children who found ways to improve their peer relationships, and classroom role plays illustrating effective ways of resolving peer
conflict.

While there is a certain amount of reasonableness inherent in such an
approach, critics have noted important deficiencies. First, the stage theorists

seem to have an unfortunate tendency to promulgate their theories on the basis of insufficient empirical evidence. Consequently, such theories as Havighurst's too often minimize some crucial individual differences. Second, the inflexible use of such stages in shaping curricula can result in a curriculum that is too concerned with the tasks of the present and insensitive to the emerging tasks of the future. Consider, for example, one of the developmental tasks Havighurst identified for adolescence: "developing intellectual skills and concepts necessary for civic competence." Does that rule out the inclusion of civics concepts in the social studies curriculum for the intermediate grades? Finally, of course, many would object to the rather explicit assumption that the schools are responsible for all the developmental tasks. In fact, one recurring controversy among both public and educators is whether the school should be responsible for such developmental tasks as "preparing for marriage and family life."

Conformity as an Educational Goal   Implicit in the conceptualization and language of Havighurst's developmental tasks is a strong sense of conforming to the status quo. Consider, for example, such tasks as these: "learning an appropriate masculine or feminine role"; "accepting one's physique . . . "; "desiring and achieving socially responsible behaviors"; "accepting and adjusting to the physiological changes of middle age." It is perhaps not unfair to say that such a strong emphasis upon conformity was both a reflection of and a contribution to a prevailing educational view that held that one of the important responsibilities of the schools was to help children and youth conform to existing societal norms.

This view was perhaps most clearly expressed in the educational movement called "life adjustment education." The phrase seems to have been first used by Charles A. Prosser, a vocational educator who offered this resolution at a conference on vocational education sponsored by the U.S. Office of Education:

> It is the belief of this conference that, with the aid of this report in final form, the vocational school of a community will be able better to prepare 20 percent of the youth of secondary school age for entrance upon desirable skilled occupations; and that the high school will continue to prepare another 20 percent for entrance to college. We do not believe that the remaining 60 percent of our youth of secondary age will receive the life adjustment training they need . . . until the administrators of public education with the assistance of the vocational education leaders formulate a similar program for the group. (U.S. Office of Education, 1951, p. 15)

The "Prosser resolution," as it became known, was immediately endorsed and became the impetus for a series of regional and national conferences on "life adjustment education." And two Commissions on Life Adjustment Education were appointed and functioned for three years each.

A review of the literature on life adjustment education suggests that the movement, while at times quite diverse in its particulars, was predicated upon some basic assumptions. First, many advocates, like Prosser, assumed that the goal of the schools was to support the status quo by tracking students into predetermined career-oriented programs. Consider, for example, this statement by Mort and Vincent (1946), two articulate advocates of "the modern school": "It is vain and wasteful to take a girl who would make a fine homemaker and try to fit her into the patterns of training which make a lawyer, or to take a boy who would be successful in business and try to fit his training to that which produces doctors" (p. 42).

A second assumption was that the curriculum should emphasize functional outcomes—practical skills and knowledge that had immediate value for the student. Thus, life adjustment curricula typically emphasized units in home and family life, the use of leisure time, and the responsibilities of good citizenship. Ravitch (1983), for example, cites a junior high course in Tulsa, Oklahoma, in which students learned how to dress appropriately, how to choose the correct shade of nail polish, and how to improve their appearance. Obviously such an emphasis upon "functional skills" would support the general thrust toward conformity. As Ravitch notes in commenting on the Tulsa course, "The object of courses like these was to teach children what kind of behavior was socially acceptable and how to adjust to group expectations" (p. 68).

A concomitant assumption was that the disciplines themselves were not important as organizing bases for the curricula. Instead, schools were encouraged to develop "core curricula" that would minimize subject-matter distinctions and integrate learnings around major themes and issues. As Oliver (1977) notes, the primary objective of the core curriculum is "to develop unified studies based upon the common needs of the learners and organized without restriction by subject matter" (p. 246). Here, for example, are some of the "centers of experience" that Van Til, Vars, and Lounsbury (1961) recommend for structuring a core program: making and keeping friends; coming to terms with my body; money—magic or madness; meet your new school.

Despite the somewhat intemperate attacks of its critics, the life adjustment movement, in retrospect, made some useful contributions. It was a sincere attempt on the part of educators to develop curricula that were responsive to the perceived needs of children and adolescents. And it provided the impetus for much local curriculum innovation that capitalized upon the teachers' knowledge of the children and their communities. However, its weaknesses doomed it to a short life. Even though the leaders of the movement were later embarrassed by the term *life adjustment* and argued that it provided for societal change and reconstruction, an analysis of the life adjustment literature suggests otherwise. The recurring theme throughout much of this literature is that this is a good society which simply must be maintained. Also, the attempt to make education more relevant too often produced curricula that trivialized learning and overemphasized the needs of the present. Finally, in too many cases it provided a curricular excuse for tracking systems that imprisoned children from poor families into low-level programs that were banal and unimaginative and denied them the opportunity to pursue academic studies needed for success in college.

The Exemplary Leaders

Two curriculum theorists seem to have been important in this period: Ralph Tyler and Hollis Caswell. Although, like most exemplary leaders, their careers spanned several of the periods demarcated here, it seems most appropriate to examine their work within the framework of the period presently under discussion.

Ralph Tyler   Tyler first gained professional attention through his participation as research director of the *Eight-Year Study* sponsored by the Progressive Education Association to evaluate and systematize the efforts of progressive schools to free their curricula from the domination of the colleges. The curriculum results of the study were summarized by Giles, Mc-Cutchen, and Zechiel (1942), who noted that curriculum development and evaluation involved attention to four basic issues: identifying objectives; selecting the means for attaining those objectives; organizing those means; and evaluating the outcomes. And it seems apparent that their work influenced Tyler in his preparation of the syllabus for the graduate course he was offering at the University of Chicago. It is this syllabus for "Education 305" (Tyler, 1950) that presents and explicates what has become known as "the Tyler rationale."

In the syllabus, Tyler noted that the first question which must be answered in developing any curriculum is, "What educational purposes should the school seek to attain?" These educational objectives can first be identified by examining three sources: studies of the learners themselves; studies of contemporary life outside of school; and suggestions from subject specialists. However, a comprehensive analysis of these three sources would yield a multitude of objectives, many of which would be in conflict. Therefore, the curriculum specialist needs to select and prioritize those objectives by using two "screens": his or her educational philosophy, and the psychology of learning. Once screened, the final objectives are then presented in a form helpful in selecting learning experiences and guiding teaching. Tyler suggested here that objectives should be formulated in a two-dimensional form: a behavioral component which identified an important learning behavior (such as the development of effective ways of thinking), and a content component drawn from the discipline or subject.

The second question is, "How can learning experiences be selected which are likely to be useful in attaining these experiences?" Here he argued for several general principles that should guide curriculum workers in selecting objectives. First, for a given objective, the student should have experiences that give him or her an opportunity to practice the kind of behavior implied by the objective. Second, the student must obtain satisfaction from carrying out the kind of behavior implied by the objective. Third, the reactions desired in the experience should be within the range of possibility for the students involved. Fourth, there are many particular experiences that can be used to attain the same objectives; a given school may develop a wide range of educational experiences for the same objectives. Fifth, the same learning experience will bring about several outcomes.

The third question is, "How can learning experiences be organized for effective instruction?" In making determinations about the organization of experiences, the curriculum developer should consider three criteria: continuity, sequence, and integration. Continuity, in Tyler's lexicon, refers to "the vertical iteration of major curriculum elements" (p. 55). There should be recurring opportunity for skills to be practiced and developed. Sequence is the principle that provides for a successive experience that the teacher can build upon and explore more deeply. And integration is "the horizontal relationship of curriculum experiences" (p. 55), which assures that important skills and concepts are reinforced from discipline to discipline.

Once the learning experiences have been identified, they should then be grouped according to certain "threads" or elements which assist in the organization of experiences. Thus, in mathematics the threads might be concepts and skills. Those threads in a sense become the elements that define the scope of a curriculum. Then learning experiences are sequenced according to certain principles (for example, chronological or whole-to-part). Finally, the curriculum specialist considers the main structural elements in which the learning experiences are to be organized. A structural element, in Tyler's rationale, can be a subject, a broad field, a core curriculum, or an undifferentiated structure.

The final question is, "How can the effectiveness of learning experiences be evaluated?" Valid and reliable curriculum-based tests should be developed and the results used to improve the curriculum.

Tyler's publication has had a lasting impact on curriculum leaders. By 1985, more than 100,000 copies of the syllabus had been purchased. It made a significant contribution by systematizing in a syncretic manner much previous curriculum theory. And curriculum workers seemed to value its clearness, its comprehensiveness, and its simplicity. Tanner and Tanner (1980) summarize their own assessment in this manner:

> *It is not a literal representation of the world of curriculum development, but an economical and simplified scheme for dealing practicably with the complex process of curriculum development. And it serves to synthesize past achievements with current practice. It cannot be dismissed lightly unless something more comprehensive and convincing can take its place. (p. 97)*

Of course, Tyler and his rationale have not been without their critics, despite the widespread impact of his ideas. Critics such as Kliebard (1970) have faulted it for its narrowness, its emphasis upon linear production, and its mechanistic rationality.

Hollis Caswell   Since Caswell's career spanned at least fifty years, beginning with his joining the faculty of Peabody College in 1929 and ending with his deanship at Teachers College of Columbia University, placing him in this period obviously distorts the continuing nature of his contributions. However, this key period seems to provide a useful context for examining his major contributions to the field since it took place roughly in the middle of his long career. (One of the most comprehensive analyses of his contributions can be found in Seguel's 1966 publication.)

To begin with, Caswell was one of the first to understand the importance of staff development as a necessary foundation for curriculum work. To that end he developed excellent study materials and bibliographies to help teachers perceive the larger issues of child development and curricular ends and used those materials in educating the teachers of Florida and other states who were working with him in a comprehensive curriculum-revision project.

Second, he put into practice on a major scale the widespread belief that teachers should be involved in curriculum development. In developing a state curriculum for Virginia, he involved ten thousand Virginia teachers in studying and discussing curricular issues. After four state-wide committees identified a set of comprehensive aims for education, several hundred teachers worked in production committees to develop experience units.

Third, he developed a useful set of organizing structures that integrated the three determiners of curricula—child interests, social meaning, and subject matter. He began by reviewing what was known about child development in order to identify important child interests. Then he turned to cultural anthropology to identify those interests that had social significance, selecting social functions that, suitably adapted to the child's development, could be used as the categories of learning. However, he also saw the importance of subject-matter content; thus, the social functions were related as appropriate to subject-matter content. The conjoining of social functions and centers of interest resulted in a scope-and-sequence chart, with the social functions constituting the scope and the centers of interest, the sequence. Thus, one of the social functions was "expression of aesthetic impulses." In grade 1, the center of interest was "home and school life." The intersection of these two would thus produce learning activities in which the child would learn how to express aesthetic impulses in home and school life. In language arts, these activities would take the form of reading and writing stories; in social studies, learning how homes in different societies reflect cultural values.

And, as Seguel notes, in his wide-ranging professional endeavors he gave the curriculum field increased prestige by giving it status as a separate department in higher education and by providing leadership to the first organization devoted solely to curricular matters, the Society for Curriculum Study.

The Major Publications

Two quite different publications are singled out here for attention: one by the distinguished Swiss psychologist Jean Piaget, and one by a somewhat anonymous committee of American educators.

The Psychology of Intelligence
Since Piaget's publishing career spans several decades during which many seminal publications were produced, it is obviously difficult to select one work as most important. However, his 1950 book, *The Psychology of Intelligence*, seems to have been especially influential since it was one of the earliest to present in a systematic manner his comprehensive view of the nature of intelligence and the child's developmental stages.

In this 1950 work he first of all clearly articulated his concept of intellectual operations. In his view, intelligent behavior is the outcome of several invariant processes: reciprocal interaction between an organism and its environment; the acquisition of mediated experience, which involves transformations within the organism; and the development of central processes of control. The operations of intelligent behavior, in Piaget's view, are the subject's actions on the environment. The essential principle throughout intelligent behavior is the degree of continuity and discontinuity. Continuity depends upon familiarity in the interactions with the environment and results in the assimilation of the experience. Discontinuity, the encounter with the unfamiliar, results in the disruption of assimilation and the initiation of accommodation. Thus, one of the essential functions of teaching from a Piagetian perspective is to introduce controlled discontinuity into the learning environment.

The level of intelligent behavior is essentially conceptualized, in Piaget's view, as the degree to which the learner is dependent on the presence of material objects in order to use these intelligent operations effectively. Thus the developmental stages he identified are organized around this essential principle. Four such stages are usually discussed in the extensive literature on Piaget: sensorimotor; preoperational; concrete operations; and formal operations. While these stages, in his view, are invariant in their sequence, they are also hierarchically related: early stages are integrated into later ones.

The sensorimotor stage, which begins with conception and lasts until about age two, is a preverbal period in which the child relies upon sensorimotor information to adapt to the environment and to acquire new behaviors. The child begins with simple reflex actions, then makes responses modified by experience; these modified responses establish a schema or a program of action. Familiar schemata developed earlier are then grouped and coordinated into new behaviors. The child then begins to make some very simple experiments with the environment, finally undertaking some rather primitive problem solving in dealing with the environment.

During the next stage, the preoperational, which lasts until about age six or seven, language and symbolic thought have their beginnings. The learner reconstructs the developments of the sensorimotor stage, integrating prior knowledge into the new intellectual structures. However, the stage is called "preoperational" because there are as yet no true operations, in Piaget's use of that term; as he defined it, an operation is an interior and reversible action which modifies knowledge and enables the learner to understand the structures of knowledge. Flavell (1963) notes four important characteristics of this period: the learner is egocentric, perceiving reality from the sole perspective of the self; preoperational thought is centered, in that the thought processes focus on a single dimension of the object of thinking; preoperational thought can also be decentered, in which the learner is able to see many dimensions of the object and relate them to each other; and preoperational thought is static, focusing on the transitory conditions of change.

During the stage of concrete operations, between ages seven and eleven, the child develops the cognitive ability to classify, order, and handle numbers, spatial operations, and all the operations of classes and relations. In a sense the concrete operations are similar to those of the prior stage, except for the fact that the child is able to use representational thought instead of direct action on the object. In this stage the child seems to have a well-integrated cognitive system by means of which he or she can act upon the environment. However, the child is still able to deal effectively in a cognitive sense only with concrete objects, not with symbolic representations of those objects.

During the final stage of formal operations the adolescent can think about both the real and the possible. Flavell (1963) notes several important characteristics of this stage. First, the adolescent can begin consideration of problems by thinking about all the possible relations which could hold true in the data and then attempting through experiment and logical analysis to find out what relations are actually true. Second, the adolescent thinker is able to handle hypothetic-deductive relationships, using hypotheses that must be confirmed or denied. Third, the adolescent can use propositional thinking, dealing with statements instead of concrete reality. Finally, the adolescent can use combinatorial analysis, being able to determine all the possible relations inherent in a problem and test them all in combination.

Educators who first learned of the Piagetian stages in the late 1950s and early 1960s were initially impressed with the research data supporting this stage theory. Two issues of application seemed paramount. First, some educators argued that curricula should reflect stage theory: the curriculum for a given stage should not make cognitive demands that children at that stage could not handle. Second, some educators were more interested in intervention, attempting to devise curricula that would facilitate cognitive development. In attempting to apply Piagetian stage theory to curriculum development, both groups faced a dilemma so aptly identified by Duckworth (1979) in this manner: "Either we're too early and they can't learn it or we're too late and they know it already." After noting the obvious difficulty of assessing the ability of thirty children to handle a dozen cognitive tasks (thus requiring 360 tasks), she reached what seems to be an eminently sound conclusion:

> The solution for the teacher, however, is not to tailor narrow exercises for individual children, but rather to offer situations in which children at various levels, whatever their intellectual structures, can come to know parts of the world in new ways. . . . And how much more to the point it is to think of a child's education as knowing and learning about how the world works than to attempt to resolve the dilemma. . . . (p. 311)

More recently, however, other researchers have been more concerned with conducting research to verify or challenge Piaget's stage theory. After reviewing all the pertinent research, Gelman and Baillargeon (1983) reach this conclusion:

> In our opinion there is little evidence to support the idea of major stages in cognitive development of the type described by Piaget. Over and over again the evidence is that the preoperational child has more competence than expected. Further, the evidence is that the concrete-operational child works out concepts in separate domains without using the kind of integrative structures that would be required by a general stage theory. (p. 214)

Education for ALL American Youth This influential volume was quite different from Piaget's work in both its genesis and its substance. First, it was the product of a committee. The National Education Association in 1935 established the Educational Policies Commission as a standing body to articulate a national policy for education. The commission first produced a policy statement advocating chiefly a social reconstruction role for the school; Kliebard (1979) notes that this statement was written chiefly by the historian Charles Beard. Their second volume was essentially a rewriting of the "Cardinal Principles." Then followed three volumes, all published in the mid-1940s, that provided specific blueprints for the schools of the United States: *Education for ALL American Youth* (1944), *Educational Services for Children* (1945), and *Education for ALL American Children* (1948). (In the discussion that follows, these three volumes will be considered as one report.)

In substance the report was essentially an argument for developmental conformism. The main section of the report portrays two imaginary communities, Farmville and American City, and delineates model curricula for their schools. In developing such curricula, the commission members strongly endorsed the key role of the teacher, with lay people serving in an advisory capacity. And those curricula were to be provided in a comprehensive system: the commission strongly recommended schooling for all children and youth from ages three through twenty. There would be a public nursery school, followed by a six-year elementary school, and then an eight-year high school, including grades 13 and 14.

The nursery school provided children with a supervised program of indoor and outdoor work and play. Children use clay, paint, and crayons, listen to the phonograph, and examine books and pictures. They work at learning how to behave as members of a democratic group. The nursery school staff includes teachers, nurses, doctors, family life consultants, nutrition experts, and mental hygiene specialists.

The elementary curriculum recommended by the commission attempted to fuse the concern for children's interests with a social reconstructionist view of the society. Although it was important from the commission's perspective for each community to develop its own elementary program—and for each child to have a curriculum responsive to his or her needs—the report also stressed the importance of common learnings: communication skills, arithmetic, social studies, science, health, and art. This rather conventional program was to be delivered in imaginative ways, however: children play house, undertake projects on animal life, and work in committees.

The secondary curriculum recommendations were much more progressive in intent and form than those for the elementary schools. The secondary curriculum, according to the commission, was to respond to ten "imperative educational needs of youth." In brief forms those needs were these: develop salable skills; maintain good health; understand the rights and duties of the citizen in a democracy; understand the significance of the family and the conditions conducive to successful family life; know how to purchase and use goods and services intelligently; understand the methods of science; develop their capacities to appreciate beauty; be able to use their leisure time well; develop respect for other persons; grow in their ability to think rationally, express thoughts clearly, and read and listen with understanding (Educational Policies Commission, 1944, pp. 225–226).

One section of the report explains in greater detail how the curriculum should be differentiated—and in so doing unwittingly betrays the conformist views of the authors. Edith of Suburbia is well-to-do and looks forward to college. Martha is a "Negro girl, daughter of a tenant farmer." Ignorant and cheerful, Martha will "probably marry in her early teens." Herbert is brilliant, but his father runs a "rather poor and run-down fruit farm." So Herbert's destiny is similarly fixed: "He will graduate next year and then help his father or get a job on another farm" (Education Policies Commission, 1944, pp. 11–13).

How influential were the commission reports? Cremin (1961) makes this assessment:

> Once they appeared, they were quickly incorporated into education syllabi across the nation. In retrospect, there is little doubt but that they summed up as well as any contemporary publications the best-laid plans of the teaching profession for American education in the post-war decades. (p. 332)

SCHOLARLY STRUCTURALISM

The Temper of the Times

In retrospect, the era of *scholarly structuralism* (1957–1967) seems to have been an interesting period of history. First, it was a time when the factors producing the turbulence of the previous period seemed to gather in strength. International tensions continued unabated. The shooting down of the U-2 reconnaissance plane in 1960 led to the cancellation of a planned summit meeting. The disastrous attempt to invade the Bay of Pigs in 1961 and the Cuban missile crisis of 1962 reminded Americans that communist forces and a Marxist government were our close neighbors. And by the end of this period, in 1967, there were 475,000 U.S. troops in Vietnam.

Racial unrest also continued to grow. In 1957, Orval Faubus, the governor of Arkansas, called out the National Guard in an attempt to bar black students from entering Central High School in Little Rock; Faubus' attempt to block the students was countered by Eisenhower's sending of federal troops to enforce a court order to remove the guardsmen. A wave of sit-ins began in 1960 at the Woolworth lunch counter in Greensboro, North Carolina. And in 1963, more than 200,000 individuals assembled in Washington, DC, to hear Martin Luther King and to show their support for equal rights for blacks. Congress responded in 1964, with an omnibus civil rights bill banning discrimination in voting, jobs, public accommodations, and several other areas. But the riots in Watts, a Los Angeles slum, in 1965, and in Newark and Detroit in 1967, indicated that serious problems still remained.

However, it was also a time in which major trends of subsequent decades were subtly prefigured. The concern for the environment was first publicly voiced during this era with the publication of Rachel Carson's *Silent Spring* in 1962; the urgent need to liberate women was forcefully articulated in Betty Friedan's *The Feminine Mystique*, published in 1963 but generally ignored until many years later. And Jack Kerouac's book *On the Road*, published in 1957, articulated many of the themes that were to be strongly expressed in the youth movement of the next period.

In education, of course, the major event was the launching of Sputnik in 1957—an event that dramatized the need for strong programs in science and mathematics in American schools. And under the prodding of President Johnson, Congress responded with massive allocations of federal aid.

The Predominant Trends

The period under consideration was an interesting one from an educational perspective. First, the early years of the 1950s had been marked by several ill-tempered attacks on progressive education by such critics as Albert Lynd and Arthur Bestor; both authors published in 1953 rather vitriolic diatribes against what they considered to be the evils of progressive education. Those assaults, along with other criticisms, resulted in a rapid collapse of progressivism in education. Then, when the Soviets launched the first space satellite in 1957, there ensued what Cremin characterizes as "a bitter orgy of pedagogical soul-searching."

In the midst of that soul-searching, Conant published his influential (1959) report on the American high school. As will be noted below, the report is essentially a somewhat conservative defense of the comprehensive high school; but its moderate tone and its sensible recommendations undoubtedly helped educators stave off the more radical critics.

However, while school administrators were reading the Conant report with often self-congratulatory smiles, scholars were already developing and implementing plans to transform the curriculum. Although Conant himself was a prestigious scholar and although scholars had often served on commissions that produced general recommendations for curricula, this was the first time in American educational history that academic scholars decided that they had a key role to play in the development of specific curricula. Largely supported by federal funds channeled through the National Science Foundation, those scholars produced numerous curricula for every major discipline in both elementary and secondary education. Cuban (1979) notes that by the end of the 1960s more than $200 million in federal funds had been invested in curriculum making—and most of that developmental work was in the hands of scholars eager to produce what some unfortunately called "teacher-proof" curricula.

In the production of those curricula, most scholars seemed much influenced by Bruner and his colleagues at the Woods Hole Conference (Bruner, 1960), who argued that curricula should be built upon the "structure of the disciplines"—the principles, concepts, and ways of knowing that were peculiar to each discipline. And those structures were to be learned by acting like a scholar. Bruner was quite explicit about this: "The school boy learning physics is a physicist, and it is easier for him to learn physics behaving like a physicist than doing something else" (p. 31).

The Exemplary Leaders

During this interesting time, two curriculum theorists seem to have made major impacts—Jerome Bruner and Joseph Schwab.

Jerome Bruner   Bruner was a psychologist from Harvard University who was selected to serve as chairman of a conference composed chiefly of scientists, mathematicians, and psychologists and convened at Woods Hole, Massachusetts, by the National Academy of Sciences. The chief purpose of the conference, convened one year after the launching of Sputnik, was to improve elementary and secondary science curricula. However, *The Process of Education*, the final conference report which was written by Bruner (1960), was a much more ambitious effort.

Bruner sets forth rather cogently in this volume a comprehensive rationale for scholarly structuralism. First, school curricula must be primarily concerned with effecting and facilitating the transfer of learning. Since school time is limited, educators must find the most efficient means of using the limited time available. This general transfer of learning can be best achieved, he argued, if the curriculum is explicitly designed to enable the learner to understand the structure of the disciplines. Rather than attempting to learn and remember numerous unrelated facts, the learner should focus on discipline-based principles, concepts, and inquiry processes. Bruner put the argument this way: "The continuity of learning that is produced by the . . . transfer of principles is dependent upon the mastery of the structure of the subject matter. . . . The more fundamental or basic is the idea he has learned, almost by definition, the greater will be its breadth of applicability to new problems" (p. 18).

The way that these structures can best be learned, he reasoned further, is by the discovery or inquiry approach, where the learner functions as a younger scientist, learning chemistry as the chemist learns it—by doing chemistry. And, in contradistinction to Piaget's position, Bruner argued that even young children could learn disciplinary structures in this manner. Or, in Bruner's words, "intellectual activity anywhere is the same, whether at the frontier of knowledge or in a third-grade classroom" (p. 14).

If the structures of the discipline were to be mastered through scientific discovery, then obviously the scholars of that discipline were in the best position to provide leadership in the development of those curricula. "Only by the use of our best minds in devising curricula will we bring the fruits of scholarship and wisdom to the student just beginning his studies," he noted (p. 19).

In later years Bruner (1973) was to call for a moratorium on developing structure-based curricula and to urge instead more socially relevant curricula: "We might better concern ourselves with how those [societal] problems can be solved, not just by practical action but by putting knowledge, wherever we find it, to work in these massive tasks" (p. 21). However, for a period of at least ten years, his ideas on transfer, structure, discovery, and readiness were to play a key role in almost every major curriculum project supported by federal funds.

Understanding those broad principles was especially important in the latter part of the twentieth century, Bruner argued, because increased scientific knowledge was able to clarify those structures in a way that perhaps was not possible before. And, obviously, the explosion of knowledge made it impossible for the student to learn everything. Therefore, learning the structures of a discipline resulted in a kind of curricular parsimony.

Joseph Schwab   Schwab was a scientist and educator at the University of Chicago at the time of the Woods Hole conference and was instrumental in developing the three different versions of the Biological Sciences Curriculum Study curriculum. His writings on curriculum span a period of at least twenty years and have proved to be rather influential in the field of curriculum theory.

Like Bruner, Schwab was early concerned with the structure of the disciplines; yet it seems fair to say that his writings on the matter demonstrate a complexity and sophistication missing from the Bruner work. As Westbury and Wilkof (1978) point out, Schwab was essentially concerned with science as a certain kind of habit of inquiry: he was primarily interested in why a particular science chooses at a point in time to emphasize one conception of verification over another. In his essay "Education and the Structure of the Disciplines" (1978) he works out this general principle by first exploring the nature of scientific claims, noting that one can understand the validity of such claims only by understanding the character and context of the discipline in which they were made. He then explores the fundamental topics which inform all the sciences: fidelity to the complexity of subject matter versus accuracy of statement about that subject matter; the understanding of patterns in a subject matter versus the identification of the elements of subject matter; and the understanding of how those patterns might be apprehended.

Rather than insisting that there is only one way of understanding the world, Schwab argues for a "permissive eclecticism," which enables the inquirer to use any valid approach to understand natural and human phenomena. He noted that few disciplines have a single structure and that the scientists in a field are too diverse in their preferences to be unanimous about one right mode of attack. In this sense, he argued, " . . . a structure is a highly flexible pattern which is continually adapted and modified to fit the particular problems and situations to which it is applied" (p. 239).

This view of the multiplicity of structures led him to certain specific recommendations for the curriculum. In the earliest grades, he pointed out, the discipline would appear as "small problems," suited to the age and ability of the child, such as the problem of classifying toys. In these earliest grades, the disciplines would appear also as "fragments of a narrative of inquiry," simple accounts of such scientific phenomena as how plants grow and animals develop. At first the subject matter for such problems and discussions would be selected for their practical importance. Beginning in junior high school, materials chosen because of their structural importance would be meshed with the practical.

At the high school level, the structures of the discipline would be introduced in another form; this time the student learns about the uncertainties, the differences of interpretation. Narratives of inquiry end in doubt or present alternative views. And now "first-order materials" replace the narrative of inquiry. The student grapples with raw data and primary sources. And the student reads original scientific papers, not interpretations of them.

Schwab's later writings on curriculum seem much more concerned with process and much less concerned with the structure of the disciplines. Four major papers, published irregularly over the period from 1969 to 1983, were concerned with what he termed "the practical": "The Practical: A Language for Curriculum" (1969); "The Practical: Arts of Eclectic" (1971); "The Practical 3: Translation into Curriculum" (1973); and "The Practical 4: Something for Curriculum Professors to Do" (1983). In these papers he established the groundwork for what has come to be known as the "deliberative" theory of curriculum. In these papers he argued for a deliberative process involving professors, content specialists, curriculum leaders, teachers, and parents in a dialogic encounter about the important practical problems of curriculum making. The outcome, he hoped, would be incremental change, and the process would be an eclectic one, drawing from several bodies of knowledge and from several perspectives.

The Major Publications

Two publications seem worthy of note: the Conant report and the PSSC curriculum project. One looked back; the other seemed to look ahead.

The Conant Report In 1956 James Bryant Conant, who had been president of Harvard University and high commissioner for Germany after World War II, was invited by John Gardner, head of the Carnegie Corporation, to undertake a major study of the American high school. It seemed like a propitious time to conduct such a study. Progressivism seemed to be reeling from the attacks of its critics. The launching of Sputnik one year after Conant began his study had shocked the public: the Soviets had achieved a technological breakthrough that seemed to mock the image of the United States as the leading nation of the world. The nation seemed to be searching for a new direction for its schools.

Thus, when the report was released in 1959, it was eagerly greeted by citizens and educators alike. Kliebard (1979) notes that eighty thousand free copies were distributed to principals, superintendents, board members, and others. Paperback copies of the report were purchased by many who ordinarily did not buy educational books.

What did they find in the Conant report? They found first a tone of reasonableness, one that Kliebard characterizes aptly in the phrase "bland common sense" (p. 231). Perhaps such a tone was especially appealing at a time when the critics seemed so strident. Beyond that general tone, they found a ringing endorsement of the American comprehensive high school. Admiral Rickover (1959) and several other critics had criticized such schools as markedly inferior to the selective high schools of Europe. Conant, however, argued strongly in their defense. While he pointed out that his study of high schools had led him to several superior comprehensive schools that were providing a sound education for all students, he based his arguments chiefly on the democratizing effects of such schools: "I believe it is important for the future of American democracy to have as close a relationship as possible in high school between the future professional man, the future craftsman, the future manager of industry, the future labor leader, the future salesman, and the future engineer" (p. 127).

He also made several recommendations about the organization and support services required in such a school. Students should not be tracked into programs that separated them from their peers, but they should be grouped by ability for most of their major subjects. Special counselors should be added to advise the academically gifted, and the schools should keep an inventory of the courses taken by the top 15 percent. And students should stay in the same heterogeneously grouped homeroom throughout their high school years.

His curricular recommendations were quite specific and somewhat conventional:

1. All students should be required to complete four years of English, three years of social studies, one year of mathematics, and one year of science.
2. Academically talented students should be required to take three additional years of mathematics, four years of one foreign language, and two additional years of science. If they wished, a second foreign language could be added.
3. All students should be required to take a senior course in American problems, as part of their social studies requirement. In this course, students, heterogeneously grouped, would have free and open discussions of controversial issues.

These recommendations were endorsed by most educators of the time. Principals and their faculties used the report as a set of criteria to judge their schools and changed their programs to bring them into line with Conant's recommendations. While it seemed both conservative and conventional in its overall thrust, perhaps such a stance was exactly what was needed at this critical juncture.

PSSC Physics   This major curriculum project of the late 1950s and early 1960s (Physical Science Study Committee, 1961) is selected as a significant publication because it seems in retrospect, as Tanner and Tanner (1980) note, to have been an "archetype for curriculum reform" (p. 546). And in many respects its history seems to encapsulate many of the lessons that might be learned from such reform movements.

In 1956 a prestigious group of scientists, headed by Jerrold R.

Zacharias from the Massachusetts Institute of Technology, met to assess the state of physics education and to develop a much stronger set of curriculum materials. While initially they seemed inclined to develop a high school course that would combine physics and chemistry, they realized that it probably would be easier to gain acceptance of a course that would fit more readily into the existing high school program.

The course they produced, with its student text and ancillary materials, seemed to meet all the requirements that Bruner had identified for effective curricula. In fact, Bruner cited the PSSC course as one of the most highly developed curriculum projects. It was developed primarily by physicists, not "educationists." It claimed to involve students in discovery and inquiry as the basic pedagogical methods for identifying the structure of physics. Students "did physics" as physicists did, at least to the extent of their ability to do so. And, although the implementation of the new course was supported by numerous federally funded teacher-training institutes, the developers had made a significant attempt to develop a "teacher-proof" curriculum that attempted to control all aspects of the instructional process.

Initially the course seemed to meet with an enthusiastic response from science educators and curriculum workers, who were impressed with its scientific rigor and its strong emphasis on discovery. It was widely adopted across the nation by school districts concerned with improving academic standards and impressed with the credentials of the committee: by 1968, the PSSC staff reported that some 200,000 students were enrolled in the course, although others challenged those figures. (See Welch, 1968, for a discussion of this controversy.)

However, criticism began to mount. Teachers complained that students found the course much too difficult. Some articulate teachers writing in the professional journals of the period noted that the course did not give them enough flexibility. And although those developing the course hoped that it would increase enrollments in physics, the data indicated instead a sharp decline, a decline that an editorial in *Science* (Abelson, 1967) blamed on the new curricula.

The most objective assessments of the quality of the curriculum and its effects on student learning yield a somewhat mixed picture. First, Sarther (1985) finds it to be of mixed quality. In a rather careful analysis of the textbooks, laboratory manuals, and teacher's guides, she found that while PSSC does seem to do an effective job of presenting the structure of physics, at least in the Brunerian sense of that term, it can be faulted on two grounds. It does not present physics as a "narrative of inquiry," to use Schwab's term. Physics is instead presented to students as a finished discipline without much uncertainty. And the so-called inquiry method embodied in the curriculum seems contrived. As she concludes, "For the most part students are not identifying questions and devising ways to answer them nor are they led to consider in any serious and sustained way the creative and critical processes involved in doing science" (p. 19).

The results on the effects on student achievement are much more positive. A research synthesis on the effects of the "new science" curricula (Shymansky, Kyle, and Alport, 1982) concluded that students who had taken PSSC physics outscored students in traditional courses by a margin of 18 percentile points, across all performance measures.

ROMANTIC RADICALISM

The era of romantic radicalism (1968-1974) seemed to many observers to be a time of national fragmentation and upheaval, one in which the fabric of the society was stretched to its breaking point.

The Temper of the Times

It was, first of all, a time of rampant violence. Martin Luther King and Robert Kennedy were both assassinated in 1968; in the same year innocent civilians were slaughtered by American troops in My Lai, South Vietnam. Joseph Yablonski, his wife, and his daughter were killed in what the courts later held as a violent attempt to settle a struggle for power in labor unions. Charles Manson and his followers were found guilty of killing Sharon Tate and six others in 1971, and George Wallace was seriously wounded by a would-be assassin in 1972. Opposition to the war in Vietnam turned violent by 1969, with the "moratorium" protests in Washington and the Chicago "Weathermen" riots.

And it was a time when youth seemed to be in the saddle. Popular writers trumpeted the glories of being young. A strongly vocal "counter-culture" developed, espousing the virtues of drug-induced hallucinogenic visions, rock music, and spontaneous "openness" in all relationships—and at the same time rejecting the "bourgeois" values of work, punctuality, and bodily cleanliness.

Finally, it was a time when the Watergate hearings shook the faith of the American people in the most central of their political institutions—the Presidency. On June 17, 1972, five men were arrested for breaking into the offices of the Democratic National Committee in the Watergate apartment complex. Two years later, on August 9, 1974, Richard Nixon resigned the Presidency rather than risk impeachment.

The Predominant Trends

This period was obviously a time of experimentation in an attempt to develop child-centered schools and programs. The experimentation took three related but different forms: alternative schools, open classrooms, and elective programs.

Alternative Schools   The alternative schools were perhaps the most radical of all. While in later years alternative schools often seemed to be very similar to the conventional schools, at the outset their faculties worked hard to make them different. The differentness was part of their reason for being, in the eyes of their advocates: since many students could not do well in the structured environment of conventional schools, they needed alternative learning environments. While these alternative schools ranged from completely unstructured "free schools" to mildly experimental schools that seemed different in only superficial ways, they did share certain characteristics. (See Glatthorn, 1975, for a fuller account of the schools and their programs.)

First, they were strongly teacher-centered: teachers often administered the schools without a principal, teachers determined the curriculum, and teachers offered many of the supportive services provided by specialists in the conventional schools. And the word *teacher* here is used in its broadest sense of anyone with expertise who could help the young grow. Alternative schools often seemed indifferent to credentials and were frequently staffed with young radicals who ridiculed the educational establishment. Second, the schools were in a real sense child-centered: curricula were shaped in response to the needs and interests of the children, and learning activities were selected primarily on the basis of their appeal to the children. Learning had to be fun. Third, those schools extended the learning environment by making extensive use of the community. In fact, one of the most highly publicized alternative schools, the Parkway Program, began as an attempt to use the city of Philadelphia as the school. Aside from a home base in a church or office building, there was no "school": students had classes in museums, offices, recreation centers, and nearby universities. Also, there was a conscious attempt to minimize the importance of tests, grades, and report cards. The most radical schools simply ignored the whole issue of evaluation; teachers in the more conventional alternative schools wrote anecdotal reports, basing their evaluations on students' self-assessments. Finally, of course, they were "schools of choice": students elected to attend the alternative, rather than being assigned to it.

Despite the attacks of critics who were alarmed at their looseness, alternative schools seem to have been generally successful in achieving their goals. In a comprehensive review of the research on these "schools of choice," Rawid (1984) noted these achievements: they seemed to produce significant growth and achievement; student attendance and behavior improved; most were able to personalize the school environment and create a sense of community; staff, students, and parents associated with alternative schools showed unusual satisfaction and approval rates.

Open Classrooms   The open classroom was perhaps an attempt on the part of the educational establishment to respond to the mood of the times. Largely influenced by developments in the best British primary schools, the open classroom movement in the United States was to a great extent a revitalization of a moribund progressivism. Although the term *open classroom* was often simply an ill-defined slogan, there were certain important characteristics. There was first of all an emphasis upon a rich learning environment. Teachers in the open classroom typically began by provisioning the classroom with stimulating learning materials and activities—centers of interest that would immediately appeal to the child and at the same time help the child learn. The emphasis in those learning centers was on concrete materials, since most advocates of the open classroom had at least a second-hand acquaintance with Piaget's research on the importance of concrete operations for the young child. Children were free to move from center to center, to work together, and to engage each other in discussion. Thus, there was little concern for order in the conventional sense of that term: the best discipline was the self-discipline that came from learning on one's own. This flexible approach to learning required a highly flexible schedule: bells were intrusive, and standard periods of instruction interfered with the natural rhythms of the child. Activity flowed into activity. In all of this the teacher played simply a facilitative role, moving from center to center, conferring with individuals and groups who seemed to need help.

How effective were open classrooms? Predictably, there were different answers. Critics attacked them for their permissiveness and lack of structure. Defenders responded with anecdotal accounts of their success. Perhaps the most accurate assessment is this balanced conclusion reached by Horwitz (1979) in his review of the research:

> At this time the evidence from evaluation studies of the open classroom is not sufficiently consistent to warrant an unqualified endorsement of that approach to teaching over more traditional methods. There is certainly enough evidence, however, to defend open classrooms as viable alternatives where teachers and parents want them. (p. 289)

Elective Programs   The elective programs were perhaps an attempt on the part of secondary schools to capture the vitality and excitement of the open classroom, which to a great extent had been limited to the primary grades. The basic concept of the elective program was a relatively simple one: instead of a student taking "English, Grade 10," the student should be able to choose from a variety of short-term courses, such as "Women in Literature," "The Romance of Sports," and "War and Peace." In this sense, of course, such "electives" are different in organizational function from a subject such as music, which students elect to study or not to study.

While Hillocks (1972) cites a 1955 *English Journal* article as the first published description of an elective program and Applebee (1974) dates the first electives as being offered in the University of Iowa laboratory school in

1960, this movement really seemed to catch hold in the late 1960s. And it was essentially a grassroots curriculum movement, emanating from classroom teachers, not university professors. Predictably, then, it was a teacher-centered curricular response. Although advocates of elective programs usually claimed that courses were developed in response to students' interests, the courses themselves tended to reflect even more strongly the predilections of the teachers. In fact, elective programs probably spread so widely in such a short period of time because they were "teacher-friendly": in many schools, teachers could develop and offer any course they wished to offer.

Obviously, their quality was quite uneven. Although Glatthorn (1980) attempted to show how reading and writing skills could be systematically built into elective courses, most courses seemed to be poorly designed—loosely connected units built around topical content. For this reason, the conclusion by several critics that the elective programs were a factor in the decline in SAT scores probably had some warrant, although there is not much empirical evidence here. (See Copperman, 1978, for a typical statement of this position.)

The Exemplary Leaders

It is perhaps symbolic that the two figures selected as representing this exciting period of innovation and experimentation were not educators in the conventional sense of that term. Carl Rogers was a psychologist, and John Holt was perhaps a professional gadfly.

Carl Rogers   Rogers was a psychologist whose name came to be used to identify a school of counseling psychology: a Rogerian counselor is one who attempts to enter into the client's world, adopt the client's frame of reference, and listen empathically without advising. Initially, of course, Rogers had been centrally concerned with counseling, not with teaching, and with working with encounter groups, not with schools. However, he seemed to achieve eminence during this period of radical experimentation in schools, and the advocates of free schools and open classrooms found his ideas on teaching so much in line with their own thinking that he became the chief apostle of nondirective teaching.

His views on teaching were perhaps most forcefully expressed in a five-minute presentation he made to a conference at Harvard Business School on "student-centered teaching." Here are some highlights from that brief presentation as reported in his biography (Kirschenbaum, 1979):

> *My experience has been that I cannot teach another person how to teach. . . . It seems to me that anything that can be taught to another is relatively inconsequential. . . . I am only interested in learnings which significantly influence behavior. . . . I have lost interest in being a teacher. . . . When I try to teach, as I sometimes do . . . it seems to cause the individual to distrust his own experience and to stifle significant learning. (p. 369)*

Rogers articulated these ideas more formally in a rather influential work, *Freedom to Learn: A View of What Education Might Become* (1969). In the introduction to this work he was explicit about the essential characteristics of meaningful learning. It has a quality of personal involvement: the whole person is actively involved. It is self-initiated: even if stimulated by some external factor, its driving force is the internal search for meaning. It is pervasive, making a significant difference to the learner. It is evaluated by the learner, not by someone else. And its essence is meaning—the integration of experience into a meaningful whole.

The rest of the book explicated these essentials and their implications for teaching and schools by presenting detailed portraits of teachers trying to function as facilitators and by explaining more carefully the basic qualities of effective teaching: congruence, empathy, and trust. He also was explicit about the methods of facilitating significant learning: using learning contracts; helping students learn how to discover; providing the needed resources for discovery and inquiry; using encounter groups in the classroom; and facilitating self-evaluation.

Although Rogers worked with several college and school faculties who were interested in a Rogerian approach to organizational revitalization, his chief contribution seems to have been his ability to articulate clearly and to practice effectively what open educators and free school advocates could only haltingly express and imperfectly implement.

John Holt   If Rogers was a counselor who did not believe in advising, then Holt might be characterized as a teacher who did not believe in teaching. And in a sense, of course, he is selected here as a representative figure of an influential group that included such other disenchanted teachers as Jonathan Kozol, James Herndon, and Herbert Kohl.

While it might seem surprising to identify a radical teacher as a major curriculum figure, Holt is selected because he and his associates represent a period of time when curriculum making itself was called into question. In Holt's view, the teacher was the curriculum. From his perspective, the schools did not need scope-and-sequence charts, clearly articulated objectives, or specified learning activities. The schools needed instead exciting and imaginative teachers who could provision a stimulating learning environment and who could involve learners in meaningful learning experiences.

Much of Holt's pedagogical philosophy seems to have been formed through his experiences at the Shady Hill School, a private progressive school in Cambridge, Massachusetts, where he joined a faculty of intelligent and exciting teachers who were just becoming aware of the open classrooms in the schools of Leicestershire, England. His success in reaching his own students and his observations of those in traditional schools led him to publish his first attack on traditional education, *How Children Fail* (1964).

It is this work which probably was most effective in reaching a large audience of unhappy liberals. The work was perhaps most aptly classified by one reviewer (Nash, 1965) as "in the genre and the tradition of Rousseau's *Emile*, Pestalozzi's *Evening Hours of Hermit*, Dewey's *My Pedagogic Creed*, and Neill's *Summerhill*" (p. 378). In the first section of the work, called "Strategy," Holt describes how children go about their central business of completing imposed tasks, avoiding risks, and willingly playing the guessing game that teachers call "discussion." He notes teachers' obsession with right answers and points out with much anecdotal evidence how such an obsession prevents teachers from hearing what children are trying to say. In the second section, "Fear and Failure," Holt observes that even in the best progressive schools, children are scared—scared of failing, scared of being kept back, scared of being called stupid. From his viewpoint, such fear comes from a culture which values success too highly, instills an overly competitive spirit among children, and overpraises good work and good behavior.

In the third section of the work, "Real Learning," Holt makes an important distinction between unreal or phony learning—disconnected and useless learning that children only appear to know—and real learning—meaningful learning that children can and do use. His experience and observations lead him to conclude that schools reward unreal learning and inhibit real learning. The last section of the book, "How Schools Fail," is a telling indictment of the schools from a radical perspective. He attacks the "tell-them-test-them" process of teaching, which convinces students that school is a place of meaninglessness—meaningless questions, meaningless answers, meaningless activities. He sees schools as jails, in which students escape by passive compliance that frees their creative energies for life outside of school.

Holt's pessimistic view of the schools became only blacker over the years. At the end of his life he had reached the conclusion that reform was impossible and that parents should educate their children at home. His impact was perhaps best assessed by Larry Hayes (1985), a former teacher and journalist who had come to know Holt well. In a reflective essay written on the occasion of Holt's death, Hayes summed up his influence in this manner:

> His books no longer are routinely assigned reading for education majors. Many of our younger teachers have never heard of him. . . . For the generation of teachers who got started in the 1960s, however, Holt helped define the basic issues in education for the nation: students' rights, local control, the curse of poverty on children. Holt had a lot of influence on teachers of that period, a lot more than he would own up to. (p. 17)

The Major Publications

Two publications are selected here for quite different reasons: one heralded the promise of open education; the other marked the end of federal involvement in curriculum making.

Crisis in the Classroom In Ravitch's (1983) view, this book "projected open education into the public limelight as nothing previously had done" (p. 245). Its author, Charles Silberman, was an experienced journalist who had been commissioned by the Carnegie Corporation to conduct a study of teacher education. However, Silberman realized that a more important story was breaking—open education might be the one movement that would revolutionize education. He interviewed American educators, traveled to England to study their schools at first hand, observed many schools in the United States that were just attempting to implement these new ideas, and became conversant with the growing literature on open classrooms.

His book began by attempting to put the movement into some societal context. He noted the protests against the Vietnam war, the rock concerts and their impact on the young, and data from polls indicating that youth were alienated and radicalized. In his words, the national crisis might "well be a religious or spiritual crisis of a depth and magnitude that has no parallel since the Reformation" (Silberman, 1970, p. 28). In the midst of this crisis, the schools had failed; they were, in his words, "grim, joyless places . . . oppressive and petty . . . intellectually barren" (pp. 10–11).

The answer, of course, was open education. He pointed to the accomplishments of British open educators, described with admiration the work of such American pioneers as Lillian Weber and Vito Perrone, and enthusiastically portrayed schools where students enjoyed learning and used their freedom wisely. He urged educators to adopt such "humanizing" approaches as the integrated day, child-centered curricula, learning by doing, and a less controlled learning environment. At times the book seemed short on specifics and marred by a tone of breathless admiration; but it seemed convincing because of its many vignettes of exciting learning.

Any reasonable assessment of its impact would probably be in accord with Ravitch's judgment; in her view, Silberman's book universalized and popularized open education. It was able to do so for several reasons. First, it came at the right time in the history of the nation. The social upheaval of the late 1960s suggested a clear need to change all the institutions of that society in order to make them more humane and responsive, however that was defined. Most of the public perhaps shared his perception that there was indeed a societal crisis.

Second, its timing was right in relation to the funds available for education. There were still large amounts of federal funding available and a general conviction that federal support was both needed and could be effective, if used wisely. Many of the alternative school projects and other similar experiments were supported with what were then known as "Title III" funds—federal monies specifically allocated to support and extend educational innovation. It seemed to be a time when proposal writers were really the most important people in the school district.

Third, it came at the right time in the history of the profession. There was a general climate of educational innovation and activism that went beyond the open classroom movement. Schools were experimenting with open space, with flexible schedules, with various forms of team teaching, and with a large number of systems labeled as "individualized instruction." The open classroom movement was just beginning to spread; thus, Silberman found a receptive professional audience, despite his attacks upon traditional schools.

Finally, of course, the book itself conveyed its message in an interesting and appealing manner. Silberman was a highly skilled writer who knew how to personalize the dry stuff of educational change. He presented fascinating portraits of educators who seemed to be making a difference, and his own conviction made his message seem even more authentic.

Man: A Course of Study   This curriculum project (Curriculum Development Associates, 1972), usually identified by the acronym MACOS, had been developed at the Education Development Center with financial support from the National Science Foundation. By the time the course development work had been completed, close to $5 million had been allocated; an additional $2 million was provided by the same source for teacher workshops and other implementation activities.

As a social studies course designed for fifth- or sixth-graders, MACOS seemed in many ways to represent the best of federally supported curriculum work. It drew heavily from Brunerian curriculum theory, taking pains to provide interesting "discovery" experiences that would help young children understand some of the basic structures of the social sciences. Its primary objective was to help children understand the basic principles of human society by having them explore questions such as: What is human about human nature?; How did humans get that way?; and What can be done to make them more so? It used concepts from anthropology and the behavioral sciences to help children make comparisons between humans and other animals and between different human cultures. Children studied such units as the life cycle of baboons and aging and dying among the Netsilik Eskimos.

Initially the new course was well received, at least by the profession. By 1974, 1,728 schools in forty-seven states were using the program. The National Council for the Social Studies praised MACOS for its "unusually sound scholarship" and noted that a survey of social studies teachers gave MACOS the highest rating of all federally supported social studies projects (National Council for the Social Studies, 1975).

However, critics both outside and within the profession began to attack MACOS. In numerous local communities across the nation, parents and other concerned citizens criticized what they perceived as its cultural relativism, faulted its attempts to spread "secular humanism," and vehemently attacked content that they perceived as shocking and too threatening for children. Some professional critics joined in the attack. Weber (1975), for example, criticized it on four grounds: fifth- and sixth-graders were not able to deal with such profound issues; the course required teachers to depend on the materials provided and minimized teacher opportunity for creativity and initiative; the materials often conveyed an "air of indoctrination"; and the course might crowd out other important content.

The controversy reached its peak when Representative Conlan attacked the course in hearings before the House Committee on Science and Technology and later in the full House's discussion of NSF funding. Conlan was almost vitriolic in his attack, charging that the MACOS materials were "full of references to adultery, cannibalism, killing female babies and old people, trial marriage and wife swapping, violent murder. . . ." He saw the course as part of a plot by a "network of educator lobbyists to control education throughout America" (U.S. House of Representatives, 1975).

Chiefly as a result of his attack and what they perceived as a groundswell of public protest, Congress terminated all funds for MACOS and other NSF-sponsored curricula, required NSF to review all courses still under development, and passed an amendment specifying that all curricula developed under NSF sponsorship be available for parental review. In a very real sense the MACOS controversy marked the end of significant federal involvement in curriculum making.

PRIVATISTIC CONSERVATISM

The Temper of the Times

The period of *privatistic conservatism* (1975–) is generally recognized as the time when a strongly conservative philosophy permeated the national consciousness. It seemed that the American people were tired of violence, of experimentation, and of protest—and yearned for peace, stability, and traditional values.

This conservative philosophy, of course, was forcefully articulated by President Ronald Reagan, the "great communicator," who was able to persuade Republicans and Democrats alike of the need for less government, reduced federal spending, and lower taxes. His two landslide victories provided strong evidence that he had captured and reflected the national mood. Other institutions followed his leadership. California was the first state to vote for a cap on taxation; its "Proposition 13" sharply limited state spending on education. In 1978 the Supreme Court by a narrow margin voted against quota systems in affirmative action plans. And in 1982, the Equal Rights Amendment was defeated after a ten-year battle for ratification.

It was also a time of increased religiosity. Fundamentalist groups especially became more active in the political arena, advancing their own candidates and giving large amounts of financial support to candidates who supported their agenda. Their agenda was concerned primarily with so-called family issues—elimination of abortion, restriction of the rights of homosexuals, and a return of Bible-reading and prayer to the public schools. Interestingly enough, the resurgence of religiosity in this country seemed paralleled by an increase in religious fanaticism abroad.

This period was also a time when the "information age" fully arrived. More than 98 percent of American households owned one or more television sets—and most of those were color models. Americans spent close to thirty-nine hours a week, according to some reports, watching television; the most popular shows at times reached audiences of more than 50 million viewers.

Finally, it was a period of widespread immigration, especially of Hispanics and Asiatics. For the decade 1971–1980, more than 44 percent of all immigrants were from South American or Central American nations; and more than 35 percent were from Asian countries.

The Predominant Trends

As noted above, this last period seems to have been a time when a conservative view of both the society and its schools held sway. Those espousing such a conservative educational view essentially argued that the chief function of the school was to transmit the culture and to prepare students for their roles in a technological society; in accomplishing such a mission, the curriculum should emphasize the scholarly disciplines, should be characterized by intellectual rigor, and should be closely monitored for its effectiveness. Emanating from this broadly conservative view of the school and its curriculum were several specific trends.

School Effectiveness and School Reform   The first significant development was a broad-based research effort to identify the key elements in effective schools, with a concomitant attempt to translate those elements into a plan for reforming the schools. Following some ground-breaking research by Brookover (see the 1979 work by him and his colleagues) and by Edmonds (1979), several researchers conducted numerous studies of effective schools in order to ascertain the elements that made them different from other schools. Others then performed meta-analyses of these studies in order to identify recurring features. One of the most useful of these, perhaps, was that performed by Purkey and Smith (1983), who after reviewing, critiquing, and synthesizing all the research were able to identify the key factors shown in Figure 2-1.

This synthesis and others similar to it provided the empirical support for a widespread school-reform movement. At the outset this movement was primarily a local effort, supported by the extension services of the several research and development centers then operating. With the publication of *A Nation at Risk* (National Commission on Excellence in Education, 1983) and several other similar reports, educational reform became a national concern, with President Reagan devoting one of his radio addresses

FIGURE 2-1. Key Factors in Effective Schools

Organizational and Structural Variables

1. The leadership and staff of the school have considerable autonomy in determining the means they will use to improve academic performance.
2. The principal plays an active role as an instructional leader.
3. The staff remains relatively stable in order to maintain and promote further success.
4. The elementary curriculum focuses on basic and complex skills, with sufficient time provided and close coordination across grade levels and across disciplines; the secondary curriculum includes a planned and purposeful program without too many electives.
5. There is school-wide staff development closely related to the instructional program of the school.
6. There is active parent involvement and support.
7. The school recognizes academic success, through symbols and ceremonies.
8. A greater portion of the day is devoted to academic subjects, with effective use made of academic time and with active involvement of students.
9. There is district support for school-based efforts.

Process Variables

1. There are collaborative planning and collegial relationships.
2. There is a pervasive sense of community.
3. Clear goals and high expectations are commonly shared.
4. There is order and discipline, with clear and reasonable rules fairly and consistently enforced.

Adapted from Purkey and Smith (1983).

to the issue. State governors and legislators were quick to respond to this burgeoning concern. By early 1985, at least two-thirds of the states had either adopted or were considering such reform measures as increasing teacher salaries, instituting career ladders or merit pay, raising school standards, increasing graduation requirements, and requiring an exit test of students. (See the summary in the February 6, 1985, issue of *Education Week.*)

A More Rigorous Curriculum   Central to this reform effort was an emphasis on "curriculum rigor." In general this slogan seemed most useful simply as a rallying cry for those who believed that a more academically challenging curriculum would best serve the needs of American youth. The most common expressions of this concern for curricular rigor were state laws and district policies mandating additional graduation requirements. Typically those stricter requirements specified additional years of science and mathematics. Obviously, in a crowded school schedule, requiring additional years of science and mathematics resulted in reduced enrollments in such elective areas as music and art.

When it came to specific recommendations for the curriculum, the advocates of curriculum rigor seemed to be pleading for a return to a somewhat traditional curriculum that emphasized the academic content of the disciplines. In a concluding chapter of a book arguing for more rigorous courses in the humanities, Finn and Ravitch (1984) were quite specific about this: "High school humanities courses must be intellectually anchored in the scholarly disciplines. . . . In the main . . . we believe that young people should first make the acquaintance of the several humanities disciplines as separate subjects . . . " (pp. 250, 251). They went on to make some very specific recommendations: English courses at the high school level should emphasize the close reading of major literary works and extensive writing in many genres; the phrase "social studies" should be "banished from the high school curriculum" (p. 260), and only history should be taught; and every student should become proficient in at least one foreign language, ". . . grappling with the best that has been written in the language, and learning how to use it to convey one's own best thoughts" (p. 260).

The "Critical Thinking" Movement   This concern for a new rigor in the curriculum also took the form of widespread interest in teaching critical thinking. Most of those in the forefront of the movement argued for the importance of critical thinking by stressing the need for better thinking in a technologically oriented "information age." Typical of these arguments was the conclusion reached by the Education Commission of the States. After analyzing the needs of the society in an information age, the Commission concluded in a special report (1982) that these were the "basics of tomorrow": evaluation and analysis skills; critical thinking; problem-solving strategies; organization and reference skills; synthesis; application; creativity; decision making given incomplete information; and communication skills. (A careful reader of the report might wonder at the uncritical thinking that produced such a poorly conceptualized list: all the skills except the last are usually subsumed under the general category of critical-thinking skills.)

While initially the interest in critical thinking seemed to focus on staff-development workshops and ancillary materials designed to help teachers acquire the skills they needed, curriculum materials were soon to follow. By 1985 a resource book published by the Association for Supervision and Curriculum Development (Costa, 1985) was able to identify sixteen curriculum projects in the area of critical thinking that were reaching a national audience; in addition, there were countless local district guides that had been quickly put together in response to what seemed to be almost a fad. By 1985 the movement had generated so much momentum across a range of constituencies that ASCD had no difficulty at all in persuading twenty-two professional associations and institutions to form a "critical thinking collaborative."

Accountability   Allied with the concern for more rigor in the curriculum was a demand that teachers and students be held more accountable. First, districts seemed to embrace eagerly several programs that attempted to hold teachers more accountable for teaching and testing the prescribed curriculum. Such programs were usually identified as "curriculum alignment projects." Although they varied in detail, they attempted to align the written and the taught curriculum, usually by monitoring what was taught, and the written and the tested curriculum, ordinarily by matching the test with the instructional objectives. (These alignment programs are discussed more fully in Chapter 11 of this work.)

Second, students were to be held more accountable. The concern for student accountability first took the form of several "promotional gates" programs that required students to demonstrate a certain level of proficiency before moving on. Such programs were usually instituted by administrators who were convinced that social promotion had been a factor in the decline in student achievement, although a large and persuasive body of research indicated quite clearly that social promotion between grades 1 and 8 was more effective than retention in developing self-image and improving achievement. (See the review by Rose, Medway, Cantrell, and Marus, 1983, for an excellent critique and synthesis of this research.) Several states also required students to pass exit tests before diplomas could be granted. Such exit tests were essentially measures of minimal competency, sampling students' ability to write clearly, to read with comprehension, and to know certain essential information about governmental processes.

These conservative responses were generally endorsed by the public; however, they met with mixed reactions from many educators. Several educational leaders seemed to feel that these reforms were long-needed correctives for policies that had been too permissive and practices that were not sufficiently challenging. Others questioned their value, especially for "at risk" youth.

Typical of these reservations were those expressed by the ASCD Task Force on the Consequences of Increased Secondary Requirements. In their 1985 report, *With Consequences for All*, the task force expressed several reservations about the impact of these policies. They first noted the concern that requiring additional years of science and mathematics might result in an unbalanced curriculum that slighted the arts and the humanities. Second, after analyzing the impact of increased graduation requirements on four groups (four-year college bound, two-year college bound, high school graduates, and drop-outs), the task force concluded that the latter two groups would be harmed by not having sufficient opportunity for vocational and supplemental studies. They also noted some undesirable side effects: increased pressure on less able students, resulting in an unfavorable climate for growth; and the overemphasis on the knowledge-transmission function, resulting from mandates and competency tests.

The Exemplary Leaders

Two figures stand out in this period for their pervasive influence: Benjamin Bloom and John Goodlad. Each in his own way made major contributions and influenced both research and practice.

Benjamin Bloom   Bloom was a psychologist and professor of education at the University of Chicago who first attracted widespread attention from the profession with the publication of what quickly became known as "Bloom's taxonomy." Although there were three handbooks in the series—one on the cognitive, one on the affective, and one on the psychomotor domain—it was the 1956 handbook on the cognitive domain that had the greatest impact. The taxonomy originally was developed by a group of college examiners to facilitate communication among themselves and colleagues about objectives and test items. They saw the taxonomy as hierarchical, with each category including more complex or abstract behavior than the previous one. The major categories posited by Bloom and his colleagues were six: knowledge; comprehension; application; analysis; synthesis; and evaluation. Each of the six major categories was further divided into two or more subcategories.

Although some critics expressed reservations about the conceptualization, the taxonomy seemed to have a significant impact on curriculum leaders and school administrators. First, many curriculum developers used the taxonomy to develop curricula; for them it was a template for designing units, ensuring that each unit included several objectives in each category. Several districts used it to evaluate curricula; for them it was a benchmark, used to assess the proportion of objectives in each category and making corrections if "higher-order" objectives seemed to have been slighted.

It also served useful instructional purposes. Teachers were first encouraged to use the taxonomy in planning their lessons, to be sure that they focused on objectives other than knowledge and comprehension. They were also encouraged to use the taxonomy in designing and assessing their tests, the chief purpose intended by its developers. The evidence from observations of and discussions with teachers indicated that for the most part they ignored such recommendations.

Finally, it seemed to have some usefulness in observing classes for supervisory purposes. It was relatively simple to develop and use an instrument which would enable the observer to determine how many questions of each type the teacher asked. The data could then be analyzed and discussed in a debriefing session, one which usually ended with the recommendation, "Next time try to use some higher-order questions."

While his work on the taxonomy was obviously influential, Bloom's theory of and research on mastery learning had perhaps an even greater impact. In discussing his work on mastery learning, it is important to make a sharp distinction between three understandings of "mastery learning": what he himself has advocated; how his students have applied his ideas in developing curricula; and what some publishers have done in commercializing mastery learning.

What does Bloom himself mean when he speaks of "mastery learning"? Perhaps the best explication of his position is in his 1976 book, *Human Characteristics and School Learning.* In this work he makes the point that he was interested in developing an explanatory theory of school learning, one which would identify the major variables in school learning and enable researchers to examine their predictive values. In the Bloom model of school learning, there are six factors. Two of these are student characteristics: the cognitive entry behaviors of the students—what they already know; and the affective entry characteristics—their motivation for the learning task and their attitudinal predispositions. A third crucial variable is the quality of instruction. And three variables relate to learning outcomes: level and type of achievement; rate of learning; and affective outcomes.

How do these variables interact? Bloom's research and the research of others indicate that the three critical variables are the cognitive entry behaviors (accounting for about one-half of the variance in achievement), the affective entry characteristics (about one-fourth of the variance), and the quality of instruction (about one-fourth of the variance). Additional research indicated that there were five important elements affecting the quality of instruction: the instructor provides clear *cues* as to what is to be learned by explaining, demonstrating, and illustrating; the instructor involves the learner in *active participation* or practice of the response to be learned; the instructor uses positive and negative reinforcement throughout the learning process; the instructor evaluates learning in order to get feedback about the effectiveness of learning; and the instructor provides corrective procedures when and where needed.

After presenting the theory and the empirical evidence testing its assumptions, Bloom (1976) reaches these conclusions:

> The major finding resulting from the application of this theory is that only minor differences need be present in the learning of different students in a particular course or subject. To put it more strongly, each student may be helped to learn a particular subject to the same degree, level of competence, and even in approximately the same amount of time if the major variables in this theory are appropriately taken into consideration in the learning process. . . . If equality of learning is possible, then the selective function of schools must be largely abandoned in favor of the developmental functions which schools must increasingly service. (pp. 208, 209)

His students and several curriculum specialists have applied this theory in developing mastery learning curricula by using a process something like the following:

1. The course is divided into several one-to-three-week units.

2. For each unit a pretest is developed and administered, to help the teacher and the students determine student readiness for the unit and to remedy any deficiencies.
3. The teacher uses whatever instructional method seems effective, keeping in mind the importance of cues, active participation, and reinforcement.
4. The students take a formative test on the unit.
5. The teacher uses test results to identify students who have not achieved mastery.
6. Students not achieving mastery are provided with the necessary correctives, usually using approaches different from those initially used.
7. Students take a different form of the test to assess mastery.

In general, the research on the effectiveness of such mastery learning units suggests that they have positive results. After conducting a meta-analysis of all the major studies on mastery learning, Burns (1979) concluded as follows: "The results presented so far indicate that mastery strategies do indeed have moderate to strong effects on student learning when compared to conventional methods of instruction" (p. 112).

Unfortunately, some programs, including a few widely published ones, so distorted mastery learning principles that they produced some negative results. These negative results probably stemmed from the fact that the developers had overemphasized discrete bits of knowledge at the expense of whole learning experiences. One widely published reading program, for example, required teachers to spend so much time teaching discrete skills that their pupils did not have time to read stories or poems. When Bloom heard about such a distorted version, he is reported to have expressed shock and dismay.

Despite the fact that some have distorted his theory, Bloom made a major contribution to curriculum—one whose effects will probably endure for some time.

John Goodlad　John Goodlad is another leading figure in the curriculum field whose career spans several periods. For more than twenty-five years he conducted research, organized centers of educational change, and taught graduate courses in the field, publishing more than twenty books and some two hundred articles. Educators tended to perceive him as a curriculum leader who understood schools, who had a clear vision of what those schools could become, and who had some tested ideas for helping them achieve their goals.

Of all his books, perhaps the most influential and significant was *A Place Called School: Prospects for the Future*, which appeared just about the time that several reform reports were being widely promulgated. Perhaps the thing that most distinguished Goodlad's book from all the rest was its broad empirical base: he and his colleagues had spent several years studying in depth 1,016 classrooms, questioning and surveying 1,350 teachers, 8,624 parents, and 17,163 students.

The picture emerging from that comprehensive study is a complex and interesting one. First, he found what perhaps was a surprising measure of support for those schools among teachers, students, and parents, who were asked to grade their schools by using the standard letter grades—A, B, C, D, and F. No school received an average grade of less than C. Most of the schools received an average grade of B, with the elementary and middle schools garnering somewhat stronger support than the high schools. Second, he found a large degree of congruence among teachers, students, and parents about the goals of education. Asking those groups to assess from their perspective the four general classes of goals (vocational, intellectual, personal, and social), he found that, as he put it, "they want it all." He expressed the finding this way:

> The message here . . . is that those closest to the schools—parents, teachers, and students—see as important all four of those goal areas which have emerged over the centuries. . . . Our data thus show no withering in goal commitments by the parent group we assembled, and indeed I do not know of serious studies that come up with a narrow list of parental expectations for the schools. When it comes to education, it appears that most parents want their children to have it all. (pp. 38–39)

From a curriculum leader's perspective, perhaps the most important findings related to the amount of time devoted to the several subject areas from level to level. At the elementary level, teachers reported that in general they allocated their instructional time in a typical week in this manner: English language arts, 34 percent; math, 20 percent; art, music, drama, and dance, 16 percent; social studies, 12 percent; science, 10 percent; physical education, 8 percent; and foreign language, 1 percent. At the middle and high school levels, he assessed time allocation to the several subjects by determining the number of full-time teachers per subject. These data yielded a picture of what he called "curricular balance." Middle school faculty allocations were as follows: English, 22 percent; mathematics, 17 percent; social studies, 14 percent; science, 13 percent; vocational education, 11 percent; physical education, 10 percent; the arts, 11 percent; foreign language, 2 percent. The high school picture was somewhat different: English, 18 percent; mathematics, 13 percent; social studies, 13 percent; science, 11 percent; vocational education, 24 percent; physical education, 9 percent; the arts, 8 percent; and foreign language, 4 percent. Note the large increase in the personnel allocations to vocational education in the high school.

His analysis of the content of that balanced curriculum yielded a rather discouraging picture. By observing classes, interviewing teachers and students, analyzing texts and tests, and examining curriculum guides, he and his research team concluded that in all the academic areas—English language arts, mathematics, social studies, and science—the emphasis was on teaching basic skills and facts. Almost no attention in any grade was given to inquiry, critical thinking, or problem solving. And the picture was especially dismal in lower-track classes.

How was that unchallenging curriculum taught? The picture here is similarly discouraging to those who believe in the importance of instructional diversity. The predominant pattern throughout all grades is what Goodlad called "frontal teaching": the teacher presenting information to the whole class, assigning and monitoring seatwork, conducting a recitation, and giving quizzes. Students seem relatively passive—listening, writing answers to questions, and taking tests and quizzes. And surprisingly, the students seem generally satisfied with their passive role.

What can be done to make schools more interesting and more exciting? Goodlad concludes the book with some very specific prescriptions, many drawn not from that study but from his long career as an advocate and orchestrator of change. The highlights of those recommendations are noted below.

1. Achieve curricular balance by reallocating time in the secondary schools: up to 18 percent to English and foreign literature and language; up to 18 percent to mathematics and science; up to 15 percent to society and social studies; up to 18 percent to the arts; up to 18 percent to vocational education. Ten percent of the time would be reserved for the student's special interests.

2. Establish several curriculum and development research centers in the major areas of the curriculum, as a means of improving the content and pedagogy of that balanced curriculum. These research centers would be supplemented by curriculum-design centers in each state that would be responsible for translating the research product in usable curriculum guides.

3. Eliminate tracking and grouping by assigning students randomly to classes in a manner that ensures heterogeneity.

4. Establish a network of "key schools" in each state, specifically charged with the responsibility of experimenting with new programs and developing and disseminating exemplary practices.

5. Divide larger schools into smaller multigrade "houses" to achieve the advantages of smallness within bigness. At the elementary level, staff those houses with teams of teachers serving from fifty to one hundred students and use part-time teachers for special-interest areas.

6. Reorganize school leadership by appointing one person to serve as headmaster or headmistress over one senior high school and the junior high and elementary schools feeding it.

In retrospect, it seems unfortunate that Goodlad's book was not given greater attention by the public. The other reports which were more successful in seizing the attention of the media and the public seemed in general much less scholarly in their grounding and much less innovative in their recommendations.

The Major Publications

In 1983 nine national "school reform" reports were issued—so many that several educational publications saw fit to publish "scorecards" and "readers' guides" to help the profession make sense of the reform literature. Two of these reports seemed especially influential.

A Nation at Risk   This publication was produced by the National Commission on Excellence in Education (1983), appointed in 1981 by the then Secretary of Education, Terrel H. Bell. The tone of the report is perhaps best reflected in its opening lines:

> *Our Nation is at risk. Our once unchallenged preeminence in commerce, industry, science, and technological innovation is being overtaken by competitors throughout the world. . . . the educational foundations of our society are presently being eroded by a rising tide of mediocrity that threatens our very future as a Nation and a people. . . . If an unfriendly power had attempted to impose on America the mediocre educational performance that exists today, we might well have viewed it as an act of war.* (p. 5)

The report then went on to present what it termed the "indicators of risk," carefully selected statistics purporting to demonstrate the gravity of the risk and to warrant the dramatic language. Some of the "indicators of risk" were the following: twenty-three million American adults and 13 percent of all seventeen-year-olds are functionally illiterate; from 1963 to 1980, average verbal scores on the Scholastic Aptitude Test fell over fifty points, and mathematics scores, nearly forty points; there was a steady decline in science achievement scores of U.S. seventeen-year-olds as measured by national assessments in 1969, 1973, and 1977.

The recommendations were straightforward, perhaps even simplistic.

1. All students seeking a diploma should be required to take the "Five New Basics" during the four years of high school: four years of English; three years of mathematics; three years of science; three years of social studies; and one-half year of computer science. College-bound students should be required to take two years of foreign language in high school, in addition to earlier study of language.
2. Schools, colleges, and universities should adopt more rigorous and measurable standards and higher expectations for academic performance and student conduct, and four-year colleges and universities should raise their requirements for admission.

3. More time should be devoted to learning the New Basics: more homework, seven-hour school days; and a 200- to 220-day school year. The schools should have firm codes of conduct; and promotion, grouping, and graduation should be guided by the academic progress of students and their instructional needs.

4. The quality of the teaching profession should be improved by raising standards for admission to teacher-education programs, increasing salaries, providing an eleven-month contract for teachers, developing career ladders for teachers, offering special incentives to attract teachers in areas of critical shortage, and appointing master teachers to assist in designing teacher-preparation programs and in supervising probationary teachers.

5. Citizens should hold educators and elected officials responsible for providing the leadership necessary to achieve those reforms. Principals and superintendents must play a key role. State and local officials have primary responsibility for financing and governing the schools; the federal government has the primary responsibility for identifying the national interest in education.

Perhaps because the language was so dramatic, the picture portrayed so dismal, and the recommendations so clear and simple, *A Nation at Risk* seemed to have a pervasive and widespread impact, especially on the public. It became the subject of television and radio broadcasts; it was discussed at parent and citizen meetings across the nation; and legislators often made reference to it as they drafted their own reform legislation.

Educators were more guarded in their reaction. Typical of the response of educators, perhaps, was a handbook prepared by the Council for Educational Development and Research (see Dianda, 1983), entitled *The Superintendent's Can-Do Guide to School Improvement: A Response to the National Reports on School Reform*. While praising some of the other reports, the authors of this handbook attacked the National Commission on Excellence report for perpetuating four "myths" about American education: the myth that the nation is at risk (the handbook challenged the validity of the data); the myth that the United States has a "high tech future" (the handbook cited Bureau of Labor Statistics challenging this view); the myth that states should finance educational reform (the handbook cited figures to show that it would be essential for the federal government to finance many of the reform initiatives); and the myth that "more is better" (the handbook questioned the simplistic notion that simply requiring more time would produce better learning).

In retrospect, perhaps, the chief value of *A Nation at Risk* is that it dramatized the issue of educational reform and moved such reform into the arena of public debate. As guidelines for educators seeking a new direction for the curriculum, it was a serious disappointment. The "Five New Basics" it advocated were simply the traditional college-preparatory curriculum recommended by other commissions in the past, with "one semester of computer science" added almost as an afterthought. And it seemed preoccupied with matters of quantity: more years of this and that, more hours in the school day, more days in the school year. Except for some superficial generalities, it had little to offer in terms of quality and content. Thus, its recommendations for the teaching of English were these:

> *The teaching of English in high school should equip graduates to: (a) comprehend, interpret, evaluate, and use what they read; (b) write well-organized, effective papers; (c) listen effectively and discuss ideas intelligently; and (d) know our literary heritage. . . . (p. 25)*

High School   This book by Ernest Boyer (1983), while not getting the media attention of *A Nation at Risk*, seems to be of better quality, was received much more favorably by educators, and thus probably had a more pervasive impact. It was the result of a two-year study of the American high school funded by the Carnegie Foundation for the Advancement of Teaching. The research staff reviewed the literature, consulted with numerous educational leaders, and spent twenty days in each of fifteen high schools. While the study lacked perhaps the breadth and comprehensiveness of the Goodlad study, it resulted in some recommendations that in many ways seemed more useful to the profession.

Boyer begins by putting the "crisis" in perspective. After reviewing critically all the evidence, Boyer concluded as follows:

> *. . . the academic report card on the nation's schools is mixed. We believe, however, that American public education is beginning to improve. After years of decline, test scores have leveled off and in some states modest gains have been recorded. . . . America is turning once again to education. (p. 1)*

He then articulates four general goals for education: help all students develop the capacity to think critically and communicate effectively; help all students learn about themselves, the human heritage, and their interdependent world; prepare all students for work and higher education; help all students fulfill their social and civic obligations through school and community service.

The high schools in this country can accomplish these goals more effectively, he concludes, if they will pursue a rather specific agenda for action. That agenda for action included recommendations covering twelve major areas: clarifying goals; the centrality of language; the core curriculum; the transition to work and learning; volunteer service; renewing the profession of teaching; instruction; technology in the schools; flexible schedules and organizational arrangements; the principal as leader; strengthening connections with businesses and universities; and the public commitment. The details of the first four of these are noted below, since they centrally impact upon curriculum.

1. Every high school should clearly articulate its goals—and those goals should focus on the four previously identified.
2. All elementary and secondary schools should give the highest priority to language; all high school students should complete a basic writing course, in which enrollment is limited to twenty.
3. A common core of learnings should constitute two-thirds of the total units required for graduation: Literature, emphasizing the reading and discussion of major works in depth; one year of United States history; Western Civilization; Non-Western Civilization, including one semester studying a single non-Western nation in depth; a two-year sequence in Science and the Natural World; Technology; two years of Mathematics; Foreign Language, beginning in the elementary school and concluding with at least two years in the high school; the Arts; Civics; Health; one semester study of Work; and a Senior Independent Project, a written report focusing on a significant social issue and drawing from several fields of study.
4. This curriculum should be provided in a single track for all students. During the last two years of high school, about half the time should be devoted to "elective clusters," carefully designed programs including advanced study in selected academic subjects and exploration of a career option.
5. All high school students should complete a service requirement—providing volunteer work in or out of the school, for not less than thirty hours a year and 120 hours over the four-year period. This requirement could be met by volunteer work in the evenings, on the weekends, and in the summer.

Several features of the Boyer report made it seem especially useful. First, it presented a balanced view of the achievement of American schools, eschewing the inflammatory rhetoric of *A Nation at Risk.* Second, it drew upon solid research, but used the research in an illuminating and interesting manner, since the book was intended to reach a large audience. Next, it offered specific recommendations about the quality of the core curriculum that provided useful guidelines for local curriculum leaders. Finally, its recommendations for required service made great sense at a time when, according to some commentators, American youth seemed self-centered and materialistic.

SUMMARY: A CENTURY OF CURRICULUM TRENDS IN RETROSPECT

In reviewing this century of curriculum history, two general observations might be made. The first is to note the pace of change. Observe that the first five periods become increasingly shorter, lasting 27 years, 24 years, 16

years, 11 years, and 7 years, respectively. The last period, privatistic conservatism, was the exception; by the time of publication of this work it had
lasted twelve years and showed no early signs of ending. With this exception noted, it would seem that futurists who have commented on the rapid
pace of change in today's society are probably correct. One therefore might
predict that future trends in curriculum will be relatively short-lived.

The second observation is to note the rhythms and directions of that
change. Here it might be useful to search for the best metaphor describing those
rhythms and directions. Now when most educators speak about the general
directions of the curriculum past and present, they seize initially on the
metaphor of the pendulum, which suggests short swings between extreme positions. Or they talk of cycles, a more abstract figure which suggests longer
periods of recurring tendencies. Neither metaphor seems to portray the past
century of curriculum history. Instead, it might be more appropriate and more
insightful to speak of separate streams that continue to flow—at times swollen,
at times almost dry; at times separate, at times joining.

In identifying such streams in our curricular history, some useful terms
are proposed by Eisner and Vallance (1974), who delineated five orientations
in the curriculum: cognitive processes (help children acquire the basic skills
and learn how to think); academic rationalism (foster intellectual growth in
the subjects most worthy of study); personal relevance (emphasize the
primacy of personal meaning); social adaptation and reconstruction (derive
educational aims from an analysis of the society); and curriculum as
technology (operationalize curricular outcomes by technological analysis of
the observable behaviors sought).

Those five curricular orientations are thus seen as streams that have
always been present throughout this past century of curricular history.
Figure 2-2 shows how these streams seem to have ebbed and flowed
throughout the separate periods. It reflects how their strength has varied and
how, during a given period, one or two have predominated. It suggests that
the strength of a given orientation at a particular period of time seems
to have resulted from powerful social forces impinging upon the curriculum.
And it makes clear that educators in general have typically espoused a
pragmatic eclecticism, one in which all five streams have at least some part of
play.

APPLICATIONS

1. Here is an exercise in prediction. Based upon what you have learned about the
   history of curriculum and what you observe happening now, when do you think
   the period of privatistic conservatism will end—and what type of period will succeed it?

2. Some have argued that there are really no new ideas in education—that all so-
   called innovations are simply refurbishings of old ideas. Based upon your
   knowledge of curriculum history, would you agree or disagree?

3. Most nationally disseminated reports recommending educational reform have very little impact. How then do you explain the seemingly profound impact made by the reform reports of the 1980s?

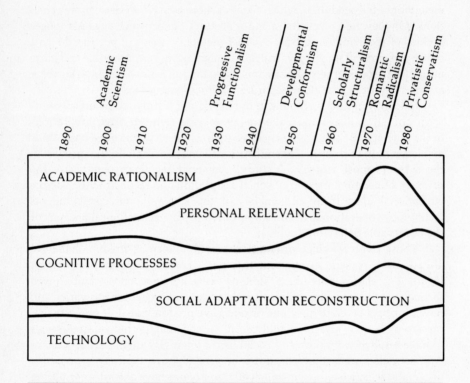

FIGURE 2–2.   The Streams of
Curricular History

REFERENCES

Abelson, P. H. (1967). Excessive educational pressures. *Science, 156,* 741.

Applebee, A. N. (1974). *Tradition and reform in the teaching of English: A history.* Urbana, IL: NCTE.

ASCD Task Force on the Consequences of Increased Secondary Requirements. (1985). Alexandria, VA: ASCD.

Bloom, B. S. (ed.). (1956). *Taxonomy of educational objectives: The classification of educational goals. Handbook 1. Cognitive domains.* New York: McKay.

Bloom, B. S. (1976). *Human characteristics and school learning*. New York: McGraw-Hill.

Bobbitt, F. (1913). *The supervision of city schools*. Twelfth Yearbook of the National Society for the Study of Education, Part I. Chicago: University of Chicago Press.

_____. (1918). *The curriculum*. Boston: Houghton Mifflin.

Boyer, E. L. (1983). *High school: A report on secondary education in America*. New York: Harper and Row.

Brookover, W. B., Beady, C., Flood, P., Schweitzer, J., and Wisenbaker, J. (1979). *School social systems and student achievement: Schools can make a difference*. New York: Praeger.

Broudy, H. S. (1971). Democratic values and educational goals. In R. M. McClure (ed.), *The curriculum: Retrospect and prospect*, pp. 113–152. Chicago: University of Chicago Press.

Bruner, J. S. (1960). *The process of education*. Cambridge, MA: Harvard University Press.

_____. (1971). The process of education revisited. *Phi Delta Kappan, 53*, p. 20–22.

Burns, R. B. (1979). Mastery learning: Does it work? *Educational Leadership, 31*, 110–113.

Changing course: A 50-state summary of major state initiatives. *Education Week*, Feb. 6, 1985, pp. 11–30.

Charters, W. W. (1923). *Curriculum construction*. New York: Macmillan.

Commission on the Reorganization of Secondary Education. (1918). Washington, DC: United States Government Printing Office.

Conant, J. B. (1959). *The American high school today*. New York: McGraw-Hill.

Copperman, P. (1978). *The literacy hoax*. New York: William Morrow.

Costa, A. L. (ed.). (1985). *Developing minds: A resource book for teaching thinking*. Alexandria, VA: ASCD.

Cremin, L. A. (1955, March). The revolution in American secondary education, 1893–1918. *Teachers College Record, 56*, 295–307.

_____. (1961). *The transformation of the school: Progressivism in American education 1876–1957*. New York: Random House.

Cuban, L. (1979a). Curriculum change and stability. In J. Schaffarzick and G. Sykes (eds.), *Value conflicts and curriculum issues: Lessons from research and experience*, pp. 139–196. Berkeley, CA: McCutchan.

_____. (1979b). Determinants of curriculum change and stability, 1876–1970. In J. Schaffarzick and G. Sykes (eds.), *Value conflicts and curriculum issues: Lessons from research and experience*, pp. 139–196. Berkeley, CA: McCutchan.

Cubberly, E. P. (1909). *Changing conceptions of education*. Boston: Houghton Mifflin.

Curriculum Development Associates. (1972). *Man: A course of study*. Washington, DC: Author.

Dewey, J. (1900). *The school and society*. Chicago: University of Chicago Press.

_____. (1902). *The child and the curriculum*. Chicago: University of Chicago Press.

_____. (1916). *Democracy and education*. New York: Macmillan.

_____. (1938). *Experience and education*. New York: Macmillan.

_____. (1964). In *John Dewey on education: Selected writings*, R. Archambaust, (ed.). New York: Random House.

Dianda, M. R. (1983). The superintendent's can-do guide to school improvement: A response to the national report on school reform. Washington, DC: Council for Educational Development and Research.

Duckworth, E. (1979). Either we're too early and they can't learn it or we're too late and they know it already: The dilemma of "applying Piaget." *Harvard Educational Review, 49,* 297–312.

Edmonds, R. (1979). Effective schools for the urban poor. *Educational Leadership, 37,* 15–27.

Education Commission of the States. (1982). *The information society: Are high school graduates ready?* Denver, CO: Education Commission of the States.

Education Policies Commission. (1944). *Education for all American youth.* Washington, DC: NEA.

Eisner, E. W., and Vallance, E. (1974). *Changing conceptions of curriculum.* Berkeley, CA: McCutchan.

Finn, C. E., Jr., and Ravitch, D. (1984). Conclusions and recommendations: High expectations and disciplined effort. In C. E. Finn, Jr., D. Ravitch, and R. T. Fancher (eds.), *Against mediocrity: The humanities in American high schools,* pp. 237–262. New York: Holmes & Meier.

Flavell, J. H. (1963). *The developmental psychology of Jean Piaget.* Princeton, NJ: Van Nostrand.

Flexner, A. (1916). The modern school. *American Review of Reviews, 8,* 465–474.

Gelman, R., and Baillargeon, R. (1983). A review of some Piagetian concepts. In P. H. Mussen (ed.), *Handbook of child psychology,* Vol. 3, pp. 167–230. New York: John Wiley.

Giles, H. H., McCutchen, S. P., and Zechiel, A. N. (1942). *Exploring the curriculum.* New York: Harper.

Glatthorn, A. A. (1975). *Alternatives in education: Schools and programs.* New York: Dodd, Mead.

_____. (1980). *A guide for developing an English program for the eighties.* Urbana, IL: NCTE.

Goodlad, J. S. (1984). *A place called school: Prospects for the future.* New York: McGraw-Hill.

Hall, G. S. (1904). The natural activities of children as determining the industries in early education. In *National Education Association Journal of Proceedings and Addresses,* pp. 443–444.

_____. (1969). *Adolescence.* New York: Arno Press and The New York Times; originally published by Appleton in 1904.

Havighurst, R. J. (1972). *Developmental tasks and education* (3rd Ed.). New York: McKay.

Hayes, L. (October 16, 1985). John C. Holt remembered as "a champion of children." *Education Week, 7,* 17.

Hillocks, G., Jr. (1972). *Alternatives in English: A critical appraisal of elective programs.* Urbana, IL: NCTE.

Holt, J. (1964). *How children fail.* New York: Pitman.

Horwitz, R. A. (1979). Effects of the "open classroom." In H. J. Walberg (ed.), *Educational environments and effects,* pp. 275–292. Berkeley, CA: McCutchan.

Johnson, P. (1983). *Modern times: The world from the twenties to the eighties.* New York: Harper and Row.

Kilpatrick, W. H. (1918). The project method. *Teachers College Record, 19,* 319–335.

Kilpatrick, W. (1921). Dangers and difficulties of the project method and how to overcome them. *Teachers College Record, 32,* 283–321.

Kirschenbaum, H. (1979). *On becoming Carl Rogers.* New York: Delacorte.

Kliebard, H. M. (February 1970). Reappraisal: The Tyler rationale. *School Review, 78,* 259–272.

————. (1979). Systematic curriculum development, 1890–1959. In J. Schaffarzick and G. Syles (eds.), *Value conflicts and curriculum issues: Lessons from research and experience,* pp. 197–236. Berkeley, CA: McCutchan.

————. (1985). What happened to American schooling in the first part of the twentieth century? In E. Eisner (ed.), *Learning and teaching the ways of knowing,* pp. 1–22. Chicago: University of Chicago Press.

Mort, P. R., and Vincent, W. S. (1946). *A look at our schools: A book for the thinking citizen.* New York: Cattell.

Nash, P. (1965). Book Reviews: How children fail. *Harvard Educational Review, 35,* 378–382.

National Commission on Excellence in Education. (1983). *A nation at risk: The imperative for educational reform.* Washington, DC: United States Government Printing Office.

National Council for the Social Studies. (1975, Nov.–Dec.). The MACOS question. *Social Education, 39,* 446.

National Education Association. (1893). Report of the Committee on Secondary School Studies. Washington, DC: Government Printing Office.

————. (1895). Report of the Committee of Fifteen. New York: Arno Press and the New York Times. Originally published in 1895 by New England Publishing Company.

Oliver, A. I. (1977). *Curriculum improvement: A guide to problems, principles, and process* (2nd Ed.). New York: Harper & Row.

Parker, F. W. (1894). *Talks on pedagogics.* New York: E. L. Kellogg.

Physical Science Study Committee. (1961). *PSSC physics: Teacher's resource book and guide.* Boston: D. C. Heath.

Piaget, J. (1950). *The psychology of intelligence.* New York: Harcourt.

Purkey, S. C., and Smith, M. S. (1983). Effective schools: A review. *Elementary School Journal, 83,* 426–452.

Ravitch, D. (1983). *The troubled crusade: American education 1945–1980.* New York: Basic Books.

Rawid, M. A. (April 1984). Synthesis of research on schools of choice. *Educational Leadership, 41,* 70–78.

Rickover, H. G. (1959). *Education and freedom.* New York: E. P. Dutton.

Rogers, C. (1969). *Freedom to learn: A view of what education might become.* Columbus, OH: Charles Merrill.

Rose, J. S., Medway, F. J., Cantrell, V. L., and Marus, S. H. (1983). A fresh look at the retention-promotion controversy. *Journal of School Psychology, 21,* 201–211.

Rugg, H. D. (ed.). (1927). *The foundations of curriculum-making.* Twenty-sixth yearbook of the National Society for the Study of Education, Part II. Bloomington, IL: Public School Publishing.

Sarther, C. (April 1985). "Structure" and "inquiry" in science education: A critique of the curriculum reform movement. Paper presented at the annual meeting of the American Educational Research Association, Chicago.

Schwab, J. T. (1969). The practical: A language for curriculum. *School Review, 78,* 1–23.

————. (1971). The practical: Arts of eclectic. *School Review, 79,* 493–542.

————. (1973). The practical 3: Translation into curriculum. *School Review, 81,* 501–522.

————. (1978). Education and the structure of the disciplines. In I. Westbury and N. J. Wilkof (eds.), *Science, curriculum, and liberal education: Selected essays of Joseph T. Schwab,* pp. 229–270. Chicago: University of Chicago Press.

————. (1983). The practical 4: Something for curriculum professors to do. *Curriculum Inquiry, 13,* 239–265.

Seguel, M. L. (1966). *The curriculum field: Its formative years.* New York: Teachers College Press.

Shymansky, J. A., Kyle, W. C., Jr., and Alport, J. (October 1982). Research synthesis on the science curriculum projects of the sixties. *Educational Leadership, 40,* 63–66.

Silberman, C. (1970). *Crisis in the classroom.* New York: Random House.

Tanner, D., and Tanner, L. N. (1980). *Curriculum development: Theory into practice* (2nd ed.). New York: Macmillan.

Taylor, F. W. (1911). *The principles of scientific management.* New York: Harper and Bros.

Tyack, D., and Hansot, E. (1982). *Managers of virtue: Public school leadership in America, 1820–1980.* New York: Basic Books.

Tyler, R. W. (1950). *Basic principles of curriculum and instruction.* Chicago: University of Chicago Press.

————. (1971). Curriculum development in the twenties and thirties. In R. M. McClure (ed.), *The curriculum: Retrospect and prospects,* pp. 26–44. Chicago: University of Chicago Press.

United States House of Representatives. (April 9, 1915). *Congressional Record-House:* H. 2585.

United States Office of Education. (1951). *Life adjustment for every youth.* Washington, DC: U.S. Office of Education.

Van Til, W., Vars, G. F., and Lounsbury, J. H. (1961). *Modern education for the junior high years.* Indianapolis: Bobbs-Merrill.

Weber, G. (October 1975). The case against "Man: A Course of Study." *Phi Delta Kappan, 57,* 81–82.

Welch, W. W. (1968). The impact of national curriculum projects: The need for accurate assessment. *School Science and Mathematics, 68,* 225–234.

Wesley, E. B. (1957). *NEA: The first hundred years.* New York: Harper.

Westbury, I., and Wilkof, N. J. (1978). *Science, curriculum, and liberal education: Selected essays of Joseph T. Schwab.* Chicago: University of Chicago Press.

3

Curriculum Theory

While *curriculum theory* is usually esteemed by scholars in the field as an important component of curriculum studies, it seems to be held in low regard by most practitioners, who often dismiss it as completely unrelated to their day-to-day work. While that impatience with the theoretical is quite understandable, the view advanced in this chapter is that sound theory can be of value to both the scholar and the practitioner. At its best, curriculum theory can provide a set of conceptual tools for analyzing curriculum proposals, for illuminating practice, and for guiding reform.

THE NATURE AND FUNCTION
OF CURRICULUM THEORY

To understand the concept of curriculum theory, it is essential obviously to understand the nature of theory in general. Here there is much disagreement among philosophers of science. On the one hand, there are those who espouse what has come to be known as the Received View of scientific theory. As Suppe (1974) points out, the Received View holds that a theory is a formalized, deductively connected bundle of laws which are applicable in specifiable ways to their observable manifestations. In the Received View, a small number of concepts are selected as bases for the theory; axioms are introduced which specify the fundamental relationships between those concepts; and definitions are provided, specifying the remaining concepts of the theory in terms of the basic ones.

As Atkins (1982) notes, there have been several criticisms of the

Received View, even in its revised formulation. First, Suppe criticized it for its narrowness in requiring axiomatization, noting that several scientific theories are not and cannot be axiomated profitably. He argued instead for a broader view of theory which emphasizes the dynamic nature of all sound theory. Other critics, such as Hanson (1958), attacked the Received View for its posture of value-neutrality; as Hanson and others have pointed out, every aspect of theory development is value-laden. Scientists do not observe objectively; their observations are profoundly influenced by their world views and their values. Popper (1962) rejected the assumption of the Received View that scientific theories can be observationally verified; in his view, theories are conjectures that, although not verifiable, can be submitted to severe tests of falsifiability.

Those who reject the positivist assumptions of the Received View tend to be classified as either realists or instrumentalists, as Atkins notes. Realists see science as a rational and empirical endeavor concerned primarily with explanatory and predictive outcomes: thus, in the view of realists, theory is a description of those structures which generate observable phenomena. And the primary feature of scientific theory is the explanation of how underlying structures and mechanisms work to generate the phenomena being studied (Keat and Urry, 1975). Instrumentalists, on the other hand, concentrate on the function the theory performs: in this view, a theory is a tool of inquiry, rather than a picture or map of the world (Kaplan, 1964). In this sense, then, a theory is not judged in terms of its truth or falsity; instead, it is assessed on the basis of the quality of predictions it demonstrates.

Thus, current philosophers of science tend to take a more open view of the nature of theory, and it is this more open view which seems especially useful in a field such as education, where theory development still seems to be in a somewhat primitive stage. For the purposes of this chapter, therefore, this broader definition of *curriculum theory* is stipulated:

> A curriculum theory is a set of related educational concepts that affords a systematic and illuminating perspective of curricular phenomena.

What are the functions of curriculum theory? Most philosophers of science argue that theory has only three legitimate purposes: to describe, to explain, and to predict. A review of curricular theory, however, suggests that many of those theories serve two additional functions. Some theorists, like Michael Apple, seem most concerned with providing educators with a critical perspective about the society and its schools. While Apple and others who share his perspective are concerned with describing and explaining curricular phenomena, their stance is an openly critical one. And some theorists, such as Ralph Tyler, seem most concerned with guiding practice. While Tyler and others whom he has influenced attempt to describe and explain, the primary intent of their work is to help educators make more reasoned choices.

The extent to which a particular theory is able to discharge its functions effectively seems to be influenced by the complexity and maturity of that theory. Here Faix's (1964) classification of the stages of theory development seems useful.

Basic theory, Stage 1, is an early speculative stage, in which a theory has not yet been correlated with empirical data. Basic theory sets up untested hypotheses, involves few variables, and employs concepts that are not systematically refined and classified. Basic theory provides only descriptive explanations and directions for more meaningful theory. Glatthorn's (1980) analysis of the curriculum into mastery, organic, and enrichment elements might be described as a basic theory.

Middle-range theory, Stage 2, includes hypotheses which have been empirically tested. An effort has been made to eliminate unlikely variables and relations by the use of models and testing. Experimental laws and generalizations result, and theory can be used to illuminate, predict, and control events. Goodlad's (1979) delineation of what he calls a "conceptual system" for guiding inquiry and practice is a good example of a middle-range theory.

General theory, Stage 3, is a general theoretical system or an inclusive conceptual scheme for explaining an entire universe of inquiry. General theory attempts to integrate the substantive knowledge produced from middle-range theories. Beauchamp's (1981) articulation of a comprehensive theory of curriculum might be seen as an attempt to present a general theory, although some would criticize the shallowness of its empirical foundation.

CLASSIFYING CURRICULUM THEORIES

In addition to Faix's attempt to classify curriculum theories in terms of their maturity and complexity, there have been several other attempts at categorization. McNeil (1985) sets up what seems to be an unilluminating dichotomy: soft curricularists and hard curricularists. Soft curricularists, in his view, are those such as William Pinar and other reconceptualists who draw from the "soft" fields of religion, philosophy, and literary criticism; hard curricularists, such as Decker Walker and Mauritz Johnson, follow a rational approach and rely on empirical data. The difficulty with such a dichotomy seems obvious. It results in a grouping together of such disparate theorists as Elliot Eisner and Henry Giroux as "soft curricularists" simply because they draw from similar research perspectives.

A tripartite classification proposed by Pinar (1978) seems equally unsatisfactory: in his formulation, all curriculum theorists can be classified as traditionalists, conceptual empiricists, or reconceptualists. Traditionalists, in his formulation, are those such as Ralph Tyler who are concerned with the most efficient means of transmitting a fixed body of knowledge in order to impart the cultural heritage and keep the existing society functioning. Conceptual empiricists, such as Robert Gagne, are those who derive their research methodologies from the physical sciences in attempting to produce generalizations that will enable educators to control and predict what happens in schools. The reconceptualists (a label he applies to his own work) emphasize subjectivity, existential experience, and the art of interpretation in order to reveal the class conflict and the unequal power relationships existing in the larger society. The basic difficulty with this tripartite formulation is that it mixes in a confusing fashion the theorists' research methodologies and their political stances as bases for categorizing theorists.

One of the most widely cited classifications of curriculum theories is the more useful one proposed by Eisner and Vallance (1974) in their *Conflicting Conceptions of Curriculum*. As they survey the field, they find five different conceptions of or orientations to the curriculum. A "cognitive-process" approach is concerned primarily with the development of intellectual operations and is less concerned with specific content. The "curriculum-as-technology" orientation conceptualizes the function of curriculum as finding the most efficient means of accomplishing predetermined ends. "Self-actualization" sees curriculum as a consummatory experience designed to produce personal growth. "Social reconstruction-relevance" emphasizes societal needs over individual needs. Theorists with this orientation tend to believe that the primary role of the school is to relate to the larger society, with either an adaptive or a reformist stance. Finally, "academic rationalism" emphasizes the importance of the standard disciplines in helping the young participate in the Western cultural tradition.

While the Eisner-Vallance system seems to make more useful distinctions than either of the two previously discussed, it does seems to err in including "technology" as a basic orientation of the curriculum. All the other four seem to designate the major sources for determining curriculum content—the cognitive processes, the person, the society, and the subject. A technological orientation is, on the other hand, concerned primarily with advocating one process for developing a curriculum—a process that could be used with any of the other four types.

The basic error of all three formulations (McNeil, Pinar, and Eisner-Vallance) is that they do not sort out curricular theories in terms of their primary orientation or emphasis. Here, Huenecke's (1982) analysis of the domains of curricular inquiry seems most productive. She postulates three different types of curricular theorizing: structural, generic, and substantive. Structural theories, which she claims have dominated the first fifty years of the field, focus on identifying elements in curriculum and their interrelationships, as well as the structure of decision making. Generic theories center their interests on the outcomes of curriculum, concentrating on the assumptions, beliefs, and perceived truths underlying curriculum decisions. Sometimes referred to as Critical Theories, they tend to be highly critical of past and present conceptions of curriculum. They seek to liberate the individual from the constraints of society using political and sociological frameworks to examine issues of power, control, and influences. The substantive theories speculate about what subject matter or content is most desirable, what knowledge is of the most worth.

While Huenecke's typology seems very useful, it seems to err in omitting one major domain—those theories such as Schwab's (1970) that are concerned primarily with the processes of curricular decision making. While Huenecke would probably argue that Schwab's work is primarily structural in its emphasis, the distinction between structure and process seems to be one worth maintaining.

It therefore seems most useful to divide curriculum theories into the following four categories, based upon their domains of inquiry.

Structure-oriented theories are concerned primarily with analyzing the components of the curriculum and their interrelationships. Structure-oriented theories tend to be descriptive and explanatory in intent.

Value-oriented theories are concerned primarily with analyzing the values and assumptions of curriculum makers and their products. Value-oriented theories tend to be critical in nature.

Content-oriented theories are concerned primarily with determining the content of the curriculum. Content-oriented theories tend to be prescriptive in nature.

Process-oriented theories are concerned primarily with describing how curricula are developed or recommending how they should be developed. Some process-oriented theories are descriptive in nature; others are more prescriptive.

The rest of this chapter will use this categorization system for examining several major curriculum theorists.

STRUCTURE-ORIENTED THEORIES

As indicated above, structure-oriented theorists of curriculum are concerned with the components of the curriculum and their interrelationships. Primarily analytical in their approach, they seek to describe and explain how curricular components interact within an educational environment. Structure-oriented theories examine questions such as the following.

1. What are the essential concepts of the curriculum field and how may they be most usefully defined? For example, what does the term *curriculum* mean?
2. What are the levels of curriculum decision making and what forces seem to operate at each of those levels? For example, how do classroom teachers make decisions about the curriculum?
3. How may the curriculum field be most validly analyzed into its component parts? For example, how does a program of study differ from a field of study?

4. What principles seem to govern issues of content selection, organization, and sequencing? For example, how can curricular elements be articulated?

In seeking answers to such questions, they tend to rely upon empirical research, using both quantitative and qualitative methodologies to inquire into curricular phenomena.

Structure-oriented theorists seem to operate at what might be termed either a macro- or a microlevel. Macrolevel theorists attempt to develop global theories that describe and explain the larger elements of curricular structure. Among such macrolevel theorists, John Goodlad seems to have made the most important contribution. In his work *Curriculum Inquiry* (1979), he describes how he and colleagues at the University of Chicago first formulated a "conceptual system" for integrating Tyler's ends-means rationale with the developmental processes Goodlad was using in his curriculum work with school districts. This early formulation was then extensively tested in the field and subjected to rigorous empirical evaluation. As a result of that testing and evaluation, Goodlad then revised the early formulation to provide for the new knowledge generated in the field studies.

He first draws from Schwab in identifying the forces that determine curricula: the needs of the polity and the economy; the common culture and its subcultures; client-perceived wants and needs; knowledge resources such as the standard disciplines; communities of inquiry or the contributions of research and scholarship; and the professional interests of teachers and administrators. These multiple sources find expression in both the funded knowledge and the conventional wisdom of the field.

In turn, those larger forces of influence interact and transact with the interests, values, needs, and wants of the sanctioning body or controlling agency. Values especially play a key role in influencing the ultimate decisions made for the curriculum at every level of decision making and in each of the four domains of curriculum work. In Goodlad's terms, these four domains interact both with each other and with the surrounding milieu. The societal domain includes those elements of curriculum inquiry and practice that deal with the larger issues of curricular policy as determined by the controlling agency, such as the federal or state government or the local school district. The institutional domain includes those elements of curriculum that operate at the school level—decisions about the selection and ordering of content that grow out of and interact with the societal elements. The instructional domain includes those elements of the curriculum determined at the classroom level—matters of emphasis, pacing, and presentation that result from and interact with the institutional decisions. Finally, the personal/experiential domain involves the elements of the curriculum as experienced by the learners themselves—elements that derive from and influence the teachers' instructional decisions.

The Goodlad conceptual system makes several contributions to the profession's understanding of curricular structure. It simplifies without

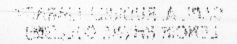

distorting a highly complex set of interacting forces. It gives appropriate attention to the political and valuational aspects of curriculum development, aspects often slighted by other theories. Its analysis of the four domains enables researchers and practitioners to make some important distinctions about curricular decision making. And the fact that it is the product of both collaborative theorizing and empirical testing is reassuring to educators justifiably skeptical of untested theories. Its only serious limitation is its high level of generality: it does not seem to deal sufficiently with other structural issues that are so crucial in the institutional domain.

Here it is necessary to turn to the work of microlevel theorists who seem more concerned with describing and explaining curricular phenomena as they occur at the institutional instructional levels. George Posner seems most representative of the microlevel theorists. Over the course of several years he has identified and analyzed several microelements of curricular structure. Typical of his theoretical work is an article (1976) co-authored with Kenneth Strike, in which they present and explicate a "categorization scheme for principles of sequencing content." By bringing to bear some useful epistemological distinctions and by analyzing the curriculum literature, Posner and Strike are able to identify five major types of content sequence.

The first principle for sequencing content they call "world-related"—the content structure reflects the empirical relationships among events, people, and things. Subtypes here include sequences based on spatial relations, temporal relations, and physical attributes. The second principle is "concept-related," in which sequences reflect the organization of the conceptual world. Thus one subtype of concept-related sequences is "logical prerequisite"—when it is logically necessary to understand the first concept in order to understand the second. "Inquiry-related" sequences are those which sequence the curriculum in relation to a particular method of inquiry, such as Dewey's analysis of the problem-solving process. "Learning-related" sequences draw from knowledge of the psychology of learning in making decisions about sequence; thus sequencing decisions based upon such assumptions as "begin with content of intrinsic interest" or "start with the easiest skills" are learning-related in nature. The final principle, "utilization-related," sequences learning in relation to three possible contexts for utilization—social, personal, and career.

As Posner and Strike point out, these categories can be considered as a set of concepts which should be useful to the curriculum developer, the curriculum evaluator, and the curriculum researcher.

VALUE-ORIENTED THEORIES

Value-oriented theorists seem to be primarily engaged in what might be termed "educational consciousness-raising," attempting to sensitize educators to the values issues that lie at the hearts of both the hidden and the stated curricula. Their intent is primarily a critical one; thus they sometimes have been identified as "critical theorists." And since many have argued the need for reconceptualizing the field of curriculum, they often are labeled as reconceptualists.

In their inquiries they tend to examine issues such as the following:

1. In what ways do the schools replicate the power differentials in the larger society?
2. What is the nature of a truly liberated individual, and how does schooling inhibit such liberation?
3. How do schools consciously or unwittingly mold children and youth to fit into societal roles predetermined by race and class?
4. As curriculum leaders determine what constitutes legitimate knowledge, how do such decisions reflect their class biases and serve to inhibit the full development of children and youth?
5. In what ways does the schools' treatment of controversial issues tend to minimize and conceal the conflicts endemic to the society?

In examining these issues, most value-oriented theorists draw eclectically from several inquiry methodologies, such as psychoanalysis, philosophical inquiry, historical analysis, and political theory.

The Major Value-Oriented Theorists

Since many critical theorists seem to focus on the person, and many others on the sociopolitical milieu, it seems appropriate to select for examination one person-oriented theorist, James Macdonald, and one milieu-oriented theorist, Michael Apple.

James Macdonald   For a period of almost two decades, James Macdonald seemed to serve as a respected gadfly for the curriculum profession, challenging educators to question their assumptions, to aspire to more worthy goals, and to reconceptualize the enterprise of curriculum making. A prolific writer, his work is so multifaceted that it is difficult to summarize. The following discussion therefore focuses on selected aspects of his works that seem most pertinent to the curriculum field.

Basic to all his work is his view of the human condition. And central to that human condition is a search for transcendence, the struggle of the individual to actualize the whole self. Much influenced toward the end of his career by the writings of Carl Jung, Macdonald used almost mystical metaphors in "A Transcendental Developmental Ideology of Education" (1974) to speak of this journey toward transcendence as the primary concern of all humans. In that journey the individual engages in a dialectic between self and society, between explicit and implicit knowledge, searching for order, creating meaning. Thus, the person is an active maker of meaning, not a passive recipient of knowledge.

In this sense, then, the goal of education is to facilitate the development of autonomous and self-actualizing individuals. As a consequence, in Macdonald's view, education is essentially a moral enterprise, reflecting in all its phases the values of those involved. It is therefore incumbent on educators to make their values explicit. Macdonald (1977) put the matter cogently in this fashion:

> *Any person concerned with curriculum must realize that he/she is engaged in a political activity. Curriculum talk and work are, in microcosm, a legislative function. We are concerned . . . with the goal of creating the good life, the good society, and the good person. . . . If we curriculum talkers are to understand what we ourselves are saying, and communicate to others, those values must be explicit.* (p.15)

Obviously, curriculum played a key role in this moral enterprise. And Macdonald (1977) construed curriculum broadly, defining it in this fashion:

> *Curriculum . . . is the study of what should constitute a world for learning, and how to go about making this world. As such it is, in microcosm, the very questions that seem to me to be of foremost concern to all of humanity.* (p. 11)

In Macdonald's view the curriculum offered by most schools is seriously distorted in its emphasis. In a critical analysis of curriculum work that draws heavily from the theories of Jurgen Habermas' *Knowledge and Human Interests* (1971), Macdonald (1975) points out that three basic cognitive interests—control, consensus, and emancipation—may be seen as the basic sources of value differences in the curriculum. Many curriculum leaders are concerned primarily with control—with defining the elements or variables involved in curriculum and developing and implementing a system of decision making for curriculum design. Such an interest is rooted in an empirical-analytic perspective and is associated chiefly with the subject-matter or disciplines approach.

A second group of curriculum theorists, Macdonald argues, are interested in consensus and rely chiefly upon what Habermas terms a hermeneutic understanding of meaning. Such an understanding of meaning, Macdonald (1975) notes, "arises in the context of different cultural life expressions such as ordinary language, human actions, and nonverbal expressions" (p. 280). In his view, Schwab's curriculum theories are oriented primarily toward consensus—a practical interest in examining what goes on in classrooms. The consensus-oriented theorists have strongly influenced developers of "problems-of-living" or "social-issues" courses, courses grounded in the assumption that conflicts can be resolved through mutual social expectations.

Finally, there is a much smaller group of curriculum theorists, he argues, who are interested in emancipation through self-reflection. Here he cites the educational theories of Ivan Illich and Paulo Freire as representative. Their work has influenced curriculum leaders who are concerned with person-centered curricula that liberate individuals through dialogic self-reflection.

This person-centered curriculum is at the heart of the ideal school as conceptualized by Macdonald. In a short monograph written with two of his colleagues (Macdonald, Wolfson, and Zaret, 1973), he envisions the school as an environment emphasizing values and humanistic processes. The curriculum here, as Macdonald conceptualizes it, is one concerned primarily with problem solving and is organized around certain areas of investigation. Students explore their environment, are provided with plentiful data sources from several perspectives, process information in multiple ways, and actively search for meaning. The student experiences the environment in both a playful, self-expressive way and also in an intellectual and reflective manner.

Although Macdonald has been criticized for being too mystical and vague, the cumulative effect of his work has been to challenge curriculum leaders to rethink their basic assumptions and to reconceptualize their field.

Michael Apple   Michael Apple is a critical theorist who seems to be primarily concerned with the relationship between the society and the school. Central to Apple's critique of the society and its schools is his use of the concept of *hegemony*. Strongly influenced by the social critics Antonio Gramsci and Raymond Williams, Apple (1979) uses the term *hegemony* to mean "an organized assemblage of meanings and practices, the central effective and dominant system of meanings, values and actions which are *lived*" (p. 113). Hegemony in this sense permeates the consciousness of the society as a body of practices and a set of meanings determined by the dominant culture. The way people construe reality, the way they allocate energies, the way they live out their daily lives are thus pervasively and deeply influenced by this system of meanings. And all the major elements of that society—the family, the schools, the churches, the workplace—work together to both transmit and remake the dominant culture.

One crucial way in which this cultural hegemony influences educators, Apple (1975) points out, is in their perception of science. In this telling critique of what might be termed "educational pseudoscientism," Apple notes that almost all educators rely upon a narrow and strict view of science, one which values only rationality and empirical data in the service of predictability and control and which ignores the close relationship between science and art, science and myth. Thus, in an attempt to achieve efficiency and smoothness of operation, the educator trivializes intellectual development by reducing knowledge to a predetermined set of discrete objectives and then structures the environment so that the students cannot deviate from the path that has been set. The curriculum field, in Apple's view, has become impoverished because it has adopted this constricting view of science, patterning its activities on models drawn from modes of endeavor based on objectivity, replicability, and the ideal of "hard" data. Behind all the work of such past curriculum theorists as Bobbitt, Charters, and Snedden, and of the systems analysts of the present, in Apple's view, is a "tacit structure of beliefs supporting the position that the complex problems of designing educational environments that are responsive to both institutional and personal meanings will be solved only if we become more certain of our actions and their observable outcomes" (p. 123).

One of the most significant ways that schools serve and reflect the dominant society is in the way educators determine what knowledge is valid. Apple and his colleague Nancy King (1977) make the point that knowledge is a type of cultural capital—and the problem of what should be taught in the schools should be examined as a form of the larger distribution of goods and services in the society: "Thus, the reforms having the greatest effect on school organization and ultimately the procedures and principles which governed life in classrooms were dominated by the language of and an interest in production, well adjusted economic functioning, and bureaucratic skills" (p. 114).

They support this conclusion in their study of a kindergarten classroom, where they found the teacher determining meanings for the children in a successful attempt to socialize them. The teacher required the children to accommodate themselves to the materials she presented. The materials were organized so that the children learned restraint: their opportunities to interact with the materials were limited by the teacher-imposed schedule. The teacher made it clear through words and actions that quietness and cooperation were the primary qualities found in "good kindergarteners." And after only a few weeks in kindergarten, the children had adopted the teacher's way of construing reality. Work was any teacher-directed activity, regardless of its nature; play included all their free-time activities. All work activities were compulsory and had to be started and finished when the teacher required. All children were required to use work materials in the same way and to produce the same kinds of results. Apple and King conclude that the experience of kindergarten is an initiation into the world of work, in which the qualities of obedience, enthusiasm, adaptability, and perseverance are more highly valued than academic competence.

CONTENT-ORIENTED THEORIES

Content-oriented theorists are concerned primarily with specifying the major sources which should influence the selection and organization of the curriculum content. For the most part, their theories can be classified in terms of their views as to which source should predominate: child-centered theories; knowledge-centered theories; or society-centered theories.

Child-Centered Curricula

Those who espouse child-centered curricula argue that the child is the beginning point, the determiner, and the shaper of the curriculum. Although the developing child will at some point acquire knowledge of subject matter, the disciplines are seen only as one type of learning. And while the child develops in and is influenced by a social environment, the needs of the society are not considered paramount; that society will best be served by the kind of mature and autonomous individual that child-centered curricula attempt to develop. As Francis Parker (1894) expressed it many decades ago, "The centre of all movement in education is *the child*" (p. 383).

During the past three decades there have been three major child-centered curriculum movements: affective education; open education; and developmental education.

Affective Education   The affective education movement emphasized the feelings and values of the child. While cognitive development was considered important, it was seen only as an adjunct to affective growth. Thus, curriculum leaders were concerned primarily with identifying teaching and learning activities that would help the child understand and express feelings and discern and clarify values. For example, George Brown (1975), who advocated "confluent education" (a curriculum approach that attempted to synthesize physical, emotional, and intellectual growth), in one of his books recommended a "fantasy body trip" as a learning activity. Students are asked to close their eyes and "move into themselves"; each person is asked to concentrate on different parts of the body, beginning with the toes; then all participants share their experiences.

In affective education, the curriculum typically is conceived as a loosely related set of activities and experiences, chosen for their relevance for and interest to the student. Often they are improvised on the spot, rather than carefully planned in advance. The teacher is considered a facilitator of learning and is encouraged not to dominate but to place the child in the center of all activity. A somewhat more structured approach to sequencing affective curricula has been offered by Shiplett (1975), who advocates this sequence of activities: those that help students become aware of concerns and problems; those that arouse the motivation to learn; those that are rewarding in themselves; and those that lead to accomplishment and mastery.

Although the advocates of affective education often reported excellent results, the research failed to substantiate their claims; and the movement seemed to die some time in the mid-1970s, following the vitriolic attacks of ultraconservative groups who argued that such affective education invaded the child's privacy, encroached on what was essentially a family responsibility, and ignored the cognitive development of learners.

Open Education As noted in Chapter 2, open education was a child-centered curriculum movement that emphasized the social and cognitive development of the child through informal exploration, activity, and discovery. Here the "whole child" was considered the beginning point and focus of curriculum work. As Lillian Weber (1971), one of the foremost exponents of open education, put it, "These questions about children seem uppermost in developing plans for the classroom, for plans were not made from the vantage point of a syllabus of demand which a child had to meet, but with relevance to children in the most immediate way. A plan fitted itself to the child" (p. 169). In fitting the plans to the child, the teacher provisioned a rich learning environment, one that emphasized the use of concrete and interactive materials organized in "learning centers."

The school day was not compartmentalized into subject periods, such as "language arts" and "mathematics." Instead, children experienced an "integrated day"; they were encouraged to solve problems that required the development of several skills and the acquisition of many kinds of knowledge. As Barth (1972) expressed it, "When a child is given freedom to explore materials in his own way, he is likely to be oblivious to categories in which adults have placed them" (p. 75).

As implied in the above discussion, open education curricularists emphasized the learning environment as an important aspect of curriculum: one assessed the child's readiness to learn, kept in mind some general outcomes for that year, and then provisioned an environment that would be stimulating and growth-producing. While the classroom teacher did very little whole-class instruction, he or she played a central role in provisioning that environment, in encouraging children to learn, in monitoring their progress, and in helping them individually and in small groups.

As a widespread movement, open education probably reached its zenith in the mid-1970s, when it gave way to the "back-to-basics" tide. Its accomplishments were simply ignored by its critics. As Walberg (1986) notes in a review of research syntheses which compared open and standard classrooms, students in open classes did slightly worse or no worse on standardized achievement tests and did substantially better on measures of attitude, creativity, cooperation, and independence.

Developmental Education Developmental education, as the term is used here, refers to any curriculum theory which stresses the developmental stages of child growth as the primary determiners of placement and sequence. As noted in Chapter 1, several earlier curriculum workers were influenced by Robert Havighurst's (1973) concept of "developmental tasks"; each major period of child development was marked by the emergence of several tasks, the successful accomplishment of which would lead to happiness. These developmental tasks became the foci of curriculum units produced by those influenced by Havighurst's work. Most curriculum workers interested in facilitating the moral development of the child use Kohlberg's (1984) stages of moral development as a conceptual framework for their curricula.

And some current curriculum leaders use a Piagetian framework in selecting, placing, and structuring appropriate learning experiences. For example, Brooks (1986) describes how the teachers in the Shoreham–Wading River (New York) schools first receive extensive training in the theory and research on cognitive development. They then learn how to assess their students' cognitive development by using a variety of formal and informal measures. Finally, they are taught specific strategies for modifying and adapting predetermined curricula to match students' cognitive levels.

In the developmental perspective, curricula tend to be seen as instruments for facilitating child development. Certain general outcomes are postulated. The child's present developmental level is assessed. Then learning activities and content are selected which will challenge the student enough to produce growth but without overwhelming the student with impossible demands. In all developmental curricula, the teacher is seen primarily as an adapter of curricula, one who learns to modify predetermined content to fit the developmental needs and capabilities of the learner.

While it seems useful to consider the child's development in selecting and placing content, there is no conclusive evidence that developmental curricula are more effective than those not embodying such a perspective.

Knowledge-Centered Curricula

Those leaders who advocate a knowledge-centered approach argue essentially that the disciplines or bodies of knowledge should be the primary determiners of what is taught. While they acknowledge that child-development research should affect decisions about placement, they pay greater attention to the structure of the disciplines or the nature of knowledge, even in matters of sequence. And while they admit that the child lives and grows in a social world, they see the society as playing only a very minor role in developing curricula. In general, curricula based upon a knowledge-centered approach might be divided into two groups: "structures-of-the-disciplines" curricula and "ways-of-knowing" curricula.

Structures of the Disciplines   As a review of the second chapter will indicate, there have been two major attempts to reform the curriculum so that it places greater emphasis upon the subjects. During the period from 1890 to 1910, the concern of curriculum leaders was to standardize the school curriculum and to bring it into closer alignment with college requirements. During the period from 1958 to 1970, the curriculum-reform movement emphasized the updating of curriculum content by emphasizing the structures of the disciplines. It is this latter period which is given chief attention here.

Those leaders advocating a "structures-of-the-disciplines" approach very forcefully assert the importance of the discipline as the beginning point and determiner of curriculum decision making. Philip Phenix (1962), one of the chief intellectual forces behind this movement, was quite direct in presenting the case:

> My thesis, briefly, is that all *curriculum content should be drawn from the disciplines*, or, to put it another way, that only *knowledge contained in the disciplines is appropriate to the curriculum*. . . . *This means that psychological needs, social problems, and any of a variety of patterns of material based on other than discipline content are not appropriate to the determination of what is taught*—though obviously such nondisciplinary contributions are essential to decisions about the distribution of discipline knowledge within the curriculum as a whole. (pp. 57–58)

The assumptions guiding the development of such a discipline-focused curriculum, as Schiro (1978) notes, are quite clear: only knowledge that can be externalized and objectified is considered worth studying; that knowledge is most systematically and usefully organized in the traditional disciplines which compose the university curriculum; the scholars of that discipline are in the best position to determine which elements of that knowledge should be selected and how those elements should be organized. As one of the earlier sources (King and Brownell, 1966) indicated, the curriculum must be an epitome of the discipline; it must have an approach and sequence which conform with that curriculum and must reflect the fundamental concepts and modes of inquiry of that discipline.

One of the central themes of such curriculum theorizing was a concern with the "structure of the discipline." As Schiro indicates, this term was often used ambiguously; it variously seemed to refer to such disparate notions as the discipline's collection of ideas, its collection of facts, its collection of concepts and principles, its collection of relations and patterns, and its methods for discovering new insights. Even the prestigious scholars involved in the Biological Science Curriculum Study project were unable to agree about the essential structures of the biological sciences; unable to resolve their basic disagreement, they produced three different curricula, each emphasizing a somewhat different approach to the structure of biology.

Having determined this structure of the discipline, the scholars then decided how it could best be taught. The answer, of course, was to teach the subject so that the learner would act like the young scholar—would do physics, not just learn about physics. As King and Brownell (1966) said, " . . . the primary *method* of teaching history at any level is that of historiography, or the *method* of the mature professional . . . " (p. 160). And as they emphasized, this method of "doing the discipline" was appropriate at any level; considerations of the child's readiness were held to be inconsequential.

Since curricula were to be developed by the scholars, the role of the teacher was to be an effective deliverer. Teachers were expected to follow the teachers' manuals very closely, producing in the classroom the "discovery learning experiences" that the scholars had decided would be effective.

As discussed in Chapter 2, such curricula were generally not effective in reforming education. Their developers were insensitive to the complex nature of schools as organizations and seemingly ignorant of teachers' needs for autonomy and control. However, when they were implemented, the research suggests that they were in general more effective than the traditional curricula in teaching concepts and in developing more positive attitudes toward the subject. (See, for example, the research synthesis on "the new science" curricula by Shymansky, Kyle, and Alport, 1982.)

Ways of Knowing This approach to the curriculum is of rather recent vintage. As Eisner (1985) notes, it grows out of several emerging research lines: cognitive science; human creativity; brain functioning; and conceptions of intelligence and knowledge. While Vallance (1985) sees this interest in ways of knowing as producing a radically different "curriculum map" that is quite distinct from the traditional disciplines, its emphasis upon knowledge and knowing seems to warrant placing it in the broader category of knowledge-centered approaches.

Briefly, those espousing such a view argue that there are multiple ways of knowing, not just one or two, and that these multiple ways of knowing should be given greater attention in the school's curriculum. Eight different ways of knowing are discussed in a recent NSSE yearbook (Eisner, 1985), and in that volume Vallance notes that there are undoubtedly several more. (All the following references to the eight ways of knowing are from this 1985 yearbook, and the explanations are paraphrases of the authors' definitions.)

Aesthetic modes of knowing are those chiefly used in the arts, although they seem essential in all spheres of human creativity. Scientific ways of knowing, used primarily in the natural sciences, rely upon theory, observation, and evidence in generating tentative explanatory hypotheses. Interpersonal ways of knowing, which are probably learned from ongoing personal relationships instead of from formal teaching, produce social intelligence and social competence. Intuitive ways of knowing refer to the ability to apprehend directly the effect of interaction taking place in a field.

Narrative ways of knowing are expressed in good stories, gripping drama, and believable historical accounts. Formal ways of knowing involve the knowledge derived from understanding the logical relationships of hypotheses and axioms—the rule-generated configurations found in such products as theorems in mathematics, strings in linguistics, and sequences in music. Practical ways of knowing involve procedural information useful in everyday life. Finally, spiritual ways of knowing produce insights through the disciplines of worship, prayer, meditation, text study, contemplation, and action.

What are the curricular implications of these several ways of knowing? Rather than providing answers, Vallance concludes with ten questions, involving such matters as the following: Which ways of knowing should be addressed through the curriculum? Is there a hierarchy of importance? What sequence would be best? Do some traditional subject areas provide better access to ways of knowing than do others?

Since this approach to the knowledge-centered curriculum is so recent, there are no research findings or reports of practice to guide curriculum workers. Instead, leaders are left with some perplexing issues to reflect about and explore.

Society-Centered Curricula

Several curriculum theorists agree that the social order should be the starting point and the primary determiner of the curriculum. However, they differ sharply among themselves about the stance the schools should take toward the existing social order; accordingly, they can best be understood by categorizing them on the basis of this factor: the conformists, the reformers, the futurists, and the radicals.

The Conformists The conformists believe that the existing order is a good one—the best of all possible worlds. While there are obviously problems in that social order, in the eyes of the conformists those problems are of lesser consequence and can be handled by mature adults. Accordingly, the essential task of the curriculum is to indoctrinate the young: help them understand the history of this society; teach them to value it; and educate them to function successfully in it. Curriculum workers with a conformist intent begin curriculum development by identifying the needs of the existing society and its institutions; then, from those needs, curriculum objectives are derived. The teacher is usually expected to serve as an advocate for the free-enterprise system, helping students understand why it is so much better than competing systems.

Curricula with a conformist thrust have been advocated in almost every period of curriculum history. Bobbitt, in his basic work *The Curriculum* (1918), argued for a social point of view, defining the curriculum as " . . . *that series of things which children and youth must do and experience* by way of developing abilities to do the things well that make up the affairs of adult life; and to be in all respects what adults should be" (p. 42). In the eyes of many critics, the career education movement of the 1970s had a conformist thrust: Bowers (1977) saw their purpose as "designed to socialize students to accept the present organization of work and technology as the taken-for-granted reality" (p. 44). And William Bennett, Secretary of Education during Reagan's second term, advocated a brand of citizenship education that had clearly a conformist intent.

The Reformers Those classified as reformers see the society as essentially sound in its democratic structure but want to effect major reforms in the social order. The major vehicle is the curriculum: courses should be developed which will sensitize students to emerging social issues and give students the intellectual tools they need to solve social problems. Thus, curriculum workers should begin the task of curriculum development by identifying social problems. Those social problems—such as racism, sexism, and environmental pollution—then become the center of classroom activity. The teacher is expected to play an active role in identifying the problems, in "raising the consciousness" of the young, and in helping students take actions to bring about the needed reforms.

The reformers seem most vocal during times of social unrest. During the 1930s, George Counts (1932) challenged the schools to take a more active role in achieving his vision of a more liberal society: the title of his book—*Dare the School Build a New Social Order?*—conveys the tone of his work. During the late 1960s and early 1970s, liberal educators advocated curricula that would be responsive to what they perceived as a "cultural revolution." For example, Purpel and Belanger (1972) called for a curriculum that would institutionalize compassion and increase students' sense of social responsibility.

The Futurists   Rather than being attuned to the present problems of the society, futurists look to the coming age. They analyze present developments, extrapolate from available data, and posit alternative scenarios. They highlight the choices poeple have in shaping this coming age and encourage the schools to give students the tools to create a better future for themselves. In a sense they might be described as reformers intent on solving the problems of the year 2000. In their view the school curricula should have such a futurist orientation, focusing on the developments likely to occur and involving students in thinking about the choices they have.

Harold Shane is typical of those futurists who argue for an activist response. In his book *Educating for a New Millennium* (1981) he urges curriculum developers to examine present trends, such as the use of chemicals to enhance memory and the application of "genetic engineering," and then consult with a range of technical experts in predicting the most likely consequences of those trends. The curricula would then be developed to enable the young to determine the kind of future they want and to make informed choices that would lead them to that future.

The Radicals   Those who regard the society as critically flawed espouse curricula that would expose those flaws and empower the young to effect radical changes. Typically reasoning from a neo-Marxist perspective, they believe the problems of the age are only symptoms of the pervasive structural inequities inherent in a technological capitalistic system. As a consequence they want to reach the masses by revolutionizing education, by "deschooling" the educational process.

One of the leading exponents of such an approach is Paulo Freire, the

Brazilian educator whose 1970 book *Pedagogy of the Oppressed* made a significant impact on radical educators in this country. In Freire's view, the goal of education is *conscientization,* a process of enlightening the masses about the inequities inherent in their sociocultural reality and giving them the tools to make radical changes in that social order that restricts their freedom. He makes the process explicit in explaining how he teaches reading. Adults learn to read by identifying words with power—words such as *love* and *person* that have pragmatic value in communicating with others in the community. They create their own texts that express their perceptions of the world they live in and the world they want. They learn to read in order to become aware of the dehumanizing aspects of their lives, but they are helped to understand that learning to read will not guarantee them the jobs they need.

PROCESS-ORIENTED THEORIES

Over the past two decades, when curriculum theory seems to have reached its maturity as a systematic field of inquiry, there have been several attempts to develop conceptual systems for classifying curricular processes and products. (See, for example, the following: Eisner and Vallance, 1974; Schiro, 1978; and Gay, 1980.) However, most of these categorization schemes are deficient on two grounds. First, they badly confuse what have been described above as value-oriented, content-oriented, and process-oriented theories. Second, they seem to give only scant attention to the curriculum-development process advocated by the theorist under consideration. Most suggest that there is some correspondence between the value or content orientation of the theory and the type of process espoused, although such connections do not seem apparent. Thus, one of Gay's (1980) "conceptual models of the curriculum planning process" is what she terms "the experiential model." Her description of the experiential model suggests that it gives predominant weight to the needs of the child as a determiner of content, is vaguely liberal in its value orientation, and emphasizes a planning process that she describes by such terms as *organic, evolving, situational,* and *inquiry-centered.* But she does not provide much detail about the specifics of the planning process.

Thus, if we are asking about alternative planning models, we will have to turn to sources other than these widely known classification schemes. One source that offers some promise is Edmund Short's (1983) paper, "The Forms and Use of Alternative Curriculum Development Strategies." His work is a recent one that seems to build upon previous efforts; it reflects a comprehensive knowledge of both the prescriptive and descriptive literature; and it seems to offer the greatest promise for analyzing and generating alternative systems.

Short's article has two explicit goals: to analyze what is known about the forms and use of alternative strategies of curriculum development, and to organize this knowledge in a way that permits one to assess the policy implications of choosing and using one or the other of these strategies. To accomplish these goals, he first identifies what he considers to be the four "key variables" in the process: the seat of curriculum development; the participants and their qualifications; the attention paid to the realities of the intended use-setting; and the value principles and assumptions of the participants. However, since he believes that objective criteria can be established for only the first three "technical" dimensions and not for the fourth axiological one, he uses only site, participants, and degree of adaptation in designing a three-dimensional analytic matrix. For each of these key variables he identifies two or more categories. Thus, in his formulation, there are two categories of "seats"—generic and site-specific. For the variable of participant expertise required, there are four: scholar-dominated; curriculum-specialist-dominated; milieus-expert-dominated; and balance-coordinated pattern. For the variable of realities of use-setting, he posits three categories: implementation as directed; limited adaptation; and open adaptation. While he notes that this $2\times4\times3$ matrix logically yields twenty-four types of strategies, he selects only three for close analysis. And for each he identifies the salient features derived from an analysis of case studies of that type.

Type I he calls "Generic/Scholar-Dominated/Implementation as Directed," the strategy chiefly used by the developers of the federally funded "alphabet" projects of the 1960s. One of the "typical features" he notes is this one: "succeeds in generating, in the schools that adopt the curriculum produced, only selectively and/or partially implemented versions of the intended curriculum—a consequence of issuing substantive directives for implementation without possessing the authority to compel compliance or sanction modifications, and of lacking on-site personnel to assist in making local adjustments necessary for accommodating the curriculum" (p. 51).

His Type II strategy he calls "Generic/Milieus-Expert-Dominated/ Limited Adaptation," a strategy he believes is dominated by the perspective of experts in the social and cultural milieus within which education takes place, "especially . . . those experts knowledgeable about certain educationally neglected segments of society for whom curriculum policy makers have authorized special programs" (p. 52), such as those for the handicapped or the non-English-proficient. One of the typical features of this strategy is this one: "runs into difficult-to-resolve accountability, ethical, or policy problems when schools that accept funds for implementation from the generic program source use them to adapt the program beyond expected limits" (p. 53).

His Type III strategy is "Site-Specific/Balance-Coordinated Pattern/ Open Adaptation," a cooperative, site-based strategy that reflects significant involvement of users. Its typical features include the following: "takes long periods of time to accomplish a given development effort; it is difficult to sustain the necessary level of involvement until completion; settlement of some tough issues and conflicts between national and local values may be deferred to the parochial interests for lack of time for adequate resolution" (p. 57).

He then sets up ten criteria for evaluating these strategies. Although he is not explicit as to how those criteria have been derived, he seems to rely upon the recommendations of curriculum experts, noting that "analysts of accumulated experience with various strategies have derived a number of criteria that corroborate one another" (p. 55). Thus, one of his criteria is this one: "it will be a strategy that gives the leading role of keeping the curriculum development process on task, and of facilitating the work of all participants in the process, to a trained specialist in curriculum development who is fully knowledgeable about what issues must be addressed and what technically useful forms decisions should take" (p. 56).

By applying those ten criteria to the three strategies previously explicated, he then determines that the Type II strategy is best.

Now there is much here that deserves serious attention. He demonstrates a comprehensive knowledge of the literature: for each type and criterion he cites several sources. And he attempts to reason inductively from the numerous case studies he obviously knows well.

However, there are some serious flaws that mar this attempt to classify and evaluate strategies. One of the basic problems is his selection of the "key variables." We are not told how these variables were selected; and the ones chosen do not seem to be those that most critically impact upon the process. Evidence of this serious omission is that only one of the thirteen "typical features" noted for the Type I strategy refers even obliquely to an element of *process*, as the term is typically used in the field: "follows a process of trial use, feedback, and refinement, until the curriculum is reasonably perfect before it is released for general use" (p. 50).

The second serious problem is with his evaluation process. Early in the article he notes the difficulty in making such assessments: "No particular set of procedures has been demonstrated to be more adequate for the task than any other" (p. 48). And he rejects the criterion of the effect of the curriculum on student achievement, arguing that the success of the curriculum in terms of such effects does not imply anything at all about the superiority of the process. In effect he seems to be arguing that a process that followed the recommendations of experts and produced a curriculum that had no measurable impact on student achievement would somehow be more desirable than one that ignored such recommendations and produced the intended results. Or to put it more simply, it's like the manager congratulating the hitter: "You had a wonderful swing—it doesn't matter that you struck out."

A System for Examining Curricular Processes

It would seem more useful to both scholars and practitioners to have available for their use a systematic means for examining curricular processes. Such an analytic system should have the following characteristics: it would include all the process elements that the research would suggest are important, thus enabling curriculum researchers to make useful distinctions between sets of recommended and implemented processes; it would be open-ended in form, thus enabling practitioners to become aware of a comprehensive set of alternatives; and it would emphasize description and analysis, not evaluation, enabling both scholars and practitioners to reach their independent conclusions about desirability.

The set of descriptors presented in Figure 3–1 represent an initial attempt to formulate such an analytic system. Certain caveats should be noted here. First, the descriptors have been drawn from a preliminary analysis of the literature and the author's own experience, but that analysis has not at this point been completely systematic and rigorous. Second, while there has been some initial success in using it to discriminate between development strategies that on the surface seem quite similar, it needs much more extensive testing and refinement. It is thus presented here as an initial formulation that invites criticism and improvement.

FIGURE 3–1. An Analytic System for Examining the Curriculum Process

1. What groups or constituencies should be represented in the developmental sessions?
2. What type of participation structure is recommended for the sessions—monologic, participatory, dialogic?
3. What shaping factors should receive significant consideration throughout the process?
4. Which curriculum element should be used as the starting point in the substantive deliberations?
5. Which curriculum elements should receive significant consideration—and in what sequence should such consideration occur?
6. Which organizing structures should receive significant consideration—and in what order: course structure, units, lessons, lesson components?
7. Should the progression from element to element or from structure to structure be predominantly linear or recursive?
8. What curriculum images and metaphors seem to influence the process?
9. What general type of problem-solving approach should be used throughout the process—technological, rational, intuitive, negotiating?
10. What recommendations are made about the form and content of the curriculum product?
11. What recommendations are made for implementing the curriculum product?
12. What recommendations are made for assessing the curriculum product?
13. What criteria should participants use to assess the quality and effectiveness of the process?
14. To what extent should developers be sensitive to the political aspects of curriculum development?

The first descriptor focuses on the participants in the process. As Short indicates, their competence and their perspective are so important that we need to have such information. The second descriptor is concerned with the general tenor of the discussions. A monologic discussion is one in which only one person participates or makes decisions, such as a college instructor developing a new course independently. In a participatory discussion, one individual clearly is in control but makes a genuine effort to solicit the input of others. A dialogic discussion is one in which there is much open discussion in an attempt to achieve consensus on key issues.

The third descriptor identifies those elements which influence curriculum decision making, even though they may not be explicitly referred to in the final document. As Figure 3-2 indicates, there are several factors that variously impact upon curriculum decisions. Thus, nursing educators who have been observed developing courses seemed most conscious of the requirements of accrediting bodies. On the other hand, teachers in a large urban district seemed chiefly concerned about "accountability procedures."

FIGURE 3-2. Shaping Factors in Curricular Deliberations

1. The developers: their espoused and practiced values; their knowledge and competence.
2. The students: their values, abilities, goals, learning styles.
3. The teachers: their values, knowledge, teaching styles, concerns.
4. The organization: its ethos and structure.
5. The administrators of that organization: their values and expectations.
6. External individuals and groups (parents, employers, pressure groups): their values and expectations.
7. Accrediting bodies: their requirements and recommendations.
8. Scholars in the field: their recommendations, their reports of research; their perceptions of the structure of that discipline.
9. The community and the larger society: what is required to maintain or change the social order.
10. Other courses in that field of study, courses taken previously and subsequently.
11. Courses in other fields which students are likely to take concurrent with the course being developed: their contents, impacts, and requirements.
12. The schedule for the course: number of meetings; length of meetings; frequency.
13. Accountability procedures: examinations, "curricular audits."

The fourth descriptor is concerned with the starting point for the substantive deliberations. As Figure 3-3 indicates, there are in this formulation several curricular elements, any one of which might conceivably be a starting point. The obvious intent here is to challenge the conventional wisdom that curriculum development must begin with a clear statement of objectives. And the fifth descriptor is concerned with those elements emphasized and the sequence in which they are considered.

The sixth descriptor focuses on the organizing structures of the course—the structural elements that give the course shape. Four structural components are included: the general structure and movement of the course itself, the units, the lessons, and the lesson components.

The seventh descriptor examines the progression of the discussion. A

FIGURE 3-3. Curricular Elements

1. Rationale, philosophy, or statement of espoused values.
2. Institutional goals or aims.
3. Knowledge outcomes for the course, the units, the lessons: concepts, factual knowledge.
4. Skill or process outcomes for the course, the units, the lessons.
5. Affective outcomes for the course, the units, the lessons: values, attitudes.
6. Content choices: elements of subject matter selected for their intrinsic worth (literary or artistic works, periods of history, important individuals, significant events, etc.).
7. Organizing elements: themes, recurring concepts, structures of linkage:

   a. Those used to link this course with courses previously or subsequently studied.
   b. Those used to link this course with other courses studied concurrently.
   c. Those used to link units in this course with each other.
   d. Those used to organize units and relate lessons in a unit to each other.

8. Teaching/learning activities.
9. Instructional materials and media.
10. Time allocations.
11. Methods for assessing student learning.

linear progression would move sequentially from element to element or from structure to structure; a recursive discussion would move back and forth in some systematic fashion. The eighth descriptor asks the researcher to be sensitive to the curricular images and metaphors that seem to influence the process. Does the developer seem to conceptualize a curriculum as a mosaic or a patchwork quilt, as a journey or series of travel experiences, as a set of steps moving from the basement to the top floor? The obvious point, of course, is that such images and metaphors reveal the pervasive belief systems of the developers with respect to that field of study—and such belief systems subtly but profoundly influence their decision making.

The ninth descriptor examines the type of problem-solving process at work. For contrary to what some deliberative theorists assert, it seems in many respects that all curriculum making is a type of problem solving. Four types of problem-solving processes have been recommended by theorists: technological; rational; intuitive; and negotiating. A technological approach to curriculum problem solving argues for a tightly controlled process assessing needs, deriving goals from those needs, performing a task analysis to identify learning objectives, determining the sequential or hierarchical relationship among the objectives, specifying instructional activities, and identifying evaluation procedures.

A rational approach to curriculum problem solving describes the somewhat looser but still logical approach advocated by Schwab and others: deliberators collect and examine pertinent data, formulate the curriculum problem, generate alternative solutions, and evaluate those solutions in order to determine which is best.

In an intuitive approach, participants are encouraged to rely upon their intuition and tacit knowledge, like Schon's (1983) "reflective practitioners" who make wise choices but cannot explain how they make those choices. And in some processes, the problem solving is more like a negotiating exchange in which bargaining and trading and making compromises seem to be the predominant activities.

The tenth descriptor examines the decisions about the form and content of the final product. Again there might be much variation here. For example, Glatthorn (1980) recommends that the final product should be a looseleaf notebook which contains only a summary of pertinent research and a list of the required and testable objectives. Teachers using the notebook thus have much latitude in how they organize the objectives and which methods and materials they use.

The eleventh and twelfth descriptors are concerned with the future—what plans are made for implementing and for testing the product. The thirteenth descriptor examines the criteria that the participants seem chiefly to rely upon in assessing the quality of their work, and the last descriptor examines the extent to which the process is sensitive to the political aspects of curriculum work.

If such an analytic system is at all valid, then it suggests, of course, that the Tyler rationale is not the only system for developing curricula; in fact, the system has been used in initial trials to analyze the significant differences between several distinct models of curriculum development. Figure 3–4 shows how the descriptors were used to analyze Doll's (1986) process, and Figure 3–5 shows how they describe the "naturalistic" process reviewed in Chapter 8 of this work.

FIGURE 3–4. Analysis of Doll's (1986) Curriculum-Development Process

1. Groups represented: teachers, pupils, administrators, supervisors, school board, lay community.
2. Participation structure: participatory.
3. Shaping factors: organizational ethos; pupil needs; teachers' values, knowledge, teaching style, concerns.
4. Starting point: institutional goals.
5. Elements considered: goals; course objectives; evaluation means; type of design; learning content; interunit linkages; interlesson linkages.
6. Organizing structures: not specified.
7. Progression: linear.
8. Images and metaphor: not used.
9. Problem-solving approach: rational.
10. Form and content of product: no specific recommendations.
11. Implementation recommendations: no specific recommendations.
12. Recommendations for evaluating product: extensive formative and summative assessments.
13. Criteria in assessing process: eleven specific criteria offered.
14. Political sensitivity: limited.

FIGURE 3–5. Analysis of Glatthorn's (1986) Curriculum-Development Process

1. Groups represented: teachers.
2. Participation structure: dialogic.
3. Shaping factors: students; teachers; administrators; scholars; other courses; schedule.
4. Starting point: knowledge and skill outcomes for course; starting point for unit planning varies.
5. Elements considered: knowledge and skill outcomes for units and lessons; unit themes; teaching/learning activities; instructional materials and media; time allocations; student assessment.
6. Organizing structures: units, lessons.
7. Progression: recursive.
8. Images and metaphors: not used.
9. Problem-solving approach: intuitive.
10. Form and content of product: open-ended "scenarios."
11. Implementation recommendations: no specific recommendations.
12. Recommendations for evaluating product: emphasis on quality of learning experiences.
13. Criteria in assessing process: none provided.
14. Political sensitivity: extensive.

APPLICATIONS

1. As noted in this chapter, there is much debate in the field about the value of curriculum theory. As you understand the nature of curriculum theory, how much professional value does it seem to have for you?

2. Most of the theoretical work in the field would be subsumed under the headings of value-centered and content-centered theories. How do you explain the fact that structure and process matters have received much less attention from curriculum theorists?

3. Several experts who have analyzed process theories claim that all attempts to develop new process approaches turn out to be simply variations of the Tyler rationale. To what extent do you agree with this assessment?

4. Use the proposed descriptive system to analyze any article or book which describes a curriculum-development process.

5. As noted in this chapter, very little work has been done in applying "ways-of-knowing" approaches to curriculum-development projects. What do you think a school curriculum would look like, in general, if it attempted to embody a "ways-of-knowing" approach to the curriculum?

REFERENCES

Achinstein, P. (1968). *Concepts of science.* Baltimore: Johns Hopkins Press.

Apple, M. W. (1975). Scientific interests and the nature of educational institutions. In W. Pinar (ed.), *Curriculum theorizing: For Reconceptualists,* pp. 120–130. Berkeley, CA: McCutchan.

———. (1979). On analyzing hegemony. *The Journal of Curriculum Theorizing,* 1, 10–43.

Apple, M. W., and King, N. R. (1977). What do schools teach? In A. Molnar and J. A. Zahorik (eds.), *Curriculum theory,* pp. 108–126. Alexandria, VA: ASCD.

Atkins, E. S. (1982). Curriculum theorizing as a scientific pursuit: A framework for analysis. Doctoral dissertation, University of Pennsylvania.

Barth, R. S. (1972). *Open education and the American school.* New York: Agathon Press.

Beauchamp, G. A. (1981). *Curriculum theory* (4th Ed.). Itasca, IL: Peacock.

Bobbitt, F. (1918). *The curriculum.* Boston: Riverside Press.

Bowers, C. A. (September 1977). Emergent ideological characteristics of educational policy. *Teachers College Record,* 76, 1.

Brooks, M. (April 1986). Curriculum development from a constructivist perspective. Paper presented at the annual meeting of the American Educational Research Association, San Francisco.

Brown, G. I. (1975). Examples of lessons, units, and course outlines in confluent education. In G. I. Brown (ed.), *The live classroom,* pp. 231–295. New York: Viking.

Counts, G. S. (1932). *Dare the school build a new social order?* New York: Day.

Doll, R. C. (1986). *Curriculum improvement: Decision making and process* (6th Ed.). Boston: Allyn and Bacon.

Eisner, E. (ed.) (1985). *Learning and teaching the ways of knowing.* Eighty-fourth yearbook of the National Society for the Study of Education, Part II. Chicago: University of Chicago Press.

Eisner, E. W., and Vallance, E. (eds.) (1974). *Conflicting conceptions of curriculum.* Berkeley, CA: McCutchan.

Faix, T. L. (1964). Structural-functional analysis as a conceptual system for curriculum theory and research: A theoretical study. Doctoral dissertation, University of Wisconsin.

Freire, P. (1970). *Pedagogy of the oppressed.* New York: Herder and Herder.

Gay, G. (1980). Conceptual models of the curriculum planning process. In A. W. Foshay (ed.), *Considered action for curriculum improvement,* pp. 120–143. Alexandria, VA: Association for Supervision and Curriculum Development.

Glatthorn, A. A. (1980). *A guide for designing an English curriculum for the eighties.* Urbana, IL: National Council of Teachers of English.

Goodlad, J. I. (ed.) (1979). *Curriculum inquiry: The study of curriculum practice.* New York: McGraw-Hill.

Habermas, J. (1971). *Knowledge and human interests.* (J. L. Shapiro, translator). Boston: Beacon Press.

Hanson, N. R. (1958). *Patterns of discovery.* Cambridge: Cambridge University Press.

Havighurst, R. (1973). *Developmental tasks and education* (3rd Ed.). New York: McKay.

Huenecke, D. (1982). What is curricular theorizing? What are its implications for practice? *Educational Leadership, 39,* 290–294.

Kaplan, A. (1964). *The conduct of inquiry: Methodology for behavioral science.* San Francisco: Chandler.

Keat, R., and Urry, J. (1975). *Social theory as science.* London: Routledge & Kegan Paul.

King, A., and Brownell, J. A. (1966). *The curriculum and the disciplines of knowledge.* New York: Kreiger.

Kohlberg, L. (1984). *Recent research in moral development.* New York: Holt, Rinehart and Winston.

Macdonald, J. B. (1974). A transcendental developmental ideology of education. In W. Pinar (ed.), *Heightened conscience, cultural revolution, and curriculum theory.* Berkeley, CA: McCutchan.

_____. (1975). Curriculum and human interest. In W. Pinar (ed.), *Curriculum Theorizing,* pp. 283–298. Berkeley, CA: McCutchan.

_____. (1977). Value bases and issues for curriculum. In A. Molnar and J. A. Zahorik (eds.), *Curriculum theory,* pp. 10–21. Alexandria, VA: ASCD.

Macdonald, J. B., Wolfson, B. J., and Zaret, E. (1973). *Deschooling society: A conceptual model.* Alexandria, VA: ASCD.

McNeil, J. D. (1985). *Curriculum: A comprehensive introduction* (3rd Ed.). Boston: Little, Brown.

Parker, F. W. (1894). *Talks on pedagogics.* New York: E. L. Kellogg.

Phenix, P. H. (1962). The disciplines as curriculum content. In A. H. Passow (ed.), *Curriculum Crossroads.* New York: Teachers College Press.

Pinar, W. F. (1978). The reconceptualization of curriculum studies. *Journal of Curriculum Studies, 10,* 205–214.

Popper, K. R. (1962). *Conjectures and refutations.* New York: Basic Books.

Posner, G. J., and Strike, K. A. (1976). A categorization scheme for principles of sequencing content. *Review of Educational Research, 46,* 665–690.

Purpel, D. E., and Belanger, M. (1972). Toward a humanistic curriculum theory. In D. E. Purpel and M. Belanger (eds.), *Curriculum and the cultural revolution,* pp. 64–74. Berkeley, CA: McCutchan.

Schiro, M. (1978). *Curriculum for better schools: The great ideological debate.* Englewood Cliffs, NJ: Educational Technology.

Schon, D. A. (1983). *The reflective practitioner: How professionals think in action.* New York: Basic Books.

Schwab, J. (1970). *The practical: A language for curriculum.* Washington, DC: NEA.

_____. (1971). The practical: Arts of eclectic. *School Review, 79,* 493–542.

Shane, H. G. (1981). *Educating for a new millennium.* Bloomington, IN: Phi Delta Kappa.

Shiplett, J. M. (1975). Beyond vibration teaching: Research and development in confluent education. In G. I. Brown (ed.), *The live classroom,* pp. 121–131. New York: Viking.

Short, E. C. (1983). The forms and use of alternative curriculum development strategies: Policy implications. *Curriculum Inquiry, 13,* 45–64.

Shymansky, J. A., Kyle, W. C. Jr., and Alport, J. (October 1982). Research syntheses in the science curriculum projects of the sixties. *Educational Leadership, 40,* 63–66.

Suppe, F. (ed.) (1974). *The structures of scientific theories.* Urbana, IL: University of Illinois Press.

Vallance, E. (1985). Ways of knowing and curricular conceptions: Implications for program planning. In E. Eisner (ed.), *Learning and teaching the ways of knowing,* pp. 199–217. Chicago: University of Chicago Press.

Walberg, H. J. (1986). Syntheses of research on teaching. In M. C. Wittrock (ed.), *Handbook of research on teaching* (3rd Ed.), pp. 214–229. New York: Macmillan.

Weber, L. (1971). *The English infant school and informal education.* Englewood Cliffs, NJ: Prentice-Hall.

4

The Politics of Curriculum

What actually is taught in the classroom results from a confluence of several often conflicting factors. Federal and state governments, professional organizations, local school boards, textbook publishers, accrediting organizations, parent and community groups, school administrators, and classroom teachers—all seem to make a difference. Those conflicting influences seem to change in their strength from time to time, and their particular impact upon a given classroom is often difficult to trace. However, any curriculum leader who wishes to develop or improve curricula needs to understand the politics of curriculum—the way those organizations and individuals attempt to influence what is taught in the schools. This chapter presents an overview of the way influences are brought to bear and then examines in greater detail those agencies that seem to have the greatest influence.

AN OVERVIEW OF THE CURRICULUM-INFLUENCE PROCESS

In understanding how several groups and individuals influence curriculum policy and curriculum development, it is important at the outset to realize that such influences do not take place in a vacuum. They occur in a complex social and cultural environment—an environment that significantly determines which belief systems and practices will gain the widest audience. Here Schon (1971) is most illuminating. As he sees it, ideas "in good currency" flow into the main stream, mediated by certain roles. New ideas incompati-

125

ble with the prevailing conceptions are suppressed within the social system, but kept alive by people in vanguard roles until a crisis occurs. At that time those new ideas might be released and spread by information networks and the mass media. However, before they are accepted, these new ideas become issues in power struggles. As Schon sees it, there are only a limited number of "slots" for new ideas, because these new ideas are attached to advocates competing for power positions. In this manner, inquiry around the ideas becomes politicized. Those that have the most powerful support become legitimated by approval from powerful people. Only then can the new ideas become public policy.

This struggle for power in the curriculum-making process seems to occur most sharply at the federal, state, and local district levels and differentially affects the recommended, the written, and the taught curriculum, to use the constructs examined in Chapter 1.

At the federal level the struggle for power occurs chiefly behind the scenes, as several influence groups and individuals attempt to persuade members of both the executive and legislative branches. Bell (1986) describes how the decision not to abolish the Department of Education during President Reagan's second term came about as the result of such behind-the-scenes maneuvering. First, the platform-drafting committee for the 1984 Republican National Convention decided to ignore pressures to abolish the department that came mainly from individuals whom Bell calls "movement conservatives"—ideologues of the far right. And, as Bell points out, key members of the platform committee were House Republicans running for office in 1984. They had read *A Nation at Risk*, they had sensed the grassroots interest in education, and they did not want to be perceived by voters as being anti-education. Although the "movement conservatives" continued to attempt to persuade Reagan to exert leadership on the issue, he was, in Bell's view, a pragmatist with different priorities. He cared deeply about tuition tax credits, vouchers, and prayer in the schools, but he saw the fate of the Department of Education as a matter of lesser consequence. Knowing there was no broad-based support to abolish the department and not caring enough to spend his political capital in fighting the battle, Reagan quietly put the proposal on the back burner and never again raised the matter with Bell.

Lobbying groups can play an important role in this hidden power struggle at the federal level. Levine and Wexler (1981) document clearly how the Council for Exceptional Children and other interest groups representing the handicapped played a determining role in the passage of Public Law 94-142, the most important national legislation affecting the handicapped. These lobbyists had developed close relationships with the staff and members of the congressional education committees, had formed close alliances with leaders in the Bureau of Education for the Handicapped, and spoke authoritatively at every Congressional hearing on the bill.

The same picture of policy being made in a highly charged and politicized environment with much behind-the-scenes lobbying is seen at the state level. A case in point is the way Pennsylvania adopted its new curriculum regulations. In 1981 a forward-looking secretary of education proposed a radical restructuring of the state's curriculum regulations, replacing lists of required courses with the specification of student competencies that could be developed in a variety of ways. For two years these changes were discussed and debated by lobbyists (chiefly those from professional organizations), by the state board of education, and by department of education officials. No action was taken; state legislators were indifferent. One legislative leader put it this way:

> *The reaction of the legislature when they were talking about these learning outcomes [the competency-based curriculum proposal] was pretty much a hands-off thing. They realized it was an issue they didn't want to get involved in. . . . Then all the reports came out in the intervening time, and there was a kind of a rush to judgment to see who was going to address this serious problem. . . . all of a sudden the national environment was "let's do these things," and so everyone wanted to have their stamp on them.* (Lynch, 1986, p. 74)

The governor published his own recommendations for "turning the tide," the House passed legislation mandating increased curriculum rigor and an emphasis upon traditional subjects (not competencies), the Senate passed a resolution directing the state board of education to take action, and the state board adopted revised curriculum regulations—all within six months' time.

In such a politicized environment at the state level, numerous groups and individuals have a differential impact. In her study of policy making in one of the eastern states, Marshall (1985) identified fifteen influence groups. Six of these groups seemed to have a strong influence: listed in order of influence, they were the governor and his executive staff; the chief state school officer; individual members of the state legislature; the legislature as a whole; the legislative staff; and education interest groups. Three seemed to have a moderate influence: the teachers' association; the state board of education; and the administrators' organization. The rest—courts, the federal government, the school boards association, noneducator groups, and researchers—had much less influence.

At the local level there is the same interplay of conflicting and coalescing influences, only there are some differences in the key actors. As the local school board sets general curriculum policy, it too is sensitive to prevailing trends in the society; in this context it makes general decisions that have been strongly influenced by the superintendent, who is responding to his or her own perception of the larger educational scene and local needs. At the same time, local pressure groups, often acting in concert with nationally organized lobbies, will attempt to influence the board's curriculum policy as it involves such specific controversial issues as sex education, evolution and creationism, and values education.

Once general policy has been determined at the district level, key decisions are then made about the written curriculum by curriculum leaders, school administrators, and teachers. At the district level, the assistant superintendent for curriculum and instruction and several subject-matter supervisors usually provide leadership in developing and improving a field of study, such as mathematics K-12. Typically, the assistant superintendent or a supervisor will appoint a committee made up of representatives of the major constituencies: a principal; a team leader or department chair; two to five teachers; and perhaps a token parent. In making decisions about the scope and sequence of that field, the committee typically uses a variety of professional sources: consults state guidelines, checks standardized tests, reviews available texts, confers with consultants, reviews guides from other districts and from professional associations, and surveys classroom teachers. When conflicts arise in their deliberations, the committee members typically resolve them through political processes—negotiating, compromising, and deferring to the most powerful. At this stage external pressure groups seem to have little influence, although the committee will usually make decisions based upon its own assessment of the community's "zone of tolerance."

The picture changes somewhat at the school level. In elementary schools the principal seems to play a key role in determining curricular priorities and in monitoring the curriculum. If conflict arises, it will usually occur between the principal and a small group of teachers who are jealous of their curricular autonomy. At the secondary level the principal will usually delegate that responsibility to a team leader or department chair, since subject-matter expertise is more important at this level. In secondary schools, curricular battles are usually waged between departments, as they compete for scarce resources.

Then the classroom door closes, and the teacher becomes the curriculum. The teacher makes decisions based upon a somewhat unconscious response to several sources: the district guide; the textbook; curriculum-referenced and standardized tests; the teacher's knowledge of and perception of the subject matter; and the teacher's assessment of pupil interest and readiness.

Thus, at different levels of curriculum decision making, the major sources of influence vary considerably, but at every level the process seems to be a highly politicized one in which issues of power and control are resolved in curriculum decision making. At this juncture a closer examination of certain of those key elements might be useful.

THE ROLE OF THE FEDERAL GOVERNMENT

In examining the role of the federal government in influencing the school curriculum, it is useful to bring to bear a historical perspective, since patterns of influence have changed over the past few decades. The discussion below, therefore, examines that role in the three most recent periods discussed in Chapter 2 of this work: Scholarly Structuralism, 1957–1967; Romantic Radicalism, 1968–1974; and Privatistic Conservatism, 1975 to the present. Prior to 1957, there was almost no federal involvement in curriculum; before the 1950s, as Kliebard (1979) notes, the activities of the federal government in education were limited to convening prestigious groups, creating professional societies, and disseminating the recommendations of prominent individuals.

1957–1967: Scholarly Structuralism

This was the period of the national frenzy to "catch up with the Russians." Largely instigated by the launching of Sputnik, it was a time of intensive and extensive federal intervention in curriculum. During this period, education seemed to be dominated by what Atkin and House (1981) call a "technological" perspective. Educational leaders were convinced that rational, technological approaches could solve the schools' problems. Teaching was seen as a technological endeavor: the essential skills of teaching could be identified and taught through a step-by-step approach. Curriculum development similarly was viewed as a rational technological enterprise: the right content could be identified by the scholars and then delivered in tested packages. Even the change process was seen from this perspective: the agricultural model of conducting research and disseminating its results through "change agents" was viewed as the only proper means for changing the schools.

And the primary intervention strategy adopted by the federal government was the development and dissemination of generic curricula. To use the constructs explicated in Chapter 1, the developers of the "alphabet-soup curricula" attempted to fuse the recommended, the written, and the taught curricula; they sincerely believed that their idealistic recommendations would be embodied *in toto* into district curriculum guides and that teachers would willingly and faithfully implement what they had produced.

The developers of these generic curricula seemed most concerned with course content: the National Science Foundation developed and supported the "Course Content Improvement Program," which in turn strongly influenced a similar program adopted by the U.S. Office of Education, called the "Curriculum Improvement Program." In the view of these leaders, *curriculum* and *content* were synonymous. That content, in their view, should be determined only by the scholars in the disciplines—not by "educationists." It was the scholars alone who understood the structures of the disciplines, who could identify the critical concepts, and who knew how to organize and sequence that content.

Once the scholars had developed these ideal curricula, the dissemination effort began. Large-scale publicity efforts were undertaken: articles appeared in the professional journals touting the high quality of the products, and sessions were held at the major professional conferences advocating the adoption of the materials. Teachers were trained in summer institutes, with rather generous stipends provided. More than thirty regional laboratories were funded to aid in the development and dissemination efforts. And the curriculum was translated into marketable packages—either textbooks produced by commercial publishers or materials sold by the developers themselves.

Initially these federally funded generic curricula seemed successful. The materials produced were significantly different from what had been developed before, especially in science and mathematics. Even the conventional textbooks produced by mainline publishing houses included concepts introduced by the scholarly curriculum projects. Early users, the most committed and knowledgeable of teachers, seemed enthusiastic.

However, resistance to these federal efforts to transform the curriculum through direct intervention began to increase at the end of this period. There was, first of all, concern about what some termed "the federal curriculum"—a fear that these federally supported curriculum projects would reduce local curricular autonomy. Others pointed out, of course, that in some fields, at least, the effect was quite the opposite. Until Project Social Studies came along, there was in effect a nationally standardized curriculum in social studies—a curriculum that was limited almost solely to recurring courses in U.S. history, a little geography in elementary schools, and a smattering of civics in junior high schools and "Problems of Democracy" in senior high schools. Project Social Studies offered more alternatives: schools could now teach economics, anthropology, and sociology, using materials that had a scholarly cachet.

There were also mounting objections to the specifics of the content. Many teachers complained that the materials were too difficult for their students. Parents and lay critics argued that the "basics" were being slighted: there was not enough attention to computational skills in the mathematics curriculum projects or to spelling and grammar in the English curricula. And there were numerous protests about the values issues embedded in many of the social studies and science curricula; many individuals and organizations felt that these nationally disseminated projects espoused values they considered too liberal and permissive. As noted in Chapter 2, these complaints reached a crescendo in the bitter controversy over *Man: A Course of Study* (MACOS).

Finally, it was obvious that these so-called teacher-proof curricula were doomed to fail, because they were put in the hands of "curriculum-proof" teachers. The developers of these curricula seemed totally oblivious to the nature of schools as organizations and to the complexities of classroom life. They somewhat naively believed that their curricula would be adopted uniformly and implemented as designed. They foolishly expected teachers to acquire, internalize, and use teaching strategies that were radically different from those they already used and that were quite demanding in their complexity.

1968–1974: Romantic Radicalism

During this period the national agenda changed. While international issues such as the war in Vietnam continued to dominate the headlines, at the grassroots level people seemed more concerned with their own individual freedoms. It was a time when "rights," not responsibilities, was the dominant slogan: black people, handicapped individuals, homosexuals, women, and non-native groups all asserted their rights to liberation and to greater power.

In this seven-year period, educational thinking at the policy-making level seemed to be dominated by what Atkin and House call a political perspective, in contradistinction to the technological perspective that had dominated the previous period. A political perspective views educational reform essentially as a political process. The legitimacy of several conflicting views is recognized. Decisions are made primarily through a process of compromise and negotiation.

It was this political perspective which seemed to influence both Congress and the several federal agencies empowered to enforce compliance with federal legislation. And their intervention strategy seemed to be a "carrot-and-stick" approach: develop specific policies mandating changes in the operation of schools and offer financial rewards to those who comply. Their impact on school curricula is best seen perhaps in an analysis of their response to pressures from two groups: those insisting on the need for bilingual education and those arguing for the educational rights of the handicapped.

Bilingual Education   As Ravitch (1983) points out, the demand for bilingual education seemed to result from a surge of new ethnocentrism that argued for ethnicity as a basis for public policy. Initially, the demand seemed modest enough. As Ravitch notes, those advocating bilingual education in the Congressional hearings of 1967 desired funding only for demonstration projects that would meet the special educational needs of Hispanic children; in their view, the aim of bilingual education was to help the Hispanic child master the English language. The Bilingual Education Act of 1968, which ultimately became Title VII of the Elementary and Secondary Education Act, covered not just Hispanic children, but all children of limited English-speaking ability, especially those from low-income families. The act was intentionally vague in key particulars: *bilingual education* was not defined, and the purpose of the act was never made explicit.

Although the act itself did not require districts to provide bilingual programs, in 1970 the Office of Civil Rights (OCR) informed every school district with more than 5 percent "national origin–minority group children" that it had to take "affirmative steps" to rectify the language deficiency of such children or be in violation of Title VI of the Civil Rights Act. The OCR guidelines were sustained and supported by the Supreme Court in its *Lau v. Nichols* decision, which directed the schools to create special language programs for "non-English-speaking children," to correct what it called "language deficiency."

Also in 1974, Congress renewed and extended the 1968 act, making several important changes in response to pressures from lobbying groups representing ethnic minorities. First, the provisions of the act covered all children, not just those from low-income homes. And instead of being primarily concerned with teaching these children how to speak English, the act recognized the importance of maintaining the native language and cultural heritage. As Ravitch notes, the 1974 act was a landmark, in that it marked the first time the Congress had dictated a specific pedagogical approach to local districts.

What had started out as a modest demonstration program to aid Hispanic students had become a mammoth program which funded the teaching of sixty-eight languages, including seven Eskimo languages and a score of Native American languages.

Educating the Handicapped   In many ways federal intervention in the education of the handicapped seemed to parallel its activities on behalf of non-native children. What began as a relatively small effort became a major establishment supported with federal funds. Prior to 1965 there seemed to be almost no concerted effort to secure federal funds to aid the education of the handicapped. However, the leaders of organizations such as the National Association for Retarded Citizens and the Council for Exceptional Children, viewing the success of the civil rights movement, began to coordinate their lobbying efforts. Their efforts quickly paid off: in 1966, the Congress established a Bureau of Education for the Handicapped, within the Office of Education, and in 1970 passed new legislation increasing the amount of aid for the education of the handicapped and expanding the definition of the term to include the learning-disabled and the socially-emotionally disturbed.

Two important court decisions provided strong impetus for further efforts. In 1971 the federal courts issued a consent decree requiring Pennsylvania to provide a free public education to all retarded children between the ages of six and twenty-one; and in 1972 the federal court in the District of Columbia held that every school-age child in the district had to be provided with a "free and suitable publicly supported education regardless of the degree of a child's mental, physical, or emotional disability or impairment" (*Mills v. Board of Education*, 1972).

Congress then responded by enacting the Rehabilitation Act of 1973, including Section 504, which Ravitch terms "the handicapped person's equivalent of Title VI of the Civil Rights Act of 1964" (p. 307). And the enactment of that legislation was quickly followed by the passage in 1975 of Public Law 94–142. In many ways this particular law was the most prescriptive educational legislation ever passed by Congress. The law not only required that every child receive an "individualized educational program" (IEP), but it even specified the content of these plans. They had to include a statement of present levels of performance; a statement of annual goals and short-term objectives; a statement of the educational services to be provided and the extent to which the child will be able to participate in regular programs; the projected date for initiation and the projected duration; and objective criteria and evaluation procedures and schedules to determine whether the objectives were being achieved. Finally, the law required the "mainstreaming" of the handicapped: such children were to be educated with the nonhandicapped, "to the maximum extent appropriate."

Whereas the development of generic content-oriented courses did not seem to make a lasting impact, the "carrot-and-stick" approach of passing and enforcing legislation had a pervasive impact, to the extent that many educational leaders of the time expressed grave concern about the intrusion of the federal government and the courts into matters that they believed were better left to local control.

1975–: Privatistic Conservatism

This period, of course, was dominated by President Ronald Reagan, who was elected on a conservative platform and who used his considerable leadership skills to implement that platform. As perceived by Terrel H. Bell (1986), then Secretary of Education, Reagan had in mind six goals relating to education: substantially reduce federal spending; strengthen local and state control; maintain a limited federal role in assisting states in carrying out their educational responsibilities; expand parental choice; reduce federal judicial activity in education; and abolish the Department of Education.

Certain of the Reagan administration's initiatives had clear implications for curriculum. In order to strengthen the state role in education and to provide equitable services for private-school students, Congress adopted under Reagan's prodding a program to award block grants to the states: Chapter 2 of the Education Consolidation and Improvement Act of 1981 consolidated more than thirty categorical programs into a single block grant to each state. An initial study *(Education Week,* 1986) of the effects of this block-grant program indicated that, in general, the Chapter 2 money had been used to support computer-based education, curriculum development, staff development, and pilot development of new programs. Although inner-city districts tended to lose the largest amount of money under the block-grant approach, 75 percent of the districts gained funds under Chapter 2; and per-pupil spending for nonpublic schools increased.

Much of this curriculum development undertaken by the states seems to have responded to Secretary William J. Bennett's agenda of "choice, content, character, and citizenship." In his initial distribution of more than $2.5 million in discretionary grants to thirty-four organizations, Bennett made eleven awards to organizations desiring to develop materials in character education and seven to those interested in strengthening the academic content of the curriculum.

The most controversial of Bennett's initiatives was his attempt to modify the federal government's approach to bilingual education. In 1985 he proposed several changes in the regulations governing the distribution of bilingual education funds: allow districts to increase the English-language component of bilingual programs; encourage them to mainstream limited-English-proficiency students more rapidly; and require districts to assume increased financial responsibility for the programs. His proposals were hailed by many who criticized the practice of teaching such students in their native language and attacked by those who saw the new proposals as jeopardizing the educational rights and opportunities of such students.

STATE ROLE IN CURRICULUM

In examining the role of the states in curriculum, two problems present themselves. The first is the fact that the states differ significantly in the extent to which they are centralized, retaining authority at the state level, or decentralized, delegating authority to the local districts. After carefully analyzing the laws of fifty states in thirty-six areas of educational policy, Wirt (1977) identified three quite different patterns of control: sixteen states were decentralized; fifteen were centralized; and nineteen were intermediate between these two positions.

The second difficulty is that the patterns of state influence have shifted with time. While education is identified by the United States Constitution as a state responsibility, in years past the states often chose to delegate that authority, at least in curricular matters, to local districts. At the height of the reform movement of the 1980s, however, most states were playing a much more active role in curricular matters. As of 1985, twenty-nine states had passed legislation requiring competency tests for students and ten states had such legislation under consideration. Thirteen states had increased the requirements for instructional time and seven were considering such an increase. Forty-three states had raised graduation requirements and five were considering such a move. And this increased concern for curricular matters was supported by a dramatic increase in funding: according to Kirst (1986), state governments increased their total spending on education from $16.6 billion in 1970 to $46.5 billion in 1980. In reviewing this trend toward increased activism, Doyle and Hartle (1985) conclude that state governments by the mid-1980s had become the most important actors in education policy making.

What has caused such an increase in the influence of the states? Doyle and Hartle posit several reasons: the increased quality and competence of state governments; the concern over school quality stimulated by reports of declining SAT scores and by the reform publications; a growing body of research on school effectiveness; an insistent public demand to make schools more accountable; and a conviction that high-quality education would ensure economic growth.

While there are these problems of differences from state to state and variations over time, there are some constants about the nature of the states' influence over curricula. In general, most states have adopted policies and procedures regulating the following matters:

1. Specifying time requirements for the school year, for the school day, and for particular subjects.
2. Mandating specific subjects, such as English and mathematics, and requiring instruction in such specific areas as alcohol and drug abuse, driver safety, and the American economic system.
3. Setting graduation requirements.
4. Developing programs for such special groups as the handicapped and those for whom English is a second language.
5. Mandating procedures for the adoption of textbooks and other instructional materials.
6. Specifying the scope and sequence of topics to be covered in various subjects and grades.
7. Mandating a testing program at specific grades in certain critical areas.

The last three matters listed—the adoption of textbooks, the scope and sequence of the curriculum, and the testing program—perhaps deserve some careful attention here. First, according to Van Geel (1979), there are twenty states that have strong textbook-adoption laws. Perhaps the strongest and most restrictive of these are found in Texas. In Texas, the state periodically adopts a small number of approved textbooks in a given field, such as secondary English grammar and composition. School districts which select their texts from that approved list receive those texts without charge from the state textbook depository. If a district wishes to adopt a text not on the approved list, then it must use its own funds. Obviously, in a time of limited educational funding, few districts bother to adopt books other than those on the approved list.

Since teachers rely greatly on the textbook in making their own curricular choices, strong adoption laws like those of Texas have the effect of standardizing the curriculum. In a sense the state controls the curriculum by selecting the texts. And the issue of textbook quality becomes a major curriculum concern in such states. This issue was dramatized in 1985 when William Honig, commissioner of education for the state of California, announced that the state board of education had rejected all the science books recommended by its committee because none of those books adequately dealt with the subject of evolution.

In dealing with the scope and sequence of the curriculum, most state offices of education seem to be at an intermediate position between centralization and decentralization. The predominant pattern is for a given subject-matter office, such as the Division of Mathematics Education, to develop and disseminate general guidelines, not to prescribe specific content and placement. These general guidelines—often called "frameworks"—typically indicate the goals to be achieved in that subject area, summarize present theory and research dealing with that subject, and recommend two or three alternative curricular patterns for achieving the goals. Local districts can then use the state frameworks in developing their own more specific curricula.

THE ROLE OF PROFESSIONAL ORGANIZATIONS

Professional organizations exercise their influence at the national, state, and local levels. At the national level such influence takes three forms. First, as noted above, professional groups such as the Council for Exceptional Children and the National Education Association are at times highly effective in lobbying for or against curriculum-related legislation. Second, several professional organizations, such as the National Council of Teachers of Mathematics, attempt to influence the written curriculum by publishing curricular guidelines or model scope-and-sequence charts. These professional publications seem to be effective in reaching only a limited audience of subject-matter curriculum specialists. School administrators and classroom teachers for the most part do not give them much attention: they are usually perceived as too "idealistic," insensitive to the realities of the classroom. Finally, they attempt to influence local practice by sponsoring institutes and workshops in which new programs and approaches are explained and demonstrated. Such "show-and-tell' sessions seem to have an impact upon participants; they return to their schools often eager to share what they have learned.

At the state level the professional organizations that seem most influential are those with large memberships and strong lobbyists—the teachers' and administrators' associations who fight to protect the interests of their constituencies. In many states the state teachers' association is so active politically that it can be the determining factor in close elections and thus has significant influence with both office holders and candidates. At the local level, professional associations attempt to influence curricula chiefly through the association-district contract. When the issue was last studied, in more than 20 percent of the local districts all across the nation, the teachers' contract required teacher participation in the selection of textbooks. (See Keith, 1981.)

THE COURTS

Increasingly, the courts seem to have played an active role in curriculum. Both federal and state courts have become so active in this area that some educators now speak of the "court-ordered curriculum."

As a consequence of several decisions by the federal courts, Van Geel (1979) points out, there is now what might be termed a constitutionally required school program. Based on his analysis of the major decisions by federal courts in the area of curriculum and program, certain salient features of such a required program emerge. First, it must be secular—but not militantly secular. The schools cannot establish a religion of secularism. Second, English may be the chief language of instruction, as long as non-English-speaking students are assisted in learning it. Third, the program must be minimally adequate for all students, even those with serious limitations of ability and capacity. Antiquated notions of sex roles may not be imposed on students by segregating them for instruction in such courses as industrial arts and home economics. Instructional materials and courses may be politically biased in favor of the free-enterprise system; but teachers and students who hold views favoring some other system of government may not be excluded from the school. As Van Geel notes, the courts in general have determined that students have a constitutional right to receive information and ideas, no matter how distasteful those ideas might seem to the local community.

State courts have taken positions similar to those supported by the federal courts. Several state courts have held that state plans for the financing of education may be unconstitutional if they result in significant differences among local districts in the level of expenditures for education; such differences, the courts have held, violate the equal-protection clause of state constitutions. As Van Geel notes, a doctrine of a "state-created right to an education" is emerging from the decisions of state courts which will have profound implications for school programs; education is no longer seen as a privilege but as a right for all. He also points out that as state legislatures become more active in adopting complex and often ambiguous educational codes, state courts will have increased influence as they resolve issues of the rights, duties, and discretionary authority allocated by those codes.

LOCAL EDUCATIONAL LEADERS

At the local district level, central office administrators and building principals seem to play key roles in influencing curriculum.

First, the typical school superintendent perceives himself or herself as relatively weak in the curriculum area and appoints a generalist as an assistant superintendent for curriculum and instruction, who then serves as the district leader in the area of curriculum. Several factors complicate the assistant superintendent's role, however. First, such individuals are usually assigned an array of responsibilities that always seem to have a higher day-to-day priority—meeting with unhappy parents, conferring with principals about the budget, planning an inservice program. Second, the assistant superintendent for curriculum in even some larger districts is expected to supervise the curriculum with little or no staff support; districts faced with budget problems typically begin to reduce personnel by reducing the size of the central office supervisory staff. Finally, the emphasis on the school as the locus of educational improvement has created confusion in the minds of many assistant superintendents about the importance of their roles in curriculum development and improvement. Despite such complicating factors, the assistant superintendent for curriculum and instruction in most districts is the sole individual exercising general supervision over the entire curriculum.

As noted above, the role of the principal in curriculum leadership seems to vary with the level of schooling. Despite the conventional wisdom that all principals should act as instructional leaders, there is growing evidence that the most effective elementary and secondary principals are quite different in this respect. (See, for example, Firestone and Herriott, 1982; and Glatthorn and Newberg, 1984.) Elementary principals in the most effective schools tend to take very active roles in curriculum leadership. They play the central role in articulating educational goals and curricular priorities, in influencing teacher perceptions about curricular emphases and approaches, in helping teachers use test results, and in aligning the curriculum. At the secondary level (especially in larger schools), however, the effective principal is more likely to delegate these roles to department heads, whose subject-matter expertise enables them to influence the curricular decision making of secondary teachers.

THE CLASSROOM TEACHER

As discussed in Chapter 1, to a great extent the teacher is the curriculum. As Connelly and Ben-Peretz (1980) note, teachers do not neutrally implement curricula; they adapt, translate, and modify given programs and develop their own. In doing so, they seem to be responding to both internal and external pressures.

The Internal Pressures

First, the teacher needs to satisfy some strong personal needs. In one major study (MacDonald and Leithwood, 1982), teachers indicated that the four strongest rewards from their perspective were affiliation, independence, usefulness, and achievement. To begin with, in making curricular decisions they felt a strong need for affiliation with students—a feeling that they were responding to students' interests, were sensitive to student concerns, and were generating student enthusiasm. Second, they needed a sense of autonomy and independence, a conviction that they had the power to make important decisions. Third, they needed to feel that they were useful—that students needed them, that they were important in the organization. Finally, there was a strong need for achievement—a need to feel that they were efficacious in achieving important learning outcomes and helping students succeed. Another major study (Leithwood, Ross, and Montgomery, 1982) found some other strong internal factors besides these: the teacher's past experience ("what works") and the teacher's attitudes and interests.

Professional motivations are also very strong. Here Doyle's continuing research is most illuminating. (See, for example, his 1986 review.) Based upon his studies, he finds that teachers are primarily concerned with classroom management, in order to make classroom life more predictable and thus more controllable. And the decisions they make about curriculum and instruction are designed to achieve those goals. They standardize the curriculum, reducing or eliminating elements of novelty. They simplify the curriculum, modifying complex elements so that they are easily managed. They routinize instruction, in order to reduce the time needed for planning.

The External Pressures

Besides responding to these personal and professional needs, the teacher is also susceptible to numerous external pressures. As Floden and his colleagues (1980) note, these sources are multiple and all seem to have some discernible influence on teachers: their research suggests that teachers are quite malleable when these pressures are brought to bear.

Which external influences are strongest? The conventional wisdom holds that the textbook is the major determiner. However, two major studies question this conventional wisdom (Leithwood, Ross, and Montgomery, 1982; and Floden and others, 1980). In both these studies, the external factors that teachers reported as being most influential were district curriculum objectives and test results. Other factors, of course, are variably influential: the values and priorities of colleagues; the requirements of administrators; the interests of students; the expectations of parents. In fact, it must seem at times to the teachers that they are power brokers, attempting to negotiate several conflicting claims.

APPLICATIONS

1. Some experts have argued that the difficulty of finding sufficient fiscal resources will shortly reduce state activity in the curriculum field. If that development does occur, and if the federal government continues to take a less active role, which sources of influence do you believe will increase in power?

2. Based on what you now know about the sources of curriculum influence, what advice would you give a superintendent who posed this question to you: "Does our district really need central office curriculum specialists?"

3. Some analysts have reached this conclusion: "All curriculum making is essentially a political process." Would you agree or disagree? Prepare a well-thought-out response to the question.

4. As the above account suggests, the federal government has for the most part abandoned the change strategy of funding the development of exemplary generic curricula. Some have argued that such an abandonment was premature—that given greater insight into the change process such a strategy might be effective. Consider two related issues: Under what circumstances would you recommend that this strategy be reintroduced? What modifications in the approach would you recommend?

5. What advice would you give this fourth-grade teacher: "My principal and the district science supervisor do not agree about what I should emphasize in teaching science. The principal wants me to spend more time on practical applications; the supervisor, on science processes."

REFERENCES

Atkin, J. M., and House, E. R. (1981). The federal role in curriculum development, 1950–80. *Educational Evaluation and Policy Analysis, 3* (5), 5–36.

Bell, T. H. (1986). Educational policy development in the Reagan administration. *Phi Delta Kappan, 67,* 487–493.

Connelly, F. M., and Ben-Peretz, M. (1980). Teachers' roles in the using and doing of research and curricula development. *Curricular Studies, 12,* 95–107.

Doyle, D. P., and Hartle, T. W. (1985). Leadership in education: Governors, legislators and teachers. *Phi Delta Kappan, 66,* 21–28.

Doyle, W. (1986). Classroom organization and management. In M. C. Wittrock (ed.), *Handbook of research on teaching* (3rd Ed.), pp. 392–431. New York: Macmillan.

Firestone, W. A., and Herriott, R. E. (December 1982). Prescriptions for effective elementary schools don't fit secondary schools. *Educational Leadership, 40,* 51–53.

Floden, R. E., Porter, A. C., Schmidt, W. J., Freeman, D. J., and Schwille, J. R. (1980). *Responses to curriculum pressures: A policy capturing study of teacher decisions about content.* East Lansing, MI: Institute for Research on Teaching.

Glatthorn, A. A., and Newberg, N. A. (February 1984). A team approach to instructional leadership. *Educational Leadership, 41,* 60–63.

Hertling, J. (1986). Block grants found to achieve gains. *Education Week* (March 12), p. 8.

Keith, S. (1981). *Politics of textbook selection.* Palo Alto, CA: Stanford University Press.

Kirst, M. W. (1986). Sustaining the momentum of state education reform: The link between assessment and financial support. *Phi Delta Kappan, 67,* 341–345.

Kliebard, H. M. (1979). Systematic curriculum development, 1890–1959. In J. Schaffarzick and G. Sykes (eds.), *Value conflicts and curriculum issues,* pp. 197–236. Berkeley, CA: McCutchan.

Leithwood, K. A., Ross, J. A., and Montgomery, D. J. (1982). An investigation of teachers' curriculum decision-making. In K. A. Leithwood (ed.), *Studies in curriculum decision-making*, pp. 14–46. Toronto, Ontario: Ontario Institute for Studies in Education.

Levine, E. L., and Wexler, E. M. (1981). *P.L. 94–142: An act of Congress.* New York: Macmillan.

Lynch, K. L. (1986). School finance policy formulation in Pennsylvania: A case study. Doctoral dissertation, University of Pennsylvania.

MacDonald, R. A., and Leithwood, K. A. (1982). Toward an explanation of the influences on teacher curriculum decisions. In K. A. Leithwood (ed.), *Studies in curricular decision making*, pp. 35–51. Toronto, Ontario: Ontario Institute for Studies in Education.

Marshall, C. (March 1985). Policymakers' assumptive worlds: Informal structures in state education policymaking. Paper presented at the meeting of the American Educational Research Association, Chicago.

Mills v. Board of Education, 348 F. Supp. 866 (D.D.C. 1972).

National Commission on Excellence in Education. (1983). *A nation at risk: The imperative for educational reform.* Washington, DC: United States Government Printing Office.

Ravitch, D. (1983). *The troubled crusade: American education 1945–80.* New York: Basic Books.

Schon, D. A. (1971). *Beyond the stable state.* New York: Random House.

Van Geel, T. (1979). The new law of the curriculum. In J. Schaffarzick and G. Sykes (eds.), *Value conflicts and curriculum issues*, pp. 25–72. Berkeley, CA: McCutchan.

Wirt, F. M. (1977). School policy culture and state decentralization. In J. D. Scribner (ed.), *The politics of education*, pp. 164–187. Chicago: University of Chicago Press.

Part 2

Curriculum Processes

5

Curriculum Planning

To a great extent the specific details of the curriculum-planning process are determined by the level and nature of curriculum work; designing a field of studies, improving a program of studies, and developing a course of study involve quite different processes, as the following chapters indicate. However, there are some general planning processes that are useful in all curriculum work. A general planning model is described in this chapter; specific adaptations are noted in the next three chapters.

Before explaining those processes in detail, it might be useful at the outset to define the term. *Curriculum planning* is used in this sense:

> The specification and sequencing of major decisions to be
> made in the future with regard to the curriculum.

A GOAL-BASED MODEL OF CURRICULUM PLANNING

Although there are several planning models available to educators, one that seems very effective for curriculum planning is the goal-based model described below. All the steps in the model are listed in Figure 5–1 and explained briefly in this section. The steps in the model are then explained more fully in the rest of this chapter.

The model begins with three organizing strategies. First, the leaders distinguish between district- and school-based responsibilities, to clarify the locus of decision making. They then decide what organizational structures

FIGURE 5–1. A Goal-Based Curriculum-Planning Model

Organize for Planning

1. Determine the locus of planning decisions: differentiate between district and school planning responsibilities.
2. Determine the organizational structures needed to facilitate planning, and set up those structures.
3. Identify leadership functions and allocate those functions appropriately.

Establish the Planning Framework

1. Align the district's educational goals with appropriate curricular fields.
2. Develop a curriculum data base.
3. Develop planning calendar based upon leaders' assessments of organizational priorities.

Carry Out Specific Planning Activities

1. Conduct needs assessment in high-priority areas by using standardized tests, curriculum-referenced tests, and other measures and data sources; use assessment results to determine the need for curriculum development or improvement.
2. Organize task forces to carry out development or improvement projects, and monitor their work.
3. Evaluate development or improvement projects.
4. Make necessary organizational changes and provisions for effective implementation.
5. Secure resources needed for new or revised curricula.
6. Provide staff development needed for effective implementation.

are needed, appointing the needed advisory groups and task forces. Finally, they allocate specific leadership functions to district and school staff.

With those organizational moves accomplished, steps are taken to establish a framework for planning. First, the broad educational goals of the district are aligned with the several fields of study, so that each field of study has a clear set of curricular goals for which it is responsible. Then the district develops a computerized knowledge base for curriculum, systematizing the information needed for good curriculum work. Leaders then assess general district priorities and from those develop a five-year planning calendar, showing the major events and foci of the curriculum-improvement process.

With the framework established, the specific planning activities are undertaken. With the goals thus stipulated, a needs assessment is conducted, using standardized and curriculum-referenced tests and other appropriate measures, as well as the data stored in the knowledge base. Task forces are appointed to carry out the development and improvement projects suggested by the needs assessment. Their work is evaluated, and appropriate plans are made to implement the new or revised program effectively.

This goal-based model has several features which recommend it. It is goal-based, ensuring that curriculum revisions are made with general outcomes clearly in mind. It emphasizes feasibility: it assists the district in undertaking only priority projects which leaders believe can be accomplished effectively. And it is systematic: planning decisions are cast in a rational framework that emphasizes orderly progression.

DETERMINE THE LOCUS OF PLANNING DECISIONS

Curriculum planning obviously occurs at several levels: at the federal level, when policy decisions and their implementation are planned; at the state level, when state offices of education plan for major changes in graduation requirements; at the district level, when the district plans to revise its mathematics field of study; at the school level, when the school revises its program of studies or adds a new course; and at the classroom level, when the teacher plans a unit of study. Since most of the important alterable decisions are made at the district and school levels, the discussion that follows focuses on these two critical levels of planning.

The central question here, of course, is the balance between district-based and school-based curricular decision making. On the one hand, there are those who argue for strong district control. Fenwick English (1980), for example, acknowledges only two levels of "curriculum management"—the state and the district. In his curriculum-management system, what occurs at the school and classroom levels is completely controlled by district policies and curriculum documents. His views seem to be shared by the leaders of many large school districts, who have attempted in recent years to standardize the curriculum throughout the entire district. For example, curriculum guides issued by the School District of Philadelphia in 1984 not only specified what was to be taught and what materials were to be used, but even indicated when it was to be taught—in every school in the city. Here, for example, is an entry from the district's secondary mathematics curriculum guide (Tobin, 1984):

Grade 7: September 24–October 19. Whole numbers. 3.5 weeks

The rationale for such standardization speaks in terms of achievement, equity, and efficiency. The first argument is that standardized curricula will result in higher achievement, although there is no evidence to support such a claim. The second is that standardization ensures equity: every student gets the same curriculum, regardless of school and teacher assignment. Critics would point out, of course, that equity is not the same as uniformity. The final argument is that the standardized curriculum is more efficient and thus more economical: the district can offer the same type of staff development, order large quantities of the same texts, and develop a single set of curriculum-referenced tests. This claim of efficiency is probably a reasonable one; the issue is whether other considerations are more important.

On the other hand, there are those who argue just as persuasively for school-based curriculum development. Gass (1979) suggests two major reasons for encouraging school-based curriculum development: schools are clamoring for autonomy; and there is some evidence that centrally developed curricula have been less successful than expected and often are not implemented as planned. Also, as Ross (1982) notes, the research suggests that teachers desire to have a more active role in curriculum development—and it is more likely that school-based processes will provide for such active participation. Additional support for school-based curricula could be inferred from the large body of school-effectiveness research which generally suggests that the school, not the district, is the primary unit for improvement. (See, for example, Joyce, 1986.) However, several reservations might be noted about granting schools too much curricular autonomy. The resulting collection of different curricula would be difficult to coordinate and manage. The process would result in much inefficiency and duplication of effort. And quality might be adversely affected, since the school-based curriculum team would probably not have as many resources as district teams.

Since there is no conclusive research on this issue, it would seem wise for each local district to resolve the matter through a clear analysis of the options, weighing such factors as the size of the district, the competence of district and school leaders, and the degree of heterogeneity throughout the district. The major issues involved here, as listed in Figure 5-2, should be discussed and resolved by the superintendent and the district leadership team; those decisions can then be used as policy guidelines for future curriculum planning.

FIGURE 5–2. Issues in District/School Curriculum Decision Making

1. May the school modify district goals so that those goals are more appropriate for the students of that school?
2. May the school reconceptualize and reorganize fields of study, using such approaches as interdisciplinary courses and "broad-fields" curricula?
3. May the school develop its own instructional objectives or modify district objectives, as long as those objectives are consonant with district goals?
4. May the school recommend which instructional processes and activities are to be used?
5. May the school make its own recommendations about the pacing of instruction?
6. May the school develop and select its own tests for evaluating student achievement?
7. May the school select its own instructional materials, as long as the materials meet district guidelines?
8. May the school evaluate its own program of studies and make needed changes, including the addition or elimination of specific courses?

DETERMINE THE ORGANIZATIONAL STRUCTURES NEEDED

With those district and school delineations made, the district leadership team should next determine which organizational structures are needed in providing ongoing curriculum leadership. Many school districts seem to err here by appointing too many standing curriculum committees. Such a mistake results in a cumbersome bureaucratic structure that only complicates curriculum planning. It is more desirable to have a simple and flexible organizational structure that can provide the continuity required and also respond quickly to changing needs. An examination of both the research and reports of effective practice suggest that the following structures would accomplish those goals.

District Curriculum Advisory Council   This is a standing committee, with members appointed by the superintendent of schools. Its membership will vary with the size of the school district; ordinarily, however, the following members or constituencies should be represented:

The superintendent or assistant superintendent
The district curriculum directors or supervisors
Secondary principals
Elementary principals
Teachers
Parents and other community representatives
Secondary school students

The advisory council, as its name suggests, serves in an advisory capacity only, recommending to the superintendent what problems require systematic attention and what processes might be used to solve those problems. Typically it would meet four times during the school year to identify problems, review planning calendars, receive evaluation reports, and review curriculum proposals. Its members would serve for a stated period of time; a rotating three-year term of office would ensure both continuity and fresh ideas.

Larger districts may wish to establish a separate community advisory council, composed of parents and representatives of the business and professional community. Most superintendents, however, seem to feel that such separate councils complicate the work of the curriculum advisory group and may even attempt to usurp certain board functions.

School Curriculum Advisory Council   Each school should also have a standing advisory group, especially if individual schools are to have a large measure of curricular autonomy. Its members should be nominated by the faculty and appointed by the principal. The school advisory council would include the principal, subject-matter specialists or grade-level leaders, teachers, and parents. Students from upper grade levels might also be included. One of the teachers and one of the parents on the school advisory council should represent the school on the district council, to ensure good communication between the two advisory groups. The school advisory council advises the principal on school-based curricular issues, in a manner similar to the district advisory council. Its members would also serve for a specified term, like those on the district council.

In smaller school districts there might not be a need for separate school councils; the district council could be composed so that it had representatives from each school. In either case, these standing groups provide the continuity required for effective planning.

Curriculum Task Forces   In addition to these two standing committees, the superintendent would appoint a number of task forces to deal with whatever major issues might need attention. These task forces would be seen as working groups, numbering perhaps from six to twelve members, depending upon the nature of the problem. Members would be appointed on the basis of the technical skills required for the job; at the same time, the superintendent should be sure that the membership is generally representative of the types of professional roles in the district. Thus, most task forces would include a curriculum specialist, a principal, and several knowledgeable teachers. If the task force needed additional technical assistance, it would request approval from the superintendent to secure a qualified consultant.

Each task force would be given a specific problem to be solved, a deadline for developing and implementing the solution, and the resources required to do the job. Ordinarily, a task force would continue in existence only until the problem had been solved. These temporary *ad hoc* groups give the school system the flexibility it needs and in this sense complement the standing bodies.

IDENTIFY AND ALLOCATE
LEADERSHIP FUNCTIONS

During the period from 1960 to 1980, a somewhat common pattern of curriculum staffing developed in most larger districts across the nation. There was an assistant superintendent for curriculum and instruction, who was expected to provide system-wide leadership. The central office staff also included several subject-matter "coordinators," who usually were responsible for coordinating the curriculum from K–12 in a designated content area. At the school level the building principal was expected to provide leadership; in larger secondary schools the curriculum responsibility was usually delegated to an assistant principal for curriculum and instruction. In larger elementary schools the principal was assisted by either grade-level team leaders or teacher-specialists, especially in reading and mathematics. At the high school level, department chairs were appointed to provide subject-matter leadership. Some middle school principals relied upon grade-level team leaders; others used department heads.

In recent years this prevailing pattern has been seriously altered. Three factors seem to be at work here. The first, of course, is money. Many districts, forced to economize by tax caps, considered central office staff the most expendable and dismissed all central office curriculum supervisors. The second factor is dissatisfaction with the prevailing pattern. Much of this dissatisfaction focused on the performance of district coordinators and school department heads; in many cases they seemed not to be providing the leadership needed. The final factor is the widespread conviction, supported by some research, that the principal should be the instructional leader. If that is the case, then, it is reasoned, district coordinators and department heads are not needed.

These interacting forces seem to have decimated the ranks of curriculum leadership, and in many districts have led to a state of uncertainty and confusion in which there is no curricular leadership. A busy assistant superintendent, suffering from role overload, attempts to respond to curricular crises. And building principals, overwhelmed by administrative responsibilities, wonder what it means to provide curriculum leadership.

The response to this crisis, it would seem, is not to return to the previous pattern and simply hire additional personnel to fill these old positions. A more useful answer is to analyze the leadership functions required at both the district and school levels, allocate these functions to those best able to perform them, and then decide what additional staff, if any, are needed—in some cases, creating new kinds of positions. This specification and allocation process can begin by having the district curriculum advisory council develop a form like the one shown in Figure 5-3. It lists all the leadership functions relating to curriculum, organizing them into four categories based upon the level and the focus of the responsibility. The intent here is to describe these functions as clearly as possible, since too many curriculum workers have only a vague understanding of their responsibilities.

The advisory council should first review the form to ensure that it includes all the functions they consider important and uses language that communicates clearly to the educators in that district. At that point, the superintendent or the assistant superintendent, with input from central office staff and the building principals, should take over the complex and sensitive task of reallocating and reassigning those functions for maximum effectiveness. The leaders should first analyze which individuals in the district are presently responsible for those functions, entering role designations in the "Now" column. In many instances they will indicate that *no one* is presently performing those functions.

After assessing how effectively those functions are being performed and how equitably they are distributed, they should next determine where changes should be made in present assignments, entering those decisions in

FIGURE 5–3. Functions of Curriculum Leadership

Function	Now	Assign	New
At the district level—for all areas of the curriculum.			
1. Articulate district curriculum goals and priorities.	Supt.	Supt.	
2. Chair district advisory council.	Supt.	Asst. Supt.	
3. Develop and monitor curriculum budget.	Supt.		Dir. Curr.
4. Develop and implement plans to evaluate curricula and use evaluative data.			
5. Identify and prioritize curricular problems to be solved.			
6. Develop curriculum-planning calendar.			
7. Appoint task forces, and review their reports, proposals, and products.			
8. Develop and monitor processes for materials selection and evaluation.			
9. Plan district-wide staff-development programs required by curricular changes.			
10. Represent district on curricular matters in relationships with state and intermediate unit curriculum offices.			
11. Evaluate district-level curriculum staff.			
12. Develop general district guidelines for aligning curricula at the school level.			

At the district level—for special areas of the curriculum.

1. Develop and implement plans to evaluate curriculum, as specified in district planning calendar.
2. Use evaluative data to identify specific curricular problems, and develop proposals to remedy them.
3. Evaluate articulation of the curriculum between elementary and middle schools and between middle and high schools.
4. Provide leadership in developing and improving K–12 curriculum materials in that special area.
5. Implement district guidelines in selecting and evaluating texts and other instructional materials.
6. Provide leadership in implementing K–12 staff-development programs for that specific area.

(continued next page)

FIGURE 5–3. *continued*

Function	Now	Assign	New

At the school level—for all areas of the curriculum.

1. Implement plans to monitor and align the curriculum.
2. Evaluate curricula at the school level and use evaluative data to identify school-level problems.
3. Ensure that important skills that cut across the disciplines are appropriately taught and reinforced in those disciplines.
4. Monitor coordination of the curriculum between those content areas where close coordination is important.
5. Develop school-based budget for curriculum needs, reflecting school priorities.

At the school level—for special areas of the curriculum.

1. Supervise teachers with respect to curriculum implementation.
2. Assist teachers in developing instructional plans based upon curriculum guides.
3. Implement school-based staff development required by curriculum change.
4. Select instructional materials.
5. Help teachers use student-evaluation results to make needed modifications in curriculum.

the "Assign" column. The entries in this column yield a clear picture of which functions can best be discharged by reassigning them to present role incumbents. In some cases, however, it will be apparent that a new role is needed: several important functions are not being performed successfully, and no one among the present staff is available and competent to assume those critical functions. The allocation of functions to a newly conceived role are reflected by placing the new role title in the "New" column. The first few entries on the form have been completed to show how the form can be used to record and analyze those decisions.

The preliminary decisions are first reviewed by central office staff and school principals and then by the district advisory council, in order to secure their input and keep them informed. The final allocations then become the basis for reconceptualizing present roles and creating any new positions needed.

The process thus enables a local district to develop its own staffing pattern, one that reflects its special needs and resources.

ALIGN EDUCATIONAL GOALS WITH CURRICULAR FIELDS

A key step in the goal-based model is determination of the goals for each field of study. There are several methods for accomplishing this task. This chapter explains one method for allocating goals to curriculum fields as an aspect of the planning process; the next chapter explains a somewhat different process for aligning and assessing the several fields for goal conformance as part of the program-improvement process.

1. Specify district educational goals. An educational goal is a general long-term outcome to be accomplished through the total educational program. Most states have developed lists of such goals to be used in all school districts. For example, the Pennsylvania State Board of Education (1985) specifies twelve "goals of quality education" and requires that the curriculum of each grade be based on those goals and the specific objectives derived from them. Districts which have the freedom and wish to develop their own goal statements might well consult Goodlad's (1984) book. This work includes an excellent set of goal statements that he developed after reviewing a large number of state and district statements. Another excellent source is the ASCD publication *Measuring and Attaining the Goals of Education* (Brookover, 1980).

2. Determine which of the educational goals should be accomplished primarily through the courses of study. Many educational leaders neglect this important step; they assume that every educational goal is a curricular goal. Thus, Pennsylvania educators, noting that the state board specifies the development of self-esteem as an educational goal, mistakenly assume that they need to develop courses and units in self-esteem. Many educational goals, like this one, can better be accomplished through other means: through instructional methods or the instructional program; through the organizational climate; through the activity program; or through the guidance program.

   For this reason, the leadership team and school faculties should carefully analyze each educational goal and make a preliminary determination of whether that goal will be primarily accomplished through organized courses of study or through some other means. In this manner they identify a shorter list of curriculum goals—those general long-term outcomes which are to be accomplished primarily through the organized curriculum. Their tentative decisions should be reviewed by the advisory councils. The input from those groups should then be used to make any needed modifications so that the resulting list represents a broad consensus.

3. Allocate the curricular goals to the several fields of study. Once the curricular goals have been identified, the leadership team with faculty input should then allocate those goals to appropriate fields of study. A system like this one seems to work. First, a small task force is appointed for each field of study. That task force reviews the list of curricular goals and determines the contribution its field can best make to that goal, indicating one of three levels: this field *emphasizes* this goal; this field *contributes* to this goal; or this field *does not contribute* to this goal. By analyzing the results from these task forces, the leadership team can ensure that every goal is emphasized by at least one field and reinforced by others and that each field has a suitable set of curricular goals.

This, obviously, is a "top-down" process—one that begins with the district's educational goals and ends with curricular goals for each field. The process, of course, can be reversed: each field can develop its own list of curricular goals, and these can be synthesized into one comprehensive district list. The outcome, not the process, is important: each field should have a clear list of curricular goals.

DEVELOP A CURRICULUM DATA BASE

A second key aspect of the planning framework is development of a comprehensive curriculum data base. The argument here is that good curriculum work requires extensive knowledge about resources, inputs, and constraints. To that end, each district should develop a computerized knowledge base that can be used in assessing needs and developing curricula. What should be included? The temptation, of course, is to collect too much information, just because it is available or seems interesting. It makes more sense to collect and organize only that information likely to be used. Figure 5–4 lists the kinds of information that seem most essential in the needs-assessment process; as will be explained in Chapter 8, a shorter list of information needs can be useful in the course-planning process.

Such information stored in a computerized data bank will greatly facilitate the work of the several task forces. Consider, for example, how the data bank would be used by a task force appointed to develop a new course for middle school students in "Personal Well-Being," one that would combine health and physical education. They would first get comprehen-

FIGURE 5–4. Information for Curriculum Data Base

Community Resources

1. People with knowledge, expertise, and influence.
2. Organizations and places useful as resources.

Students

1. Date of birth, sex, and ethnic identity.
2. Eligibility for federal or state assistance programs.
3. Parents' occupations and marital status.
4. Verbal and mathematical abilities and IQ scores.
5. Talents, skills, and special interests.
6. School achievement: standardized test scores and curriculum-referenced test scores.
7. English proficiency; native language if other than English.
8. Limitations: physical, emotional, and learning disabilities.
9. Learning styles and cognitive levels.
10. School record: subjects studied, grades, and attendance.
11. Career and educational plans.
12. Extracurricular activities.
13. Community activities.

Faculty

1. Subjects and grades certified to teach.
2. Present assignment.
3. Special interests and competencies.
4. Recent professional development: courses, workshops, etc.

School

1. Courses offered and enrollments.
2. Extracurricular activities and student participation.

Other Resources

1. State curriculum guides.
2. Curriculum guides from other districts.
3. Other sources of learning objectives.
4. Professional materials and resources for teachers.

---

sive data about the students likely to take the course, in order to become aware of students' needs, limitations, and capacities: "About 15 percent of the students will have limited English proficiency; we may need a separate section or special materials for them." Next they would get data on student participation in extracurricular activities and note that very few students participate in activities that require a high level of physical exercise: "We should include a unit that deals explicitly with the value of and opportunities for in-school aerobics activities." They then would retrieve information about other professional resources available—state curriculum guides, guides from other districts, banks of learning objectives: "A nearby district has just started a pilot program similar to the one we're planning; let's see how it's going." Then they would take a look at faculty data: "The teachers we plan to use do not seem to have an up-to-date knowledge of nutrition; we had better plan some special staff development here and beef up the teacher's guide for that unit." Finally they would examine community resources: "The hospital dietitian has offered to share her films on good nutrition for the young." For them the curriculum data base is invaluable.

DEVELOP A PLANNING CALENDAR

One of the central leadership functions is to develop and monitor the district's curriculum-planning calendar, a master calendar which assists district leaders in making systematic plans for curriculum evaluation and development.

As Figure 5–5 suggests, the planning calendar should include the six steps listed as "specific planning activities" in Figure 5–1. Note that a distinction is made between major and other fields, simply to assist in the planning process, not to depreciate the importance of such areas as art and industrial arts. And provision is made for evaluating the several programs of study. Note that in this example, the district has chosen to do a needs assessment each year of one major and one other field and one program level. With such a schedule, the district would be able in a five-year period to assess all major fields, five other fields, and every program level.

FIGURE 5–5. Curriculum-Planning Calendar

Major Projects	1988–89	1989–90	1990–91
1. Needs assessment, major fields	Lang. arts	Math	Science
2. Needs assessment, other fields	Ind. arts	Art	
3. Needs assessment, programs	Middle	Elem.	High
4. Task forces appointed, at work		Lang. arts	Math
		Ind. arts	Art
5. Evaluate projects		Lang. arts	Math
		Ind. arts	Art
6. Organizational provisions		Lang. arts	Math
		Ind. arts	Art
7. Resources selected and provided		Lang. arts	Math
		Ind. arts	Art
8. Staff development			Lang. arts
			Ind. arts

The superintendent and the district leadership team should begin by mapping out tentatively a five-year plan which would indicate year by year the major projects to be undertaken. They should make these decisions based upon their own analysis of district needs and their own priorities for improvement. The decision about how many projects should be initiated will, of course, be influenced by their perception of district needs and resources. A large school district with well-staffed curriculum and evaluation offices could obviously plan for many more projects than a smaller district with an overextended staff. A newly appointed superintendent given a mandate by the board to improve the curriculum would want to plan for a more ambitious and comprehensive development program than a superintendent who has been presiding for several years over a district that seems to be making excellent progress.

Those tentative decisions should be reviewed by district and school administrators and supervisors and then be shared with the district advisory council for their input before a final form of the calendar is developed. The final form of the calendar can then be used by leaders in developing budget requests, appointing task forces, and monitoring their progress.

CONDUCT NEEDS ASSESSMENT

The next major step in the model is to conduct a needs assessment. This term *needs assessment* seems to be used often in the profession without much understanding of what is involved. Here Kaufman's (1982) definition seems most useful: a needs assessment is a process of identifying gaps between what is and what should be. In his comprehensive review, he identifies and analyzes seventeen needs-assessment models. His analysis of these seventeen models leads him to conclude that they share several major shortcomings: they focus on internal elements, ignoring the societal impact and payoffs; they shy away from empirical data, relying too much on people's perceptions; they place too much emphasis on such "middle-level" concerns as learner characteristics, methods, and test scores, slighting long-term outcomes; most are really status surveys and thus give too much attention to "what is"; and most are not sufficiently comprehensive, limiting attention to only a few components.

To deal with these deficiencies, he advocates a rather complex and sophisticated model that would use multiple data about inputs, processes, products, outputs, and outcomes and would be sensitive to both the internal organization and the external society. The major drawback to the model he advocates is that it would seem to be too complicated, time-consuming, and expensive for most districts to implement.

A simpler needs-assessment model that avoids many of the pitfalls noted in Kaufman's review could be built upon several of the elements explained in this chapter and in Chapter 12. (Note that this section explains the needs-assessment process in developing a field of study; the next chapter explains how to assess needs in improving a program of studies.) First, the district would develop a comprehensive curriculum data base, as noted above. This would provide information about what Kaufman and others call the two major "inputs"—the teachers and the learners. Next, the district would develop for each field a clear set of curricular goals, using the processes described above. These specify the ends to be accomplished. Then the district would evaluate selected fields of study, assessing the major components of the field explained in Chapter 1: the written curriculum; the supported curriculum; the taught curriculum; the tested curriculum; and the learned curriculum. Thus, if a district is concerned with assessing curricular needs in a single field of study, the process is a rather straightforward one.

On the other hand, if a district wishes to make a needs assessment that focuses on a general curriculum goal (not a single field), then the process is slightly more complex. This process is explained below, using as an example the general goal of "enhancing creativity."

The process begins with a vague sense of deficiency. Some individual or group asks, "Are we doing all we can in the curriculum to enhance creativity?" (Note that the question focuses on the curriculum; if a broader assessment of an educational goal is desired, then other components, such as the guidance and activity programs, would also be included.) A task force is appointed to answer the question; they begin their work by identifying those fields of study which have indicated that they emphasize or contribute to this goal. In this case, it would be likely that these fields would make such a claim: English language arts; home economics; art; music; science.

The task force would then proceed to examine the written curriculum in those fields: Do the written guides give sufficient and explicit attention to the goal of enhancing creativity? They then would turn to the supported curriculum, examining budgets, schedules, and materials: Does the district provide sufficient funds for creative materials? Do texts and other instructional materials emphasize creativity in their approach and content? Are these fields of study allocated sufficient time to include creative activities?

They would then consider the more complicated matter of the taught curriculum. Here they would focus on two critical issues: Do teachers actually teach those units in the written guide that were designed to enhance creativity? Do the teachers teach in a manner that fosters creative thinking? Obviously these questions would require evaluators to observe a representative sample of classrooms.

The tested curriculum would next warrant scrutiny: Do curriculum-referenced and teacher-made tests make adequate provisions for assessing creativity? And finally they would attend to the learned curriculum: Are the students actually learning to think creatively and to produce creative works? This question could be answered through several data sources: results from tests of creativity; results from surveys of teachers, parents, and students; and an evaluation of a representative sample of student creative products.

The results of these several processes would then be used to determine which elements of the curriculum need strengthening or to suggest perhaps that a new course should be added to the curriculum.

ORGANIZE, EVALUATE, CHANGE, PROVIDE RESOURCES

The next steps in the planning process involve development and implementation strategies more fully explained in subsequent chapters. After determining whether to strengthen existing elements or add new ones, the leaders appoint another task force to take over the responsibility of developing the recommended solution. Their work is evaluated by expert review and systematic field testing. Any necessary organizational elements are changed, such as the school schedule, teacher assignments, or grouping practices. Then plans are made to secure the necessary material resources required by the new or improved program.

PROVIDE STAFF DEVELOPMENT

One of the most effective means of ensuring successful implementation of new curricula is to integrate effective staff-development programs with any major curricular change. Many curriculum projects of excellent quality have not been implemented successfully because they were not supported with the right kind of staff development. The discussion that follows focuses on the planning of staff-development programs as they relate to the general curriculum-planning process; Chapter 9 examines staff development as a means of supervising the taught curriculum, and Chapter 10 offers detailed suggestions for using staff development during the implementation stage.

One of the major planning issues is the timing of staff development as it relates to curricular change. Although there are many variations in the specifics of this issue, there are two general models that have been used successfully: staff development precedes and leads to curricular change; and staff development follows and supports curricular change.

In the first model, staff-development sessions are held prior to any major curriculum change. The intent here is to update teachers' knowledge about new developments in the field, to give them the skills they need in writing curriculum and instructional materials, and to provide an opportunity for them to exchange and try out such materials. In general, this is the planning model used in the highly successful National Writing Project. (See Keech and others, 1979, for a comprehensive evaluation of this approach.) James Gray, the individual chiefly responsible for the Bay Area Writing Project, the precursor of the National Writing Project, explicitly rejected curriculum change as the major intervention strategy. His knowledge of the research on the change process led him and his colleagues to begin with a highly effective staff-development model that showed teachers new ways of teaching writing. As teachers explored the new process approach and developed instructional materials, they began gradually to change the curriculum.

The chief advantage of this approach is that it tends to result in a teacher-produced curriculum of high quality. The teachers involved in the staff-development program become local experts who have a better understanding of the field; and the materials they produce have usually stood the test of rigorous trials in the classrooms. The chief drawback to this model is that it can result in piecemeal change; the curriculum becomes a collection of interesting exercises and lacks an integrating conceptual framework.

In the second model, staff-development sessions are held subsequent to the curriculum change. The new curriculum is developed; then those who developed the curriculum identify the new knowledge, skills, and attitudes required for successful implementation. Those new learnings then become the basis for a series of staff-development programs offered immediately prior to the introduction of the new program and during its implementation stage. This essentially is the model used in most curriculum-development and implementation projects. A very effective use of this model is reported by Romberg and Price (1983), in their account of the Curriculum Review Project of the Berea (Ohio) public schools. One of the factors that seemed to account for the success of this project was that the developers were sensitive to the culture of the local schools and made a specific attempt to change the beliefs and traditions of the teacher-implementors.

The chief advantage of this model is the close fit between the curricular change and the staff development. If planned carefully, the staff-development program equips the teachers with the skills they need to implement the new curriculum. The chief drawback is that it can place the teacher in a passive role: "Here is your new curriculum, and this is how you teach it."

APPLICATIONS

1. Some specialists argue for a simpler planning model, one that would require less time and fewer resources. If you wanted to simplify this goal-based model, how would you do so? Indicate the specific steps that would occur in your simplified model.

2. In the school district about which you are most knowledgeable, would you recommend a separate community advisory council, rather than appointing representatives to a general council? Explain the reasons behind your decision to set up a separate council or to appoint to a general one.

3. In the school district you know best, how would you balance the need for district management of the curriculum with the need for school autonomy? Use the questions in Figure 5-2 as guidelines for resolving this issue.

4. How would you allocate leadership functions in that same district? Use the form shown in Figure 5-3 to answer this question, indicating how you think functions should be allocated.

5. Develop a planning calendar you would use in a district you know well. Use the form shown in Figure 5-5.

6. Some experts in the field have recommended a more complex needs-assessment model, one that would make extensive use of such measures and processes as parent interviews, community surveys, student interviews, and futures-forecasting techniques. If you were in a district leadership position, would you recommend using one of these more complex processes instead of the more sharply focused model described here? Justify your answer.

REFERENCES

Brookover, W. B. (1980). *Measuring and attaining the goals of education.* Alexandria, VA: Association for Supervision and Curriculum Development.

English, F. W. (1980). *Improving curriculum management in the schools.* Washington, DC: Council for Basics Education.

Gass, J. R. (ed.). (1979). *School-based curriculum development.* Paris: Centre for Educational Research and Innovation.

Goodlad, J. I. (1984). *A place called school: Prospects for the future.* New York: McGraw-Hill.

Joyce, B. R. (1986). *Improving America's schools.* New York: Longman.

Kaufman, R. A. (1982). Needs assessment. In F. W. English (ed.), *Fundamental curriculum decisions,* pp. 53–67. Alexandria, VA: Association for Supervision and Curriculum Development.

Keech, C., Stahlecker, J., Thomas, S., and Watson, P. (1979). *National Writing Project evaluation report.* Berkeley, CA: University of California.

Pennsylvania State Board of Education. (1985). Chapter-5 curriculum regulations. Harrisburg, PA: Author.

Romberg, T. A., and Price, G. G. Curriculum implementation and staff development as cultural change. In G. A. Griffin (ed.), *Staff development,* pp. 154–184. (82nd Yearbook of the National Society for the Study of Education, Part II). Chicago: University of Chicago Press.

Ross, J. A. (1982). The influence of the principal. In K. A. Leithwood (ed.), *Studies in curriculum decision making,* pp. 54–67. Toronto: Ontario Institute for Studies in Education.

Tobin, A. (1984). Pacing schedules and sample lessons for standardized curriculum: Mathematics, grades 7–12. Philadelphia: School District of Philadelphia.

6

Improving the Program of Studies

As explained earlier, the program of studies is the total set of organized learning experiences at a given level of schooling—all the courses offered at the elementary, middle, or high school level. From time to time it is useful for educational leaders to implement a systematic process to assess and improve the program of studies offered at one or more of these levels. This chapter suggests such a process, after reviewing some recent attempts to reconceptualize programs of study. It should be noted here that the chapter focuses on *improving* an existing program, rather than developing a completely new program, since few educators have the opportunity of developing new programs of study.

RECONCEPTUALIZING PROGRAMS OF STUDY

Before discussing the assessment and improvement strategies, it might be useful here to examine briefly some widespread attempts to reconceptualize schools' programs of study. For the most part those attempts have been motivated by dissatisfaction with the discipline-based curriculum (which uses the standard disciplines as the fields or organizing centers of learning.) There are those who argue that the traditional disciplines, such as science and mathematics, are rigid boxes that fragment knowledge unduly. (See Cawelti, 1982, for a recent statement of this position.)

As a consequence, there have been several attempts to break away from the standard academic disciplines as ways of organizing knowledge. Such attempts have a long history. In fact, one of the by-products of the progressive era was widespread interest in developing curricular models that transcended or ignored the traditional disciplines. One of the most pervasive models of this period was the *core curriculum* movement, which flourished in the 1940s and still persists as a curricular model for many middle schools. In one widely disseminated model of the core curriculum, the ninth-grade student would have two periods a day of learning experiences related to personal interests, three periods a day of "common learnings" (one continuous course that would help students develop life competencies), and one period of health and physical education (Educational Policies Commission, 1952). And the organizing center of the common-learnings course was not the disciplines, but the needs of youth.

Some of those basic principles of the core curriculum still influence current attempts to reconceptualize the curriculum. While there are many possible ways of categorizing those attempts, most can be classified as attempts either to develop interdisciplinary courses or to achieve a total restructuring of the program of studies.

Interdisciplinary Courses   Interdisciplinary courses are courses of study that either integrate content from two or more disciplines (such as English and social studies) or ignore the disciplines totally in organizing learning experiences. Integrated approaches often take the form of "humanities" courses that include content from literature, history, art, and music. Such humanities courses can be organized in terms of cultural epochs ("The Renaissance"), area studies ("American Studies"), ethnic identity ("The Black Experience"), or themes ("The Utopian Vision"). While such courses include material from several disciplines, there is still a strong sense of the disciplines informing the decisions about content and sequence. At the elementary level, while not concerned with "humanities courses," innovative teachers have always developed interdisciplinary units, such as "Our Animal Friends," that draw from such subject areas as language arts, social studies, science, and art.

Courses or units that ignore or transcend the disciplines are almost always thematically structured. Thus, a team of teachers might develop a course in "The Nature of Conflict," which would embody concepts from literature, biology, anthropology, philosophy, and psychology. The planning focuses on key concepts and skills, with no regard for their disciplinary sources. Or an elementary team might cooperatively develop an integrated unit on "Families First," which would integrate content from social studies, reading, and language arts.

Interdisciplinary courses of both types can be offered either as a substitute for the standard required courses ("take American Studies instead of junior English and American history") or as enrichment electives ("take our new humanities course in addition to junior English and American history").

The research on interdisciplinary courses has been neither extensive nor deep. However, the few well-designed studies available suggest that such interdisciplinary courses are as effective as the standard courses in teaching basic skills. (See Vars, 1978, for a review of such studies.)

Restructured Programs of Study Reformers who have been critical of the standard discipline-based curriculum have expressed impatience with modest attempts to reform it by adding interdisciplinary courses. They have advocated instead a total restructuring of the curriculum, arguing that only a completely fresh reconceptualization can bring about meaningful change. Typical of such advocates is Mortimer Adler, creator of the *Paideia* proposal (1982). Adler recommends that the school curriculum be perceived as "three columns of learning"—column one, the acquisition of organized knowledge (language, literature, fine arts, mathematics, natural science, history, geography, and social studies); column two, the development of intellectual skills (reading, writing, speaking, listening, calculating, problem solving, observing, measuring, estimating, and exercising critical judgment); and column three, the enlarged understanding of ideas and values (through discussion of books and other works of art and involvement in artistic activities).

Despite the attractiveness of such proposals, most educators believe that the disciplines will persist. One reason for such persistence, of course, is the force of tradition: curricula have been discipline-based for several hundred years, and such time-honored educational traditions are difficult to change. Then there are the practical arguments: teachers are trained and certified in the disciplines, and textbooks are written for the disciplines. Finally, there is an intellectual basis for continuing discipline-based curricula. As several writers have pointed out, each discipline has its own special way of knowing, its own syntax of inquiry; consequently, they assert, attempts to ignore the disciplines might produce students who do not know how to think mathematically or artistically. (See Schwab, 1962, for an especially cogent statement of this position.)

IMPROVING THE PROGRAM OF STUDIES

While it is unlikely that there will be widespread interest in these total reconceptualizations, there is a continuing concern for improving the program of studies. Some of that concern results from external pressures. An accrediting body, such as the Middle States Association of Secondary Schools, is scheduled to conduct an evaluation. The state department of education issues new curriculum requirements for all schools. The local board decides to increase graduation requirements, or the superintendent asks each principal to determine where reductions in the instructional budget might be made with the least damage to the educational program. In a sense, all these mandates are external demands for assessing and improving the program of studies. While such externally mandated reviews are useful and necessary, they are no substitute for an internally motivated assessment that responds to the special concerns of those directly involved with that school—its administrators and faculty. This section, therefore, explains a process that a school district can use on a systematic basis to assess and improve the program of studies in its schools.

Developing the Assessment Agenda

The first step is to develop the assessment agenda. District administrators, school administrators, key faculty members, and parent leaders should meet to discuss these issues:

- How often should program assessment be undertaken?
- Which program-assessment issues should be addressed?
- What levels of schooling should be examined?
- What resources are available?

These questions should be answered, of course, by weighing assessment priorities ("Are we most concerned with our middle school?"), by noting any forthcoming external reviews ("When is the high school scheduled for its next accreditation visit?"), and by reflecting about the importance of program assessment ("How much time and effort should we really be putting into this process?").

One of the key components of the assessment agenda is the set of assessment issues. The five major issues which might be considered are listed briefly here and then discussed at length in the following sections. They are:

1. Goal-curriculum alignment: To what extent does the program of studies reflect and respond to the school district's goals?
2. Curriculum correlation: To what extent do learning experiences in the various subjects correlate with each other at a given grade level?
3. Resource allocation: To what extent does the district's allocation of resources to the program of studies reflect district priorities and provide for equity of opportunity?
4. Learner needs: To what extent does the program of studies respond to present and future needs of the students?
5. Constituent satisfaction: To what extent are teachers, students, and parents satisfied with the program of studies?

The decisions about the assessment agenda can be formalized in a program-assessment calendar, such as the one shown in Figure 6-1.

Aligning District Goals and the Curriculum

In the previous chapter, the process of aligning goals with specific fields of study was explained as a critical step in the goal-based planning model. This

FIGURE 6-1. Program-Assessment Calendar

Year	Level	Assessment Issues
1987–88	Middle schools	Goal-curriculum alignment Resource allocation Learner needs
1988–89	Elementary schools	Goal-curriculum alignment Resource allocation Constituent satisfaction
1989–90	High schools	Goal-curriculum alignment Resource allocation Curriculum correlation

chapter suggests a slightly different procedure to use when the focus is on improving a program of studies.

The first step is to identify the school's curriculum goals—those educational goals to which the curriculum is expected to make a major contribution. As indicated in Chapter 5, too often educators assume that all educational goals are curriculum goals. Such an assumption ignores the fact that some goals might best be met through noncurricular means. Consider this goal, one found in many goal statements:

The student will develop a positive self-image.

In general the research suggests (see, for example, Brookover and Erickson, 1975) that self-image is chiefly affected by the expectations of others, such as peers, parents, and teachers, and by the role one chooses for oneself. Since the curriculum makes only a relatively minor contribution, this educational goal probably should not be identified as a curriculum goal.

One useful way of making such a determination is to survey the faculty, using a form such as the one shown in Figure 6-2. Rather than simply distributing and collecting the forms without discussion, it makes more sense to provide time at a faculty meeting for a general discussion of the issues, to let teachers meet in small groups for fuller discussion, and then to ask them to complete the survey after such analysis and reflection. After the surveys have been completed, the faculty should meet again to discuss the results in an attempt to achieve a consensus. In general, any educational goal which at least half the faculty believe should be met primarily through the curriculum should be considered a curriculum goal for the school.

The next step is to determine to what extent and in what subjects these curriculum goals are being met. The objective here is to develop a matrix which shows in graphic form each goal and the contributions of each sub-

FIGURE 6–2. Identification of Curriculum Goals

To the Faculty: Listed below are the educational goals of the school. In your opinion, to which of these educational goals should the school's curriculum make a major contribution? Write the letter *C* after each educational goal to which you think the curriculum should make a major contribution. We should note here that not all these educational goals necessarily have to be curriculum goals. Some goals, for example, might be achieved primarily through the extracurricular program, with the curriculum making only a minor contribution.

1. Develop a positive self-image. _____

2. Value own ethnic identity and accept people
   of other ethnic groups. _____

---

ject, grade by grade. Figure 6–3 shows part of such a matrix, to illustrate the format and content desired here. The curriculum goals are listed down the left-hand side. Across the top are the required subjects offered by the school. (Note that only required subjects are listed; since not all students take electives, the contributions of electives should not be assessed here.) Each subject column is further subdivided into grade levels, since it is important to analyze grade-level progression. The entries note major curriculum units which make a major contribution to each goal.

How can the data for this matrix best be obtained? Two ways are possible. One method is to do a goal analysis of the curriculum guides for all major subjects. A member of the leadership team can go through a guide systematically, entering in the matrix the titles of units that relate to a particular goal and listing any units that do not seem directly related to any of the goals. One drawback of this process is that the matrix reflects only what is in the written guides, not what is actually taught.

For that reason, districts may prefer to build the matrix by surveying teachers. The form can be a simple one, with these directions:

> Listed below are our school's curriculum goals. Consider each goal. If you teach a unit of study that relates directly to or makes a major contribution to that goal, enter the title of the unit. Please keep in mind that we are trying to identify only major units of the curriculum that make major contributions; therefore, you should not note any incidental attention you give to this goal.

Since the objective is to get valid data from individual teachers, this survey should probably be completed by individuals without consultation or discussion with colleagues. Teachers working in groups often claim to be teaching a particular unit because they sense pressure from colleagues to be doing so.

FIGURE 6–3. Curriculum Goals and Subject Contributions

Goal	English Language Arts	
	Grade 4	Grade 5
Think critically and solve problems creatively.	Solving personal problems	Solving school problems

The results collated in the matrix should then be reviewed by the leadership team, keeping these questions in mind:

1. Is each curriculum goal adequately addressed in at least one of our required subjects? This question examines the basic goal-curriculum relationship, to ensure that every goal is dealt with in at least one subject.
2. Are complex curriculum goals reinforced appropriately in two or more subjects? This question is concerned with reinforcement across the curriculum. A complex goal, such as the development of critical thinking, should appear as a focus in several subject areas.
3. Is each goal appropriately developed and reinforced from grade to grade? This question examines the developmental sequence from grade to grade, to be sure that each goal is sufficiently reinforced.
4. Are we avoiding unnecessary duplication and overlap from subject to subject and from grade to grade? This question focuses on the particular units to be sure that unnecessary duplication is avoided.
5. Does each required subject seem to be making an adequate contribution to the curriculum goals of the school? This question focuses on a given subject and examines its contributions to all the goals.

The results of the alignment process can lead to several responses. One response is to reconsider the set of curriculum goals. If it turns out that a curriculum goal is not adequately treated in at least one of the required subjects, then perhaps that goal might better be assigned to some other aspect of the educational program, such as the activity program. A second response is to add a new required course or sequence of courses specifically designed to address a particular goal. Thus, if it appears that critical thinking is not sufficiently stressed in any of the subjects, a required course could be developed which students would have to take at some point in their program. The third response to a perceived deficiency—and perhaps the most effective—would be to determine with teachers in each department how they could develop new units in their courses which would specifically relate to goals not receiving adequate treatment.

Correlating Curricula

Correlating curricula is a process of aligning the contents of two or more subjects—of relating what is taught in English, for example, to what is taught in social studies. Obviously, correlation is most essential in schools with a departmentalized structure. An elementary teacher in a self-contained classroom is probably able to achieve whatever correlation is necessary without special intervention. In the same way, a group of teachers working closely together in an interdisciplinary team are probably able in their own way to effect the correlation they consider desirable. In departmentalized schools, however, teachers in each subject often go their own separate ways, so that what is taught in one subject has no relationship to what is taught in the rest of the program.

There are some good reasons for a closely correlated curriculum, as long as the integrity of individual disciplines is not violated. Teachers in one subject can call upon and develop the skills students have learned in another discipline, without having to take the time to teach those skills themselves. So the chemistry teachers know that they can expect students to be able to handle quadratic equations. Important skills that transcend a given discipline, such as retrieving and evaluating information, can be reinforced from subject to subject, without excessive repetition. The sense of isolation that seems endemic to departmentalized teaching can be reduced as teachers discuss their curricula and develop correlated units of study. And students begin to see more clearly how their learning is related.

There are some obvious drawbacks, however, in excessive or misdirected correlation. In some cases misdirected efforts to correlate can impose unduly restrictive constraints upon teachers. Consider, for example, the problems in trying to correlate American history and American literature. The period of the American Revolution is vitally important in American history deserving intensive treatment from a historical perspective, but the literature of that period is considered by most experts to be insignificant as literature and merits only brief consideration. A second drawback is that some attempts to impose correlation can result in a situation where one is perceived as a "service" subject that exists chiefly to serve the needs of other disciplines. English often suffers this fate: "That's the English teacher's job" is the common cry across the disciplines.

For these reasons a problem-solving approach to correlation is emphasized, where school leaders work with classroom teachers in determining subject by subject how much correlation is needed. The process begins with a survey, using a form such as that shown in Figure 6–4. Notice that it first asks about five general sets of skills and concepts that seem to have applicability across the curriculum: library and study skills; reading skills other than basic comprehension; academic writing skills, such as summarizing an article; mathematics skills; and English grammar. The data from this section of the survey can be collated and shared with the faculty to help them determine how to proceed.

FIGURE 6–4. Curriculum-Correlation Analysis

Department/team _____

Directions: Our school has decided to undertake a study of curriculum correlation to determine how what is taught in the various subjects can be mutually reinforcing. Consider the subject you teach and answer the following questions based upon your knowledge of your own subject.

1. What library/study skills do you think your students should have in order to perform more successfully in your subject?

   Grade 10 _____

   Grade 11 _____

   Grade 12 _____

2. What special reading skills (other than comprehension skills) do you think your students should have?

   Grade 10 _____

   Grade 11 _____

   Grade 12 _____

3. What academic writing skills do you think your students should have?

   Grade 10 _____

   Grade 11 _____

   Grade 12 _____

4. What mathematics skills do you think your students should have?

   Grade 10 _____

   Grade 11 _____

   Grade 12 _____

5. What knowledge of English grammar (parts of speech, parts of the sentence) do you think your students should have?

   Grade 10 _____

   Grade 11 _____

   Grade 12 _____

6. List below any units of study you presently teach which you think could profitably be correlated with units in other subjects, or any new units with a correlated approach that you might be interested in developing.

   Grade 10 _____

   Grade 11 _____

   Grade 12 _____

These data will usually indicate two sorts of problems in correlation. One problem occurs when one or more departments indicate that the curriculum requires the intensive development of one of the basic skills. Suppose it happens, for example, that several departments indicate that their students should know certain basic library skills. There are essentially three options available here to administrators. One would be to develop a new course which would teach the required skills; such a new course would serve the needs of all departments. A second option would be to ask one department (in this case reading/language arts) to assume primary responsibility, with each department then adding its own special content. The third option would be to decide that each department should teach in its own way the library skills its students need. A fuller discussion of these options as they relate to academic writing and critical thinking is presented in Chapter 14.

In some cases the problem is misalignment of content: the ninth-grade science curriculum requires a mathematics skill that the mathematics curriculum places in tenth grade. In such instances the two departments should confer to determine which adjustment seems more feasible—to change the science curriculum so that the skill is not required until the later grade, or to change the mathematics curriculum so that the skill is taught in the earlier grade.

In the same manner the responses to the last question, dealing with the possibilities of developing correlated units, can be shared with the appropriate departments or teams, to see if such units might be cooperatively planned. It might happen, for example, that the mathematics teachers, learning about a unit in logical thinking taught by the English teachers, would suggest a correlated unit which would include an analysis of valid and invalid uses of statistics in reasoning.

Thus correlation is achieved through a problem-solving process of determining need, assessing the options, and making decisions that seem best for the students.

Analyzing Resources Allocated to Curricula

The third process for assessing and improving the program of studies is to analyze the resources allocated to the several curricula. The resource-allocation analysis provides data relevant to these related issues:

- Does the school's allocation of resources reflect its educational priorities? The assumption here is that the manner in which resources are allocated should reflect the system's priorities.
- Does the school's allocation of resources seem adequate for achieving the outcomes desired? If certain important educational outcomes are desired, then those classes will need adequate time, appropriate staffing, and suitable class size.

- Does the allocation of resources seem to be cost-effective? This question essentially examines the relationship between the number of students served and the resources required to serve them.
- Is the allocation of resources equitable? This question is concerned with whether the needs of all students are being met in an equitable fashion. In too many instances, less able students receive less than their share.

The examples shown in Figure 6–5 illustrate the types of data that might be analyzed in answering those questions. Obviously, additional data could be included, such as classroom space, instructional costs, noninstructional costs, and overhead and indirect costs. However, that additional information would contribute only some refinements to the basic data presented in Figure 6–5 and therefore might be omitted without harm to the analysis.

FIGURE 6–5. Analysis of Curriculum Resources

Subject	Required Elective	Enrollment	Number of Sections	Faculty Assigned	Minutes per Week
Art	Elective	250	14	1	80
Phys. Ed.	Required	1500	50	6	120
Russian	Elective	36	3	0.6	200

A special note might be made about the importance of analyzing time allocations. Several studies (see, for example, Stallings, 1980) indicate quite clearly that the time allocated to a particular area of the curriculum is directly related to student achievement in that area. One useful standard for assessing time allocations has been provided by John Goodlad (1984). After reviewing the time allocations in the numerous schools he studied and assessing his own extensive experience in curriculum development, he concluded that the following allocations would be desirable for the three upper grades of elementary school: language arts, 1.5 hours a day; mathematics, 1 hour a day; social studies, 2.5 hours a week; science, 2.5 hours a week; health and physical education, 2.5 hours a week; arts, 3.5 hours a week. In many states, of course, minimum time allocations are stated in the school code; where the district has some flexibility, however, allocations should be closely examined.

In examining those data in relationship to the questions noted above, the leadership team might decide that certain reallocations would strengthen the overall program. Such reallocations might take several forms: increasing or decreasing time allotments; increasing or decreasing section size; increasing or decreasing the number of teachers assigned.

Assessing Learner Needs

One of the most important analyses of the program of studies involves the extent to which the curriculum seems to respond to both present and future needs of the learners. However, to argue for the importance of such an analysis is not to assert that learner needs must always be the primary determiner of curriculum. As explained in Chapter 3, there are other sources that might be just as or more important, depending upon the orientation of curriculum planners. But even curricula that have been influenced primarily by other sources should give some attention to present learner needs if they are to be successful in eliciting student interest. And all curricular orientations seem to accept the importance of preparing students for the future, even though they construe that preparation differently.

If such an assessment is therefore important, it must be done carefully and conscientiously; it should not be perceived as a meaningless exercise undertaken just to satisfy administrators or some external group. The process should begin by involving the faculty in a systematic study that results in an explicit statement of present and future learner needs. How this is done will obviously vary with the local situation; however, the process explained below is one that should work well in most systems.

Begin by setting up a small task force or committee composed of one district administrator, one or more school administrators, and several key faculty members. Their first task should be to develop a tentative draft of present learner needs. Two points should be stressed about this needs analysis. First, it should focus on the developmental needs of the age group enrolled in that school, not on the needs of all children and youth. The assumption is that the district's goals speak to the broader needs of all students; the needs analysis is concerned solely with the age group served by that school. Second, it should be concerned primarily with those needs that might best be served through the curriculum, since the emphasis is on assessing the educational program, not other aspects of schooling.

The task force should use two general sources of information: publications and people. First, they should undertake a systematic examination of current publications dealing with that age group. For each age level—the children in elementary schools, the preadolescents and early adolescents in middle schools, and the youth in high schools—there are numerous sources that synthesize the research on the psychological, physical, social, and intellectual needs of that population. The task force would be wiser, perhaps, to limit themselves to careful study of a smaller number of the best sources (perhaps no more than five or six), rather than attempting a comprehensive survey. They should also use whatever expert advice they can get from both district personnel (such as school nurses, counselors, social workers, and psychologists) and from professionals in the community.

Their draft report might take the form of the one shown in Figure 6-6. That document synthesizes the most current and reliable information about

FIGURE 6-6. Adolescent Needs and Curricular Responses

The research suggests that young adolescents have these needs:

Their program of studies therefore should probably respond in these ways:

1. Understand the physical changes occurring and the special nutritional needs that result.

1. Health education units and science units emphasizing that such changes are normal and stressing importance of good nutrition.

2. Develop greater physical coordination in a nonthreatening environment.

2. Physical education experiences that build coordination without overemphasizing competition.

3. Increase level of cognitive development, moving from semiformal to formal operations.

3. Units in all appropriate subjects that include a mix of concrete and abstract learnings.

4. Become more sophisticated in their political reasoning.

4. Units in social studies that help them examine complexities of current political issues.

5. Increase level of moral development.

5. Units in social studies, science, and English that help them examine complex moral issues.

6. Develop clearer sense of personal identity.

6. Units in English that explore issues of personal identity and self-awareness.

7. Maintain balance between growing sense of autonomy and continuing need for peer approval.

7. Units in social studies that explore the nature of peer influence from a sociological perspective.

middle school learners. Observe that it first states the need and then suggests a curricular response.

Their second major task is to identify future needs of the learners. Here the intent is not to play the role of futurist and attempt to develop elaborate scenarios about the twenty-first century. Instead the goal is to identify rather predictable features of the next twenty years that should influence the kind of education provided for today's students. Here the task force can turn to two types of documents for assistance. First, there were several commission reports written during the early 1980s which both examined the present performance of schools and addressed specifically the issue of future curricular needs. Three that seem worth checking are the National Science Board (1983) report, *Educating Americans for the 21st Century;* the Education Commission of the States (1982) study, *The Information Society;* and the College Board (1983) report, *Academic Preparation for College.* Second, there are several books available which look more broadly at the issue of planning for the future. While some of these seem unduly speculative, one that seems especially worthwhile is the Phi Delta Kappa (1984) handbook.

This section of the draft report might take the form shown in Figure 6–7. Again, a future development is indicated and then a curricular response is suggested.

The draft report on present and future needs should then be analyzed and discussed by the faculty, meeting in small groups, with perhaps one member of the task force leading each group. Out of those discussions should emerge a final draft reflecting a faculty consensus. That process results in a final document which can then be used in assessing the program of studies. The process obviously is a time-consuming one, but the commitment of large amounts of time seems warranted. Not only will the faculty have produced a highly useful document, but teachers will also have had an opportunity to analyze and discuss some very critical issues.

How can this document be used in assessing the program of studies? Two processes might be considered. The first is a mapping of what might be called the "needs-responsive curriculum"—those aspects of the curriculum that specifically respond to the needs which have been identified. A form similar to the one shown in Figure 6–8 should be distributed to departments or teams of teachers, who should meet in small groups to discuss the ques-

---

FIGURE 6–7. The Future and the Curriculum

The experts predict that the future will be marked by these developments:

1. The world becomes a "global village."

2. New immigrant groups continue to arrive in this country in large numbers.

3. The information age arrives: a glut of information made available by computers.

4. Television becomes increasingly dominant as a medium of communication and entertainment.

5. The family continues to change—more family instability, more one-parent families.

6. The technology continues to change, with the job market changing frequently and unpredictably.

The curriculum should probably respond in these ways:

1. Units in social studies and English that increase students' awareness of national interdependence; foreign language study made available to all students.

2. Units in English and social studies that emphasize our immigrant past and the contributions of immigrants.

3. Units in all appropriate subjects on information retrieval, evaluation, and application.

4. Units in English that emphasize critical viewing.

5. Units in social studies that put such changes in perspective.

6. Units in English and social studies that emphasize career-mobility skills, rather than examining particular careers.

FIGURE 6–8. The Needs-Responsive Curriculum

Directions: The following curriculum characteristics have been suggested by our analysis of our students' present and future needs. Consider each characteristic. If you feel that the curriculum in your subject in some way reflects that characteristic, then indicate specifically how it does so.

Department: English language arts

A needs-responsive curriculum should have these characteristics:	Our curriculum reflects these characteristics in these ways:
1. Helps students develop a global perspective.	1. Students read some contemporary literature written by European and Asian writiers.

tion and respond to the survey. The results can then be reviewed by the leadership team to determine areas of strength and weakness.

It might be useful here to distinguish between the goal-curriculum alignment process and the mapping of the needs-responsive curriculum. The goals usually are very general statements that apply to all levels of schooling and are ordinarily produced at the state or district level. The goal-curriculum alignment process attempts to align larger curriculum entities, such as units of study, with these very general outcomes. The statement of needs is produced at the school level and focuses on the more specific needs of a given age level, and the mapping process seeks detailed evidence of how a given curriculum responds to those needs. However, since the alignment and mapping processes are somewhat similar in approach, it might be desirable to use only one, not both, during a given assessment project.

The other process for assessing the needs-responsive curriculum takes an entirely different approach. Each homeroom or adviser-room teacher is asked to identify three students from that homeroom and conduct an in-depth interview to ascertain the students' perceptions of how well the program of studies responds to the needs identified. If the homeroom group is heterogeneous in abilities, the teacher should choose one student from each ability level. The interview might open with a statement of this sort:

> The teachers in our school have been thinking about students your age and the kinds of things they should be learning. We'd like to find out from some of our students how they feel about what they are learning. You've been selected because I think you have some good ideas about what you're studying. I'm going to read a statement about what our faculty believes you should be learning. I would then like you to answer in two ways. First, tell me if you agree that those things are important to learn. Then tell me in which subjects, if any, you are learning those things.

The teacher, of course, should caution students not to make statements critical of particular teachers, since the intent is not to evaluate teachers but to examine the program of studies.

Each teacher should then be asked to prepare a written summary of the results of the interviews. Time should also be provided for small groups of homeroom advisers to meet together to discuss their findings. The written summaries should be reviewed by the leadership team to identify specific ways in which the program of studies does not seem sufficiently responsive to learner needs.

Both these processes will have identified certain needs-based deficiencies in the existing program of studies. The leadership team can then decide how to respond to those deficiencies. One response, obviously, is to decide that a particular need should not be addressed in the curriculum. Upon further reflection, the leaders might determine that a particular need can better be satisfied through some other educational means or through some other agency. The more likely response is to suggest to appropriate teams or departments that they spend more time deciding how they could make their curricula more responsive. Thus, if it is apparent that none of the school's courses is concerned with the need to develop a global perspective, several departments might be asked to examine how their curricula might be suitably modified. The social studies, English, music, art, and home economics departments would need to be involved in this instance.

Assessing Constituent Satisfaction

The last assessment process involves measuring constituent satisfaction; *constituent* is used here as an umbrella term that includes students, teachers, and parents as constituents whom the curriculum serves. This is not to suggest that all groups need to be surveyed; especially at the elementary level, measures of pupil perceptions tend not to yield valid results. The leadership team should decide which groups should be surveyed, and whether the total population or only a sample should be included. Thus, the leaders might decide to survey all teachers, a stratified sample of 20 percent of the students, and all parents.

Ordinarily, the survey should focus on the entire program of studies, not on individual subjects or the instructional processes. However, a faculty committee should be charged with the responsibility of developing the specific items to be included. The items shown in Figure 6–9 suggest the types of items that might well make up the survey. Observe that the survey shown in Figure 6–9 attempts to assess satisfaction with several dimensions of the program of studies: present relevance; future value; interest; the required/elective balance; difficulty and challenge; subject correlation; and curricular equity. These seem to be the aspects where constituent satisfaction is most salient.

The results of these surveys require careful analysis before steps are

FIGURE 6–9. Student Survey

To the Student: Below you will find several statements about the subjects you are studying this year. Consider each statement and decide how much you agree with it. Circle one of these responses to show how much you agree or disagree with that statement:

SA	strongly agree	D	disagree
A	agree	SD	strongly disagree
?	uncertain		

Remember also to read the question at the end of this survey.

Statement	Your Response				
1. I am learning things that seem useful to me now.	SA	A	?	D	SD
2. I am learning things that will be helpful to me in the future.	SA	A	?	D	SD
3. I am learning things that seem interesting to me.	SA	A	?	D	SD
4. I think I should have a chance to take more electives.	SA	A	?	D	SD
5. The things I am studying seem much too difficult for me.	SA	A	?	D	SD
6. The courses I am taking make me think and develop my abilities.	SA	A	?	D	SD
7. The courses I am taking seem connected with each other; what I learn in one course ties in with what I learn in the other courses.	SA	A	?	D	SD
8. The bright students in our school have better courses than students who are not so bright.	SA	A	?	D	SD

Is there some course not offered by our school which you would like to see offered? If so, list it below. You may list more than one course if you wish.

_____

taken to improve the program of studies. The leadership team should examine the data with these questions in mind:

1. Are there major discrepancies in the extent to which teachers, parents, and students seem satisfied with the program of studies? If so, what do those discrepancies mean?
2. Where general dissatisfaction is expressed with some dimension of the program of studies, what changes might best be made?

It should be stressed here that constituent satisfaction is only one standard by which a program of studies should be assessed. The leadership team and the faculty should use one or more of the measures discussed above to supplement this particular analysis.

Taken together then, these five assessment processes can yield some highly useful data which the leadership team and the faculty can use in improving the program of studies.

APPLICATIONS

1. Compare the process suggested above with that recommended by one of the accrediting bodies. What do you perceive to be the advantages and disadvantages of each? What local factors might affect the one you would recommend to a school district?

2. There are those who argue that speculating about the future is a futile pursuit, since the future is so unpredictable. Many also point out that if we teach students how to think, how to communicate, how to read, and how to solve problems, there is no need to worry about the future. How would you respond to such arguments?

3. Try your hand at reconceptualizing the curriculum. Choose a level of schooling you know best (elementary, middle, high). Identify the way you would organize learning (using some of the disciplines, if you wish) and indicate what percentage of time would be devoted to each broad field.

4. Develop a detailed program-assessment calendar for a school that you know. Include the following: the program-assessment issues to be analyzed; the individuals primarily responsible; and the dates by which the final assessments should be made.

REFERENCES

Academic preparation for college: What students need to know and be able to do. (1983). New York: The College Board.

Adler, M. J. (1982). *The Paideia proposal: An educational manifesto.* New York: Macmillan.

Brookover, W. B., and Erickson, E. L. (1975). *Sociology of education.* Homewood, IL: Dorsey Press.

Cawelti, G. (1982). Redefining general education for the American high school. *Educational Leadership, 39,* 570–572.

Educational Policies Commission. (1952). *Education for all American youth—A further look.* Washington, DC: National Education Association.

Goodlad, J. I. (1984). *A place called school: Prospects for the future.* New York: McGraw-Hill.

National Science Board Commission on Pre-College Education in Mathematics, Science, and Technology. (1983). *Educating Americans for the 21st century.* Washington, DC: National Science Board.

Phi Delta Kappa Commission on Schooling for the 21st Century. (1984). *Handbook for conducting future studies*. Bloomington, IN: Phi Delta Kappa.

Schwab, J. T. (1962). The concept of the structure of a discipline. *Educational Record, 43*, 197–201.

Stallings, J. (1980). Allocated academic learning time revisited, or beyond time on task. *Educational Researcher, 9*, 11–16.

The information society: Are high school students ready? (1982). Denver: Education Commission of the States.

Vars, G. F. (1978). *Bibliography of research on the effectiveness of block-time, core, and interdisciplinary team teaching programs*. Kent, OH: Kent State University.

7

Improving a
Field of Study

When a school district decides to improve a field of study, it usually is concerned with strengthening one subject area, such as English language arts, over several grade levels. Such a decision typically emerges from an awareness of a deficiency: there is poor articulation between the various levels of schooling; teachers are no longer using existing guides; or the present curriculum has become outdated. This chapter describes a process for effecting such improvements, after noting some attempts to reconceptualize fields of study.

RECONCEPTUALIZING FIELDS OF STUDY

Whereas attempts to reconceptualize programs of study usually are concerned with proposals for minimizing the rigid demarcations between the disciplines, those involving fields of study ordinarily focus on eliminating the rigidity imposed by graded curricula. Proponents of such approaches argue that curricula organized by grade level (grade 10 English, grade 6 mathematics) militate against individualization and result in "batch processing" that ignores individual differences. They argue for curricula that are not bound to grade levels but that instead facilitate individual progress.

The idea of minimizing the importance of grade levels in designing curricula is not new, of course. As early as 1919, Carleton Washburne working in the Winnetka schools developed an individualized program that emphasized self-paced progress. The pupils worked as long as they needed on self-instructional and self-correcting materials, progressing to subsequent units on the basis of teacher-administered tests. (See Washburne and Marland, 1963, for a fuller discussion.)

While there are several current models for a nongraded curriculum, most seem to be varieties of two basic ones: the diagnostic-prescriptive model and the elective model.

Diagnostic-Prescriptive Models   Diagnostic-prescriptive models of the curriculum begin by structuring the field of study as a series of sequential nongraded levels of learning. Thus, elementary mathematics might be organized into eighteen levels, instead of six grades. Each level in turn comprises several sequential modules or units. Thus, in Level 3 mathematics there might be sixteen modules arranged in a developmental sequence, so that Module 2 builds on Module 1 and leads to Module 3. The curriculum is thus conceptualized as a linear series of tightly sequenced learning experiences, ordered without respect to grade level. The student moves through this linear sequence at an individualized pace. The teacher diagnoses the student's present level of achievement, prescribes the appropriate placement ("begin with Module 4, Level 3"), and monitors the student's progress through a series of formative and summative tests.

How effective are the diagnostic-prescriptive models? The answer is difficult to determine, since it is almost impossible to sort out the effects of the curricular structure itself from those of the instructional system. However, a recent review of several so-called individualized programs indicates that, while they seem to be superior at the college level, they are not demonstrably more effective in elementary and secondary schools (Bangert, Kulik, and Kulik, 1983).

Elective Models   Elective models are quite different in concept from the diagnostic-prescriptive models. Whereas developers of diagnostic-prescriptive models conceptualize the curriculum as a linearly ordered sequence, those advocating elective models view the curriculum as a multipath network. The contrast is illustrated in Figure 7-1. The elective curriculum is usually delivered as an array of minicourses typically lasting 6, 9, 12, or 18 weeks. (See Oliver, 1978, for a useful description of the various elective options.) And since those minicourses usually are offered to students from several grade levels, they achieve nongrading in their own way.

The content of a given elective course is usually determined by an individual teacher or a team of teachers, who for the most part draw upon their own special interests and their perceptions of student interest. Thus, an English department might offer electives with titles such as the following:

The Black Experience
Hispanic Literature
The Dialects of the South
Conflict: Literature of Battle
Looking at Television with a Critical Eye
Communicating with Computers
Utopias, Real and Imagined

FIGURE 7–1. Individualized and Elective Systems Contrasted

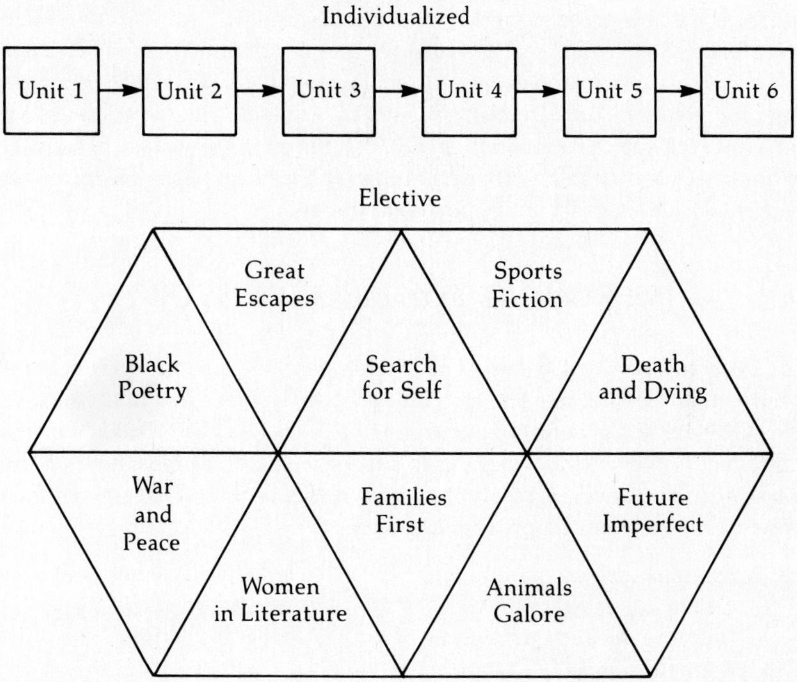

Individualized

Unit 1 → Unit 2 → Unit 3 → Unit 4 → Unit 5 → Unit 6

Elective

Great Escapes · Sports Fiction · Black Poetry · Search for Self · Death and Dying · War and Peace · Families First · Future Imperfect · Women in Literature · Animals Galore

The research on the effectiveness of the elective model is even less conclusive than that assessing the diagnostic-prescriptive models. Although several writers blamed the elective program for the "educational crisis" of the early 1980s, there is no hard evidence to support such a conclusion. (See Copperman, 1978, for one such attack.) In fact, there are only a handful of studies that even attempted to assess electives systematically. Hillocks' (1972) study of English electives is one of those few. After reviewing over one hundred such programs, he concluded on a rather optimistic note:

> Given the time to study, plan, and evaluate their work, English teachers, with their newly awakened sense of professional dignity, may manage to revolutionize the teaching of English. . . . For that reason alone, elective programs . . . will have been worth the effort. (p. 123)

While most objective observers tend to agree that electives were often poorly designed, the issue of whether well-designed programs could be as effective as the standard curriculum must still be considered unresolved.

What of the future of diagnostic-prescriptive and elective models? First, it seems quite likely that the extensive use of the computer in the classroom will make diagnostic-prescriptive models increasingly widespread, since the computer facilitates diagnosis, prescription, and assessment. The elective model at this point in time seems to have been a short-lived fad; its openness and lack of structure are considered suspect by those concerned with standards and rigor. Most leaders in the field seem to take for granted that the graded curriculum will persist because it is so deeply entrenched in the ways in which schools are organized, teachers are assigned, students are grouped, and materials are written. However, the process described below for improving the field of study can be applied in a way that will permit nongrading, if local administrators and teachers decide that such an option is desirable.

IMPROVING THE FIELD OF STUDY

The process described below is a teacher-centered process that relies on teacher input; a rationale for such an approach is presented in the next section. Obviously, it is only one of many ways that a field of study might be improved; however, it has been used successfully by several school districts and seems to achieve the results desired without requiring excessive time or money. The steps in the process are these:

1. Establish project parameters
2. Orient for mastery
3. Map the desired curriculum
4. Refine the map
5. Develop curriculum materials
6. Suggest time allocations
7. Select and develop tests
8. Select instructional materials
9. Provide for staff development

Each of these steps will be explained in detail in the sections following the rationale. Although the English language arts curriculum is used for most of the examples, the process has worked equally well with several other fields of study.

A Rationale for a Teacher-Centered Process

This teacher-centered process has been developed as a solution to a problem perhaps first identified by Goodlad (1977). As discussed in Chapter 1, his studies of school curricula indicated that there are in fact five different curricula that exist almost as separate entities: the *ideal* curriculum (in this work termed the *recommended* curriculum), that set of recommendations proposed by the scholars and experts in the field; the *formal* curriculum (identified in this work as the *written* curriculum), the curriculum embodied in the school district's curriculum guides; the *perceived* curriculum (in this work called the *taught* curriculum), that curriculum which the teachers believed they were teaching; the *operational* curriculum which an observer would observe; and the *experiential* curriculum (in this work called the *learned* curriculum), the curriculum that students are learning.

The ideal curriculum, he noted, rarely influences either the written or the taught curriculum: the written curriculum often is completely ignored by the classroom teacher; the teacher and an observer do not agree as to what the teacher actually taught; and students do not learn all that the teacher attempts to teach. His conclusions have been supported by several subsequent studies which have focused on the teacher as curriculum maker. (See, for example, Cusick, 1983.) Those studies present this general picture: classroom teachers (especially secondary teachers) in making decisions about what to teach rely primarily on their knowledge of the subject, their teaching experience, and their perceptions of their students, giving only cursory attention to the district curriculum guide.

Obviously, then, a process is needed that will at least bring the recommended, the written, and the taught curricula into closer alignment. The recommended curriculum should not be ignored: what teachers teach should reflect the best current knowledge about that subject, tempered by the realities of the classroom. And the written and the taught curricula should be more congruent. Otherwise curricular anarchy results, with each teacher doing what he or she wants to do.

The process described below attempts to accomplish these objectives. It begins with the teachers, determining what they think should be taught. It reviews their decisions in light of the best current knowledge. And it produces written guides that reflect that synthesis of the recommended and the taught. Observe that this improvement process therefore is not concerned primarily with improving the written materials; it is concerned with the much larger issue of improving teaching and learning in that field throughout the district.

Establish Project Parameters

The first task, obviously, is to define the scope of the project. In addition to providing for the necessary budget support, administrators need to answer several questions.

What Grade Levels Will Be Included?   The usual answer here is to improve the entire field, from kindergarten to grade 12. However, there are other options which might be considered: improve the elementary, and then add middle and high school levels; improve the middle and then add elementary and high; improve the high school and then build backwards to middle and elementary.

Which Ability Levels Will Be Included?   If the schools group by ability levels, then the district has to decide whether it will produce a different guide for each level or produce one basic guide that will then be supplemented with other materials. The mastery-curriculum theory posits a curriculum that can be mastered by all students (except for perhaps those in the lowest decile of achievement); it therefore seems to make more sense to produce one basic mastery guide which is then supplemented with special materials for more able students.

Who Will Direct the Improvement Project?   Most districts have found that a small task force is most efficient and effective. It should include one district administrator, one or two school administrators, the district supervisor for that field, at least one teacher-leader from each level to be included, and one parent representative. The task force should probably be led by one of the district administrators or the district supervisor.

How Much Time Will Be Needed?   Although the answer will vary with the size of the district, the scope of the project, and the resources available, most districts have found that one school year is sufficient for the entire project.

Orient for Mastery

With the project parameters set, the process begins with an orientation of all teachers who will be affected by the improvement program. The project leader should prepare materials summarizing the project and stressing two basic features: the improvement program will rely heavily on teacher input; and the improvement program will focus on the mastery curriculum only. As explained in Chapter 1, the mastery curriculum is that part of a field of study which meets two criteria: it is considered essential for all students; and it requires careful structuring and organization for optimal learning. District curriculum efforts should focus on the mastery curriculum; the organic curriculum and the enrichment curriculum can be strengthened at the school level, chiefly through staff development.

Map the Desired Curriculum

With that orientation accomplished, the next phase is mapping the desired curriculum—finding out what teachers think *should* be taught in that field of study, at their grade level. Note that the intent is to determine what teachers believe should be taught, not what they actually teach. Although several experts (see English, 1980, for example) advocate mapping to determine what teachers actually teach, several studies indicate quite clearly that teachers in effect know better than they teach. For a variety of reasons, they do not teach what they think should be taught: they lack materials; they believe they are constrained by administrators' or parents' preferences; and they are not sure that colleagues would approve. (See Lieberman and Miller, 1984, for an excellent picture of the conflicts teachers experience in making decisions about classrooms and curricula.) Therefore, it seems desirable to find out what they think they should be teaching, rather than simply formalizing the unnecessary compromises they have made. In a sense, then, the process attempts to tap the classroom teacher's perception of the "ideal," as well as that of the scholars.

The best way to map the desired curriculum is to survey the teachers grade by grade. The survey instrument is a crucial element here, since the content and structure of the instrument will very much affect the kinds of data elicited. An expert in the field (either someone from the district or an external consultant) should develop a draft of the form by considering several crucial issues (Figure 7–2 shows a portion of a form used to map the social studies curriculum in a suburban school district):

FIGURE 7–2. Mapping the Social Studies Curriculum: Skills

THE EXPERTS RECOMMEND THAT . . . .
1. Skill development is an important aspect of social studies goals. A skill is the ability to do something well—"knowing how."
2. Social studies skills are best developed through sequential instruction and practice, from kindergarten to grade 12.
3. The social studies curriculum should emphasize the important skills of *acquiring information:* reading skills; study skills; reference and information-searching skills; and the use of the computer in acquiring information.
4. The social studies curriculum should emphasize the skills of *oranizing and using information:* critical thinking and decision-making skills.
5. The social studies curriculum should emphasize the skills needed for effective *interpersonal relationships and social participation:* personal skills, group skills, and social and political participation skills.

What information-acquiring skills do you think should be taught for mastery at your grade level?

1

2

3

What information-organizing skills do you think should be taught at your grade level?

1

2

3

What interpersonal and social skills do you think should be taught at your grade level?

1

2

3

- What elements of the mastery curriculum will be mapped? The objective is to elicit only essential information, not to clutter up the process with unnecessary detail. English teachers, for example, might decide that they do not want to get specific data about punctuation or usage items, since those matters are extensively covered in most English textbooks.
- What strands will be used for the mapping process? The strands are the elements that make up a given field of study—the divisions of that field. Obviously, any given field of study could be analyzed differently in terms of its strands. Some, for example, would argue that English language arts comprises only three strands: language, literature, and composition. The objective is to identify strands that make sense to the teachers—to conceptualize the field as they do, not as the experts do.
- How detailed should the mapping data be? Some who use mapping prefer to get very detailed data—long lists of specific objectives. Extensive experience with mapping suggests that more general data at this stage of the process are desirable. The specific objectives can be produced at a later stage of the process.
- Will the survey form include a summary of the recommendations of experts, so that teachers can make more informed decisions? One advantage of including such information is that the process of completing the mapping form also serves to educate teachers about recommended practice. There is a concern, however, that such summaries might influence teachers to recommend content that they would probably not really want to include. Someone who knows the teachers well should make this decision.

That draft of the survey form should be tested with a small group of teachers to be sure that the directions are clear, that the strands seem appropriate, and that the structure of the form will elicit the kinds of information desired.

Teachers should then have an opportunity to complete the form during an inservice day or a faculty meeting. They should be notified in advance of the mapping process, in case they wish to bring along textbooks, lesson-plan books, or existing curriculum guides. Should the teachers complete the form together in small teams, or should they work alone? Either approach can be used. The team approach provokes good discussion; the individual approach prevents assertive teachers from dominating too much. The decision should be made perhaps by the principal, since he or she probably best understands faculty work habits.

The returns should then be collated on a large scope-and-sequence chart which shows the strands, the grade levels, and the teachers' responses. Figure 7–3 shows a portion of such a chart. Note in this example that the chart also shows responses school by school, since such information can help leaders identify special staff-development needs.

FIGURE 7-3. Results of the Mapping Process: Grade 7 English

The following chart shows how the English language arts teachers in our three middle schools responded in indicating where they believe the parts of speech should be taught for mastery. The tallies indicate the number of teachers so responding for each part of speech.

Grammar: Parts of Speech

North	South	Central
Noun—2	Noun—3	Do not
Verb—2	Verb—3	wish to teach
Adjective—2	Adjective—3	parts of speech
Adverb—2	Adverb—3	in grade 7
	Determiner—3	
	Conjunction—3	
	Pronoun—3	
	Preposition—3	

Refine the Map

The next phase of the process is refining the map—reviewing the first version of the scope-and-sequence chart and making the necessary modifications. Here the advice of an expert in the field might be needed, unless there are local leaders who have a deep and current knowledge of that field. The results should be reviewed with these questions in mind:

1. What important skills and concepts have been omitted and should be included? Have the teachers ignored some important recommendations of the experts?
2. What less important content has been included that might be dropped in order to reduce the overall content load? Have teachers tried to accomplish too much?
3. What skills and concepts seem to be misplaced by level and might better be taught at some lower or higher level? Does placement reflect current knowledge about cognitive development?
4. Where is there unnecessary duplication and repetition? Should some concepts and skills be taught for mastery at more than one grade level?
5. Does each strand show a desirable development from grade to grade? Is there good progression in relation to difficulty and complexity?
6. Is there good balance from grade to grade? Are some grades overloaded?
7. Does the scope-and-sequence chart respond adequately to state and district mandates concerning student competencies?

It is this phase especially where the influence of the ideal curriculum is paramount: the recommendations of the teachers are checked against the best judgment of the scholars and the experts.

The results of that critique are reflected then in a revised scope-and-sequence chart which should be distributed to all administrators and classroom teachers involved. The teachers especially should have an opportunity to critique the revision, focusing on the changes that have been made. If a majority of the teachers object to the inclusion or placement of any specific item, then that item should be changed to reflect majority wishes. The intent is to develop a consensus curriculum, one that teachers will support.

Develop Curriculum Materials

The revised scope-and-sequence chart shows the grade-level placement of the major skills and concepts, strand by strand. The task force now needs to resolve this important issue: what curriculum materials are needed to help teachers implement the improved curriculum?

There are three likely options for the curriculum materials: a *curriculum guide*, a *curriculum-objectives notebook*, and a *curriculum-scenario book*.

The standard *curriculum guide*, described in detail in Chapter 8, is perhaps used most often by districts. Its main components are the specific learning objectives and the activities suggested for each objective. If it is decided that a standard curriculum guide is needed, then a team of teachers should first use the general skills and concepts identified in the scope-and-sequence chart to develop the specific objectives. Thus, if the scope-and-sequence chart includes "nouns" as a concept in the grammar strand for grade 8, then the team might develop this list of objectives:

1. Define *noun*.
2. Identify nouns in sentences.
3. Define *concrete* and *abstract noun*.
4. Identify concrete and abstract nouns in sentences.
5. Use concrete and abstract nouns appropriately in sentences.
6. Define *proper* and *common noun*.
7. Identify proper and common nouns in sentences.
8. Use proper nouns in sentences, capitalizing correctly.

That list of specific objectives is developed by analyzing the general skill or concept and determining what specific knowledge would be most appropriate for a given grade level. For each objective or set of objectives, the team would then identify the necessary learning activities.

The distinguishing feature of the curriculum guide is its comprehensiveness. It ordinarily covers every grade level and, besides the detailed objectives and activities, includes a statement of the philosophy, suggestions for evaluation, and lists of materials. It often is bound and printed with an impressive cover.

The second option is to produce a *curriculum-objectives notebook.* The curriculum notebook is a looseleaf notebook which contains the following: a summary of the research on how to teach that subject; a copy of the scope-and-sequence chart in reduced form; and a list of the objectives for those grade levels taught by the teacher to whom the guide is issued. Thus, a seventh-grade teacher would have a copy of the seventh-grade objectives only. The objectives are developed through the same process described above.

The distinguishing features of the curriculum-objectives notebook are its simplicity and flexibility. Only the essentials are included for only the grade level needed. Learning activities are not suggested; it is assumed that teachers can develop their own activities or can learn from staff-development programs how to use varied learning activities. There is an important message implied by this format: "Achieve these mastery objectives in any reasonable way you wish." The flexibility is of two sorts. First, the looseleaf format makes it easy for teachers to add, delete, and modify. They are encouraged to make the notebook their own: to include their own learning materials; to insert their lesson plans; to add professional articles they find useful. The second type of flexibility results from listing the objectives only. Teachers thus have a great deal of freedom both in how they organize those objectives for teaching and in how they teach. If some teachers wish to teach integrated units, they may; if some wish to focus on discrete skills, they may do so.

The *curriculum-scenario book* is the term given here to describe a collection of learning scenarios. The team takes each general concept or skill and asks, "What mix of learning activities, learning materials, and learning objectives can result in quality learning experiences?" Thus the team working on the concept *noun* might produce these scenarios, among others:

1. Have students read the section from Helen Keller's autobiography where she first learns that things have names. Introduce the concept of nouns as names. Discuss the importance of naming as an aspect of using language. Discuss as well the danger of reification—of believing that whatever is named, is real.
2. Have students write noun poems—poems made of lists of very specific nouns. Discuss the importance of specificity. Ask students to think about the usefulness of general nouns. Advanced students may be interested in the "abstraction ladder" of the general semanticists.

Notice that the scenarios emphasize the holistic nature of the learning experience; the objectives are there, but they are implicit and do not dictate what occurs. In addition to the learning scenarios, the scenario book would also include a copy of the scope-and-sequence chart and a summary of the research.

Which of these three choices is best? The answer depends on the needs of the system and the maturity and competence of the teachers. The curriculum guide probably best serves the needs of a school district in which administrative control is important and in which teacher experience is limited. The curriculum notebook is perhaps best in a district which wishes to give mature and competent teachers a great deal of freedom while still emphasizing the importance of the mastery learning objectives. The scenario book perhaps best serves the needs of those districts whose leaders feel they can be more concerned with the quality of the learning experiences and less concerned with the specification of objectives.

Suggest Time Allocations

At some point in the improvement process, the leadership team should suggest time allocations to be used in teaching that subject. As noted previously, several studies (see Stallings, 1980) indicate that the time allocated to a particular area of the curriculum is related to achievement in that area. If 40 percent of the time in English is devoted to the study of grammar and 10 percent to writing, then achievement in grammar will be sharply ahead of achievement in writing.

There are several ways in which time allocations can be set. One method uses the several strands as the basis for establishing time allocations at a district level. The curriculum-improvement task force reviews the recommendations of experts, reflects on district curricular goals, and recommends time allocations for each strand of the curriculum. These recommendations are made part of the final curriculum report.

A variation of this method relies more upon teacher input about time and strands and sets allocations level by level. A district supervisor poses the question to all teachers in the district who teach that subject at a given level of schooling: "As you think about the students in our middle schools, what percentage of time do you think we should allocate to each strand of this curriculum?" The supervisor helps the teachers agree on time allocations that reflect their perceptions and at the same time are responsive to district priorities. Here is how one group of middle school social studies teachers answered the question:

History: 50 percent
Map and study skills: 20 percent
Geography: 15 percent
Civics: 10 percent
Other: 5 percent

A third method focuses on unit planning at the school level. At every grade level in each school, teachers are asked to submit at the start of every marking period a unit-planning proposal, indicating for each unit the unit objective, the important concepts and skills emphasized, and the number of instructional periods allocated. The principal reviews these plans and discusses with the teachers any proposals that seem to reflect unwise allocations of time.

A fourth method relies upon staff development. Rather than specifying district guidelines or checking on unit plans, a member of the leadership team uses staff-development sessions to raise with the teachers issues of time allocation and achievement, to encourage teachers to discuss openly with each other how they allocate time, and to assist teachers in making decisions about time that reflect their knowledge of the learners and the district's curricular priorities.

Obviously, these methods can be used together, since in effect they complement each other.

Select and Develop Tests

The testing aspect of curriculum improvement involves both selection of the appropriate standardized tests and development of curriculum-based tests. First, the task force should consult with measurement specialists in the district to select standardized tests that adequately reflect the improved curriculum. This is an important consideration, since performance on standardized tests is often used as a measure of school success. While the issue is most critical in reading and mathematics, it also needs careful consideration in any area of the curriculum where standardized tests are used.

Curriculum-based or curriculum-referenced tests are also needed. These are locally developed examinations that are based solely on the district's curriculum. They can be used both to assess student achievement and to ensure that teachers are implementing the mastery curriculum. If teachers know that their students will be tested on specific content, they are more likely to emphasize that content.

How many curriculum-based tests are needed at each grade level? The answer seems to vary with the district and the level. The Pittsburgh school district has developed a comprehensive program of curriculum-based tests (called Monitoring Achievement in Pittsburgh) that tests all students once at each grade level. (See Rifugiato and Wilson, 1983, for a fuller discussion of this program.) In many high schools, curriculum-based tests are administered as semester and final examinations.

Since these tests are often used as measures of student progress, school success, and even teacher performance, it is essential that they be developed with the utmost care, to ensure reliability and validity. The advice of measurement specialists will be required, and every form of the tests should be used in pilot studies before the tests are administered throughout the district.

Select Instructional Materials

The improved curriculum will probably require new instructional materials. The task force should develop guidelines for evaluating materials, pointing out any special features that the improved curriculum might require. ("All language arts texts must give special attention to the composing process.") An instructional materials committee should then use those guidelines in reviewing and selecting materials that will provide the best support for teachers implementing the improved curriculum.

It should be stressed here that the textbooks should serve the curriculum, not dictate it. In too many instances, districts reverse the process. They purchase a basic text and then use the publisher's scope-and-sequence chart as the basis of their own curriculum. The folly of such an approach is apparent to anyone who understands how school textbooks are designed. To sell well, they must appeal to a mass market; as a consequence, textbook authors often include content that they know is inappropriate, only because they believe the market demands it. Thus, almost every elementary language arts series includes a great deal of grammar, even though most experts in the field believe that such content is totally inappropriate at the elementary level.

Provide for Staff Development

There are two major issues to consider in planning for staff development: timing and content. Since resources are limited, staff-development sessions must be held at a time when they will be most effective. As explained in Chapter 5, two approaches seem to be successful in the timing of staff development. One approach begins with and emphasizes staff development. The teachers in a given field of study meet for several sessions to review the research, to reflect about the recommendations of experts, to exchange ideas about teaching that subject, and to develop and share materials. The materials they produce—units of study, sample lessons, and student learning materials—in a sense become the improved curriculum. Thus, the curriculum grows out of the staff development. All that is needed is some work at the end to systematize and formalize what they have produced. Many new composition curricula, for example, have been developed in this way.

The second approach provides the staff development at the crucial implementation stage. Once the improved project has been completed, instructional leaders conduct a series of staff-development sessions to help teachers understand the new program, to assist teachers in acquiring the new skills they will need, and to work with teachers in fleshing out the details of the improved program. In this manner, the staff development is seen as supportive of the curriculum. Either of these approaches can work well. The important consideration is to provide good staff development at a time when teachers seem to need it.

What is good staff development? Here the answer is clear. Over the past decade there have been numerous research studies whose results yield a clear picture of what staff development should be. Those results are summarized in Figure 7-4. While it may not be possible for a district to offer staff-development programs that meet all those guidelines, they should be given serious consideration whenever staff-development programs are planned. (The guidelines have been synthesized from the following reviews of the research: Lawrence, 1979; Berman and McLaughlin, 1978; and Joyce and Showers, 1980.)

These nine steps taken together can help a district improve any field of study. Obviously they are time-consuming, but there are no shortcuts to educational quality.

FIGURE 7-4.   Summary of Research on Effective Staff Development

Duration
   1. The program should be ongoing and continuous.

Management
   1. The principal should participate actively but should not dominate.
   2. Teachers and administrators should plan the program jointly.
   3. There should be regular project meetings in which participants review progress and discuss substantive concerns.

Content
   1. The program should provide a necessary theoretical base for the new skills.
   2. The program should give primary attention to the specific skills teachers believe they need.
   3. The content should be timely, directly related to job needs.

Learning Activities
   1. The program should make extensive use of hands-on activities and demonstrations of new skills.
   2. The program should provide for the trial of those new skills in simulated or real settings.
   3. The program should make it possible for teachers to get structured feedback about their use of those skills.
   4. The program should provide opportunities for observation in other classrooms and schools.

Site
   1. The program should be school-based, not university-based.

Instructors
   1. Local teachers should be the instructors, with minimal use of outside consultants.

APPLICATIONS

1. If you wanted to develop a series of elective English courses for high school students, how could you ensure that all students would develop their reading and writing skills, regardless of the electives they chose?

2. Design a mapping form for a subject you know well. In designing the form, consider the issues posed in this chapter's discussion of such forms.

3. Develop a detailed planning schedule that you could follow in improving a field of study in a local school district.

4. How do you account for the fact that the ideal curricula of the scholars and experts have had such little impact on the written or the taught curriculum?

5. Suppose you are part of a grade 5 team of teachers. You decide that you would like to give the pupils some choices about the social studies content by offering some elective units. How would you ensure that all pupils mastered the requisite skills, regardless of the content emphasis?

REFERENCES

Bangert, R. L., Kulik, J. A., and Kulik, C. C. (1983). Individualized systems of instruction in secondary schools. *Review of Educational Research, 53,* 143–158.

Berman, P., and McLaughlin, M. W. (1978). Federal programs supporting educational change. In *Implementing and sustaining innovations.* Washington, DC: U.S. Office of Education, R-1589, No. 8, HEW.

Copperman, P. (1978). *The literacy hoax.* New York: William Morrow.

Cusick, P. A. (1983). *The egalitarian ideal and the American high school: Studies of three schools.* New York: Longman.

English, F. W. (1980). Curriculum mapping. *Educational Leadership, 37,* 558–559.

Goodlad, J. I. (1977). What goes on in our schools. *Educational Researcher, 6,* 3–6.

Hillocks, G., Jr. (1972). *Alternatives in English: A critical appraisal of elective programs.* Urbana, IL: National Council of Teachers of English.

Joyce, B. R., and Showers, B. (1980). Improving inservice training: The messages of research. *Educational Leadership, 37,* 390–392.

Lawrence, G. (1979). *Patterns of effective inservice education: A state of the art summary of research on materials and procedures for changing teacher behaviors in inservice education.* Tallahassee, FL: Florida Department of Education.

Lieberman, A., and Miller, L. (1984). *Teachers, their world, and their work: Implications for school improvement.* Alexandria, VA: Association for Supervision and Curriculum Development.

Oliver, A. I. (1978). *Maximizing mini-courses: A practical guide to a curriculum alternative.* New York: Teachers College Press.

Rifugiato, F. J., and Wilson, H. A. (1983). *A guide to the MAP project.* Pittsburgh, PA: Pittsburgh School District.

Stallings, J. (1980). Allocated academic learning time revisited, or beyond time on task. *Educational Researcher, 9,* 11–16.

Washburne, C. W., and Marland, S. P., Jr. (1963). *Winnetka: The history and significance of an educational experiment.* Englewood Cliffs, NJ: Prentice-Hall.

8

Processes for Developing New Courses and Units

From time to time, administrators, supervisors, or teachers will decide that a new course is needed. In some cases they will determine that an existing course should be completely redeveloped with a fresh perspective. ("Let's rewrite our American history course—the old course just isn't working any more.") In some instances they will see the need for a new course to fill a gap newly perceived in the existing program. ("We need a course in *Career Planning*.") And elementary teachers will often sense the need for a new integrated unit. This chapter explains how to develop a new course or unit using two contrasting processes: the standard *technological* process, and what is termed here a *naturalistic* process. The intent, it should be noted, is not to suggest that one process is better than the other, but only to contrast two divergent processes that might be used in different subject areas, at different grade levels.

THE TECHNOLOGICAL PROCESS OF CURRICULUM PLANNING

The term *technological process* is used here to describe any curriculum-development model which emphasizes the importance of defining terminal learning objectives early in the process and then identifying the steps needed to accomplish those objectives. While there are many variations of the technological process, it tends to be a rational, systematic, ends-oriented model. Its basic principles were perhaps most clearly articulated by Tyler (1949), and its details are probably most clearly explained in manuals written for industrial training. (See, for example, Mager and Beach, 1967.) Its systematic nature and its efficiency make it the preferred process in most industrial and military training. While details of the process will vary from specialist to specialist, in general it moves in an orderly sequence through certain specified steps (for a current and useful explication of the details of the technological process, see Wulf and Schave, 1984):

1. Determine the course parameters—a rationale for the course, its general goals, its probable time schedule.
2. Assess the needs of the learners.
3. On the basis of those needs and the goals previously specified, identify the course objectives, the terminal outcomes desired.
4. Determine the optimal sequence for those course objectives and cluster related objectives into unified learning experiences.
5. For each objective, identify learning activities that will enable the learners to achieve those objectives.
6. Select instructional materials that will support the learning activities.
7. Identify methods by which the attainment of those objectives will be assessed.
8. Systematize all these decisions in a curriculum guide.

It should be noted here that, while the steps identified above are usually followed in that sequence, the most competent technological developers use them in a recursive, iterative fashion and do not apply them in a mechanistic, unthinking manner.

Each of these steps will be described in detail below, using as an example a course for high school students in career planning.

Determine Course Parameters

The first step is to determine course parameters by establishing a rationale for the course—a statement of the principles guiding the developers and an argument for the course. Posner and Rudnitsky (1982) recommend that the rationale deal explicitly with the society-centered values, the child-centered values, and the subject-centered values that inform the course.

With the rationale established, the curriculum specialist then makes a determination about the goals of the course—the general outcomes desired. (The term *curriculum specialist* is used here to designate any administrator or supervisor with responsibility for and training in curriculum development; he or she may organize a team of colleagues to assist in the process.) A course goal is a very general statement of the intended outcomes; typically, a one-semester course would have no more than three goals. Thus, the goal for the career course might be stated in this fashion:

> This course will help students develop their career-planning skills.

A new integrated unit for fourth grade might have this as its goal:

> This unit will help the pupils understand that there are many different kinds of careers and that each career has value to the society.

With the course or unit goal established, the developers then consider the matter of the course schedule—for what length of time will it last, how often will it meet, and for how many minutes per session. This step is usually accomplished by the curriculum specialist through consultation with those responsible for administering the organization, typically the director of curriculum or the school principal.

Assess the Needs of the Learners

The next step is needs assessment; a need is perceived as a gap between a present and a desired state. Thus, the needs-assessment process evaluates the present state of the learners in relation to the general outcomes expected. The data for the needs assessment can come from several sources: achievement scores; surveys; observations; interviews; measures of performance. In the case of the career-planning course, the curriculum specialist might decide to use these methods for determining learner needs: a survey of all juniors and seniors focusing on their career plans and career questions; a survey of teachers' perceptions of students' career-planning needs; and interviews with guidance counselors to elicit their opinions about the same issue.

Identify Course Objectives

The curriculum specialist would next take the critical step of identifying the course objectives. This is usually accomplished by first doing a task analysis of the outcome desired. In the case of the career-planning course, the specialist would ask: Given what is known about how career choices are best made, what specific skills must be mastered? The results of the task analysis are then checked against the needs-assessment data as a means of determining which of those skills should be stressed for the intended population. The result would be a comprehensive list of course objectives, stated in measureable terms. Figure 8–1 shows a list that might be developed for this course in career planning.

Sequence and Cluster Course Objectives

With the objectives determined, the next step is to determine the optimal sequence in which those objectives should be mastered. In an excellent analysis of the nature of curricular sequence, Posner and Strike (1976) identify these types of sequence which might be used:

1. World-related: space, time, physical attributes.
2. Concept-related: class relations, propositional relations, sophistication, logical prerequisite.
3. Inquiry-related: logic of inquiry, empirics of inquiry.
4. Learning-related: empirical prerequisite, familiarity, difficulty, interest, human development, internalization.
5. Utilization-related: procedure, anticipated frequency.

Curriculum specialists who use the technological process usually opt for a learning-related sequence, determining the optimal sequence by examining the relationships between the objectives and then assessing the entry-level skills, knowledge, and attitudes of the learners. In the case of the career-planning course, the order in which the objectives are listed in Figure 8-1 is one that many curriculum specialists would use as the optimal sequence in a course of this sort: the sequence as shown establishes a conceptual basis, moves to the student's awareness of self, and orders the rest of the objectives in what seems to be chiefly a temporal sequence.

Once the specific objectives are sequenced appropriately, the next step is to cluster related objectives into unified learning experiences, such as units of study or instructional modules. The specialist examines the entire list, assesses the constraints of the schedule, reflects about student interest and attention span, and determines which objectives should be placed together in a unified set of learning experiences. Thus, the specialist might determine that objectives 1 and 2 in Figure 8-1 might make a good brief introductory unit, which would establish the conceptual base for what follows.

Identify Learning Activities

For each objective stated, the curriculum specialist would then identify one or more learning activities which would be specifically shaped to help the learners master the objective. The learning activities are usually seen as an ordered set of learning experiences which move the learner step by step to the objective. Consider, for example, objective 7 in Figure 8-1:

> In a well-organized essay, explain at least two factors that have influenced your career values.

The following learning activities could be prescribed:

1. Identify several possible factors that might influence career values: culture, ethnic group, family, peers, gender, region in which you were reared, school experiences, physiological factors.
2. By reflecting about yourself and your values, identify two of those which seem to have had the greatest influence.
3. Check your perceptions and gather supporting information by discussing the question with parents and friends.
4. Develop a plan for your essay; have the preliminary plan reviewed by your teacher and a classmate.
5. Use the revised plan to write the first draft of the essay.
6. Ask a classmate to edit your essay and give you feedback about the essay.
7. Write a revised draft of the essay.

Note that learning activities are chosen primarily on the basis of their fit with the objective; only those activities which move the student step by step to the objective are prescribed.

FIGURE 8–1. Course Objectives: Career Planning

1. Define these three terms in a way that distinguishes them from each other: *job, career, vocation.*
2. Define these terms correctly: *talent, skill, value.*
3. Describe two career-related talents that you believe you possess to a high degree.
4. List four career-related skills that you possess.
5. Explain three ways in which you might acquire additional career-related skills.
6. Explain the two career values that seem most important to you.
7. In a well-organized essay, explain at least two factors that have influenced your career values.
8. In a well-organized paragraph, explain how you would distinguish between a highly reliable source and a less reliable source of career information.
9. Identify three reliable sources that provide current information about career opportunities and requirements.
10. Using those sources, identify three careers for which you possess the necessary talents and which would adequately respond to your career values.
11. Identify the education and experience you would need for securing an entry-level position in each of those three careers.
12. Describe the processes by which you would obtain the required education and experience.
13. Explain three sources of information you would use in locating an entry-level vacancy in one of the three careers selected.
14. Write a career resume which you could use in applying for one of those positions.
15. Demonstrate that you know how to handle a job interview by role-playing such an interview.
16. In a well-organized essay, explain three factors that might cause you to change careers.

Select Instructional Materials

With the objectives and activities identified, the next step is to select the instructional materials that will help accomplish the objectives and support the learning activities. A systematic search would be made for texts, films, computer software, video tapes, and other instructional media. Since career education was for a while a high national priority, it would be simple to locate a variety of instructional materials. It should be noted here, however, that only materials which specifically fit the intended objectives are identified.

Identify Assessment Methods

The specialist would next determine which assessment methods are needed. Some assessment is done to evaluate readiness for a unit and to diagnose learner needs; some is done to provide the student and teacher with formative feedback to determine whether remediation is needed; and some is done to make summative judgments for grading purposes. In addition to the usual written tests, the specialist might decide to make use of other assessment methods, such as interviews, observations, or performance tests.

The specialist planning the career course, after consultation with measurement specialists, might decide on the following tests: one diagnostic test to determine specific learning needs of each student; one short formative test for each lesson; one longer formative test for each group of five lessons; and one final summative test covering the entire course.

Develop the Curriculum Guide

The final step is to systematize all these decisions into a curriculum guide. While the format varies from district to district, most guides developed from the processes described above include the following components:

1. A rationale for the course or a statement of the philosophy that guided the course planners.
2. A list of the objectives, ordered in the desired sequence.
3. The recommended learning activities, displayed graphically so that their relationship to the objectives is very clear. In some cases activities are described under each objective; in some guides, the objectives and activities are arranged in parallel columns.
4. A list of recommended instructional materials.
5. Copies of tests and suggestions for other assessment activities.

The Technological Process Summarized

Observe certain key features of the technological approach. The basic flow of the decision-making process might be described as progressing from specific to general or as "bottom-up"—specific outcomes are identified and then clustered into related sets of learning experiences. Objectives play a central role: they are specified early in the design process and control the selection of learning activities and instructional materials. The process essentially is thus ends-oriented: methods are determined on the basis of the extent to which they accomplish specified outcomes. And the process is primarily a linear one. While many advocates of the technological process provide for feedback and correction in the development stage, for the most part the steps proceed in linear fashion—do step 1, then step 2, and so on.

There are several advantages of this technological approach, when used by an expert or team of knowledgeable people. It seems orderly and systematic and thus might be more readily mastered by those less skilled in curriculum work. It seems efficient, since all decisions are made in relationship to outcomes. And, when the outcomes can be rendered into precise sequential objectives, it is perhaps very effective, since those objectives tightly control the activities used. For these reasons, the technological approach has been widely used in military and industrial training.

However, it has several significant limitations. It seems insensitive to the politics of curriculum making. Most curricular decisions in schools are inherently political, since they involve issues of power and "turf." The new course in career planning, for example, might be opposed by any teachers who include career units in the courses they already teach; they would see the new course as dealing with content they believed they owned. The technological process also seems to slight the importance of learning activities: learning activities are selected only if they accomplish some predetermined objective. It could be argued that some activities, such as group inquiry, have intrinsic worth, regardless of their fit with a particular set of learning activities.

Furthermore, the technological process does not reflect the reality of curriculum planning. As Walker (1971) notes, most major curriculum projects have not followed the technological model; the leaders of such projects have tended to operate in ways that might be described as less systematic, and more discursive and interactive. (It should be noted here that Walker seems to have been the first to argue for a naturalistic process.) Finally, the technological process is insufficiently responsive to the realities of teacher planning. Several studies (see, for example, Clark, 1983) indicate quite clearly that teachers tend not to begin their planning by identifying objectives. They often begin by deciding on useful activities and consider objectives only at a later point in the planning process.

THE NATURALISTIC PROCESS OF CURRICULUM PLANNING

An awareness of these limitations of the technological process and extensive work with curriculum specialists and teachers have led to the development of a special version of the naturalistic process. The process attempts to embody these characteristics:

- It attempts to be sensitive to the political aspects of curriculum making.
- It places greater emphasis on the quality of the learning activities.
- It attempts to reflect more accurately the way curricula have actually been developed.
- It takes cognizance of the way teachers really plan for instruction.

In the discussion which follows, the steps in the process are described in the order in which they ordinarily would be taken, although other sequences could just as well be followed. In fact, the process has been conceptualized as an interactive and recursive one, in which flexibility is emphasized. To illustrate these steps and to highlight comparisons with the technological approach, the discussion again uses the development of a new course for high school students in career planning. It then shows how an elementary team would use the same process in developing an integrated unit.

Assess the Alternatives

Before developing a new course, the naturalistic process begins with a systematic examination of the alternatives to a new course. Although many of those using a technological approach begin in the same manner, some technological developers seem to move too quickly from the identification of need to the development of the course.

To understand why this assessment of alternatives is important, consider how the initiative for a new course usually develops. Someone with a stake in the outcome—such as a principal, department head, or teacher—assumes that a new course is needed. How does such a conviction develop? Typically, it arises as a consequence of what March and Olsen (1976) call the "garbage-can" model of decision making—key individuals toss solutions into the organizational "garbage can" and then search for problems that might accommodate those solutions. A new principal is appointed and looks for an innovative curriculum project in order to create the impression that he or she is a "mover and shaker." A group of influential business people, unhappy with the quality of applicants for entry positions, put pressure on the superintendent to "do something about career education." A teacher whose existing courses are attracting fewer students sees the new course as a means of avoiding reassignment to the middle school.

Only in rare instances does the conviction emerge from a rational analysis of the data available. Even though most experts urge curriculum supervisors to use such information sources as test scores, parent surveys, and student interviews, such data are often sought to justify a predetermined solution, not to establish the need for a given response.

For this reason it is important for someone in authority—such as the director of curriculum or the principal—to examine the alternatives before allowing the decision to offer a new course to move ahead too quickly. Any new course is costly. It involves, first of all, what economists call "opportunity cost"—every student who takes the new course loses in the process the opportunity for some other educational experience. It also involves substantial development cost—the time and efforts of those responsible for planning it. And finally it involves significant implementation costs—the funds needed to staff the course, provide facilities, and secure the necessary equipment and materials.

What are the alternatives to offering a new course? Several alternatives are available for those interested in a new course in career planning.

- Ignore the need, based on the assumption that somehow adolescents will acquire the career-planning skills they need without organizational intervention.
- Ask some other agency to respond to the need. Decide that helping adolescents make wise career choices is the responsibility of the family, or the business community, or the YMCA—not the school.
- Provide for the need through the activities program. Arrange for

assemblies, career-planning days, or career clubs; develop programs for the homeroom.

- Use noncurricular methods of responding to the need. Put career materials in the library; buy computer software on career planning and make it available in the guidance suite; increase the guidance staff, adding specialists in career planning.
- Integrate the skills into existing courses. In each existing subject, include units in the careers that emphasize career-planning skills.

It is not suggested here that any of these alternatives is necessarily better than offering a new course. The point is simply that the alternatives should be examined before finally deciding that a new course is needed.

Stake Out the Territory

If it still appears that a new course is the most desirable option, then the next step is to stake out the territory. In general, the process of staking out the territory is very similar to that of identifying course parameters. The planning team considers the students for whom the course is intended, makes some initial determinations about the schedule, and tentatively identifies the coverage of the course. (Note that the active parties in the naturalistic process are identified as a planning team, in contradistinction to the curriculum specialist, since teams of teachers more typically are involved in using the naturalistic process.)

However, there is an important difference between identifying the course parameters and staking out the territory—a difference connoted by the metaphors used. The identification of course parameters tends to be more definitive and final; the staking out of the territory is a more tentative and open-ended boundary-setting process.

By consulting with those in authority, by examining whatever data are readily available, and by reflecting about the perceived need for the course, the team determines some tentative answers to the following questions:

1. For which group of students is the course primarily intended? What grade levels will be included? What ability levels?
2. Will the course be elective or required?
3. What is the probable duration of the course—a marking period, a term, a year?
4. What weekly schedule at this stage seems most desirable—how many times a week should classes meet, and how long should each class meeting be?
5. What will the course cover? What is the content? What general ideas and skills do we hope to develop?
6. Will the written materials focus only on the mastery curriculum, or will they also include organic and enrichment content? (See Chapter 1 for an explanation of these concepts as they relate to course development.)

7. How will the new course relate to existing courses in the school's program of studies? Is it part of a proposed sequence of courses? Is it intended to relate closely to the content of other courses?

In order to assist in further development, the course territory should be described in a course prospectus. The course prospectus presents the answers to the questions listed above—and does so in a manner that will both guide planners and inform others. In the case of the career course, the prospectus might read as follows:

> We're thinking about offering a new course tentatively entitled "Thinking about Careers." As we see the course now, it would be an elective offered to all juniors and seniors, although our hunch is that it would probably appeal most of all to those not presently interested in higher education. It would probably run for one term, meet three times a week, for a total of about forty classroom hours. As we presently conceptualize the course, it would help students examine their career values, assess career skills, learn how to retrieve career information, and do some systematic career planning. It would probably de-emphasize the study of particular careers and focus on processes instead. Our written materials will include only the mastery component, not enrichment or organic content. All of these notions are very tentative; we need the advice of anyone competent and interested.

Observe that the description is general and the language tentative. The intent is to identify broad boundaries that will be flexible enough to accommodate the ideas of all those who will later be involved in the more detailed planning. And the tentative language clearly suggests that no final decisions have been made.

Develop a Constituency

As noted above, all curriculum making has a political aspect. Those developing the new course wield power to advance their own interests. While genuinely concerned with improving the education of students, they are also motivated by personal interests: to enhance their reputations, to make their positions more secure, to win the attention of superiors. And those opposed to the course resist for similarly personal reasons. While articulating sincere professional reservations, they are also moved by personal needs. They are jealous of the course developers and resent the attention the developers are receiving. They are worried about the impact of the new course on enrollments in their department. And since resources always seem scarce, they are justifiably concerned about where the money will come from.

For this reason it is important throughout the naturalistic process for course planners to build a constituency for the new course—to mobilize support and neutralize likely opposition. How much time and energy are devoted to such politicking will depend, of course, upon the likely impact of the proposed change and the extent to which the course seems to have broad-based support.

How is such support developed? While the specific answers will depend upon local factors, there are some general strategies that seem to be effective.

Win the Support of the Powerful   Early in the process, course planners should try to secure the endorsement of those with power. Several studies (see, for example, Leithwood and Montgomery's 1982 review) indicate that in most schools the principal plays a key role as the curriculum gatekeeper. If the principal supports a curriculum change, the process moves along well. If the principal opposes the change, major problems develop: meetings are canceled, requisitions are delayed, space is unavailable. Central office supervisors who try to impose curricular changes on resistant principals soon discover the folly of such attempts.

Respect the Opposition   One of the most effective ways of building support is manifesting an attitude of respect for those who oppose the course. While motivated by their own personal reasons, they also probably have some legitimate professional concerns. Listening and responding to those concerns is not only politically wise but also professionally sound.

Share the Power and the Glory   Make the new course "our course," not "my course." Open up the planning process to all those who want to participate. Make a special effort to involve the undecided. Spread the credit around in all public discussions: "We're making good progress in finding speakers—thanks to the special efforts of Dr. Walker."

Be Suitably Modest   Avoid making extravagant claims about the wonders of the course. Most teachers are a bit cynical about educational innovations and are more attracted by understatement: "We don't pretend that we can make them all better decision makers, but maybe they'll become just a little wiser in thinking about careers."

Be Prepared to Negotiate   The process of getting a new course approved often requires the art of negotiating. Especially when the opposition seems strong, course planners should give themselves room to bargain, by asking publicly for more than they hope to get: asking for four periods, hoping to get three; asking for two classrooms in the expectation of getting one.

All these strategies will require time. For that reason the process of developing a constituency is not initiated and then dropped; instead, it should continue throughout both the planning and implementation stages.

Build the Knowledge Base

As noted in Chapter 5, another fundamental step which should be initiated early is building the knowledge base—retrieving and systematizing information about the students, assessing faculty readiness, analyzing the relevant research, and identifying available materials and programs. Too often those using the technological process slight this crucial step: course planners begin with a cursory "needs assessment" of the students, ignore those who will be teaching the course, slight the research, and act as if nothing else has ever been done in the field before. Their subsequent decisions are less effective because they are less informed.

The questions listed in Figure 8–2 can guide the development of the knowledge base, as it relates to course development. Note that the questions here are not as comprehensive as those suggested in Chapter 5; since local course planners usually have limited resources, only the most important questions are listed.

The student questions are designed to help planners understand the constraints imposed by the characteristics of those likely to take the course. In contrast to the usual "needs assessment," which often turns out to be a useless documentation of the obvious ("students need to reflect about their career values"), this component of the knowledge base reminds developers of the reality they face in implementing the course successfully. Will the course attract less able, unmotivated students? Will many of them have serious reading problems? Will they have trouble understanding abstract concepts?

The teacher questions are intended to guide the developers in deciding how detailed the course planning should be and how much staff development will be required. Comments of the following sort illustrate how the answers might impinge on the planning process:

"We'll have to use teachers not too interested in teaching the course, so we can't expect too much extra time from them."

"This is a new field for most teachers; we'd better be rather explicit as to where to find materials."

"The course will be taught by a few of our most competent people, so we don't need to go into a lot of detail about teaching methods."

The research questions focus on course content and teaching/learning methods. Stated generally here so that they can apply to any new course, they perhaps should be rephrased more specifically by the planners so that they can be answered more readily. Thus, those developing the career-planning course might seek answers to these more specific questions:

- What do we know about the career values of adolescents?
- What do we know about general patterns of career choice? How stable are career decisions?
- What do we know about changing occupational trends?

FIGURE 8-2.   Questions To Answer in Building the Knowledge Base

The Students

Consider the students likely to take the course and find out . . .

1. What is the IQ range?
2. What levels of cognitive development are represented?
3. What is known about their academic achievement?
4. What are their predominant values and attitudes?
5. What similar learning experiences have they had before?

The Teachers

Consider the teachers likely to be assigned to the course and find out . . .

1. How interested are they in teaching the course?
2. How much do they know about the content likely to be covered by the course?
3. How effective are they as teachers?

The Research

Consider the course territory and find out . . .

1. What research is available that will help planners determine course content?
2. What research is available that will help planners select teaching/learning activities?

What's Available

Consider the course territory and find out . . .

1. Have similar courses have developed by national curriculum centers?
2. Have similar courses been offered by other schools?
3. What materials (texts, films, video tapes, computer software) are readily available in the field?

- What do we know about the skills needed for career decision making?
- What instructional methods seem to be most effective in developing decision-making skills?

Finally, the questions on "what's available?" help the planners profit from the experience and work of others. If they locate an excellent program developed by a major curriculum center, they may decide to adopt it with modifications. If they examine courses that seem to have been successful in other schools, they can make better decisions about organizing content and selecting learning activities. And if they are able to locate very useful instructional materials, they can give those materials a key place in the units and lessons developed. As will be noted below, sometimes it is useful to find excellent materials first, and then choose objectives to fit the materials.

Block in the Unit

With the knowledge base developed, the next step that should usually be taken is to block in the units—to determine the number and focus of each unit of study that will make up the new course. Note that while the recommended direction is top-down (from general to specific, from unit to lesson), in some cases it might be desirable to reverse the flow—to identify lessons and then cluster lessons into units.

In blocking in the units, planners make tentative decisions about these issues:

1. How many units of study are planned?
2. How many lessons will there probably be in each unit?
3. What is the general objective of each unit?
4. What is the optimal sequence of the units?

One "unit-blocking" process that seems to work well in most disciplines is the following one. First, identify the probable number of units by reviewing the course territory and assessing the interest span of the learners. "We're planning a one-semester course that will meet three times a week, and many of the learners will probably have a short attention span, so maybe we need about seven to nine units—some two weeks long, some three weeks long."

Then tentatively identify the general objective of each unit. The unit objective, as the term is used here, is the one general outcome desired at the end of the unit. It might be a theme that ties the lessons together ("the changing American family"), an overarching concept that subsumes several more specific concepts ("ethnicity"), or a general skill that embraces many behaviors ("choosing the right college"). At this stage of the planning, the unit objective can be stated imprecisely, in terms that are not necessarily measurable. Initially the list of tentative unit objectives can be a random collection of good ideas, which will later be refined and systematized.

How can the tentative unit objectives be produced? One method that seems to work well is to convene the planning team, review with them the course prospectus and the knowledge base, and then ask, "What do we really want the students to learn?" The discussion that ensues should be somewhat free-wheeling, with the leader accepting any ideas offered. The intent is to develop a somewhat comprehensive list that can next be refined.

Here is a list of the tentative unit objectives that might be produced by those developing the career course:

Understanding your career values
Learning about your skills and aptitudes
Thinking about the education you need
Retrieving and using career information
Career-mobility skills
Matching self and careers
Learning from other people—parents, successful role models

Changing occupational needs
Reading the want ads
Preparing a resume
Different ways of looking at careers—jobs, careers, vocations.

Once the tentative list of unit objectives has been developed, the planning team should review the list in order to refine it. The refining process attempts to reduce the number of unit objectives to match the number of units previously identified, and to ensure that the final list closely matches the course territory. Questions of the following sort should be asked:

- Which unit objectives might be combined?
- Which unit objectives are of low priority and might be eliminated?
- Which unit objectives are tangential to the central thrust of the course and might be eliminated?

The refining stage is also the best time to make a tentative decision about the number of lessons. In making this decision, the team should reflect about the complexity and importance of the unit and the attention span of the learners, realizing, of course, that the decision is only a preliminary one. Making a preliminary decision at this point in the planning process enables the planners to be sure that they have not listed too many unit objectives. It also provides some information that will be useful when they get to the next stage of planning each unit in detail.

Thus, the team planning the career course might produce a final list such as the following one, in which both the unit objectives and the probable numbers of lessons are indicated:

Careers, jobs, and vocations: 6
Looking at yourself—skills, aptitudes, values: 6
Changing occupational needs: 6
Retrieving and using career information: 9
Matching self and careers: 6
Thinking about further education: 9
Finding the first full-time job: 9

The final step in this stage of blocking out the units is determining the optimal sequence. Again, as with the technological process, course planners would have several types of sequences available to them. However, those using the naturalistic process ordinarily combine several types of sequence, giving considerable weight to student interest and the rhythms of the school year. They typically ask such questions as the following:

- What unit will quickly capture student attention?
- How does the flow of units match the school calendar?
- Which units will best get them through the doldrums between semester exams and the spring break?
- Which units are most complicated and need some foundation units?
- Which unit would make a strong ending?

Obviously the units in the career-planning ccourse could be sequenced in several possible ways, each of which might work for a particular group of students.

Plan Quality Learning Experiences

With the units blocked out, the next stage in the process is planning quality learning experiences—designing a set of learning experiences that together will lead to the unit objective. It is at this stage perhaps that the naturalistic process differs most significantly from the standard model; it therefore might be useful at this point to clarify the distinction.

In the technological model, the objectives drive the planning process. They determine the activities and influence the choice of materials. The intent is to control the learning process to ensure that a predetermined end is achieved. And the process is linear and unidirectional, as Figure 8–3 suggests.

In the naturalistic process the planners attempt to design quality learning experiences—stimulating teaching/learning transactions that will produce several desirable outcomes, some of which might occur serendipitously. They think about the learners—their learning styles, their motivations, their abilities. They keep in mind the unit objective, as the general outcome to be attained, and reflect about the more specific objectives it comprises. They search for excellent materials that will have high interest value and good in-

FIGURE 8–3. The Technological Process

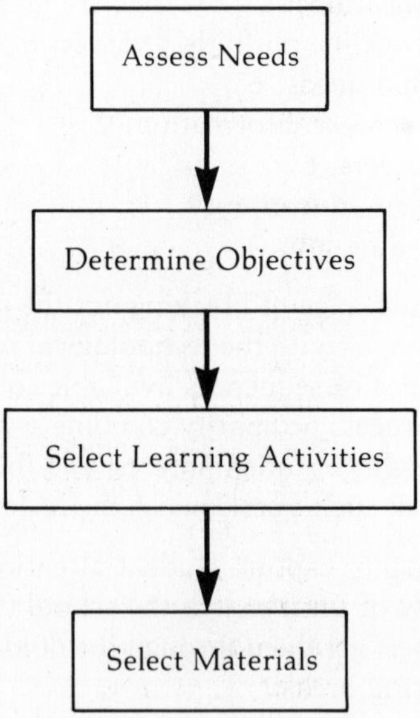

structional payoff. They reflect about learning activities that will appeal to the learners, will challenge them to think, and will give them an opportunity to be creative.

Sometimes the specific objectives will dominate their thinking, as in the technological approach. Sometimes, however, planners will begin by thinking about materials, and will derive an objective from a particularly fine text or film. "I know of an excellent film on career values—let's show it." And often they will begin by thinking about a learning activity, something intrinsically worthwhile regardless of its outcome. "I think it would be a good idea for the students to interview their parents about their career values, just as a way of getting to see their parents in a different light."

Thus, in the naturalistic model, objectives, materials, and activities are all examined in an interactive and recursive manner as components of quality learning experience. Figure 8-4 illustrates this process.

FIGURE 8–4.   The Naturalistic Model

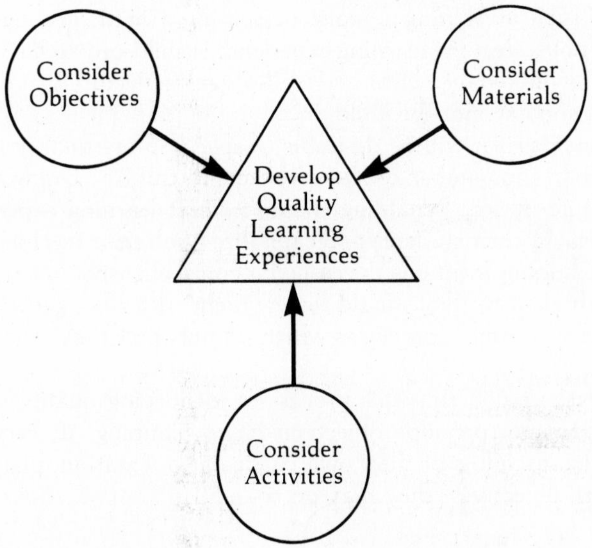

The intent is to develop plans for quality learning experiences—meaningful learning transactions mediated by the teacher. Such quality learning experiences should meet several important criteria:

1. The learning experience is meaningful—it provides an opportunity for students to discover meaning, to make sense of their experience, to integrate knowledge.
2. The learning experience is involving—its nature is such that it is likely to

involve all students, not just a few, in the active processing of experience. Some of that active processing will be mental, and perhaps not always observable, but it will not be a passive receiving of information.

3. The learning experience is multiple—it requires the use of many learning styles, modalities, and talents.

4. The learning experience is ethical—it does not require deception on the part of students or teachers or in any way diminish the dignity of participants.

5. The learning experience is challenging—it requires the students to acquire new information, but also to process that information, to synthesize it, to apply it, and to create new forms.

6. The learning experience is appropriate—for both the context (the school classroom) and the participants (the students and the teacher).

7. The learning experience is relevant—it relates directly to the unit objective. It is not included simply because it is interesting.

Notice that the criteria do not include "the learning experience is enjoyable." Some learning requires hard work and, occasionally, drudgery—such as writing a story or solving a math problem. And the criteria do not state, "the learning experience is child-centered." Some learning can be facilitated by a clear and well-organized lecture that derives from the subject content, not the child.

In many cases it will be desirable to specify more quality learning experiences than the number of lessons seems to call for. Doing so will give teachers some options, enabling them to select learning experiences that would appeal to their students and capitalize upon their teaching strengths. After the planning team has developed a comprehensive list of productive learning experiences, they should review them critically against the criteria specified above. Any experiences which do not meet those tests should be eliminated.

Observe, finally, that this process of identifying quality learning experiences does not preclude objectives-based planning. If, because of the nature of the discipline or their own curricular orientation, planners prefer to start with objectives, they may do so.

Develop the Course Examination

The naturalistic process places less emphasis on assessment. Rather than developing in advance several detailed assessment devices, course planners ensure that teachers are given the staff development needed to make their own ongoing assessments. However, a final course examination is usually included, both to help teachers make a summative assessment and to aid administrators in aligning the curriculum. (See Chapter 11 for a discussion of curriculum alignment.)

Develop the Learning Scenarios

Instead of using the standard curriculum guide, the naturalistic process culminates in the production and dissemination of *learning scenarios* for each unit of study. A learning scenario, as the term is used here, is a more flexible and open-ended guide to assist the teacher in implementing the new course. It includes these components:

1. A clear and detailed statement of the unit objective.
2. A suggested number of lessons.
3. A list of recommended quality learning experiences, phrased in a way that integrates objectives, activities, and materials.
4. Reprints of articles, maps, and photographs that teachers could use in making lesson plans. Observe that resources are not just listed—they are included. (The copyright law allows such professional use in a teacher's guide if three conditions are met: proper credit is given; the guide is not sold for profit; and the articles are not reproduced for student use.)

An example of a learning scenario is shown in Figure 8–5, p. 216.

Adapting the Naturalistic Model for Elementary Grades

The naturalistic model can also be used effectively at the elementary level, making some simple modifications in the model. Assume that a fourth-grade team of teachers, teaching in self-contained classrooms, decide to plan together a unit on "communication," using the naturalistic model. The steps they would take are as follows.

Stake Out the Territory   They begin by defining the boundaries of the unit, considering the pupils, the schedule, the general content of the unit, and the length. They would produce a prospectus for themselves and the principal which might read like this:

> We would like to work together in developing an integrated unit on communications for our fourth-graders. It will be for all our pupils; we'll try to reach even the least able and challenge the gifted. As we see it now, it will emphasize language arts but will also include some content from social studies, science, music, and art. We think we will need about an hour each day for the unit, probably for a three-week period.

Develop the Knowledge Base   They begin this phase by getting good information about their pupils, reviewing their abilities and checking with second- and third-grade teachers to determine what was taught in

FIGURE 8-5. Learning Scenario: Self-Understanding and Career Planning

Course: Career Planning

Unit objective: At the end of the unit it is hoped that the students will have a clearer sense of their talents, skills, and values as they relate to the career-planning process. The goal is to help students become somewhat more realistic as they think about careers—but not to box themselves in or aim too low. Keep reminding them that weak talents can be developed, that new skills can be acquired, that values change with age and experience.

Suggested number of lessons: 6 to 8

Quality learning experiences: (These are listed in what seems to be a desirable sequence, but you should feel free to modify the order as you see fit.)

1. Have students write a paper which they could share with peers, parents, and counselors on "My Ideal Career." Provide some good prewriting discussion and allow time for revision. This is a good initiating activity; the paper will provide you and the student with some baseline data—how the student thinks about self and careers before the unit starts.
2. Conduct a discussion of the nature of talents (the general aptitudes that we possess, such as a talent for music), skills (specific career-related behaviors we have mastered, such as being able to use a word processor), and values (those aspects of life we consider worthwhile, such as liking to be outdoors). Emphasize: people have multiple talents and skills; the strengths of those talents and skills vary for each individual; while all talents and skills have intrinsic worth, our culture accords them varying merit; all of us have different values as they relate to careers.
3. Help students analyze test scores and grades as a way of understanding themselves. If possible, ask the guidance counselor to prepare a test-and-grade profile for each student and to discuss the uses and limitations of test scores and school grades in assessing talents, skills, and values.
4. Have each student develop a talent profile. Identify the range of talents people possess—mechanical, verbal, mathematical, scientific, musical, physical, artistic, interpersonal, managerial. Chart your own highs and lows on the profile, to illustrate that talents are differentially strong in one individual.

(continued next page)

earlier grades about communication in general. They discuss their own expertise and background in the field. They review the research on the cognitive development and communication interests of the age group. And they take some time to see what is available, checking especially on instructional materials.

Block in the Unit Now they proceed to block in the unit. They have tentatively considered the general content and think they can spend three weeks on the unit before pupil interest wanes. They move now to consider the general outcomes that they hope to achieve, producing this tentative statement:

FIGURE 8.5 *continued*

5. Help each student develop a skills inventory. Most students will probably believe that they have few career-related skills. Help them reflect about their part-time jobs, their school experiences, and their community experiences as sources of skills that can be used in a job.
6. Ask students to interview one or both parents about parental career values. Emphasize that the goal here is not to intrude on parents' privacy (the results will not be shared with classmates or the teacher), but to get a broader understanding of parents and to see whether parent values have influenced student values. Stress that most studies show similarities between core values of parents and of children. Teach students how to conduct a supportive interview, one that helps the interviewee be reflective about self. The students should probably summarize the results of the interviews in their journals, only to systematize what they know—but these summaries need not be shared with the teacher. You may wish to check just to be sure that they were written.
7. Arrange for students to take the values section of the program called SIGI (System of Interactive Guidance and Information). This is a software program produced by Educational Testing Services and available in the guidance office, which gives students some useful information on their career values. The results will need some discussion in class.
8. As a culminating activity, ask students to write a final paper on the topic, "Seeing myself in relation to careers." They'll probably need some prewriting help in organizing all the information they have collected. This will also provide a good opportunity for teaching students how to present information in a table or a figure, and how to integrate tables, figures, and text.
9. As an enrichment activity for those with special interests in the subject, discuss how culture shapes career values. Ask them to speculate about the career values of an Eskimo and those of an urban factory worker.

Additional resources: You'll find in the following pages some resources you might find helpful: a recent article on parent and teen values; an article by Calvin Taylor on talent profiles; a review of Howard Gardner's work on multiple intelligences; and an excerpt from a recent book on the work values of Soviet citizens.

We hope that by the end of the unit the pupils will have a beginning knowledge of what communication is, will understand the many ways people communicate with each other, will know something about how animals communicate, and will improve their own communication skills. Since we're trying to integrate some social studies, we also think we would like to introduce the idea of regional dialects; it would fit in well with our fourth-grade social studies unit on geographic regions.

With those general outcomes in mind, they discuss together the flow of the unit, moving to a more specific level but still not talking about precise learning objectives. They tentatively decide on a sequence of topics such as this one:

1. A general and simplified model of the communication process: a message sender sending a message to a message receiver, with feedback following. (Gifted pupils can explore the concepts of *signal* and *code.*)
2. People communicate in spoken and written words—the differences between the two media.
3. People communicate in nonverbal language.
4. People communicate with art and music.
5. People communicate with different dialects.
6. People communicate with machines—and machines with each other.
7. People communicate with animals—and animals with each other.

Develop Quality Learning Experiences   With those general topics listed and sequenced, they then brainstorm about the quality learning experiences they need. Again, as with the career unit, they begin with an activity, with learning materials, or with an objective. Here are some they might produce:

- Have pupils explore the use of nonverbal language by giving each an index card with a message they are to communicate without words. After several have done so, lead them in an analysis of what forms of nonverbal communication are most important. (Topic 3.)
- Ask two pupils to role-play a scene where one invites the other to a birthday party. Then have each member of the class write an invitation. Have them discuss the differences between the two forms, stressing the interactive nature of face-to-face spoken communication. (Topic 2.)
- Arrange to place telephone calls to fourth-graders in other dialect regions. Prepare pupils beforehand by having them list questions they want to ask about that region and its dialect. Stress that there are no "funny ways of talking." Each dialect sounds right to its own speakers and different to others. (Topic 5.)

Develop the Unit Test   The team would cooperate in developing the end-of-unit test, assessing all the learnings they considered important.

Develop the Learning Scenarios   As with the career unit, the teachers would systematize and package their work in a learning scenario.

The Naturalistic Model Summarized

The naturalistic model is characterized by several features which set it off from the technological model. It is looser, more flexible, and less rational, with many attributes of what Kirst and Walker (1971) call "disjointed incrementalism." It is more responsive to the political realities of curriculum making. It tends to be a "top-down" process, moving from the larger unit to the smaller lesson. It seems to be more in accord with the way teachers actually plan. And it gives equal weight to objectives, activities, and materials, rather than giving primary attention to objectives.

Its advantages seem clear. It should result in curricula that are more likely to be implemented, rather than shelved. Since it addresses the political reality of schools and since it is in accord with teachers' actual planning styles, it should have greater appeal to both principals and teachers. And it should result in more interesting and challenging learning experiences, since it emphasizes the intrinsic quality of the experience.

Its main drawback is its looseness. Especially in the hands of the inexperienced, it can result in a seemingly random collection of entertaining activities that seem unrelated to the intended outcomes.

APPLICATIONS

1. Consider this issue: should the choice of the technological or naturalistic process be influenced by the nature of the educational organization? If so, in what types of organizations should each be used?
2. To test your ability to use the technological model, do the following:
   1. Identify the parameters of a new course you might develop.
   2. List the learning objectives for the course.
   3. For one objective, identify the learning activities you would recommend.
3. To test your ability to use the naturalistic model, do the following:
   1. Describe the territory of a new course.
   2. List all unit objectives.
   3. For one unit, write at least four quality learning experiences.
4. Some who have used the naturalistic process have suggested that it is more suitable for elementary grades than for secondary. If you were an elementary principal, would you recommend that your teachers use the naturalistic process?

REFERENCES

Clark, C. M. (1983). *Research on teacher planning: An inventory of the knowledge base.* East Lansing, MI: Institute for Research on Teaching.

Kirst, M., and Walker, D. F. (1971). An analysis of curriculum policy making. *Review of Educational Research, 41,* 479–509.

Leithwood, K. A., and Montgomery, D. J. (1982). The role of the elementary principal in program improvement. *Review of Educational Research, 52,* 309–339.

Mager, R. F., and Beach, K. M., Jr. (1967). *Developing vocational instruction.* Palo Alto, CA: Fearon Publishers.

March, J. G., and Olsen, J. D. (1976). *Ambiguity and choice in organizations.* Bergen, Norway: Universitetsforlaget.

Posner, G. J., and Strike, K. A. (1976). A categorization scheme for principles of sequencing content. *Review of Educational Research, 76,* 665–690.

Posner, G. J., and Rudnitsky, A. N. (1982). *Course design: A guide to curriculum development for teachers* (2nd Ed.). New York: Longman.

Tyler, R. W. (1949). *Basic principles of curriculum and instruction.* Chicago: University of Chicago Press.

Walker, D. F. (1971). A naturalistic model for curriculum development. *School Review, 80,* 51–65.

Wulf, K. M., and Schave, B. (1984). *Curriculum design: A handbook for educators.* Glenview, IL: Scott Foresman.

Part 3

Curriculum Management

9

Supervising the Curriculum: Teachers and Materials

Too many curriculum leaders focus unduly on the written curriculum, neglecting the taught curriculum and the supported curriculum. Obviously such a neglect is unwise and counterproductive. An excellent written curriculum will have little impact if it is not taught well and supported with appropriate materials. This chapter, then, examines how to improve these two often-slighted aspects of curriculum.

SUPERVISING THE TAUGHT CURRICULUM: CURRENT APPROACHES

Leaders concerned with supervising the taught curriculum have available to them several current approaches to supervision. The four that seem to have the greatest value are Hunter's (1984) *essential elements of lesson design,* Glickman's (1985) *developmental supervision,* Costa and Garmston's (1985) *cognitive coaching,* and Glatthorn's (1986) *differentiated professional development.* The first three are reviewed in this section; the last is explained more fully in the next section.

Hunter's "Essential Elements"

During the middle of the 1980s, the work of Madeline Hunter seemed to be the dominant mode of supervision: several state offices of education, in fact, had given the Hunter approach their official blessing and encouraged its adoption through workshops for administrators, supervisors, and teachers. Although Hunter herself advocated a number of "templates" that could be used to analyze and improve teaching, her "elements of lesson design" attracted the most attention. By reviewing the theory of and research on learning, Hunter was able to identify the following elements of good lesson design:

Anticipatory set: Developing in students a mental set that causes them to focus on what will be learned.

Objective and purpose: Stating what is to be learned and how it will be useful.

Input: Giving students information about the knowledge, skill, or process they are to achieve.

Modeling: Demonstrating the process or skill.

Guided practice: Directing the student practice of the new process or skill.

Independent practice: Assigning independent practice of the process or skill.

What made the Hunter "elements" so popular with practitioners? First, they were based on sound theory, even though the research base seemed thin to some critics. Second, they gave educators a common vocabulary to discuss teaching: everyone could talk about "anticipatory set" and know what was meant. Finally, they seemed "teacher-friendly": they did not require teachers to adopt new behaviors but instead helped teachers systematize what they had already been doing.

Her approach, however, was not without its critics—most of whom were university professors, not practitioners. Those critics faulted the model, first of all, because it offered a narrowly constricted view of teaching. Sergiovanni (1985) made the point that she conceived teaching and learning only as "an instructional delivery system," a conception that saw teaching as sending information through a pipeline to passive students. Others were unhappy because the elements seemed to be derived from the direct instruction model of teaching and slighted other models, although Hunter argued that the elements could be used flexibly in any model of teaching.

Although many administrators who had adopted the Hunter "elements" approach reported enthusiastic reception on the part of teachers and noted many positive effects, the early research on its impact on achievement indicated that it was not more effective than standard approaches to supervision. (See Stallings, 1986.)

Glickman's Developmental Supervision

Carl Glickman's (1985) "developmental supervision" is characterized by two important features that set it off from Hunter's work. First, he argues that the development of teacher thought should be the focus of supervisors' work with teachers—helping teachers increase their conceptual level of development. He posits three levels of development: low abstract (the teacher is confused, lacks ideas, wants to be shown, gives habitual responses to varying decisions); moderate abstract (depends on authority, identifies one dimension of instructional problem, generates one to three ideas about solutions, needs assistance from experts); and high abstract (uses various sources to identify problems, generates multiple ideas, chooses for self the action to be taken).

This "thought-oriented" approach permeates the four ways he believes supervisors can help teachers grow: by offering direct assistance (what is usually called "clinical supervision"); by providing inservice education; by working with teachers in curriculum development; and by helping them carry out action research.

Although Glickman admits that the results on developmental supervision have been "predictably mixed," both features make the model seem very useful for curriculum leaders. He recognizes the fact that teachers are different and require different approaches. And he broadens the prevailing understanding of supervision by emphasizing the importance of inservice, curriculum-development, and action research.

Costa and Garmston's Cognitive Coaching

Like Glickman, Costa and Garmston (1985) emphasize the importance of teacher thinking. However, their approach seems quite different. Rather than using all the approaches that Glickman advocates, they give their attention exclusively to direct assistance or clinical supervision. However, it is clinical supervision with a profound difference. They are not concerned initially with skills; they believe it more productive to emphasize teacher thinking. As the supervisor works with teachers in this cognitive coaching mode, the supervisor has these goals: to create and manage a trusting relationship; to facilitate teacher learning by restructuring teacher thinking; and to develop teacher autonomy. Those goals are achieved primarily through in-depth conferences, in which the supervisor listens actively, questions insightfully, and responds congruently.

Although the authors indicate that their approach has been based on current theory and sound research on adult development, they do not offer any empirical evidence about its effectiveness. Its emphasis on teacher thinking and its concern for teacher autonomy both seem to be useful from the standpoint of curriculum leaders. There are, however, two problems that would seem to limit its effectiveness. First, it would seem to require a great deal of time on the part of administrators and supervisors to use it effectively with all teachers. Second, it demands a high level of skill: the "cognitive coach" is really acting as a sensitive counselor.

DIFFERENTIATED PROFESSIONAL DEVELOPMENT

Differentiated professional development (Glatthorn, 1986) is essentially a reconceptualization of the supervisory function, one that attempts to broaden the practitioner's view of supervision. Glatthorn argues that one of the reasons that educational leaders neglect the taught curriculum is that they hold a very narrow view of supervision. Too often it is equated with clinical supervision—the intensive process of observing a teacher, analyzing observational data, and giving the teacher feedback about such data. There are several reasons why such a narrow view is unproductive. First, clinical supervision is so time-consuming that principals especially find it impossible to provide it for everyone. Second, clinical supervision is only one of several means for facilitating the professional development of teachers; other processes, as Glickman notes, should be used. Also, not all teachers need clinical supervision; experienced, competent teachers need some options. Finally, most models of clinical supervision do not give sufficient attention to major aspects of curriculum. For these reasons, leaders who wish to improve the taught curriculum need to reconceptualize the supervisory process—to see it more broadly, and to differentiate its use in relation to teacher need.

Such a reconceptualization, Glatthorn notes, can make a modest contribution to what Sergiovanni (1986) calls a "theory of practice for supervision"—a theory that takes account of the complex messiness of classrooms and teaching, that uses the practical language of classroom life, that is sensitive to the way teachers and supervisors construe classroom meanings, and that is explicitly designed to improve teaching and learning. In this attempt to reconceptualize supervision, it seems useful to substitute the term *professional development* for those activities ordinarily subsumed under the heading of *supervision*. The advantage of using new terminology is that it facilitates the task of reconceptualizing the field by distancing users from the restrictive assumptions implicit in the old language. In this reconceptualization, *professional development* is used in this sense:

> All those systematic processes used by school administrators, supervisors, and teachers to help teachers grow professionally.

Those professional development processes are divided into four distinct yet related tasks: staff development, informal observations, rating, and individual development.

Staff Development

Staff development is used here to designate all those district- and school-sponsored programs, both formal and informal, offered to groups of teachers in response to organizational needs. The importance of staff development has been noted in Chapter 5, as an aspect of the planning process, and in Chapter 7, as a critical ingredient in improving a field of study. There are several issues that seem important here in examining staff development as an aspect of broader professional development.

First, staff development can be both formal and informal. Formal staff-development programs are those with a specific agenda, a set schedule, and a structured set of experiences. Typically such formal programs are skill-focused. And the research on such skill-focused programs suggests that they will be more effective if they embody the tested practices recommended in Chapter 7.

However, even the best formal programs seem to make two major errors. Too many seem unduly concerned with the linear transmission and translation of knowledge into practice, using consultants who, in effect, say, "Here is the research on effective teaching; let me explain how you should use it." For example, contributors to the 1983 National Society for the Study of Education yearbook on staff development recommend that those planning the content of staff development should begin by examining the results of the Beginning Teacher Evaluation Study, a research project conducted in the late 1970s, in second- and fifth-grade classrooms. (See Howey and Vaughan, 1983.)

While there is an obvious need for teachers to be informed about such research, much better results could be achieved by using an approach which Buchmann (1985) calls "conversation about teaching," a dialogic encounter of peers. Buchmann describes the tone of such conversation in this fashion:

> *In conversation, ideas . . . collide and mingle with one another and are diluted and complicated in the process. The pleasant tone of conversation is inimical to doctrinaire notions. In conversation, one may differ and still not disagree; the defensive, corrective, and didactic aspects of rhetoric are out of place. People do not insist that partners follow; it is enough that they enter into conversation. Thus, conversation respects great differences and ranges easily over different provinces of meaning: dreams, play, science, and action.* (p. 449)

Thus we might imagine a dialogic staff-development session in which a linguist, a district language arts coordinator, an English department chair, a principal, and several English teachers are holding a conversation about the teaching of grammar, discussing the contributions of contemporary grammars, the functions of teaching grammar, the implications of research on the teaching of grammar, and the possibilities of conducting classroom-based research on students' use of language.

The second error reflected in too many district staff-development programs is that they are too individualistic and neglect organizational needs. Here the position taken by Fielding and Schalock (1985) in their review of staff development seems to be a reasonable one:

> *[Staff] development rarely responds to overall district priorities for improvement. Inservice activities are more likely to deal with a series of discrete and unrelated topics or a common theme. It appears that one of the most important responsibilities of central office staff is to anchor plans for staff development to long-term district goals. (p. 56)*

So formal staff-development programs can be effective if they reflect sound research, create a spirit of dialog, and respond to district goals. However, they should be supplemented with an array of informal staff-development approaches. Ineffective principals and supervisors complain that they do not have time for staff development; effective leaders use whatever time is available. They work with small groups of teachers during preparation periods, over lunch, and in faculty meetings in a less systematic and structured fashion, sharing ideas, discussing current educational issues, and engaging in some informal problem solving.

As noted in previous chapters, staff development of both the formal and informal types is essential throughout the curriculum development and improvement process. If staff development has helped teachers change their perceptions of a subject, develop the materials to be used in implementing the new curriculum, and acquire the skills needed to deliver it, then it is quite likely that the written, the taught, the tested, and the learned curricula will be in much closer congruence.

Informal Observations

Informal observations are brief, unannounced classroom visits, lasting perhaps from five to fifteen minutes. Some term these informal visits "walk-throughs"; some experts in the corporate world call such informal observations "managing by walking around."

The process of making numerous brief and informal observations can serve several purposes. It is a useful way of making the principal and the supervisor more visible and less office-bound, thus reducing the isolation that most teachers feel. It provides excellent opportunities for both principal and supervisor to reinforce and praise good teaching—catching teachers doing something right. It can provide useful data about curriculum implementation. And it can alert leaders to curricular and instructional problems before they become critical.

How much value do such informal observations have? Here there is an interesting paradox. While many of the standard texts on supervision disparage such visits and insist that all observations should be for a full period and should be preceded by a conference, the research suggests otherwise. Several reviews of the research on effective schools (see, for example, Squires, Huitt, and Segars, 1981) conclude that in such schools the educational leader is highly visible, frequently monitors the classroom, stays well informed about daily life in the school, and demonstrates an interest in instruction by spending much time in the classroom. All these functions can be accomplished through informal observations. And in every school system where the author has helped institute a program of informal observations, the teachers have welcomed the process as long as it is not linked to the rating system.

Although there does not seem to be any research available on how to make informal observations most effective, the experience of successful principals and supervisors who use this process suggests that the following guidelines should be useful:

1. At the outset, administrators and supervisors should resolve through discussions with teachers whether the data from informal observations will be used as part of the teacher evaluation or rating process. Teachers will more readily accept the process if it is clear that informal observations are not linked with teacher evaluation, although many administrators would like to use such information in rating teachers.

2. Informal observations should be frequent and numerous. Effective principals and supervisors report that they attempt to make at least ten informal observations each week by reserving time in their weekly schedules. And most find it helpful to make the informals on a systematic basis, one week focusing on a particular grade level ("What's our fourth-grade program like?") and the next on a particular field ("How much science is being taught in our intermediate grades?")

3. Immediate feedback is important. If the observer is pleased with what has been observed, then a smile, a gesture of approval, or a brief note may be enough. If some concerns are felt, a brief face-to-face conference is perhaps needed. At such a conference, the concern should be expressed only as a very tentative reaction: "I was there only for five minutes, of course, but I did note that you were discussing a book that I believe is taught in tenth grade—can you clarify this for me?"

4. The informal observations will probably have more value if observers vary their focus. Sometimes it is useful to concentrate on *what* is being taught—its level of difficulty and interest for the learners. At times the *pace* of instruction and curriculum delivery should be noted—how much the teacher has covered so far. At times the *method* should be the center of attention. And at times the *learners* should be the concern.

Rating

In the reconceptualization, the term *rating* is used in this sense:

> The process of making formative and summative assessments of teacher performance for purposes of administrative decision making.

The term is chosen to distinguish this formal assessment function from a more general act of evaluation, which in the context of this reconceptualization is construed to mean a judgment about the quality of performance made on any occasion for a variety of purposes. This distinction between rating and evaluation is intended to clarify the conceptual confusion that is so prevalent in our professional discourse. One interesting example of the conceptual confusion is McGreal's monograph titled *Successful Teacher Evaluation* (1983), which really seems to be a treatise on teacher supervision.

Perhaps some examples of the two concepts would provide more clarity. You make an informal observation of a teacher with a disorderly class. You make a judgment: you do not like what you see. You observe a teacher for the purpose of diagnosing teaching style. You try your best to be objective, but you find yourself smiling in approval. You conduct a staff-development session and ask one of the teachers to demonstrate a particular skill. You are not happy with the demonstration. In each instance you have made an evaluation—a judgment about quality. Despite all attempts to be objective, it is probably impossible to observe the act of teaching without making judgments. Most teachers would not want an observer to pretend that he or she had not made any judgments about their performance. And there is some evidence that supervisors who are candid about their assessments are judged to be more effective than those who do not provide evaluative feedback. (See Gersten, Green, and Davis, 1985.)

Now consider a contrary example. You visit a teacher's class in September with a rating form in hand, in which very explicit criteria are stated along with the standards of performance. You observe the class and complete the rating form. You confer with the teacher and say, "Your performance in that class was not satisfactory; I hope your supervisor will be able to help you improve before the next rating observation." You have made a formative rating. You make several more formative rating observations throughout the year. Then in May you make a summative assessment based upon all your data and say to the teacher, "Your performance this year was unsatisfactory; your contract will not be renewed."

Perhaps one more analogy will help. The gymnast performs a set of exercises in a meet. The coach watches and says, "Your approach was faulty; we'll have to work on that." The coach has made an evaluation. The judges were also watching. They hold up their scorecards with numerical scores on each. The judges have made a rating.

What rating systems are most effective? After studying thirty-two school districts reported to have effective rating systems, Wise and his colleagues (1984) reached five conclusions. (Their term *teacher evaluation* is used below, instead of the narrower term *rating*, since many of the systems included processes that in the reconceptualization are considered primarily developmental):

1. To succeed, the teacher-evaluation system must suit the goals, management style, conception of teaching, and community values of the school district.
2. Top-level commitment to and resources for evaluation are more important than the particular kind of checklist or procedures used.
3. The school district should decide about the main purpose of the rating system and then match the process to the purpose.
4. The evaluation process must be seen to have utility: it is cost-effective, valid, and reliable.
5. Teacher involvement in and responsibility for the process improves the quality of teacher evaluation.

Obviously these conclusions suggest that several types of rating systems can be effective. However, if the purpose is administrative decision making, then a criterion-based system using multiple observations seems preferable. One process that has been used effectively in several districts is described below.

Together, administrators, supervisors, and teachers analyze the job of teaching and the research on effective teaching. From those reviews they develop a comprehensive set of criteria dealing with the three important aspects of the teacher's role. First, they define the noninstructional aspects of the teacher's role. In most cases a short list of noninstructional responsibilities is all that is necessary: supervise students in noninstructional settings; communicate with parents; attend faculty meetings and staff-development sessions as required; carry out other assigned duties.

Then, by reviewing the research they identify the essential instructional skills that can be directly observed, such as providing a clear lesson structure. Finally, they identify the essential instructional skills that are probably not always directly observable, such as making valid tests. This research-based list of the "essential observables" and the "essential nonobservables" plays a crucial role in both rating teachers and helping them grow professionally. Therefore, care should be taken in ensuring that the list includes only those skills well supported by the research. One formulation of these skills is shown in Figure 9–1.

The essential observable skills become the basis of a Rating Observation Form which identifies each skill and for each one specifies several indicators of performance. A portion of one such form is shown in Figure 9–2. That form is then used in making a rating observation. The rater tells the teacher that he or she will be observing the class some time next week in order to rate performance. The teacher is familiar with both the criteria and the indicators and understands clearly that the purpose of the observation is to rate, not to improve instruction. The rater arrives with the rating observation form in hand. The rater observes solely to rate: he or she makes careful notes throughout the lesson about the teacher's performance in rela-

FIGURE 9–1. Essential Skills of Teaching

The following list of essential skills is intended to provide general guidelines for administrators, supervisors, and teachers. While based on a careful review of the literature and a reflective analysis of shared experience, it is not intended as a definitive prescription of "the best way to teach." Other cautions need to be noted:

1. The list focuses on the instructional role of the teacher; it does not address the important noninstructional responsibilities.
2. The list does not speak directly to the skills of lesson planning and communicating. As will be noted below, effective planning and clear communication lie behind several of the skills listed below.

ESSENTIAL SKILLS OBSERVABLE IN CLASSROOM INSTRUCTION

Lesson Content and Pace

1. Chooses content for the lesson that relates directly to curriculum goals, is at an appropriate level of difficulty, and corresponds with assessment measures.
2. Presents content of lesson in a way that demonstrates mastery of subject matter.
3. Paces instruction appropriately.

Climate

4. Creates a desirable environment that reflects appropriate discipline and supports the instructional function.
5. Communicates realistically high expectations for students.
6. Uses instructional time efficiently, allocating most of time to curriculum-related instruction.
7. Keeps students on task.

(continued next page)

tion to each of the criteria and then makes a holistic rating of the entire class. Then the rater holds a rating observation conference, informs the teacher of the general rating, reviews the specific strengths and weaknesses, and in conjunction with the teacher lays out a professional development plan for remedying any perceived deficiencies.

The essential nonobservable skills are assessed through conferences and the analyses of such relevant documents as teacher plans (yearly, term, unit, and daily plans), teacher-made tests, and teacher record book and grades. Suppose, for example, that the rater wishes to assess test-related skills. The rater informs the teacher that such an assessment will take place: "I'd like to work with you in assessing your tests; bring to the conference a test you plan to give, one you have given and scored, and some indication of how you use test results." The conference is held and the assessments are made; again, specific suggestions for improvement are provided. The teacher's performance of noninstructional responsibilities is assessed by means of the rater's day-to-day observations of such performance, recorded in an anecdotal record.

FIGURE 9-1. *continued*

Instruction

8. Provides organizing structure for classroom work: reviews, gives overview, specifies objectives, gives clear directions, summarizes, makes relevant assignments.
9. Uses instructional strategies, learning activities, and group structures that are appropriate to objectives, respond to student needs, and reflect sound learning theory.
10. Ensures active participation of students in learning activities.

Assessment

11. Monitors student learning and uses evaluative data to adjust instruction.
12. Questions effectively: asks clear questions; asks questions at appropriate level of difficulty; varies types of questions.
13. Responds effectively to student answers: allows sufficient wait time, gives prompt and corrective feedback, praises appropriately.

ESSENTIAL SKILLS NOT DIRECTLY OBSERVABLE IN CLASSROOM INSTRUCTION

1. Develops long-term plans that reflect curricular priorities and adequately deal with all aspects of written curriculum.
2. Uses tests that are consistent with instructional objectives.
3. Grades student learning fairly, objectively, and validly.

The above list of skills has been synthesized from several reviews of the research on teaching effectiveness. Three sources have been especially useful:

Berliner, D. C., (1984). The half-full glass: A review of the research on teaching. In P. Hosford (ed.), *Using what we know about teaching.* Alexandria, VA: Association for Supervision and Curriculum Development.
Brophy, J. E., and Good, T. L. (1986). Teacher behavior and student achievement. In M. C. Wittrock (ed.), *Handbook of research on teaching* (3rd Ed.), pp. 328–375. New York: Macmillan.
Rosenshine, B., and Stevens, R. (1986). Teaching functions. In M. C. Wittrock (ed.), *Handbook of research on teaching* (3rd Ed.), pp. 376–391. New York: Macmillan.

All these formative data are drawn together in a summative rating conference: the rater reviews with the teacher the teacher's performance of the noninstructional responsibilities, summarizes the results of all the rating observations, synthesizes the results of the conferences at which the nonobservable skills were assessed, and provides a final holistic rating of the teacher's performance for that year. The conference ends with a view to the future: how will the teacher build upon strengths and remedy any deficiencies?

Obviously, such a rating system will require a great amount of administrator and supervisor time if it is to be thorough—much more time than is perhaps warranted in relation to the value of the process for teachers who are known to be highly competent. Therefore, the reconceptualized model proposes two rating tracks: standard rating and intensive rating. The standard rating is used for career teachers whose performance is clearly satisfactory; it is a *pro forma* compliance with the state school code, usually involving one observation and one final conference. An intensive rating is used for all probationary teachers, for any teachers being considered for

FIGURE 9-2. Portion of Rating Observation Form

Teacher's Name _____ Rater _____

Class _____ Date and Time _____

Rating Code:

1, unsatisfactory; 2, satisfactory; 3, more than satisfactory; NA, not able to make a judgment.

1. Chooses content that relates directly to curriculum goals and assessment measures, at appropriate level of difficulty.

   1 Chooses unrelated content, too difficult or too easy.

   2 Chooses related content, with appropriate difficulty.

   3 Chooses related content, with appropriate difficulty, relates content to student needs and interests.

Rating _____

Observations Supporting Rating

Teacher Comments

Overall Rating for This Class: _____

1. Which essential teaching skill(s) does this teacher seem to use most successfully?

2. Which essential teaching skill(s) does this teacher need to improve?

special promotion, and for teachers whose level of performance is questionable. The intensive rating involves several observations by two or more observers, with a conference following each observation.

Individual Development

Individual development includes all the processes used by and with individual teachers to help them grow professionally. In contrast to staff development, the work is with the individual, not the group; and the needs of the individual, not the needs of the organization, predominate. For two reasons, a differentiated system of professional development is recommended—one that gives teachers some options in the type of developmental processes used. (A fuller explanation of how to implement a differentiated system can be found in Glatthorn, 1984.) First, as noted above, most principals are too busy to provide clinical supervision to all teachers. Second, teachers vary significantly in their conceptual development, in their learning styles, and in their professional needs; they thus should be provided with different types of developmental services. Accordingly, the differentiated system offers three options for individual development: intensive, cooperative, and self-directed.

Intensive development is what is ordinarily called "clinical supervision," although it is more broadly construed. It is an intensive and systematic process, in which a supervisor, an administrator, or an expert teacher works closely with an individual teacher in an attempt to effect significant improvement in the essential skills of teaching. While the intensive development is most needed by inexperienced and struggling teachers, it can be provided for any teacher who wants to work with a skilled educational leader to bring about significant improvement in teaching performance. In providing intensive development, the leader works closely with the teacher in determining which of several processes will be used. Rather than relying solely on planning conferences, observations, and debriefing conferences, they examine together a wide array of processes to determine which ones might be most effectively employed:

1. Planning conferences: conferring with the teacher on yearly planning, semester planning, unit planning, and daily planning.
2. Student-assessment conferences: conferring with the teacher about assessing student progress, testing, grading, and record keeping.
3. Diagnostic observations and diagnostic feedback: observing all significant transactions in a classroom in order to diagnose priority developmental needs and providing appropriate feedback.
4. Focused observations and feedback: observing one particular aspect of teaching and learning (such as classroom management) and providing appropriate feedback.
5. Video-tape analysis: making a video tape of teaching and analyzing it with the teacher in order to complement direct observation.
6. Coaching: developing a particular teaching skill by providing a rationale, explaining the steps, demonstrating those steps, providing a supportive environment in which the teacher can use the skill, and giving the teacher feedback.
7. Descriptive student feedback: surveying students for their perceptions of the classroom by asking them to offer descriptive (not evaluative) feedback.
8. Directed observation of a colleague: structuring and guiding an opportunity for the teacher to observe a colleague using a specific skill.

Thus, intensive development provides a variety of supportive services; and, to be most effective, those services are provided in a systematic manner. First, after an initial orientation session, the supervisor makes a diagnostic observation, one in which all important classroom interactions are recorded and analyzed in order to determine patterns of behavior. The supervisor analyzes those diagnostic data and tentatively identifies which skills can best be developed over the next two to three months. The supervisor and the teacher then confer about the observation. They review together those observational data and any other information they have and decide together on the skill-development agenda for the months ahead.

They formalize this decision in a Professional Development Plan, which lists the skills to be developed, the resources to be used, and the deadlines to be met.

They then begin to work together on the first skill. The supervisor coaches the teacher on the use of that skill. Then the supervisor makes a focused observation of one of the teacher's classes, gathering data just on the skill being developed. They confer again to decide whether more coaching and observing for that skill are needed or whether they should move to the next skill. It is an intensive process of diagnosing, developing a growth plan, coaching, holding a focused observation, and then assessing the next move. Obviously, it takes a great deal of time to implement effectively; the hope is, however, that only a few teachers in each school will be involved in such intensive development.

Cooperative development is an option usually provided only to experienced and competent teachers; it enables small groups of teachers to work together in a collegial relationship for mutual growth. It is intended to be a teacher-centered, teacher-directed process which respects the professionalism of competent teachers. While it requires administrative support, it does not require inordinate amounts of administrator or supervisor time; the expectation is that the cooperative groups can direct their own growth. In doing so, they may decide to use a variety of processes: observing and conferring about each other's classes; exchanging classes; collaborating on action research; and developing curricular and instructional materials.

Self-directed development is an option usually provided to experienced and competent teachers who wish to work on their own, rather than as part of a cooperative team. Teachers who choose this option identify a small number of professional-growth goals for the year and work independently in attempting to accomplish those goals. In a sense, the self-directed model is akin to the "management-by-objectives" assessment process, except that it is completely nonevaluative. The administrator or supervisor simply acts as a supportive resource for the teacher in the self-directed mode.

In general, teachers should be able to choose which of these three options they prefer, with the understanding that all probationary teachers will be involved in the intensive mode and that the principal will be able to identify tenured teachers who should also be involved in this mode. A form facilitating these choices is shown in Figure 9–3. These three individual development options provide teachers with a choice and enable supervisors and administrators to focus their supervisory efforts on those teachers in the intensive mode who most need their skilled services.

The Interrelationship of the Four Processes

How do these four processes for professional development interrelate? Obviously they are closely related. The data derived from informal observations can be used to supplement the information derived from rating

FIGURE 9–3. Options for Professional Development

Teacher's Name _____ School _____ Date _____

Basic Assumptions:

1. All teachers will participate in system-based and school-based staff development.
2. All teachers will be observed informally several times during the year.
3. All teachers will be rated by an administrator.

Teacher's Preferred Option: (Check one)

_____ For this year I prefer not to participate in any special professional-development activities other than those outlined above.

_____ For this year I prefer to work cooperatively with colleagues using the processes identified below.

_____ For this year I prefer to work in a self-directed mode using the processes identified below.

Preferred Developmental Processes: (Check all those which at this point seem desirable.)

_____ Observe a colleague and confer about observation.

_____ Exchange classes with a colleague and confer about exchange.

_____ Develop new course of study.

_____ Develop and try out new instructional materials.

_____ Improve an advanced teaching skill.

_____ Conduct action research.

_____ View and analyze video tapes of own teaching.

_____ Plan and implement an independent study program.

_____ Enroll in graduate course or special workshops.

_____ Other _____

observations and can play an important part in assessing staff-development needs. The rating process can help the supervisor or administrator identify those teachers who need intensive development. The activities undertaken in all the options for individual development can be linked with on-going staff-development programs. And the staff-development program can provide needed support for the individual development. All the processes obviously play a key role in improving the taught curriculum.

However, having administrators and supervisors examine these processes separately and analytically has clear advantages, since each requires different skills, provides different kinds of information, and employs different processes. In such an examination, the author has found it most useful to work with individual school districts to assist them in developing their own model, rather than presenting them with a formulaic solution. Thus, some districts link rating and individual development rather closely; others keep them quite distinct. Some emphasize curriculum alignment in the informal observations; other focus on instructional processes. Some offer teachers only the cooperative and intensive options; others provide the full array. Since such matters are much affected by district size, administrative philosophy, and available resources, they are best resolved at the district level.

One particular local option needs to be emphasized here. As each district develops its own model, it determines who will be primarily responsible for each of the four approaches. Some districts limit the informal observations to administrators; others expect supervisors to be involved. Some require that rating be done only by administrators; others expect input from the supervisory staff. Some districts use assistant principals for the intensive development; others use supervisors or expert teachers. Some expect administrators to direct staff development; others see this as a supervisory function. Rather than beginning with a set of foreordained conclusions about these important matters, the "professional-development" approach suggested here enables local districts to resolve these issues in a way that makes most sense to their administrators, supervisors, and teachers.

Although the differentiated model has been found to be feasible and acceptable to teachers (see Glatthorn, 1984), there again is no empirical research that proves it to be more effective than other approaches. Curriculum leaders, therefore, would be well advised to study all four approaches carefully (as well as any others that seem useful) and choose or develop a model that seems to respond best to their own district's needs.

SUPERVISING THE SUPPORTED CURRICULUM

In Chapter 1 the *supported curriculum* was defined as all the resources provided to ensure the effective implementation of the curriculum: the time allocated to the curriculum; the personnel assigned to plan and implement the curriculum; and the instructional materials required for the curriculum. Since time and personnel allocations have been discussed in Chapter 6, this chapter focuses on the instructional materials as a central aspect of the supported curriculum. The importance of developing an effective system for selecting and using instructional materials cannot be overemphasized. As noted in Chapter 4, the textbook plays a central role in influencing what teachers select to teach and how they teach it. In most classrooms the use of texts and ancillary materials is the predominant mode of teaching and learning: one study (Durkin, 1978) discovered that students spent as much as 70 percent of instructional time directly involved with textbooks, workbooks, dittos, and other seatwork activities.

Given that importance, it is especially discouraging to note how little systematic attention is given to the textbook-selection process. One survey by the Educational Products Information Exchange (1978) determined that nearly half the teachers surveyed had no role at all in choosing the instructional materials they were using and that those who were involved reported spending only one hour a year in reviewing and selecting texts. What is needed, obviously, is a sound process for supervising the selection and use of materials—one that recognizes the central importance of the supported curriculum. The procedures outlined below, drawn from a review of the literature on textbook selection, should provide a useful beginning for local leaders who wish to review their current selection and adoption procedures. (The discussion that follows uses the term *text* to refer in general to any instructional material that plays a central role in the curriculum; Chapter 14 discusses some current developments in computer software.)

Develop a Statement of Board Policy and Administrative Procedures   The board policy should delineate the functions of instructional materials; specify the roles of the board, school administrators, and teachers in selecting materials; and indicate the rights of citizens to question the use of particular materials. That policy should be supplemented with a more specific set of administrative procedures for implementing those policies. The administrative procedures should specify how materials will be selected, how citizens can register complaints, and how administrators should respond to such complaints.

Appoint the Textbook-Adoption Committee   The committee should be a representative one—large enough to include broad representation and small enough to work efficiently. At a minimum, the committee should be composed of one school principal, a supervisor in that field, one teacher from each school which will be using the text, an instructional-materials specialist, and a parent. Although Gall (1981) recommends limiting the committee to five or six members in order to increase efficiency, larger districts will probably find it wiser to increase the size in order to ensure adequate representation of all schools involved. The committee should be able to secure the help of a disinterested consultant, if members feel that they need technical assistance. Muther (1985) recommends that the committee be led by an "autocratic manager" who is nonbiased and does not vote.

Train the Committee   Since the committee will play such a central role in the adoption process, the committee should be trained in the following skills: understanding board policy and district procedures; maintaining ethical and professional relationships with publishers; understanding current research in the field; assessing district and teacher needs; evaluating instructional materials; and monitoring the implementation and use of instructional materials.

Provide the Committee with Selection Resources   The committee should also have easy access to selection resources. Two types of resources are especially needed. First, the committee should have access to catalogs of available materials; one of the best resources here for nonprint materials is Sive's *Selecting Instructional Media* (1983), which is a catalog of catalogs, listing hundreds of comprehensive and subject-specific catalogs. Several catalogs of print materials are now available as computerized catalogs, making it possible to conduct sharply focused searches for materials. Second, the committee should have access to objective reviews of materials. The journals published by the several subject-centered professional groups (such as the National Council of Teachers of English) often include such reviews. Two other excellent sources of a more general sort are the journal *Curriculum Review,* which includes reviews of materials and articles about current developments, and the Educational Products Information Exchange (EPIE), which publishes evaluative profiles of textbook materials.

Determine How Teachers Will Probably Use the New Materials   In order to make a wise decision, the adoption committee needs good information about how teachers will probably make use of the materials. Here the committee should survey, interview, and observe teachers to secure answers to these questions:

- For which groups of students will the text be used?
- Will the text be used primarily in class or outside of class?
- Will the text be used chiefly to teach skills and concepts or to provide guided and independent practice?

To understand the importance of this information, contrast two groups of teachers teaching mathematics in elementary school. One team comprises specialists in a departmentalized setting; they have been well trained in modern approaches to mathematics and are highly skilled in explaining concepts. They want a mathematics text to be used primarily as a source of problems for pupils to work on in class and at home. The other teachers are teaching several subjects in a self-contained classroom. They do not have a deep or current understanding of mathematics. They want a mathematics text which can explain concepts clearly and which can reduce their preparation time. Those two contrasting uses of the text require quite different textbooks.

Develop a Sharply Focused and Weighted Set of Criteria for Selection   Muther (1985) notes the dangers involved in using long checklists that include too many criteria. They lead the committee to "select by elimination": the committee spends a great deal of time searching for the perfect text, one which has all the content and qualities specified on the checklist. In the process they ignore some excellent texts that fall short on just one or two of the less important criteria. She also believes that such long checklists exert pressure on publishers to assemble texts that have bits and pieces of many kinds of content, simply to satisfy checklist users. As a result, she recommends that the committee list only three criteria and weight those criteria in order of importance. One modification has been found to be useful here: the committee also identifies certain basic requirements that all texts should meet, such as being free of racial and sexist stereotyping and being at an appropriate level of difficulty.

District leaders who have the time and the resources needed may also wish to use the Annehurst Curriculum Classification System (Frymier, 1977), which uses ten characteristics (experience, intelligence, motivation, creativity, emotion, personality, sociability, verbal expression, auditory expression, and motor perception) to describe both pupils and materials. The objective of the ACCS is to enable educators to match pupils and materials, so that achievement and attitudes can be improved. The research on the use of the ACCS has yielded mixed results. (See Cornbleth, 1979; and Berneman and Dexter, 1979.)

One useful way of summarizing all these matters is to record them in a set of specifications, similar to those shown in Figure 9–4.

FIGURE 9–4. Specifications for Elementary Language Arts Texts

For Which Pupils:

All pupils (except those with limited English proficiency) in grades 1–6.

How Will Texts Probably Be Used:

Most teachers will use them in class, as the primary source for language arts instruction. Pupils will frequently read the text independently, discuss what they have read, and then do practice exercises.

Basic Requirements:

1. Texts should be free of racial, ethnic, and sexist stereotyping.
2. Texts should be written so that they can be read by all pupils who will use them, but should not be too simple or childish.

Major Selection Criteria: (Listed in order of importance)

1. The texts emphasize a process approach to writing, giving special attention to prewriting and revision.
2. The texts include a number of integrated units that show the interrelationships of writing, speaking, listening, and reading.
3. The texts reflect an informed view of language learning: good form is stressed as an aid to clarity, not as a set of rigid rules; pupils are encouraged to value their own language and to accept the languages of others; grammar is presented as a system of language structures, not a collection of abstract terms and rules.

Ancillary Materials Required:

1. Testing program.

Identify Five Texts That Best Meet the Requirements and the Criteria   The committee should then use the set of specifications to identify five texts or series that meet the criteria and then rank these five in order of merit.

Get Teacher Input on the Top Five Texts   At this point all teachers who will be using the text should be given an opportunity to review the top five identified by the committee and give their own input. Perhaps the best way to do this is for the committee member representing that school to meet with the teachers from that building, explain the requirements and criteria, and discuss the five texts which have passed the initial screening. The teachers should be encouraged to discuss the merits of each of the texts and then to express their own preferences, with the understanding that the final decision will be made by the committee, not by a majority vote.

Select the Best Text   The committee should then meet, review teacher input, take a fresh look at the five texts, and then make their final choice.

Develop a Service Contract with the Publisher   Muther and other specialists in the field of text adoption recommend that, before an order is placed, the district should develop a service contract indicating what services it expects the publisher to provide. Services that can be requested include the following: giving the district the right to photocopy certain portions; training teachers in use of the materials; helping teachers place pupils appropriately in the program; correlating the text with the district curriculum; assisting schools in ordering materials; and providing follow-up assistance when problems develop. Obviously, such services will be costly to the publisher, and the amount of service provided will likely be contingent on the size of the order.

Train the Teachers in the Use of the Texts and Provide Materials to Correlate the Texts with the Curriculum   Teachers will need assistance before school begins on how to use the texts most effectively. They also should receive correlation charts showing how the text correlates with the district curriculum. (Chapter 11 explains this matter more fully.)

Monitor the Use of the Texts   Too many districts purchase expensive textbooks and then consider the matter closed. Experts in the field point out the necessity of monitoring closely the use of the texts to be sure that they are being used appropriately and to identify problems with them. The selection committee can be given this responsibility, although Muther recommends that a separate monitoring committee be established. Once problems have been identified, then corrective action should be taken.

If these steps are taken, it is likely that the supported curriculum will be more effective.

APPLICATIONS

1. On the basis of your experience in schools, do you believe that teachers should have some options about the types of supervisory services they receive? Be prepared to support your position with well-reasoned arguments.

2. Glatthorn recommends that each district should develop its own differentiated system of professional development. Sketch out the main components of a system that you think would work well in a district with which you are acquainted. Decide which components you would emphasize (staff development, rating, informal observations, individual development), which options (if any) you would provide to teachers, and who would be responsible for the several components.

3. The list of essential teaching skills presented in this chapter is only one way of describing and analyzing effective teaching. Review the research on teacher effectiveness and develop your own list of essential teaching skills, one that you could use in supervising teachers.

4. Using a form like the one shown in Figure 9-4, develop a set of specifications for textbooks in a subject field you know well.

5. One of the issues that confronts larger districts is whether all the elementary schools in that district should use the same basal reading series. What position would you take on this issue? What reasons would you advance in support of your position?

REFERENCES

Berneman, L. P., and Dexter, C. V. (April 1979). Annehurst Curriculum Classification System: Effect of matching materials and students on achievement, on task behavior, and on interest. Paper presented at annual conference of the American Educational Research Association, San Francisco.

Buchmann, M. (1985). Improving education by talking: Argument or conversation? *Teachers College Record, 86,* 441–453.

Cornbleth, C. (April 1979). Curriculum materials and involvement in learning activities. Paper presented at annual conference of the American Educational Research Association, San Francisco.

Costa, A., and Garmston, R. (1985). *The art of cognitive coaching: Supervision for intelligent teaching.* Sacramento, CA: California State University.

Durkin, D. (1978). *What classroom observations reveal about reading comprehension.* Technical Report #106. Urbana, IL: University of Illinois.

Educational Products Information Exchange. (1978). National survey and assessment of instructional materials: Two years later. *EPIEgram, 5,* 1–3.

Fielding, G. D., and Schalock, H. D. (1985). *Promoting the professional development of teachers and administrators.* Eugene, OR: Center for Educational Policy and Management, University of Oregon.

Frymier, J. R. (1977). *The Annehurst Curriculum Classification System: A practical way to individualize instruction.* West Lafayette, IN: Kappa Delta Pi.

Gall, M. D. (1981). *Handbook for evaluating and selecting curriculum materials.* Boston: Allyn and Bacon.

Gersten, R., Green, W., and Davis, G. (April 1985). *The realities of instructional leadership: An intensive study of four inner city schools.* Paper presented at the annual meeting of the American Educational Research Association, Chicago.

Glatthorn, A. A. (1984). *Differentiated supervision.* Alexandria, VA: Association for Supervision and Curriculum Development.

————. (March 1986). Reconceptualizing supervision. Paper presented at conference of National Commission on Supervision, San Francisco.

Glickman, C. D. (March 1986). Development as the aim of supervision. Paper presented at the annual meeting of the Association for Supervision and Curriculum Development, Chicago.

Howey, K. R., and Vaughan, J. C. (1983). Current patterns of staff development. In G. A. Griffin (ed.), *Staff development.* (Eighty-second yearbook of the National Society for the Study of Education, Part 2.) Chicago: University of Chicago Press.

Hunter, M. (1984). Knowing, teaching, and supervising. In P. L. Hosford (ed.), *Using what we know about teaching,* pp. 169–193. Alexandria, VA: Association for Supervision and Curriculum Development.

McGreal, T. L. (1983). *Successful teacher evaluation.* Alexandria, VA: Association for Supervision and Curriculum Development.

Muther, C. (1985). *The pitfalls of textbook adoption and how to avoid them.* (Video cassette and user's manual.) Alexandria, VA: Association for Supervision and Curriculum Development.

Sergiovanni, T. J. (1985). Landscapes, mindscapes, and reflective practice in supervision. *Journal of Curriculum and Supervision, 1,* 5–17.

————. (1986). A theory of practice for clinical supervision. In J. S. Smyth (ed.), *Clinical supervision: Theory, research, and practice.* London: Croom-Helm.

Sive, M. R. (1983). *Selecting instructional media* (3rd Ed.). Littleton, CO: Libraries Unlimited.

Squires, D. A., Huitt, W. G., and Segars, J. K. (1981). Improving classrooms and schools: What's important. *Educational Leadership, 39,* 174–179.

Stallings, J. (April 1986). Report on a three-year study of the Hunter model. Paper presented at the annual conference of the American Educational Research Association, San Francisco.

Wise, A. E., Darling-Hammond, L., McLaughlin, M. W., and Bernstein, H. T. (1984). *Teacher evaluation: A study of effective practices.* Santa Monica, CA: Rand Corporation.

10

Curriculum Implementation

Previous chapters have discussed the processes used in developing new courses and in improving programs and fields of study. Each of these processes represents a type of curriculum change—and the literature on educational change suggests that, to be successful, those new and improved curricula will require careful support throughout several stages. The discussion which follows examines these critical stages, after analyzing briefly the nature of curricular-change processes.

THE NATURE OF CURRICULAR CHANGE

To understand the nature and importance of the curricular-change process, consider this scenario:

> A supervisor and a team of teachers produce a curriculum guide during the summer. With suitable fanfare, they distribute the new guide to the teachers in September and provide one hour of "inservice" about the new curriculum. The teachers give the guide a cursory examination and put it aside. As they plan the first two or three units for that year, they rely on the text they have always used, draw from their knowledge of the subject, and flip through the guide to see if they are generally on target. After the first few units, they file the guide and teach what they have always taught.

How typical is this scenario? As Fullan and Park (1981) note, the answer depends upon several key factors. Figure 10–1 summarizes the most important elements identified in their review of the research on curriculum implementation. When those elements are strongly present, a high level of implementation can be expected; when they are only weakly present or are absent, lower levels can be anticipated.

FIGURE 10–1. Elements of Curriculum Implementation

A high level of curriculum implementation can be expected if . . .

1. Teachers perceive the need for the new curriculum.
2. The curriculum changes are not unduly complex and are clearly explained to teachers.
3. Quality materials supporting the new curriculum are made available to teachers.
4. Previous attempts in the district to change curricula have been successful.
5. Principals are strongly encouraged to take responsibility for implementing the new curriculum in their schools and are given the necessary training.
6. Teachers have had substantial input into the new curriculum and are provided with the necessary staff development.
7. There is strong school-board and community support.
8. There is a carefully developed implementation plan which makes specific provisions for monitoring implementation.
9. Administrators take the necessary steps to prevent and respond to the problem of "overload"—when teachers feel overwhelmed and overworked in implementing the new curriculum.
10. Principals play an active role in advocating and supporting the new curriculum.
11. Teachers have an opportunity to share ideas and problems with each other and receive support from supervisors and administrators.

(Adapted from Fullan, F., and Park, P. (1981). *Curriculum implementation: A resource booklet.* Toronto, Ontario: Ontario Institute for Studies in Education.)

Are such variations important? The research indicates that they are. In assessing the effects of a second-grade "adaptive education" program, Leonhardt (1974) discovered that the degree of implementation explained 35 percent of the variance in achievement. And Hess and Buckholdt (1974), in evaluating the effects of a "Language and Thinking" program for primary pupils, determined that the mean percentage of mastery for pupils in the classrooms of "high implementors" was 83 percent, compared with 59 percent for those in classrooms of "low implementors."

Obviously, it is therefore generally desirable for a new curriculum to be implemented with its main features intact. This is not to suggest, however, that complete fidelity is desired. In challenging the belief that teachers should function as the "faithful implementors" of curricula, Connelly and Elbaz (1980) argue forcefully for a quite different conceptualization—one in which teachers are perceived as partners in developing curricula and as active, deliberating agents in transforming new materials. In examining this conflict between what some have termed "fidelity" and "mutual adaptation," Huberman (1983) seems to strike a reasonable compromise: "The inference . . . is *not* that one should retreat into improvisation but that one should try actively to deliver as many of the necessary ingredients as possible" (p. 23) [italics in original].

How can curriculum leaders ensure that those necessary ingredients are delivered? The answer, as will be seen below, is a complex one. Although the suggestions which follow have been drawn from a review of the literature on curricular change, two cautions should be noted in following these recommendations. The first is that the nature of the school as an organization will very much influence the change process to be used. In arguing for what they term a "contingency approach" to planned change, Corbett and Dawson (1981) note that eight local factors can affect the implementation of change: district priorities; availability of incentives; availability of resources; organizational characteristics; the political coalitions present; the success of prior projects; the local environment; and the complexity of the change itself.

The second caution is that the scope of the curriculum project itself needs to be assessed. Large-scale projects will probably require the systematic applications of all the recommendations given below. Smaller projects requiring minimal change can be implemented with less attention to change strategies.

Thus, the recommendations presented below should be seen as guidelines to be interpreted flexibly, not as a formula that should be followed rigidly.

EFFECTIVE ACTIONS IN THE
STRATEGIC PLANNING STAGE

The first stage in the change process is what Herriott and Gross (1979) call the *strategic planning* stage. It is the stage that actually antedates the development or improvement of the curriculum. The research on successful educational change in general would suggest that the following steps should be taken in the strategic planning stage.

Develop an Overall District Plan for Curriculum Development and Improvement As explained in Chapter 5, a comprehensive plan is needed if problems of overload are to be prevented. By assessing district needs, by reviewing external requirements from the state or accrediting agencies, and by calculating district resources, curriculum leaders should develop a master plan which indicates year by year which new courses are to be developed, which programs of study are to be improved, and which fields of study are to be strengthened. Figure 10–2 shows one district's master plan; an alternative form can be found in Chapter 5.

FIGURE 10–2. A Master Plan for Curriculum
Development and Improvement

Year	Curriculum Project	Personnel Primarily Affected
1987–88	Develop new critical-thinking courses for middle school.	Middle school principals; supervisors; social studies, science, mathematics, English teachers.
1988–89	Improve high school program of studies in preparation for Middle States evaluation.	High school administrators, department heads, teachers.
1989–90	Improve social studies curriculum, K–12.	All elementary teachers, elementary principals, supervisors, secondary social studies teachers.
1990–91	No major projects initiated.	

In Developing the Master Plan, Incorporate a Strategy of Systematic Incrementalism   This second guideline speaks to the need of avoiding radical curricular change which requires major modifications of the organization or significant alterations in the teachers' role; it makes more sense in general to develop or adopt what Loucks and Zacchei (1983) call a "classroom-friendly" innovation. Obviously there will be times when a new technology, such as the computer, will compel more radical changes, but in general incremental curriculum change will result in a higher level of implementation.

Develop a Constituency for the Planned Curriculum Change   To be successful, the new project needs to have the support of all those centrally affected. The curriculum leader should move systematically to enlist the support of board members, district administrators, school principals, parent leaders, and teachers. There is a special need, of course, both to inform and to enlist the active support of the teachers who will be affected. Here some research by Loucks and Hall (1979) is especially helpful. Their studies of teachers involved in educational changes indicate that teachers move through various "stages of concern" as the innovation progresses. At the strategic planning stage, the teachers' concerns focus chiefly on information: what change is contemplated—and what are its details? The curriculum leader should hold discussion sessions with teachers to inform them about the general outlines of the project, to solicit their active participation, and to invite their input.

Appoint the Task Force   A task force or project team should be designated to assume primary responsibility for the curricular-change effort. Most districts find that a team of twelve to fifteen is large enough to secure adequate representation from all constituencies but not so large that it is unwieldy. Typically the task force or team should include one or more representatives from these groups: district administrators; district supervisors; school administrators; school department heads or team leaders; teachers; and parents. In high school curriculum projects, student representation is sometimes desirable as well.

A project leader should also be identified—a key educational leader who knows the curriculum field and is skilled in working with groups of colleagues. Loucks and Hall (1979) call the project leader the "local facilitator," a role that they believe can best be performed by a district curriculum coordinator or staff developer. This local facilitator, they note, should be someone who meets several criteria: has legitimacy; is central in the communication network; and has the time, the skills, the clout, and the resources to do the job. As they see the role, the local facilitator or project leader acts as *cheerleader* (building commitment through constant encouragement), *linker* (linking external and internal resources), and *troubleshooter* (helping teachers solve problems).

Determine the Pace and Scope of Change   One of the initial tasks of the project team should be to determine how rapidly and broadly the curricular change will be introduced into the district. Large-scale changes should probably be introduced the first year on a pilot basis, so that the team can assess and improve the new curriculum.

Secure the Needed Resources   With that determination made, the project team should next secure the resources needed for the successful accomplishment of the project. A detailed project calendar showing the time needed should be developed and disseminated. A realistic project budget indicating the funds needed should be planned and submitted. And personnel and material needs should be calculated and specified.

Make Specific Provisions to Secure Continued Input from Teachers   As will be noted throughout this chapter, significant teacher input is needed in every stage of the curricular-change process. Such input is needed not only to enlist the support of teachers, but also to improve the quality of the final product and to ensure effective implementation and institutionalization. Connelly and Elbaz (1980) cogently make the point that the teacher's knowledge of the "practical" is essential for curricular quality:

> . . . we are committed to thinking of the teacher as a knower of the practical. . . . teacher's thinking is characterized by questions of what ought to be done to encourage the growth that is the purpose of their work, and their thinking takes into account the prescriptive wishes of stakeholders in their intellectual environment. (pp. 110, 111)

Anticipate and Make the Necessary Organizational Changes
The last step in the strategic planning stage is to anticipate and make the

necessary organizational changes. A new curriculum or an improved program of studies will often require such organizational modifications as new teaming arrangements, changed time allotments, new role definitions, and alterations in space allocation and utilization. Such changes should be anticipated and the necessary modifications made.

How much time will these strategic planning steps require? The answer obviously will vary with the scope and complexity of the project. Most districts find that five to eight months is adequate.

EFFECTIVE ACTIONS IN THE INITIATION STAGE

The strategic planning has been completed, and a new curriculum has been developed—or an existing one has been improved. Now the initiation stage begins. The initiation stage is that period of time when the new curriculum is first introduced to the teachers and used in the classroom: it is the "lift-off" stage of the curriculum project. If the first year of the new curriculum is seen as a pilot year, then that whole year can be seen as the initiation stage. If the project is introduced to the entire system in the first year, then the first few months can be viewed as the initiation stage. Like the strategic planning stage, it will be most successful if effective leadership is provided.

Provide the Required Staff Development for Those Who Will Be Initiating the Project   Staff development for curriculum change is an on-going process that requires attention throughout the project. One of the critical times when staff development is essential is at the beginning of the initiation stage. According to Loucks and Hall's "stages of concern" theory, teachers at the initiation stage will typically express both personal and management concerns: "How will the new curriculum affect me?" and "How can I manage all the materials I will need?" The staff development at this stage can deal with these concerns in several ways.

First, the staff-development sessions should be used to give teachers who will be using the new program complete information about the specific changes expected. The importance of such clear understanding is underscored in Herriott and Gross's (1979) research: they found that many innovations were not successfully implemented because teachers never fully understood the nature of the change. In clarifying the specific changes anticipated, the project team might wish to make use of what Loucks and Crandall (1982) term a *practice profile*. The practice profile of any innovation describes the critical components of the change and presents a precise list of implementation requirements. It thus can be used both to communicate the nature of the change and to assess the extent of implementation. A portion of a practice profile is shown in Figure 10–3.

FIGURE 10-3. Excerpt from Practice Profile: Reasoning
and Problem-Solving Course

COMPONENT 1: Instructor role

1	2	3
Instructor poses some problems; requires students to pose problems; encourages students to develop alternative solutions.	Instructor poses all problems; guides students to one of several "acceptable" solutions.	Instructor poses all problems; directs students to "right" answer.

Code: _____ variations to the right are unacceptable; variations to the left are acceptable.

In communicating these changes, the leaders should encourage the teachers during the initiation stage to follow the new curriculum guides with as much fidelity as possible. Most of those who have researched the process of educational change conclude that teachers should make changes and adaptations only after they have followed the program prescriptions somewhat faithfully for a year at least. (See, for example, Huberman, 1983.)

The second focus of the staff development should be to give the users of the new program specific assistance in translating the curriculum documents into instructional plans. A member of the project team who understands both the new curriculum and the world of the teachers should take teachers through the entire instructional planning process. The leader should begin by showing the teachers how to develop a yearly plan with appropriate time allocations. Then the leader should take a typical unit from the new materials and show teachers how to develop unit and daily plans based on the new guide. Teachers can then work in teams in developing additional units under the direction of the leader. In this way some of their management concerns will be addressed.

Finally, the staff-development sessions should help teachers improve in their use of instructional skills which the new curriculum requires. If, for example, they will be expected to make frequent use of cooperative learning groups, they will need specific help with organizing such groups, structuring their work, monitoring their progress, and assessing their achievement.

Be Sure All Materials and Equipment Required Are Available and Readily Accessible   This step seems obvious, yet it is one that is too often slighted by busy administrators and supervisors who neglect to place orders in sufficient time. Thus teachers arrive in September eager to begin the new project and find that texts have not arrived, the computer software was never ordered, and the VCR doesn't work.

Secure the Active Support of District Administrators, Supervisors, and School Principals At the initiation stage, strong administrative support is essential. Obviously the superintendent should communicate his or her full endorsement of the program. As noted above, the district supervisor must play those roles that Loucks and Hall describe as "cheerleader," "linker," and "troubleshooter." And the building principal must make it clear that he or she is completely behind the new project.

Monitor the Teachers' Use of the New Curriculum During its Initiation—but Avoid Premature Evaluation The initiation stage should be seen as a time when users "de-bug" the new program, testing out its feasibility in real classrooms. Accordingly, principals should be required to work closely with the teachers in noting problems and successes. However, most researchers and practitioners would support Fullan and Pomfret's (1977) recommendation that evaluation during the initiation stage should be concerned with facilitating local system capabilities through feedback, rather than with judging success or failure. It should be more formative and less summative in its emphasis. And Seidman (1983) notes that evaluation during the initiation stage should not be unduly concerned with compliance; he cites several studies which indicate that an excessive concern with teacher compliance may actually interfere with successful implementation.

The initiation stage ordinarily is a time of high commitment to and great enthusiasm for the new curriculum. If teachers have been involved in developing it and have been trained in the ways described above, they will usually initiate the project with high expectations for its success. However, the enthusiasm and commitment of the initiation stage are typically short-lived; leaders should be prepared for the predictable problems that will develop during the implementation stage.

EFFECTIVE ACTIONS DURING THE IMPLEMENTATION STAGE

The implementation stage occurs when there is widespread adoption of the new curriculum. All teachers are following the new curriculum guide, which has been revised on the basis of feedback from the initiation stage. And, as Fullan and Pomfret note, teachers should be encouraged during the implementation stage to experiment systematically in making and adopting their own variations. The following suggestions should be useful in making the implementation stage a successful one.

Continue Providing Staff Development for Teachers Staff development continues to be important during the implementation stage. However, it will have a different emphasis now.

First, some staff-development time should be devoted to an analysis of the effects of the new curriculum. Loucks and Hall's (1979) work suggests that the many teachers in the implementation stage will be concerned about the consequences of the new curriculum—"How is the new curriculum affecting my students?" It therefore would be useful to provide opportunities for teachers to share their perceptions about student response to and achievement with the new curriculum. As will be noted below, the evaluation during the implementation stage should be more directly concerned with student achievement; and the staff-development sessions should provide a useful forum for analyzing and interpreting these results.

Second, time should be provided for the development and sharing of instructional materials. As noted above, the implementation stage should be a time of some experimentation; therefore, some of the sessions should be devoted to collaborative development of teaching and learning materials.

Finally, the staff development should provide an opportunity for peer coaching. Several studies (see, for example, Showers, 1984) indicate that peers can be effective in coaching their colleagues in the acquisition of new skills. Effective teachers who successfully used the new curriculum in the initiation stage should help first-time users polish the needed technical skills.

Increase Administrative Pressure on Teachers to Use the New Curriculum While teachers should be encouraged to develop their own variations, they should not be permitted to ignore the new project. As Miles (1983) notes, change projects were most successfully institutionalized when a powerful central office administrator put considerable pressure on users to implement the new program. While this strong pressure initially resulted in some reduced commitment on the part of teachers, that lowered commitment was only temporary. When teachers received the necessary assistance and support, their use and commitment increased.

Make Provisions for Systematic Evaluation During the implementation stage, the evaluation should emphasize the summative assessment of results. Are students achieving the outcomes intended? Here the use of curriculum-based tests is strongly recommended. The data from such tests should give district and school leaders useful information about the effects of the new curriculum.

This is not to suggest that formative evaluation should be ignored. In fact, the summative data will have validity only if there is good formative data on the extent of use. Here the "practice profile" can play a different role. It now can be used to assess the extent to which teachers are actually implementing key features of the new program.

Solve Emerging Problems Even if the new curriculum was carefully de-bugged in the initiation stage, somewhat predictable problems will develop in the implementation stage. Leaders should be alert to the following problems and take the steps needed to deal with them:

- Students have trouble acquiring the skills which the new curriculum requires. If, for example, the new curriculum emphasizes group inquiry, students will need specific training in the new behaviors required in such an approach. Teachers will need specific assistance in providing such training.
- Parents are confused about the new program. Parents used to traditional curricula will feel some anxiety and uncertainty about new approaches. Principals should work closely with the parents' organization in developing programs that will answer parents' questions and deal with their doubts.
- Budget cuts threaten the new program. Miles (1983) notes that funding cuts are a frequent manifestation of what he calls "environmental turbulence"—problems within the organization that threaten successful institutionalization. School boards which were eager to provide funds for the new curriculum in the initiation stage too often forget the importance of sustaining the change with adequate fiscal support. Here the superintendent must play a key role in planning for and securing the needed support.

If such problems are anticipated and dealt with, it is more likely that the implementation stage will be successful.

INSTITUTIONALIZATION—THE FINAL STAGE IN THE CHANGE PROCESS

The curriculum change has been successfully implemented. How can it then be institutionalized so that it becomes a somewhat stable part of the district's educational program? Here Miles' (1983) research (summarized in Figure 10-4) is illuminating. He notes eight key variables that should be present if the change is to become part of the system. A review of that list will suggest quite clearly that the key actions of the earlier stages—administrative support and pressure, organizational changes, and consistent support and assistance for teachers—are the essential ingredients required for the institutionalization of change. Thus, if leaders have worked systematically throughout the strategic planning, the initiation, and the implementation stages, then it is very likely that the curriculum change will be institutionalized—it will become a stable part of the district's educational program.

However, certain developments requiring continued administrative attention might be noted here. First, evaluation should continue to emphasize summative outcomes. Data from one or two years of implementation will not be sufficient to establish long-term effectiveness. Multiyear assessments will yield more valid findings. Principals should continue to monitor the use of the curriculum, but such monitoring may be less frequent and systematic.

Second, staff development should continue, but with less intensity. At the institutionalization stage, teachers are internalizing what they have learned from the once-new curriculum. They need some opportunity to reflect about what they have learned and to share their insights.

Finally, provisions should be made for periodic updating of the curriculum. Several data sources can be used to refine the curriculum still further: student achievement results; information from classroom observations; and surveys of teachers' judgments and perceptions. Change thus becomes a cycle of renewal, not a one-time innovation.

FIGURE 10–4. Variables Affecting Successful Institutionalization

The research suggests that educational changes are more likely to be institutionalized when the following factors are present:

1. There is strong and continuing administrative commitment to the change.
2. Administrators mandate the innovation for all teachers.
3. There is strong administrative pressure on users to implement the solution.
4. Administrators make the necessary organizational changes to support the innovation.
5. There is consistent administrative support for users.
6. Administrators provide continuing assistance to users.
7. There is increased user effort, resulting from administrative pressure and assistance.
8. Increased user effort leads to increased user commitment.

Adapted from Miles, M. B. (November 1983). Unraveling the mystery of institutionalization. *Educational Leadership, 41,* 14-19.

APPLICATIONS

1. Assume that you are the leader of a project team developing a new social studies curriculum for grades K–12 for your district. Develop a master planning schedule which would show a time line and the key steps that you and the team would take.

2. The recommendation by Miles that principals should exert strong and continuing pressure on the teachers seems to contradict the advice of those who believe in more democratic leadership. By reflecting on your experience and your knowledge of the literature on leadership, decide whether you follow or reject Miles' recommendation.

3. Some have argued that in a time of rapid change the schools should adopt "quick-fix" approaches to curriculum change, in which the entire cycle is markedly shortened. What is your view on this issue?

REFERENCES

Connelly, F. M., and Elbaz, F. (1980). Conceptual bases for curricular thought: A teacher's perspective. In A. Foshay (ed.), *Considered action for curriculum improvement*, pp. 95–119. Alexandria, VA: Association for Supervision and Curriculum Development.

Corbett, H. D., III, and Dawson, J. A. (1981). *To teach its own: School contingencies in the process of planned change*. Philadelphia: Research for Better Schools.

Fullan, M., and Park, P. (1981). *Curriculum implementation: A resource booklet*. Toronto, Ontario: Ontario Institute for Studies in Education.

Fullan, M., and Pomfret, A. (1977). Research on curriculum and instruction implementation. *Review of Educational Research, 47*, 335–397.

Herriott, R. E., and Gross, N. (1979). *The dynamics of planned educational change: Case studies and analysis*. Berkeley: McCutchan.

Hess, R., and Buckholdt, D. (April 1974). *Degree of implementation as a critical variable in program evaluation*. Paper presented at the meeting of the American Educational Research Association, Chicago.

Huberman, A. M. (November 1983). School improvement strategies that work: Some scenarios. *Educational Leadership, 41*, 23–31.

Leonhardt, G. (April 1974). *Evaluation of the implementation of a program of adaptive education at the second grade (1972–73)*. Paper presented at the meeting of the American Educational Research Association, Chicago.

Loucks, S. F., and Crandall, D. P. (1982). *The practice profile: An all purpose tool for program communication, staff development, and improvement*. Andover, MA: The NETWORK.

Loucks, S. F., and Hall, G. E. (April 1979). *Implementing innovation in schools: A concerns-based approach*. Paper presented at the meeting of the American Educational Research Association, San Francisco.

Loucks, S. F., and Zacchei, D. A. (November 1983). Applying our findings to today's innovations. *Educational Leadership, 41*, 28–31.

Miles, M. B. (November 1983). Unraveling the mystery of institutionalization. *Educational Leadership, 41*, 14–19.

Seidman, W. H. (1983). Goal ambiguity and organizational de-coupling: The failure of "rational systems" program implementation. *Educational Evaluation and Policy Analysis, 2*, 399–413.

Showers, B. (1984). *Peer coaching: A strategy for facilitating transfer of training*. Eugene, OR: Center for Educational Policy and Management.

11

Aligning the Curriculum

Curriculum alignment is a process of ensuring that the written, the taught, and the tested curricula are closely congruent. In too many schools there is little correspondence between the district curriculum guides, the teacher's instructional plans, and the assessment measures. Curriculum alignment attempts to remedy this situation in order to improve student achievement.

A RATIONALE FOR CURRICULUM ALIGNMENT

The argument for curriculum alignment is clear enough. It begins by asserting the need for a close fit between the written curriculum and the taught curriculum. The written curriculum, it is assumed, represents a district-wide consensus about instructional objectives and their relative importance for a given group of learners. If developed in the manner outlined in previous chapters, it reflects the input of curriculum experts, subject-matter specialists, district administrators and supervisors, and classroom teachers. Since it thus represents an informed consensus, it should be the determining element in what is taught day by day.

If the district does not take reasonable steps to ensure that the guides are followed, the evidence suggests that many teachers will make unwise choices of content. In one study, for example (Fisher et al., 1978), a teacher who taught nothing about fractions over a period of ninety days (even though the topic was mandated by the state for that grade) explained the omission by saying, "I don't like fractions." Her reaction is not too atypical. As Schwille et al. (1981) noted, a teacher's decisions about content are influenced by the perceived effort to teach a particular area, the perceived difficulty of that area for the students, and the teacher's feelings of enjoyment while teaching that area. Obviously, then, the district must take reasonable steps to ensure that a teacher's content choices reflect an informed consensus, rather than resulting from such idiosyncratic factors.

There is also an obvious need for a close fit between what is taught and what is tested. As Natriello and Dornbusch (1984) note, student effort and achievement will be enhanced if students believe that the evaluation systems are valid and fair. And valid and fair assessment systems require curriculum-based tests that correspond adequately with what was taught. Standardized tests will not suffice, since the content of standardized tests does not correspond closely with what is usually taught in the classroom. In one study (Freeman et al., 1980) it was determined that almost half the items in a standardized mathematics test used in many districts covered content not taught at a particular grade level.

These arguments for curriculum alignment have not totally persuaded the profession. Some educators and researchers are concerned that administrative attempts to align closely the written and the taught curricula will reduce teacher autonomy and creativity. And others have pointed out the dangers of making the test too important: the test becomes the curriculum, and teachers focus all their efforts on preparing students for that test.

Such reservations, it should be noted, support the principles of the mastery curriculum articulated in Chapter 7. As explained there, district curriculum guides should encompass only the mastery curriculum—those aspects of the curriculum that are both essential and structured. District guides should not deal with the organic elements—those that do not require structuring; or the enrichment elements—those not essential for all students. Obviously, then, the alignment process should focus only on the mastery curriculum. Since neither organic nor enrichment components are assessed or monitored, the teacher will thus have an important measure of autonomy.

ORGANIZING THE ALIGNMENT PROJECT

The first important step is to organize the alignment project and to allocate responsibilities. The project is a complex one, involving several critical steps, and it will probably operate most effectively if it systematically involves all those who can contribute. Each district, of course, will develop its own organization and management system for the project; the system oulined below has been derived from an analysis of several successful alignment projects.

One effective way to begin is to appoint a curriculum-alignment task force, a respresentative group that will be responsible for planning and coordinating the project. The task force should include an appropriate number of representatives from the following constituencies: district administrators; district supervisors; school administrators; teachers; and parents. At the outset the task force should develop its own planning guide, indicating the steps to be taken, the deadline for each step, and those responsible for each step. A special point should be made here about the allocation of leadership responsibilities. Rather than simply assuming that the principal will play the key leadership role at the school level, the task force should attempt to identify and develop a leadership team at each school, so that the talents of many individuals are utilized and responsibility is shared. Figure 11-1 shows a form that can be used to assist in such planning. It lists all the steps in the alignment project and provides space for deadlines and the names of those responsible for each step.

In the discussion that follows, certain assumptions will be made about those providing leadership, simply for purposes of illustration; however, each district should develop its own system for allocating leadership responsibilities.

One of the initial decisions the task force should make is the scope of

FIGURE 11-1. Alignment-Project Planning Guide

Project Step	Deadline	Primarily Responsible	Assists
1. Determine scope of project.			
2. Orient school administrators.			
3. Orient teachers.			
4. Orient students and parents.			
5. Revise curriculum guides.			
6. Identify mastery objectives.			
7. Develop curriculum-based tests.			
8. Correlate mastery objectives with instructional materials.			
9. Develop planning aids.			
10. Help teachers use planning aids.			
11. Monitor teacher use of planning aids.			
12. Develop test-reporting materials.			
13. Help teachers use test reports.			
14. Help school administrators use test reports.			
15. Use test reports in evaluating curriculum.			
16. Provide staff development for school administrators.			
17. Provide staff development for teachers.			
18. Monitor and evaluate the alignment project.			

the alignment project: which subjects at which grade levels will be included? The alignment project of the Los Angeles Unified School District (see Niedermeyer and Yelon, 1981) covers reading, mathematics, and language from K-6; the Monitoring Achievement in Pittsburgh project covers mathematics, reading, grammar/composition, and critical thinking/social studies from K-12 (see Rifugiato and Wilson, 1983). The decision will, of course, be affected by such considerations as the size of the district, the resources available, and administrator's perceptions of needs.

The task force should then make plans to orient all the key groups to be involved in and affected by the alignment project. The first group to be oriented should probably be the school principals. They should have in-depth preparation to enable them to both discharge their own respon-sibilities and explain the project to others. The principals can then at the school level orient both their own faculties and parent groups.

IDENTIFYING THE MASTERY OBJECTIVES

With the orientation completed, the task force should turn their attention to the critical task of identifying the mastery objectives. (As explained in Chapter 1, the mastery objectives are those objectives that are essential for all and require careful structuring.) Since that list of mastery objectives will be used in developing both the curriculum-based tests and the teachers' alignment materials, it is essential that the task be done with care and due deliberation. If the district has developed a curriculum that focuses only on mastery objectives, then the task is a very simple one: the objectives have already been identified for each grade level. If the district is basing the align-ment project on existing guides that do not embody the mastery approach, then subject-matter committees should be assigned the task of identifying the key objectives.

The subject-matter committees should begin by reviewing and revising the guides, if revision seems indicated. Even the best guides become out-dated; and it is obviously unwise to base an alignment project on an inade-quate curriculum. Once necessary revisions have been made, the committee should identify for each grade the mastery objectives—the key skills, con-cepts, and information that students are expected to master. (A sample list is shown in Figure 11-2.)

Three types of objectives should probably not be included in the mastery list:

- Objectives that are too difficult to assess with district-made tests. Most districts, for example, would probably choose not to assess listening skills, since valid listening tests are very difficult to develop, ad-minister, and score. Similarly, most affective outcomes (such as "ap-preciating poetry") are difficult to measure validly with objective tests.

FIGURE 11–2. Sample Mastery-Objectives List

GRADE 5. SOCIAL STUDIES: PEOPLE OF AMERICA

Maps, Globes, and Graphics Skills

1. Locate Canada on globe.
2. On an outline map of Canada, identify each province.
3. On an outline map of Canada, with locations of cities indicated, identify: Montreal, Vancouver, Toronto, Winnipeg, Calgary.
4. Use scale on map to estimate distance between two Canadian cities.
5. Identify major ethnic groups and their relative sizes from bar graph.

- Objectives that are not considered essential for all students. Many district guides include content which has been identified in this text as enrichment material: objectives that are not really basic for all students but simply broaden the curriculum or challenge the more able.
- Objectives which have been emphasized at some previous grade level or which will be emphasized at some future grade level. While many district guides include objectives which are to be "reviewed" or "introduced," only those objectives to be emphasized at that particular grade level should be identified in the alignment project. It is expected that teachers will review as necessary and will feel free to introduce skills and concepts as the occasion arises.

These preliminary lists of grade-level mastery objectives should then be reviewed by classroom teachers. At the elementary level, the reviews should be made by grade-level teams; third-grade teachers, for example, should have an opportunity to review the mastery lists for all areas for which they are responsible. At the secondary level, the review should be conducted departmentally. This teacher review is essential, since teachers will be expected to teach and test for the objectives on the final list.

The task force should then undertake a final review of the mastery lists. One of the important questions to be raised at this juncture is whether the skills and concepts can be taught for mastery within the time allotted. How much time should be allotted to mastery objectives? The Pittsburgh alignment project suggests a figure of 60 percent of the total instructional time available; the remaining time is provided for remediation and enrichment.

DEVELOPING CURRICULUM-BASED TESTS

That graded list of mastery objectives should then be used to develop curriculum-based tests. Since these tests play such a key role in the alignment project, they should be developed with the advice of measurement experts who can guide the development of the tests and also assess the tests for reliability and validity. Test development is a highly complex process that requires very specialized technical skills. If districts do not have their own evaluation experts, they may wish to use the services of professional and commercial organizations which will develop such tests on a contractual basis.

Measurement experts usually recommend that a process like the following one be used in developing and assessing the curriculum-based tests. (Those requiring more information about the development of curriculum-based tests should consult one of the standard references: Bloom, Hastings, and Madaus's 1971 text provides a comprehensive treatment of evaluation; the Morris, Fitz-gibbons and Henderson 1978 kit is also very helpful.)

1. Determine test scope and frequency. Will curriculum-based tests be administered at the conclusion of each unit, at the end of each semester, or at the end of the school year? More frequent testing provides administrators and teachers with formative data that can be used to monitor student progress and take corrective actions; however, frequent testing reduces instructional time and seems to increase teacher resistance to the project.

2. Determine how many forms of each test will be required. Larger school systems may require several alternative forms for each test, in order to ensure test security. For smaller systems, two forms for each test will probably suffice.

3. For each objective, develop a pool of test items. Be sure that the test items validly assess the objective. Do not use "comprehension" items, for example, to assess "application" objectives.

4. Construct the pilot forms of the tests by selecting a sample of test items, grouping the items in some logical manner, and preparing clear instructions.

5. Develop a scoring system which will provide administrators, teachers, and students with the information they require in order to understand and use test results. Administrators will need information about overall achievement; teachers will need diagnostic information about classes and individual students; and students will want grades.

6. Have content specialists review the tests to ensure that items are valid, that the answers are correct, and that the sampling reflects curricular priorities. Administer the pilot forms of the test to groups of students in order to measure test reliability.

The process outlined above obviously describes the development of objective tests, the type most commonly used in alignment projects. Many districts, however, have seen fit to supplement those objective tests with certain performance tests, especially in the area of written composition. Those performance tests will require quite different methods of development and assessment.

Obviously the process of developing curriculum-referenced tests is a complex and time-consuming one. These tests are so important, however, that such an expenditure of time and effort is fully warranted.

CORRELATING THE MASTERY LIST AND INSTRUCTIONAL MATERIALS

With the tests prepared, the subject-matter committees should turn their attention to the instructional materials. By reviewing texts currently in use and checking their content against the mastery list, the committees should first establish whether new basal texts will be required. Quite often the development of the mastery-objectives list will highlight deficiencies in existing texts—deficiencies that were not apparent when teachers alone determined what they would teach.

The committees should then develop objectives-materials correlation charts for each grade, in order to assist teachers in using instructional materials. On the left of the chart are listed the mastery objectives; across the top, the titles of both basal and supplementary texts, including, of course, any new texts which will be ordered. Each mastery objective is then keyed to specific pages in the texts. A sample correlation chart is shown in Figure 11-3. Although many publishers make such correlation charts available to districts which have purchased their texts, such publisher-produced charts are not sufficiently reliable for use in the alignment project.

The correlation process thus accomplishes two important goals. It provides a means for the district to ensure that adequate instructional materials are available; and it helps teachers make their instructional plans.

FIGURE 11-3. Sample Objectives-Text Correlation Chart

GRADE 10. SCIENCE: BIOLOGY

Mastery Objectives	Life Sciences	Modern Biology
1. Define *ecosystem*	pp. 75–78	pp. 14–18
2. Identify three common air pollutants	pp. 78–79	pp. 19–20
3. Explain probable causes of acid rain	pp. 82–83	

DEVELOPING INSTRUCTIONAL-PLANNING AIDS

The next important component of the alignment project is the instructional-planning aids. These are materials which will assist teachers in developing and implementing instructional plans. Besides helping teachers plan, they also can facilitate discussions between administrators (or supervisors) and teachers about the planning process. Two major types of planning aids play an important role here.

Yearly Planning Matrix   Teachers will first need help in making tentative plans for the school year, to ensure that all mastery objectives are taught and reinforced and that adequate time has been provided. One way of helping them accomplish these goals is by providing a yearly planning matrix, like the one shown in Figure 11–4. The teachers first list the mastery objectives, grouped according to subject-matter subdivisions. They then indicate the report or marking period when they plan to teach this objective for mastery and when they expect to reinforce that objective. They then estimate the total number of instructional periods required.

FIGURE 11–4.   Sample Yearly Planning Guide

GRADE 8.   ENGLISH LANGUAGE ARTS (Literature)

Mastery Objective	Report Period				Total Time Required
	First	Second	Third	Fourth	
1. Define *character*	T		R		2 Periods
2. Identify three means of character portrayal	T		R		2 Periods
3. Infer character's motivations	T	R	R		4 Periods

CODE: T, teach for mastery; R, reinforce

One effective way of using the yearly matrix is as follows:

1. The teacher submits to an instructional leader the yearly matrix, with entries noted in pencil. The penciled entries reflect the teacher's tentative decisions about yearly planning.
2. The instructional leader and the teacher confer about the yearly plan, discussing issues of sequencing and time allocation and making

any changes they both agree are necessary. The revised decisions are then recorded in ink.

3. The yearly matrix is posted in the classroom so that students and classroom visitors can be informed. As the teacher teaches or reinforces a mastery objective, the appropriate entry is circled.
4. The teacher is expected to bring the yearly matrix to any supervisory or evaluation conferences.

The yearly matrix thus serves several important purposes.

Unit-Planning Guides   Teachers will also need help with their unit planning. Two approaches can be used in deriving unit plans from the yearly matrix. In fields such as mathematics and science, where units are built from closely related objectives, the teacher can begin with the yearly matrix, list related objectives in unit clusters, and check to see that the time allocations seem appropriate for that grade level. In this approach the objectives shape the unit.

In fields such as English and social studies, where several types of objectives are often included in one unit, teachers will need special help in learning how to integrate mastery objectives into thematic units. Most teachers will find it helpful to begin by "roughing in" the unit—identifying the unit theme, determining the approximate length of the unit, specifying the major unit generalizations, and identifying the key resources. They then turn to the yearly matrix and select appropriate objectives for that unit, checking off each objective as it is included in a particular unit. They then make a final check to be sure that all objectives have been included in at least one unit. Figure 11–5 shows one form that can be used in integrating mastery objectives into a thematic unit. In this approach the unit theme influences the selection of the objectives.

These unit-planning guides should also play an important role in the supervision process. They can assist the supervisor and the teacher in discussing curricular priorities, in reflecting about planning approaches, in determining instructional methods, and in examining issues of individualization and remediation.

In addition to the yearly and unit-planning aids, some school districts expect teachers to indicate in their daily lesson plans which mastery objectives will be covered. Others feel that teachers should have more flexibility and autonomy in daily planning. The research does not provide any clear guidance here. Although well-structured lessons are usually associated with increased achievement (see Berliner, 1984), there is no evidence that the quality of written lesson plans is related to student achievement. Some teachers can write good plans but cannot deliver them effectively; other teachers can deliver well-structured lessons without committing plans to paper. (For an excellent review of the research on planning and achievement, see Peterson, Marx, and Clark, 1978.)

FIGURE 11–5. Sample Unit-Planning Chart

GRADE 10. ENGLISH. Second Report Period

UNIT THEME: The Changing American Family

LENGTH OF UNIT: 10 periods

Thematic Generalizations

> 1. Understand how American family is changing.
> 2. Understand reasons for changes.

Common Readings

> 1. *My Antonia*
> 2. *Life with Father*
> 3. *Kramer vs. Kramer*
> 4. Selected articles from current magazines

Mastery Objectives to Be Emphasized

> 1. Write expository essay of causal analysis.
> 2. Identify author's bias in an essay of opinion.
> 3. Identify three means of character portrayal.
> 4. Infer character's motivations.

Also, some districts provide pacing charts that indicate when a given set of objectives should be taught and approximately how much time should be devoted to each group of outcomes. While such charts can be helpful to teachers who need assistance with pacing, most teachers seem to view the pacing charts as too controlling. Their use would seem to reduce teacher autonomy in planning, teaching, and providing remediation. The purposes of such pacing charts can perhaps be better realized through supervisor-teacher discussions about yearly and unit planning and by team or departmental discussions of time allocation and instructional pacing.

The intent of all the instructional-planning aids should be to help teachers plan more effectively, not to control their classroom decision making.

DEVELOPING REPORTING MATERIALS

The task force should also determine, in consultation with administrators, supervisors, and teachers, what reporting materials will be required in the alignment project. The following types of materials have been used in several successful projects:

1. The *planning report* summarizes for each class the student performance on the previous year's summative examination. The report is distributed to teachers in workshops that precede the opening of school

in September; teachers use the report to determine which objectives need additional review and which students require special attention.

2. The *class diagnostic summary* is provided to teachers after each test administration. It gives information about the test results of all the students in the class, objective by objective. The teacher uses this report to plan posttest remediation and to make adjustments in the yearly and unit forms.

3. The *individual student report* provides comprehensive information for each student; it also is distributed after each major testing. It gives the student's name and indicates for all objectives the number correct and incorrect. The individual student report is made available to teachers, the student, and the student's parents.

These reports, which provide a great deal of useful information, can be produced at relatively little cost through the use of computers.

PROVIDING STAFF DEVELOPMENT FOR THE ALIGNMENT PROJECT

Once all these decisions have been made and materials have been developed, the school administrators and teachers should then be provided with the in-depth training they will need to make the project successful. Part of this staff development should occur, of course, before the project begins, to prepare both groups for the requirements of the alignment project. Much of it, however, should be made available on a continuing basis throughout the year as problems develop. The specific content of the staff development will, of course, depend upon local needs. In general, however, the following topics might be included in the staff development for principals:

1. A rationale for curriculum alignment.
2. Orienting teachers and parents about alignment.
3. Helping teachers use test reports.
4. Helping teachers make yearly and unit plans.
5. Monitoring teacher planning and instruction.
6. Using test reports to evaluate the school's program of studies.
7. Using the alignment project to make supervision more effective.
8. Evaluating the alignment project.

The staff development for the teachers will include some similar topics, with a different emphasis. The following topics would probably be helpful:

1. A rationale for curriculum alignment.
2. Identifying mastery objectives.
3. Using mastery objectives in yearly and unit planning.
4. Using test reports to plan instruction and monitor progress.
5. Locating and using instructional materials.

6. Teaching for mastery objectives.
7. Communicating test results to students and parents.

The staff-development workshops for both administrators and teachers should also be used to get participants' input about improving the project. Even well-planned projects will need refinement and revision, and the staff-development sessions provide an excellent opportunity for groups to raise problems and suggest solutions.

MONITORING AND EVALUATING THE ALIGNMENT PROJECT

Throughout its operation the alignment project should be monitored to be sure it is working as planned and then evaluated to assess its overall effectiveness. Two types of monitoring are required. First, district administrators should be responsible for monitoring project mangement, seeking answers to the following questions:

1. Have all necessary instructional materials been provided, and are correlation charts accurate?
2. Are tests being administered and scored on schedule?
3. Are staff-development sessions being conducted as planned, and are they judged by participants to be helpful?
4. Are principals and supervisors helping teachers plan effectively, teach to mastery objectives, and use test results to modify instruction?

Several methods can be used to answer these questions. First, those responsible for carrying out the steps identified in the planning guide should be expected to submit periodic reports noting dates when key steps were carried out and identifying any problems that developed. Second, as noted above, some time during each staff-development session should be used to identify problems and assess progress. Regularly scheduled administrative and faculty meetings can also be used, of course, to assess the progress of the project. Finally, a representative sample of administrators and teachers should be interviewed, perhaps once every two months, in order to survey their perceptions and probe their concerns.

The second type of monitoring focuses on the teachers' implementation of the project at the classroom level. The intent here is for school administrators to ensure that teachers are carrying out their responsibilities, but to do so in a professional manner that does not create an atmosphere of distrust. This goal can be accomplished if principals present the project as a means of helping teachers, not as a method of controlling them. All of the following activities, therefore, should be carried out in that spirit. First, of course, the submission of the yearly planning matrix will enable the principal and the teacher to discuss together such essential matters as the organizing of objectives, the optimal sequencing of instruction, and the allocation of instructional time as a reflection of curricular priorities.

Also, the unit plans should facilitate professional discussions between supervisors and teachers. The review of those plans will enable the supervisor and the teacher to discuss issues of unit planning, time allocation, instructional methods, assessment of student learning, and remediation strategies. Since these unit plans are so important, some districts require teachers to submit them for review; others simply expect teachers to develop such plans and review them with colleagues and supervisors, without requiring the plans to be submitted.

Finally, the alignment project can support an objectives-focused supervisory process. Instead of being concerned primarily with instructional methods, supervisors can focus on outcomes. In preobservation conferences they can help the teacher assess what progress has already been made and determine what mastery objectives should be emphasized in the week ahead. The preobservation conference should also provide both with an opportunity to reflect about assessment concerns: How will student learning be assessed? What will be an acceptable level of student achievement for a given lesson and a series of lessons? In their observations they can focus on the clarity of objectives and the evidence of student mastery. And in the postobservation conference they can help the teacher use student-achievement data as a means of diagnosing instruction.

Such outcomes-focused supervision enables the supervisor and the teacher to examine data objectively and to concern themselves with the essential issue of student learning, rather than emphasizing instructional methods. Issues of method are raised only if the data suggest that students did not achieve at the agreed-upon level. As Niedermeyer (1976) notes, "One of the most obvious advantages of using the . . . model is that the interaction between administrators and teachers is referenced to empirical evidence of student accomplishments, rather than to beliefs or opinions about what is 'right' or 'works' " (p. 4).

The summative evaluation of the alignment project can make use of two measures. First, the perceptions of administrators, supervisors, and teachers should be surveyed at the end of each school year. Figure 11–6 shows one type of survey form that can be used. The more important measure, of course, is student achievement. School districts should maintain and carefully analyze the results of both curriculum-based and standardized tests, noting trends over a multiple-year period of time. If the project has been designed carefully and implemented professionally, districts should find that student achievement increases. As Niedermeyer and Yelon (1981) note in their report of the Los Angeles project, evaluators who reviewed the project judged it to be one of the most promising efforts to improve urban schools.

FIGURE 11–6. Survey of Perceptions about Alignment Project

DIRECTIONS: Listed below are several statements about our alignment project and its components. Circle the symbol that best represents the extent to which you agree or disagree about the statement:

SA strongly agree   D disagree
A agree   SD strongly disagree

Statement		Your Perception		
1. The list of mastery objectives helped teachers plan, teach, and assess learning.	SA	A	D	SD
2. The objectives-materials correlation charts helped teachers plan and use materials.	SA	A	D	SD
3. The yearly planning matrix helped teachers make effective plans for the year.	SA	A	D	SD
4. The unit-planning guides helped teachers develop and implement unit plans.	SA	A	D	SD
5. The curriculum-based tests provided useful information to administrators and teachers.	SA	A	D	SD
6. The alignment project improved the professional climate of the school.	SA	A	D	SD
7. The alignment project seemed successful in improving student learning.	SA	A	D	SD

Please provide brief responses to the two items below.

8. The main advantage of the alignment project was

9. The alignment project could be improved by

Please check below to indicate your professional role; there is no need to sign your name.

_____ District administrator   _____ District supervisor

_____ School administrator   _____ Team or department leader

_____ Classroom teacher

APPLICATIONS

1. Be prepared to discuss or write about your views on this statement:

    Curriculum-alignment projects are unnecessary attempts by administrators to control teachers and damage the climate of trust essential in effective schools.

2. Using the form shown in Figure 11-1 (or your own modification of it), develop an alignment-project planning guide that could be used in a school district with which you are acquainted.

3. One of the issues raised in this chapter is the need for pacing charts. Based upon your knowledge of classroom teachers, would you consider such charts helpful or intrusive?

4. What advice would you give this elementary teacher: "We're being judged on our pupils' success on district tests. Since I think that's unfair, I'm thinking about doing a little quiet coaching for the tests."

REFERENCES

Berliner, D. C. (1984). The half-full glass: A review of research on teaching. In P. Hosford (ed.), *Using what we know about teaching.* Alexandria, VA: Association for Supervision and Curriculum Development.

Bloom, B. S., Hastings, J. T., and Madaus, G. F. (1971). *Handbook on formative and summative evaluation of student learning.* New York: McGraw-Hill.

Fisher, C. W., Berliner, D. C., Filby, N. N., Marliave, R. S., Cahen, L. S., and Dishaw, M. M. (1978). *Teaching behaviors, academic learning time, and student achievement.* San Francisco: Far West Laboratory for Educational Research and Development.

Freeman, D., Kuhs, T., Porter, A., Knappen, L., Floden, R., Schmidt, W., and Schwille, J. (1980). *The fourth grade mathematics curriculum as inferred from textbooks and tests.* East Lansing, MI: Institute for Research on Teaching, Michigan State University.

Morris, L. L., Fitz-gibbons, C. T., and Henderson, M. E. (1978). *Program Evaluation Kit.* Beverly Hills, CA: Sage.

Natriello, G., and Dornbusch, S. M. (1984). *Teacher evaluation standards and student effort.* New York: Longman.

Niedermeyer, F. C. (1976). *A basis for improved instructional leadership by school administrators.* Los Alamitos, CA: Southwest Regional Laboratory for Educational Research and Development.

Niedermeyer, F. C., and Yelon, S. (1981). Los Angeles aligns instruction with essential skills. *Educational Leadership, 38,* 618–620.

Peterson, P. L., Marx, R. W., and Clark, C. M. (1978). Teacher planning, teacher behavior, and student achievement. *American Education Research Journal, 15,* 417–432.

Rifugiato, F. J., and Wilson, H. A. (1983). *A guide to the MAP project.* Pittsburgh, PA: School District of Pittsburgh.

Schwille, J., Porter, A., Belli, A., Floden, R., Freeman, D., Knappen, L., Kuhs, T., and Schmidt, W. J. (1981). *Teachers as policy brokers in the content of elementary school mathematics.* East Lansing, MI: Institute for Research on Teaching, Michigan State University.

12

Curriculum Evaluation

Evaluation has an ancient history. As Guba and Lincoln (1981) point out, a Chinese emperor in 2200 B.C. required that his public officials demonstrate their proficiency in formal competency tests. And in the United States, the concern for evaluating the schools can be traced at least as far back as the recommendations of the Committee of Ten, which at the end of the nineteenth century became perhaps the first example of "evaluative standards" for the nation's secondary schools (National Education Association, 1969). However, in recent years, the interest in curriculum evaluation especially has seemed to increase markedly. The public's insistence on educational accountability, the experts' demands for educational reform, and the educators' concomitant need for evidence of results have all contributed to this current interest in theories and methods of curriculum evaluation. Unfortunately, much of this interest seems to have resulted in an ill-conceived obsession with test results. A broader perspective and more diversified approaches both seem necessary.

It is hoped that this desired breadth and diversification have been reflected throughout this work. Chapter 6 described a comprehensive assessment model that can be used in improving a program of studies. Chapter 8 emphasized the importance of evaluating new courses of study. Chapter 10 explicated an approach especially useful during the implementation stage. And Chapter 11 described how evaluation can be used to effect improved alignment. The intent of this chapter is to bring all these approaches into focus and to provide for greater understanding of the evaluation process. To that end it begins by proposing a broad definition of the term *curriculum evaluation*. It then describes several current evaluation models. It concludes by proposing a comprehensive and eclectic process that can be used to evaluate a field of study, perhaps the most difficult task that evaluators face.

CURRICULUM EVALUATION DEFINED

That broader perspective mentioned above requires a less constricting view of both the purposes and foci of curriculum evaluation. In acquiring a broader understanding of purpose, two concepts delineated by Guba and Lincoln (1981) seem especially useful: *merit* and *worth*. *Merit*, as they use the term, refers to the intrinsic value of an entity—value that is implicit, inherent, and independent of any applications. Merit is established without reference to a context. *Worth*, on the other hand, is the value of an entity in reference to a particular context or a specific application. It is the "payoff" value for a given institution or group of people. Thus, a given English course may seem to have a great deal of merit in the eyes of experts: it may reflect sound theory, be built upon current research, and embody content that experts deem desirable. The same course, however, may have relatively little worth for a teacher instructing unmotivated working-class youth in an urban school: it may require teaching skills which the teacher has not mastered and learning materials which the students cannot read. In this sense, then, curriculum evaluation should be concerned with assessing both merit and worth.

The foci of curriculum evaluation also need to be expanded. To use the concepts of this present work, curriculum evaluation should be concerned with assessing the value of a *program of studies* (all the planned learning experiences over a multiyear period for a given group of learners), a *field of study* (all the planned learning experiences over a multiyear period in a given discipline or area of study), and a *course of study* (all the planned learning experiences for a period of one year or less, in a given field of study). All three levels of curriculum work are important. And there are substantive differences between evaluating a program of studies and a field of study and differences of scope between evaluating a field of study and a course of study.

The foregoing analysis yields this stipulative definition of *curriculum evaluation*:

> The assessment of the merit and worth of a program of studies, a field of study, or a course of study.

CURRENT EVALUATION MODELS

How can the merit and worth of such aspects of curriculum be determined? Evaluation specialists have proposed an array of models, an examination of which can provide useful background for the process presented in this work.

Tyler's Objectives-Centered Model

One of the earliest evaluation models, which continues to influence many assessment projects, was that proposed by Ralph Tyler in his monograph, *Basic Principles of Curriculum and Instruction* (1950). As explained in this work and used in numerous large-scale assessment efforts, the Tyler approach moved rationally and systematically through several related steps:

1. Begin with the behavioral objectives which have been previously determined. Those objectives should specify both the content of learning and the student behavior expected: "demonstrate familiarity with dependable sources of information on questions relating to nutrition."
2. Identify the situations which will give the student the opportunity to express the behavior embodied in the objective and which evoke or encourage this behavior. Thus, if you wish to assess oral-language use, identify situations which evoke oral language.
3. Select, modify, or construct suitable evaluation instruments, and check the instruments for objectivity, reliability, and validity.
4. Use the instruments to obtain summarized or appraised results.
5. Compare the results obtained from several instruments before and after given periods in order to estimate the amount of change taking place.
6. Analyze the results in order to determine strengths and weaknesses of the curriculum and to identify possible explanations about the reason for this particular pattern of strengths and weaknesses.
7. Use the results to make the necessary modifications in the curriculum.

The Tyler model has several advantages. It is relatively easy to understand and apply. It is rational and systematic. It focuses attention on curricular strengths and weaknesses, rather than being solely concerned with the performance of individual students. And it emphasizes the importance of a continuing cycle of assessment, analysis, and improvement. However, as Guba and Lincoln point out, it suffers from several deficiencies. It does not suggest how the objectives themselves should be evaluated. It does not provide standards or suggest how standards should be developed. Its emphasis on the prior statement of objectives may restrict creativity in curriculum development. And it seems to place undue emphasis on the pre-assessment and post-assessment, ignoring completely the need for formative assessment.

Stufflebeam's Context-Input-Process-Product Model

These obvious weaknesses in the Tyler model led several evaluation experts in the late 1960s and early 1970s to attack the Tyler model and to offer their own alternatives. One of those alternatives which had the greatest impact was that developed by a Phi Delta Kappa committee chaired by Daniel Stuf-flebeam (1971). This model seemed to appeal to educational leaders because it emphasized the importance of producing evaluative data for decision making; in fact, decision making was the sole justification for evaluation, in the view of the Phi Delta Kappa committee.

To service the needs of decision makers, the Stufflebeam model provides a means for generating data relating to four stages of program operation: context evaluation, which continuously assesses needs and problems in the context in order to help decision makers determine goals and objectives; input evaluation, which assesses alternative means for achieving those goals to help decision makers choose optimal means; process evaluation, which monitors the processes both to ensure that the means are actually being implemented and to make the necessary modifications; and product evaluation, which compares actual ends with intended ends and leads to a series of recycling decisions.

During each of these four stages specific steps are taken:

1. The kinds of decisions are identified.
2. The kinds of data needed to make those decisions are identified.
3. Those data are collected.
4. The criteria for determining quality are established.
5. The data are analyzed on the basis of those criteria.
6. The needed information is provided to decision makers.

The Context-Input-Process-Product (CIPP) model, as it has come to be called, has several attractive features for those interested in curriculum evaluation. Its emphasis on decision making seems appropriate for administrators concerned with improving curricula. Its concern for the formative aspects of evaluation remedies a serious deficiency in the Tyler model. Finally, the very detailed guidelines and forms provided by the committee provide step-by-step guidance for users.

The CIPP model, however, has some serious drawbacks associated with it. Its main weakness seems to be its failure to recognize the complexity of the decision-making process in organizations. It assumes more rationality than exists in such situations and ignores the political factors that play such a large part in such decisions. Also, as Guba and Lincoln note, it seems very difficult to implement and expensive to maintain.

Scriven's Goal-Free Model

Michael Scriven (1972) was the first to question the assumption that goals or objectives are crucial in the evaluation process. After his involvement in several evaluation projects where so-called "side effects" seemed more significant than the original objectives, he began to question the seemingly arbitrary distinction between intended and unintended effects. His goal-free model was the outcome of such dissatisfaction.

In conducting a goal-free evaluation, the evaluator functions as an unbiased observer, who begins by generating a profile of needs for the group served by a given program. (Scriven is somewhat vague as to how this needs profile is to be derived.) Then, by using methods that are primarily qualitative in nature, the evaluator assesses the actual effects of the program. If a program has an effect that is responsive to one of the identified needs, then the program is perceived as useful.

Scriven's main contribution, obviously, was to redirect the attention of evaluators and administrators to the importance of unintended effects—a redirection that seems especially useful in education. If a mathematics program achieves its objectives of improving computational skills but has the unintended effect of diminishing interest in mathematics, then it cannot be judged completely successful. His emphasis on qualitative methods also seemed to come at an opportune moment, when there was increasing dissatisfaction among the research community with the dominance of quantitative methodologies.

As Scriven himself notes, however, goal-free evaluation should be used to complement, not supplant, goal-based assessments. Used alone, it cannot provide sufficient information for the decision maker. And some critics have faulted Scriven for not providing more explicit directions for developing and implementing the goal-free model; as a consequence, it probably can be used only by experts who do not require explicit guidance in assessing needs and detecting effects.

Stake's Responsive Model

Robert Stake (1975) has made a major contribution to curriculum evaluation in his development of the responsive model, since the responsive model is based explicitly upon the assumption that the concerns of the stakeholders—those for whom the evaluation is done—should be paramount in determining the evaluation issues. He makes the point this way:

> To emphasize evaluation issues that are important for each particular program, I recommend the responsive evaluation approach. It is an approach that trades off some measurement precision in order to increase the usefulness of the findings to persons in and around the program . . . . An educational evaluation is responsive evaluation if it orients more directly to program activities than to program intents; responds to audience requirements for information; and if the different value perspectives present are referred to in reporting the success and failure of the program. (p. 14)

Stake recommends an interactive and recursive evaluation process which embodies these steps:

1. The evaluator meets with clients, staff, and audiences, to gain a sense of their perspectives on and intentions regarding the evaluation.

2. The evaluator draws upon such discussions and the analysis of any documents to determine the scope of the evaluation project.

3. The evaluator observes the program closely to get a sense of its operation and to note any unintended deviations from announced intents.

4. The evaluator discovers the stated and real purposes of the project and the concerns that various audiences have about it and the evaluation.

5. The evaluator identifies the issues and problems that the evaluation should be concerned with. For each issue and problem, the evaluator develops an evaluation design, specifying the kinds of data needed.

6. The evaluator selects the means needed to acquire the data desired. Most often the means will be human observers or judges.

7. The evaluator implements the data-collection procedures.

8. The evaluator organizes the information into themes and prepares "portrayals" which communicate in natural ways the thematic reports. The portrayals may involve video tapes, artifacts, case studies, or other "faithful representations."

9. By again being sensitive to the concerns of the stakeholders, the evaluator decides which audiences require which reports and chooses formats most appropriate for given audiences.

Clearly, the chief advantage of the responsive model is its sensitivity to clients. By identifying their concerns and being sensitive to their values, by involving them closely throughout the evaluation, and by adapting the form of reports to meet their needs, the model, if effectively used, should result in evaluations of high utility to clients. The responsive model also has the virtue of flexibility: the evaluator is able to choose from a variety of methodologies once client concerns have been identified. Its chief weakness would seem to be its susceptibility to manipulation by clients, who in expressing their concerns might attempt to draw attention away from weaknesses they did not want exposed.

Eisner's Connoisseurship Model

Elliot Eisner (1979) has drawn from his background in aesthetics and art education in developing his "connoisseurship" model, an approach to evaluation which emphasizes qualitative appreciation. The Eisner model is built upon two closely related constructs: connoisseurship and criticism. Connoisseurship, in Eisner's terms, is the art of appreciation—recognizing and appreciating through perceptual memory, drawing from experience to appreciate what is significant. It is the ability both to perceive the particulars of educational life and to understand how those particulars form part of a classroom structure. Criticism, to Eisner, is the art of disclosing the qualities of an entity that connoisseurship perceives. In such a disclosure, the educational critic is more likely to use what Eisner calls "nondiscursive" language—language that is metaphorical, connotative, and symbolic. It uses linguistic forms to present, rather than represent, conception or feeling.

Educational criticism, in Eisner's formulation, has three aspects. The descriptive aspect is an attempt to characterize and portray the relevant qualities of educational life—the rules, the regularities, the underlying architecture. The interpretive aspect uses ideas from the social sciences to explore meanings and to develop alternative explanations—to explicate social phenomena. The evaluative aspect makes judgments in order to improve the educational processes and provides grounds for the value choices made, so that others might better disagree.

The chief contribution of the Eisner model is that it breaks sharply with the traditional scientific models and offers a radically different view of what evaluation might be. In doing so, it broadens the evaluator's perspective and enriches his or her repertoire by drawing from a rich tradition of artistic criticism. Its critics have faulted it for its lack of methodological rigor, although Eisner has attempted to refute such charges. Critics have also argued that use of the model requires a great deal of expertise, noting the seeming elitism implied in the term *connoisseurship.*

DEVELOPING AN ECLECTIC APPROACH

Although the models above seem sharply distinct from each other, there is some evidence of congruence in current theories of evaluation. This congruence is quite evident in the ASCD monograph, *Applied Strategies for Curriculum Evaluation* (Brandt, 1981), in which seven experts in evaluation were asked to explain how their "evaluation model" would be used in evaluating a secondary humanities course. While the models proposed by the experts (Popham, Bonnet, Stake, Scriven, Eisner, Webster, and Worthen) differed in many of their details, there were several common emphases in the approaches: study the context; determine client concerns; use qualitative methods; assess opportunity cost (what other opportunities the student is missing by taking this course); be sensitive to unintended effects; and develop different reports for different audiences.

By using these common emphases along with insights generated from analyzing other models, it is possible to develop a list of criteria which can be used in both assessing and developing evaluation models. Such a list is shown in Figure 12–1. Districts with sufficient resources to employ an expert consultant can use the criteria to assess the model proposed by the consultant; districts developing a home-grown process can use the criteria to direct their own work.

The criteria will obviously result in an eclectic approach to evaluation, one which draws from the strengths of several different models. Such an eclectic approach is reflected in the discussion which follows. It describes a process which has been used successfully in evaluating a field of study; the same process can be used as well to evaluate a course of study; only the scope of the evaluation is reduced.

FIGURE 12–1.   Criteria for a Curriculum-Evaluation Model

An effective curriculum-evaluation model . . .

1. Can be implemented without making inordinate demands upon district resources.
2. Can be applied to all levels of curriculum—programs of study, fields of study, courses of study.
3. Makes provisions for assessing all significant aspects of curriculum—the written, the taught, the supported, the tested, and the learned curricula.
4. Makes useful distinctions between merit (intrinsic value) and worth (value for a given context).
5. Is responsive to the special concerns of district stakeholders and is able to provide them with the data they need for decision making.
6. Is goal-oriented, emphasizing objectives and outcomes.
7. Is sensitive to and makes appropriate provisions for assessing unintended effects.
8. Pays due attention to and makes provisions for assessing formative aspects of evaluation.
9. Is sensitive to and makes provisions for assessing the special context for the curriculum.
10. Is sensitive to and makes provisions for assessing the aesthetic or qualitative aspects of the curriculum.
11. Makes provisions for assessing opportunity cost—the opportunities lost by those studying this curriculum.
12. Uses both quantitative and qualitative methods for gathering and analyzing data.
13. Presents findings in reports responsive to the special needs of several audiences.

EVALUATING A FIELD OF STUDY

"How good is our K–12 science curriculum?" The answer to this question comes from evaluating a field of study—a multigrade sequence of learning experiences in one discipline, subject area, or field. Such evaluations are almost always made for a single purpose—to identify strengths and weaknesses in order to plan for improvements. The process of evaluating a field of study includes five important phases: preparing for the evaluation; assessing the context; identifying the evaluation issues; developing the evaluation design; and implementing the evaluation design.

Preparing for the Evaluation

The preparations for the evaluation include three major steps: setting the project parameters; selecting the project director and the evaluation task force; and preparing the evaluation documents.

In setting the project parameters, district administrators in consultation with the school board should determine both the purpose and the limits of the project. They should first of all be clear about the central purpose of the review, since purpose will affect both issues to be examined and methods to be used. In identifying the limits of the project, they should develop answers to the following questions:

1. How much time will be allocated and by what date should the evaluation be completed?
2. What human, fiscal, and material resources will be provided?
3. Which fields will be evaluated?
4. What constituencies will be asked for input? Specifically, will parents, community representatives, and students be involved?

With those parameters set, the project director and evaluation task force should be selected. The project director should be a consultant or a member of the district staff who has considerable technical expertise in curriculum evaluation. The task force should function as an advisory and planning group, making recommendations to and monitoring the performance of the project director. It should probably include a total of ten to twenty individuals, depending upon the size of the district, and have adequate representation from these constituencies: board; school administrators; teachers and other faculty members; and parents and community organizations. If administrators wish, secondary students can be included, if it is felt that their input can be useful.

The project director and the task force can then begin to assemble the documents necessary for the program review. The following documents would typically be needed:

1. A statement of the curriculum goals for that field.
2. A comprehensive description of the community and the student body.
3. A list of all required courses in that field, with time allocations and brief descriptions of each course.
4. A list of all elective courses in the field, including time allocations, course descriptions, and most recent enrollment figures.
5. A random selection of student schedules.
6. Syllabi or course guides for all courses offered.
7. Faculty schedules, showing class enrollments.

Other materials, of course, will be required as the review gets under way; but the above-listed materials are important at the outset.

Assessing the Context

The next stage in a comprehensive evaluation of a field of study is to assess the context. While this stage is obviously of critical importance for an outside evaluator, it is also essential in district-directed projects. The context-assessment stage enables the evaluators to identify both the salient aspects of the educational environment which impinge upon the field of studies and the critical needs of the learners. In assessing the context the evaluators typically should seek answers to the following questions:

1. What are the prevailing attitudes, values, and expectations of the community?
2. What significant aspects of the school district impinge upon the field of study: size; leadership; organizational structure; fiscal resources?
3. What are the special characteristics of school facilities that impinge upon or constrain this field of study?
4. What are the special characteristics of the student body: scholastic aptitude; achievement; home background; ethnic identity; social and physical development?
5. What are the special characteristics of the faculty: experience; educational values; overall competence; educational background?
6. What is special about the school organization: nature of leadership; organizational structure?

The context assessment should result in a report which calls attention to the salient aspects affecting the field of study and identifies the special needs of the learners.

Identifying the Evaluation Issues

The next step in the process is to identify the evaluation issues, to be sure that the evaluation is sensitive to the special concern of the stakeholders and will provide the information needed. Here the distinctions between the several aspects of the curriculum are essential: the written, the supported, the taught, the tested, and the learned curricula all subsume quite different assessment issues.

Also, each of these five must be assessed if the results are to be at all valid. In too many curriculum evalations, the team evaluates only the written curriculum (the official course guides) and the learned curriculum (the results on achievement tests). No valid inferences can be drawn from such an assessment, since the other three important components have been ignored. Suppose, for example, that the students in a particular district do not perform well on measures of critical thinking in social studies, even though district guides include such units. District administrators cannot be sure about the causes of the problem. It might well be that teachers have chosen not to teach those units because they lack the training and materials necessary. Only a comprehensive assessment can yield the information needed to make improvements.

As Figure 12-2 indicates, those five components subsume more than fifty different issues. Obviously, not all these issues will be used in every evaluation. Here it is essential for the evaluation team to identify the issues by surveying and interviewing stakeholders. That list of issues can be used to survey such constituencies as board members, school administrators, faculty, and parents, using a form similar to the one shown in Figure 12-3. The responses can then be analyzed to determine which issues should be evaluated, given the constraints previously identified. The surveys, of course, should be supplemented with interviews of key individuals to provide supplementary data.

FIGURE 12-2. Evaluation Issues: Field of Study

THE WRITTEN CURRICULUM

Goals

1. Are the goals of this subject clearly and explicitly stated and readily accessible to those who need to refer to them?
2. Are those goals congruent with relevant curricular goals of the school district?
3. Are the goals in accord with the recommendations of experts in the field?
4. Are the goals understood and supported by parents?
5. Are the goals understood and supported by school administrators?
6. Are the goals understood and supported by classroom teachers?
7. Are the goals understood and supported by students?

Scope and Sequence of Level Objectives

1. Have the goals of this field been analyzed into a set of grade-level (or achievement-level) objectives that identify the important concepts, skills, and attitudes to be attained?
2. Are those level objectives sufficiently comprehensive so that they adequately reflect the goals of this field?
3. Are those level objectives clearly displayed in some form (such as a scope-and-sequence chart) that facilitates understanding and use?
4. Are the level objectives in accord with and do they reflect the recommendations of experts in the field?
5. Does the grade placement of objectives reflect the best current knowledge of child development?
6. Does the grade placement of objectives provide for sufficient reinforcement without undue repetition?
7. Is the grade placement of objectives appropriate in relation to their difficulty for learners at that level?
8. Are the objectives appropriately distributed over the grades so that there is balance between the grades?

(continued next page)

FIGURE 12-2. *continued*

Written Course Guides

1. Are there written course guides for this field covering all grade levels?
2. Are those guides readily available to administrators, teachers, and parents?
3. Does the format of the guides facilitate revision and amplification?
4. Do the guides clearly specify grade-level objectives in a format and manner that facilitate use?
5. Do the guides make appropriate distinctions between mastery, organic, and enrichment outcomes and focus primarily on the mastery outcomes?
6. Do the guides indicate clearly the relative importance of the mastery outcomes and suggest time allocations that reflect their importance?
7. Do the guides suggest ways of organizing the objectives into learning units, without requiring a particular type of unit organization?
8. Do the guides recommend (but not mandate) teaching/learning activities that seem likely to lead to the attainment of the relevant objectives?
9. Do the teaching and learning activities recommended reflect the best current knowledge about teaching and learning and are they qualitatively excellent?
10. Do the guides suggest appropriate evaluation processes and instruments?
11. Do the guides recommend appropriate instructional materials and other resources?

THE SUPPORTED CURRICULUM

Time

1. Has the school district clearly specified time to be allocated to this field of study at each level of schooling?
2. Does the time allocated to this field seem appropriate in relation to the district's goals, the goals of the field of study, and the recommendations of experts?
3. Do school master schedules and administrative guidelines on time allocation appropriately reflect district allocations?

Materials

1. Is the quantity of instructional materials adequate in relation to student enrollments?
2. Are the learning objectives of the instructional materials consonant with the objectives of the written course guides?
3. Do the instructional materials reflect the best current knowledge in this field of study?
4. Are the instructional materials free of gender bias and ethnic stereotyping?
5. Are the instructional materials written at an appropriate level of difficulty?
6. Are the instructional materials designed and organized in a manner that facilitates teacher use?
7. Do the instructional materials reflect sound learning principles, providing adequately for motivation, explanation, application, reinforcement, and enrichment?

Staff Development

1. Does the district provide on-going staff-development programs that help the teachers use the curriculum guides effectively and involve teachers in improving the guides?

THE TAUGHT CURRICULUM

1. Do the teachers allocate time to this field of study in accordance with district and school guidelines?

(continued next page)

FIGURE 12-2. *continued*

2. Do the teachers allocate time to the several components of this field of study in a way that reflects curricular priorities?
3. Do the teachers teach for the objectives specified for that grade?
4. Do the instructional methods used by the teachers reflect the best current knowledge about teaching that field of study and are they qualitatively excellent?
5. What unintended effects does this curriculum have on teaching?

THE TESTED CURRICULUM

1. Does the district provide curriculum-based tests that adequately reflect and correspond with the objectives stated in the course guides?
2. Are such tests valid and reliable measures of performance?
3. Does the district make use of standardized tests that provide norm-referenced data on achievement in this field of study?
4. Do any standardized tests used by the district adequately reflect and correspond with the objectives stated in the course guides?

THE LEARNED CURRICULUM

1. Do pupils believe that what they are learning is useful and meaningful?
2. Do pupils achieve the specified objectives at a satisfactory level?
3. What unintended learning outcomes are evidenced?
4. What are the opportunity costs for pupils involved in this field of study?

FORMATIVE ASPECTS

1. By what processes was this field of study developed, and did those processes provide for appropriate input form all constituencies?
2. What specific provisions are there for continuing input from those constituencies?
3. What specific provisions are there for revising and modifying the program of studies?

FIGURE 12-3. Survey Form: Evaluation Issues: Mathematics

DIRECTIONS: As you probably are aware, our school district will soon begin to evaluate the mathematics curriculum in our district. Listed below are the questions we might ask in such an evaluation. Tell us how important you think each question is. Read each question and then circle one of the following symbols:

VI: I think this question is *very important.*
I: I think this question is *important.*
LI: I think this question is *less important.*

Your responses will help us decide which questions to study.

Question	Your Response		
1. Are the goals of this subject clearly and explicitly stated and readily accessible to those who need to refer to them?	VI	I	LI

Developing the Evaluation Design

With the evaluation issues identified, the project director and the task force should cooperatively develop the evaluation design. One useful framework for such a design has been proposed by Worthen (1981). For each evaluative question (or evaluation issue, to use the terminology employed here), identify the information required, the sources of information, and the methods for collecting that information. Thus, in an example used by Worthen, if the evaluation proposes to answer the question, "Do student attitudes demonstrate that the curriculum is producing the desired results?", the attitudes of students with regard to the values and concepts taught constitute the information required. Students are the source of information; and the methods employed might include a comparative design using attitude scales and simulated situations requiring an attitudinal response.

In identifying the methods for collecting information, evaluators should be certain to include qualitative approaches. As noted above, current evaluation theory gives strong emphasis to such qualitative methods as interviews and observations in assessing curriculum impact.

Those decisions—about the issues, the information required, the sources of information, and the methods for collecting information—should form the basis of a detailed evaluation plan, which would include as well the specific tasks to be undertaken, the names of those responsible for each task, and the deadline for accomplishing the task.

Implementing the Evaluation Design

With the design developed, the evaluation team can move expeditiously to implement the design and report the results. Two matters should be stressed here. First, the implementation process should be a flexible one: if new issues develop or if additional data sources become apparent, they should be built into a revised design and incorporated into the implementation process. Second, the results should be reported in ways that will accommodate the special needs of the several audiences. Thus several reports might be envisioned: a summary written in plain language for the public; an action plan presented to the board and school administrators; a detailed technical report for the broader educational community.

APPLICATIONS

1. Choose one of the issues identified for the field of study evaluation. Use the Worthen framework in developing a design for that issue.

2. Select one of the models described and write a detailed explication and critique of that model.

3. Suppose a classroom teacher posed this question to you: "I want to evaluate my own course. I don't know much about statistics. Can you tell me how to evaluate it in a way that won't take too much time?" Write the answer you would give that teacher.

REFERENCES

Brandt, R. S. (ed.). (1981). *Applied strategies for curriculum evaluation*. Alexandria, VA: Association for Supervision and Curriculum Development.

Eisner, E. W. (1979). *The educational imagination: On the design and evaluation of school programs*. New York: Macmillan.

Goodlad, J. I. (1984). *A place called school: Prospects for the future*. New York: McGraw Hill.

Guba, E., and Lincoln, Y. (1981). *Effective evaluation*. San Francisco: Jossey Bass.

National Educational Association. (1969). *Report of the Committee of Ten on Secondary School Studies*. New York: Arno Press and the *New York Times*. (Originally published in 1893 by the U.S. Government Printing Office.)

Scriven, M. (1972). Prose and cons about goal-free evaluation. *Evaluation Comment, 3* (4), 1–4.

Stake, R. E. (ed.). (1975). *Evaluating the arts in education: A responsive approach*. Columbus, OH: Merrill.

Stufflebeam, D. L. (1971). *Educational evaluation and decision-making*. Itasca, IL: Peacock.

Tyler, R. W. (1950). *Basic principles of curriculum and instruction: Syllabus for Education 305*. Chicago: University of Chicago Press.

Worthen, B. R. (1981). Journal entries of an eclectic evaluator. In R. S. Brandt (ed.), *Applied strategies for curriculum evaluation*, pp. 58–90. Alexandria, VA: Association for Supervision and Curriculum Development.

Part 4

Current Trends in the Curriculum

13

Current Developments in the Subject Fields

One of the best ways to understand general developments in the curriculum is to examine trends in the specific subject areas. While there are certain innovations that transcend the disciplines, such as those to be discussed in the next chapter, most of the important changes take place and are worked out in the subject areas themselves. This chapter will examine those developments in the major fields that ordinarily constitute the common curriculum: English language arts; reading; social studies; mathematics; science; foreign language; and the arts. In each case the discussion begins with a review of the recent history of that field, starting with the curricular reform movement of the post-Sputnik era, and concludes with a description of current trends.

ENGLISH LANGUAGE ARTS

The discussion that follows focuses on all the language arts except reading; reading is considered so important that it is given special attention in the following section.

The Past Three Decades in English

During the period from 1957 to 1967, identified in this work as a time of "scholarly structuralism," the school curriculum was chiefly affected by two parallel forces: the interest of scholars from the academy in reforming the curriculum; and the allied concern of curriculum leaders with identifying the structure of the discipline. Spurred by the publication *The National Interest and the Teaching of English*, published under the aegis of the National Council of Teachers of English (1961), the federal government took a more active interest in the field. Federal funds, previously reserved for science and mathematics, were made available for Project English; and the National Defense Education Act of 1964 provided the resources for research, curriculum centers, and summer institutes.

Perhaps the most influential publication of the period was *Freedom and Discipline in English*, a report from the College Entrance Examination Board Commission on English (1965), which recommended a curriculum built upon the "tripod" of language, literature, and composition. Although this tripartite conceptualization of the field came to predominate among curriculum workers, most of the scholarly work focused on language study. Linguists and teachers worked collaboratively in summer institutes, fashioning new curricula that emphasized structural or transformational grammar. Despite the infusion of federal funds and the resulting efforts of scholars, however, these attempts to reform the English curriculum did not seem to be effective. As Squire and Applebee (1968) noted in their study of 158 excellent English programs, the taught curriculum looked much as it always had: literature was taught without much concern for its structure; traditional grammar held sway; and writing was confined to the "500-word theme."

The term *romantic radicalism*, used in this text to describe the brief period between 1968 and 1974, captures the two key motifs of the rhetoric of that time: a romantic view of the child and a radical critique of the schools. The key event at the international level in the field of English was the Dartmouth conference which brought together specialists in the teaching of English from the United States and England. As reported in two companion volumes (Muller, 1967; Dixon, 1967), the conference provided an opportunity for British educators to persuade their American counterparts of the virtues of such approaches as the child-centered curriculum, improvisational drama, informal class discussions, and imaginative writing.

In the classroom, however, the major development was the rapid spread of elective courses, perhaps an outgrowth of the British "open classroom" movement. Rather than requiring all students to take the same course, English departments offered a wide array of teacher-developed minicourses, usually lasting a quarter, trimester, or semester. Although Hillocks (1972) believed that the elective programs might "revolutionize the teaching of English for all students" (p. 123), their impact was not long-lasting. Conservative critics such as Copperman (1978), who attacked elective programs for their lack of rigor, gave needed support to school administrators eager to eliminate the elective "frills" and return to the basics.

That return to the basics is the primary characteristic of the period that began in the mid-1970s and continued up to the time of this present work.

One of the major controversies of the period, however, was how those basics were to be defined. Both the general public and some of the more vocal experts outside the field construed English basics rather narrowly. In their view, the desired outcomes for the study of English were limited to a knowledge of traditional grammar, a mastery of language "correctness," and an appreciation of the standard literary classics.

Leaders in the profession, however, espoused a more comprehensive perception of the discipline. In a widely disseminated document entitled "Essentials of English: A Document for Reflection and Dialogue" (National Council of Teachers of English, 1983), the Commission on the English Curriculum presented a list of essentials that had certain notable characteristics. (See the discussion in the next section for a fuller account of these recommendations.)

- It advocated a study of language that emphasized language change and language differences, rather than language correctness.
- It emphasized the study of literature for personal involvement, recommending that masterpieces of both the present and the past be studied.
- It offered a comprehensive list of "communication skills" that included reading for meaning, writing for personal development, speaking and listening, and using the media with awareness.
- It included creative, logical, and critical thinking as important elements.

Emerging Trends in English Language Arts

Four emerging developments in English curricula seem to be significant. The first is a widespread interest in the composing process and a concomitant attention to diverse types of writing. Motivated primarily by the widely disseminated National Writing Project, the developers of English curriculum guides are stressing the importance of an inclusive writing process that gives due attention to prewriting and revision, rather than focusing solely on the final product, and are emphasizing varied forms of writing for real audiences and purposes, rather than limiting writing to standard school essays written to satisfy the demands of a teacher. An allied development here is the increasing use of the computer to facilitate the composing process. While such use will not directly affect the curriculum, it should result in teachers giving more attention to composition in the curriculum.

The second development is a more comprehensive and diversified view of the student's response to literature. While previous curriculum guides stressed the interpretive and evaluative responses, more enlightened approaches encourage students to respond personally and creatively to the work studied. The intent is to help students find personal meaning in literature, not to develop young literary critics. Thus, a teacher introducing a poem begins by asking, "How does the poem touch you—what connections does it make with your life?" Only later are issues of analysis and evaluation raised.

At the same time, forward-looking districts are giving specific attention to the teaching of critical thinking in English. As part of a general nationwide interest in teaching thinking (see Chapter 14), curriculum leaders and experts such as Staton (1984) have been urging English teachers to see thinking as central to all classroom uses of language. However, at the district level this emphasis on critical thinking in English seems most often to take the form of units on the critical analysis of the mass media and advertising.

Finally, there is renewed interest in integrating the English language arts. While such interest can be traced back at least to *English for Social Living* by Roberts and his colleagues (1943), the present emphasis seems to have resulted from the recent theoretical work of Moffett (Moffett and Wagner, 1976), who argues cogently that language is a holistic phenomenon, and the research of scholars such as Goodman (1980), who have provided evidence that integrated, language-centered reading programs can be effective. One of the integration models gaining most attention was that proposed by the Speech Communication Association (Allen and Brown, 1976), which used the five functions of language as the framework for curricula: informing; expressing feeling; imagining; ritualizing; and controlling. Those five functions, intersecting with five context dimensions (mass communication, public communication, small-group communication, dyadic communication, and intrapersonal communication), resulted in a matrix of twenty-five cells, each of which involves both message initiation and reception.

How are these developments to be translated into effective curricula? Four publications seem to offer guidance to curriculum workers. The first, *Three Language-Arts Curriculum Models: Pre-Kindergarten through College* (Mandel, 1980), is a collection of essays that describe the "competencies," the "heritage," and the "process" models of curricula. The competencies model emphasizes the mastery of specific skills, developed incrementally through carefully designed instructional systems. The heritage model stresses the understanding of the cultural tradition, chiefly through the study of language and literature. The process model emphasizes discovery through personal inquiry in a stimulating environment. While the authors of the essays attempted to produce distinctive curricular models for the several levels, they seem to have been not completely successful. As Early (1983) points out, the essays are really critiques of teaching-learning procedures, not of ideal curricula, and display considerable overlap.

The second, *A Guide for Developing an English Curriculum for the Eighties* (Glatthorn, 1980), emphasizes a process for developing an English curriculum, rather than prescribing specific content. The work recommends a teacher-centered process that attempts to integrate the best current knowledge of the field with the tested experience of classroom teachers. Rather than advocating a single approach, this monograph recommends an eclectic process that uses the best of several approaches. Early considers the work a highly useful one:

. . . I know from experience, my own and that of teachers with whom I have worked, that [Glatthorn] . . . has described a workable plan for organizing a curriculum. . . . Most teachers welcome the structure Glatthorn insists on because it makes it possible for them to use the freedom he leaves them for choosing content. (p. 205)

The third publication is the "Essentials of English" report referred to above (National Council of Teachers of English, 1983). Figure 13–1 summarizes the outcomes recommended by the commission. As is apparent, the goals are broad-based and comprehensive and would provide a useful beginning point for curriculum leaders. It should be noted, however, that many of the outcomes listed are what Glatthorn (1980) calls "organic" and should not be used in a mastery approach.

The final source, *Academic Preparation for College: What Students Need to Know and Be Able to Do* (College Board, 1983), while focusing on preparation for the college-bound, is also a useful guide for planning curricula for terminal students. The goals proposed here for reading and literature, for writing, for speaking and listening, and for language are very similar to those recommended by the *Essentials of English* report. The thinking outcomes are presented in the College Board report as "reasoning" skills and are included in a separate listing of "basic academic competencies" for all subjects.

These volumes together should provide sufficient guidance for local curriculum workers interested in both substantive and process guidelines for the English curriculum.

FIGURE 13–1. The Essential Goals of English

LANGUAGE

1. Learn how the English language has developed and is changing.
2. Understand that usage varieties are shaped by social, cultural, and geographical differences.
3. Recognize that language is a powerful thinking and learning tool.
4. Become aware of how grammar represents the orderliness of language and makes communication possible.
5. Recognize how context influences the structure and purpose of language.
6. Understand how language can act as a unifying force among citizens.

LITERATURE

1. Realize the importance of literature as a mirror of human experience.
2. Be able to identify with fictional characters and gain insights from involvement with literature.
3. Become aware of important writers from diverse backgrounds.
4. Become familiar with past and present masterpieces.
5. Develop effective ways of talking and writing about literature.
6. Experience literature as a way to appreciate the beauty of the language.
7. Develop habits of reading that carry over into adult life.

(continued next page)

FIGURE 13–1. *continued*

COMMUNICATION SKILLS

Reading

1. Recognize that reading is a pleasurable activity and a means of acquiring knowledge.
2. Learn how to approach reading as a search for meaning.
3. Develop the skills necessary to comprehend a variety of forms.
4. Learn to read accurately and make valid inferences.
5. Learn to judge literature critically on the basis of personal response and literary quality.

Writing

1. Learn to write clearly and honestly.
2. Recognize that writing is a way to learn and develop personally.
3. Learn ways to generate ideas for writing, to arrange those ideas, to find appropriate modes for expressing them, and to evaluate and revise.
4. Learn to adapt expression to various audiences.
5. Learn the techniques of writing for, appealing to, and persuading others.
6. Recognize that precision in manuscript form is a part of effective writing.

Listening

1. Learn that listening with understanding depends on determining a speaker's purpose.
2. Learn to attend to detail and relate it to the overall purpose of communication.
3. Learn to evaluate messages and effects of mass communication.

Using Media

1. Become aware of the impact of technology on communication and recognize that understanding the electronic modes requires special skills.
2. Realize that new modes of communication demand a new kind of literacy.

THINKING SKILLS

Creative Thinking

1. Learn that originality derives from the uniqueness of the individual's perceptions.
2. Learn that inventiveness involves seeing new relationships.
3. Learn that creative thinking derives from several receptive and expressive abilities.

Logical Thinking

1. Learn to create hypotheses and predict outcomes.
2. Learn to test the validity of an assertion.
3. Learn to understand logical relationships.
4. Learn to construct logical sequences.
5. Learn to detect fallacies in reasoning.
6. Recognize that "how to think" is different from "what to think."

Critical Thinking

1. Learn to ask questions.
2. Differentiate between subjective and objective viewpoints, fact and opinion.
3. Evaluate intentions and messages of speakers and writers.
4. Make judgments based on criteria that can be supported.

Source: Paraphrased from *The Essentials of English: A Document for Reflection and Dialogue*, National Council of Teachers of English, 1983.

READING

Although reading in the strictest sense is one of the language arts (usually construed to cover reading, writing, speaking, and listening), it has so much importance, especially in the early grades, that it is given separate consideration as a curriculum field.

Early Developments in the Field of Reading

In the three decades from 1950 to 1980, three developments perhaps stand out. The first was an intense debate over the value of phonics instruction. In the 1940s and 1950s, most basal texts and most school programs emphasized word recognition as the basic strategy, in which pupils were taught to develop a "sight vocabulary," recognizing whole words in reading passages where word choice was tightly controlled. During the same period more innovative educators and schools emphasized an "experience" approach, in which the child's experiences, expressed in the child's own words, became the basis of reading instruction. Both approaches came under attack by both educators and lay critics who believed that instruction in phonics or decoding strategies would be more valuable.

To a great extent the issue has been resolved, at least from the standpoint of those who value empirical evidence. For beginning reading, at least, an emphasis on decoding strategies will be beneficial. Chall's 1967 review of all the studies up to that point concluded that decoding programs had more value than other approaches; additional studies since that time, such as Becker and Carnine's (1980), confirm that earlier finding. However, Calfee and Drum (1986) point out the hazards in translating these findings into beginning reading programs that stress only decoding: the advantage of phonics training is typically small; reliance on rote drill and practice as the primary vehicle for decoding instruction is unwise; decoding instruction should not crowd out the time given to developing comprehension skills.

A second important development during the preceding decades was an interest in dialect differences and the extent to which they interfered with the reading process. Perhaps sparked by the concern for the civil rights of blacks and other minorities, several educators became concerned about the problems those minority groups had in reading texts that were insensitive to dialect differences. As Shuy (1979) notes, their basic argument was that the mismatch between the minority child's language and the language used in the basal texts created undue difficulties for the child. Several reviews, including Shuy's, conclude that sound, syntax, and meaning differences may interfere with oral reading but not with silent reading comprehension. One review (Pflaum-Connor, 1978) also found no advantages for black-dialect speakers in reading texts written in black dialects.

An interesting explanation of the reading problems experienced by minority children is offered by Simons (1979). After reviewing several studies of the interactions between minority children and teachers, he concludes that teachers spend an undue amount of time correcting the speech of black children; he infers that such responses take away from the time that should be devoted to reading instruction and suggest to the minority children that the teacher disapproves of their language and them.

The third major development of those decades was an interest in reading readiness and its implications for curriculum. The earlier view held that children became ready to read through normal developmental processes that could be accelerated by providing "readiness" activities. As Chall (1983) notes, there is now a movement away from such a global approach to readiness to an attempt to identify specific underlying abilities that can be developed in beginning reading programs. A review of several studies suggests that the following types of instructional activities would be helpful to the child who is just beginning to read: providing rich language experiences; training in sound blending, in which children are taught how to blend individual sounds into words; and developing metalinguistic awareness— helping the child become more conscious of such elements as word boundaries in spoken sentences, the phonemic composition of words, and the syntactic rules governing sentence production.

Recent Trends in Reading

Three rather recent developments seem to have profoundly changed the way reading is understood and taught. The first is the awareness that the ability to read probably progresses through clearly demarcated stages, in which different skills and different methods are needed. Perhaps the most clearly formulated of such stage approaches is Chall's (1983) six-stage model:

Stage 0: Prereading. Birth to age 6. During this stage it is important to nurture all aspects of the child's language and to help the child understand the nature and importance of reading.

Stage 1: Initial reading or decoding. Ages 6 to 7. Acquiring letter sound correspondences is crucial.

Stage 2: Fluency. Ages 7 to 8. The child automatizes decoding and begins to focus on meaning.

Stage 3: Reading to learn. (Not defined by age.) Reading becomes a tool for exploring subject matter in school and for handling daily affairs.

Stage 4: Multiple viewpoints. High school. Texts are more demanding and comprehension is more difficult: the student must hold one set of ideas in mind while acquiring new information.

Stage 5: Reconstruction. College and beyond. The student views the text from multiple perspectives and brings to the text a critical mind.

Obviously the Chall model has clear implications for the reading curriculum.

The second major development of the present period is the emergence of schema theory as a means of understanding and facilitating the reading process. Schema theory, a contribution of cognitive psychology, holds in brief that each individual has stored in the mind certain mental structures or frameworks, derived from both experience and instruction, that are used to understand and make meaning from new experiences. Schema theorists who have considered the reading process (see, for example, Adams and Collins, 1979; and Spiro, 1977) believe that reading is an active meaning-making process. The reader notes the topic of the passage and activates schemata relevant to that topic. These schemata have slots for information which are filled with information from the text. If the text does not provide that information, the reader fills in what is needed, drawing from the relevant schema. Thus, if the reader does not have an appropriate schema for a given text, comprehension will be inhibited.

Several specialists in the field have attempted to translate schema theory and metacognitive approaches (becoming aware of one's cognitive processes) into practical instructional approaches. One of the more useful is that proposed by Palincsar and Brown (1984). They identify from the literature six important comprehension skills: understanding the purposes of reading; activating relevant background knowledge; allocating attention so that it is focused on major elements, not trivia; evaluating content for internal consistency and compatability with prior experience; monitoring reading to ensure that comprehension is occurring; and drawing and testing inferences of several kinds. It would seem useful to develop all these skills through well-organized reading curricula.

The third development is an increased awareness of the importance and complexity of adult literacy. Calfee and Drum (1986) note that contemporary concern for the problem dates back at least to 1969, when James E. Allen, Jr., the Commissioner of Education, announced the Right to Read program. Although the federal Right to Read office set up reading centers for adults and distributed sets of materials, Calfee and Drum conclude that the program was "lost in the turmoil of the 70s and never moved beyond the initial rhetoric" (p. 804). This concern for adult literacy seems to have been rekindled in the 1980s with the growing realization that a technological society required highly literate adults. In a historical review of the field, Resnick and Resnick (1977) concluded that the current demand for a high level of literacy is unprecedented.

How successful are adult literacy programs? The results are not very promising, as Chall and Stahl (1982) see them. They note that literacy training programs in the army have not been very successful. Even those community- and work-based programs that seem to be effective have not succeeded either in attracting adults to take the courses or to complete them once enrolled. And they point out that those adult literacy programs in revolutionary Third World societies that have claimed a high success rate have not been evaluated by disinterested researchers.

SOCIAL STUDIES

In many ways the history of the social studies curriculum is similar to that of English. As the following discussion will reveal, early attempts at reform resulted in seemingly little change; and the current period seems marked by some confusion of aims.

The Past Three Decades in Social Studies

The post-Sputnik curriculum reform movement, which first affected science, mathematics, and foreign languages, seemed initially to make a major impact on the field of social studies as well. Over forty curriculum-development projects of national scope were initiated under the aegis of the U.S. Office of Education's Project Social Studies and the National Science Foundation. All the USOE project centers were located at universities, and the curriculum efforts clearly reflected an academic orientation. The projects attempted to identify the structure of the social science disciplines and to teach their key concepts and generalizations. In the views of those scholars, the discipline was the focus. Most of the projects, consequently, focused on one of the social sciences; thus, there were curriculum projects in economics, geography, anthropology, history, and sociology. And in almost every instance the recommended teaching and learning activities emphasized inquiry: the student was to be engaged with primary sources, acting as a younger social scientist.

The period following the curriculum-reform era has been characterized by Jarolimek (1981) as a time when social studies was in disarray. The projects had run their courses, and there were no funds available in significant amounts for new projects. The civil rights movement of the late 1960s and early 1970s and the war in Southeast Asia both produced strong pressures for social studies courses to be more relevant and student-centered: the response at the local level was the development of courses in ethnic studies, women's studies, environmental studies, and peace studies. The elective framework provided a facilitating structure for such relevant offerings; Jarolimek notes that "mini-courses at the secondary level grew as profusely as mushrooms after a fall rain" (p. 9). And many social studies teachers turned to "values-clarification" activities as a means of motivating students and making courses seem more appealing.

The backlash was perhaps predictable. In what seemed to many to be a well-orchestrated response, several conservative organizations and local parent groups attacked any course that raised questions of values and morality. *Man: A Course of Study*, a course that attempted to involve fifth-graders in an examination of values from an anthropological point of view, seemed to be a favorite target; the furore even resulted in Congressional hearings, since federal funds had been used to produce that particular curriculum package. And even parents and other citizens with more moderate views began to raise questions about social studies curricula that slighted the American past and gave short shrift to citizenship education. The "back-to-the-basics" movement of the late 1970s thus resulted in the elimination of most elective courses, the rejection of relevance as a criterion for selecting content, and a return to somewhat standard offerings.

Several studies of the status of the field suggested a somewhat discouraging picture at the time of the present work. (The following synthesis is drawn from Superka, Hawke, and Morrissett, 1980; Shaver, Davis, and Helburn, 1979; and Ponder, 1979.) First, the discipline-centered projects of the post-Sputnik era do not seem to have made a lasting impact; even generous estimates suggest that they were being used in only 20 percent of the school districts of the nation. Second, despite a widely held belief that there was little uniformity in the social studies, a standard organizational pattern had firmly taken hold. Figure 13–2 shows the sequence of what Superka, Hawke, and Morrissett call "a virtual nationwide curriculum . . . held rather firmly in place by state laws, district requirements, textbook offerings, and tradition" (p. 365).

FIGURE 13–2. Dominant Organizational Patterns for Social Studies

K— Self, school, community, home

1— Families

2— Neighborhoods

3— Communities

4— State history, geographic regions

5— U.S. history

6— World cultures, Western hemisphere

7— World geography or history

8— American history

9— Civics or world cultures

10— World history

11— American history

12— American government

Commercially produced textbooks constituted the primary resource; in grades 4 to 12, 90 percent of the social studies classes surveyed used one or more textbooks (Weiss, 1978); and two-thirds of class time was spent using print materials, primarily textbooks (EPIE, 1976). Those textbooks, however, seemed much improved over earlier ones. Close analyses of the texts by several researchers revealed the following characteristics: the texts were more racially and ethnically pluralistic; provided a less stereotyped view of females; were less narrowly nationalistic; embodied more inquiry activities; and incorporated more social science concepts and methodologies.

Despite these improvements in the texts, the taught curriculum had changed very little. The whole-class lecture-recitation method dominated, and students were tested primarily on their ability to remember and reproduce information. Experience-based curricula and inquiry learning were rare. Teachers were the final arbiters of the curriculum actually delivered; and those teachers tended to support a somewhat traditional view of the field.

Emerging Trends in the Social Studies

The first important trend to note is an increase in the social studies requirements for graduation. As of 1980, most states mandated only two years of social studies during the four years of high school (National Association of Secondary School Principals, 1980). However, largely as a result of the several national commission reports and the concomitant concern for "curriculum rigor," by 1985 several states had increased or were considering increasing that requirement to three years.

The second major development seemed to be an increasing flexibility in the organizing framework for the scope and sequence of social studies. While the National Council for the Social Studies (1984) recommended a scope and sequence that very closely resembles the dominant patterns noted in Figure 13–2, they also sketched in three optional structures for grades 6 to 12 that they believed would afford local districts greater flexibility. Thus, in grade 8, these optional frameworks were offered:

Option 1—U.S. History with emphasis on social history and economic developments
Option 2—Economics and law-related studies
Option 3—Interdisciplinary study of the local region

Others proposed more radical patterns. Crabtree (1983), for example, recommended a three-dimensional planning grid. One dimension of her framework is composed of the three participatory systems—the political, the social, and the economic. A second includes four learning perspectives: systems perspective, historical perspective, geographic perspective, and global perspective. And in each of the cells generated by the intersection of those two dimensions are the four basic learning domains—knowledge, cognitive skills, attitudes, and participatory skills.

A third developing trend seemed to be the increasing attention given to global issues. Even conservatives suspicious of "one-worldism" realized that there were certain ineluctable factors that made global education a necessity: the rise of multinational corporations; the rapid development of technologies that transcended national boundaries; the economic interdependence of nations; and the televised immediacy of world conflict. Such factors, Crabtree (1983) argues, make a global perspective a necessity for contemporary students; they must understand that all people across the world share common problems and are interrelated through worldwide economic, technological, and social systems.

Finally, there was evidence of a resurgence of interest in moral and character education. While "values clarification" had become widely questioned by the profession, there was continued interest in Kohlberg's "moral education" as a means of developing greater complexity in moral reasoning processes. (One of the best sources for the curricular implications of Kohlberg's work is Mosher, 1980.) Here Lockwood's (1978) review of the research on values clarification and moral development seems pertinent. While he concludes that the research on values clarification does not suggest that it has a positive impact on self-esteem, self-concept, and personal adjustment, his review of studies on Kohlberg's moral education leads him to believe that "the direct discussion approach [of Kohlberg-based moral education] generally produces significant development in moral reasoning" (p. 358).

Whereas moral education is concerned with the process of moral reasoning, character education seems more content-oriented. According to the developers of the Character-Education Curriculum (American Institute for Character Education, n.d.), character education is based upon fifteen values "shared by all major world religions and cultures": courage; conviction; generosity; kindness; helpfulness; honesty; honor; justice; tolerance; use of time and talents; freedom of choice; freedom of speech; citizenship; right to be an individual; right of equal opportunity and economic security (p. 3). While character education did not seem to be widely supported by leaders of the social studies profession, there was evidence of growing grassroots acceptance: the 1985 newsletter of the American Institute for Character Education reported that institute materials were being used in fourteen thousand classrooms in forty-three states.

MATHEMATICS

Except for the short-lived reform movement of the post-Sputnik era, the mathematics curriculum has perhaps undergone less change than other disciplines. However, as the discussion below will note, greater change seems likely to occur during the coming decade.

The Past Three Decades in Mathematics

During the late 1950s, the mathematics curriculum was under serious attack from the experts. A traditional curriculum inherited from the nineteenth century relied heavily on drill, presented mathematics as a collection of discrete skills, separated algebraic and geometric thinking, and slighted the importance of mathematical thinking and reasoning. The response of the scholars was to produce "the new math," a reconceptualization of the discipline delivered through projects that often bore the name of their university home, such as "Illinois math," "Ball State math," and "Maryland math."

While these projects differed in their details, they were all characterized by certain key features. First, the emphasis was on the structure of mathematics, as the scholars saw that structure. And the structure turned out to be a deductive axiomatic approach that emphasized abstract concepts and principles. Second, that structure was presented in what Bruner (1960) called a "spiral curriculum"—one in which concepts were introduced in simple form in the early grades and then redeveloped in increasingly complex forms in later grades. Third, new content was included: the theory of sets, typically ignored in the traditional curriculum, was often introduced as early as first grade. Also, the language used to present that structure was made as precise and as unambiguous as possible; previously esoteric terminology such as *commutative property* became part of the lexicon of mathematically naive elementary teachers. Finally, teachers were encouraged to use an inquiry approach in presenting the new mathematics; problem solving, not drill, was to be the focus of instruction.

Although several writers have used the term *revolution* to describe the adoption of the new mathematics curricula, systematic research on the extent of implementation suggests a much less radical impact. Gibney and Karns' (1979) summary of the National Science Foundation study of the status of mathematics education after twenty years of reform yields this picture:

- At the elementary level, the core mathematics curriculum is still based upon computation with whole numbers, fractions, and decimals; however, the written curriculum has expanded to include geometry, measurement, probability, statistics, graphs, equations, inequalities, and properties of number systems.
- At the secondary level, the most frequently taught courses are still general mathematics, algebra, and geometry; new topics in the written curriculum include functions, vector approaches to geometry, computer processes, and calculus.
- Case studies of the taught curriculum suggest much less impact of new curricula. Observers noted only a few instances where modern mathematics was emphasized. Little attention was being given to inquiry learning; teachers were assigning and reviewing problems, just as they had done for decades previous.

- The textbook was still the dominant instructional resource. And, as Stake and Easley (1978) noted, the ten most frequently used texts were clearly traditional in orientation and similar to each other in almost every respect.

Even though there was not systematic and widespread implementation of the new mathematics curriculum, there has been continued interest in the effects of this new approach on student achievement and attitude. Although critics such as Kline (1973) attacked the new math for causing a decline in computational skills and producing negative attitudes toward mathematics, the research suggests that modern mathematics curricula were generally effective. In a careful meta-analysis of 134 studies comparing "old" and "new" math, Althappilly, Smidchens, and Kofel (1983) reached this conclusion:

> The aggregate findings of the experiments with modern mathematics for the last 30 years show that there have not been many detrimental effects of the "new math," either on achievement or on attitude. On the contrary, the evidence points toward beneficial effects in terms of improvement in the overall achievement and attitude when the mathematics curriculum contained "modern mathematics." (p. 491)

Emerging Trends in Mathematics

If trends in the subject areas are strongly influenced by the widely disseminated pronouncements of professional associations, then trends in mathematics are relatively easy to identify. For here the National Council of Teachers of Mathematics has played a very active role. First, the NCTM published a very useful set of guidelines for the teaching of mathematics entitled *An Agenda for Action: Recommendations for School Mathematics of the 1980s* (National Council of Teachers of Mathematics, 1980). Then, with support from the National Science Foundation, their Priorities in School Mathematics Project (PRISM) surveyed several thousand classroom teachers, college instructors and mathematics-teacher educators, supervisors of mathematics, principals, and school-board and parent-organization presidents about most of the issues covered in the Agenda's recommendations. The general recommendations and a summary of the survey results are shown in Figure 13–3; details of the survey results are reported in the publication *Priorities in School Mathematics: Executive Summary of the PRISM Project* (National Council of Teachers of Mathematics, 1981).

Besides these somewhat general recommendations, *An Agenda for Action* also included several specific curricular recommendations:

- Expand the "basics" to include problem solving; applying mathematics in everyday situations; alertness to the reasonableness of results; estimation and approximation; appropriate computational skills; geometry; mea-

FIGURE 13-3. Recommendations for School Mathematics and Survey Responses

1. Problem solving must be the focus of school mathematics in the 1980s.

   This recommendation was strongly supported by all groups surveyed.

2. The concept of basic skills in mathematics must encompass more than computational facility.

   Teachers and lay respondents gave strong support; only supervisors and teacher educators were lukewarm.

3. Mathematics programs must take full advantage of the power of calculators and computers at all grade levels.

   While there was general support among all groups for this recommendation, lay respondents were even stronger than the professional group.

4. Stringent standards of both effectiveness and efficiency must be applied to the teaching of mathematics.

   There was generally strong support for the following teaching approaches: manipulative materials; small-group activities; out-of-class activities; more homework. There was less support for an increased emphasis on mathematics laboratories and the use of laboratory investigations.

5. The success of mathematics programs and student learning must be evaluated by a wider range of measures than conventional testing.

   Minimal support was given to increasing emphasis on competency testing and norm-referenced testing.

6. More mathematics study must be required for all students, and a flexible curriculum with a greater range of options should be designed to accommodate the diverse needs of the student population.

   About half of the lay group surveyed (the only group queried about this recommendation) recommended four years of mathematics during high school; there was generally strong support for increasing curricular options, within the bounds of identified needs.

7. Mathematics teachers must demand of themselves and their colleagues a high level of professionalism.

   All groups strongly supported improved preservice and inservice education for mathematics teachers.

8. Public support for mathematics instruction must be raised to a level commensurate with the importance of mathematical understanding to individuals and society.

   There did not seem to be strong support here: two-thirds of the respondents felt that general problems confronting teachers deserve priority over problems specific to the teaching of mathematics.

Source: National Council of Teachers of Mathematics, *Priorities in School Mathematics: Executive Summary of the Prism Project,* 1981.

surement; reading, interpreting, and constructing tables, charts, and graphs; using mathematics to predict; and computer literacy.
- Develop curriculum materials that integrate and require the use of the calculator and the computer in imaginative ways.
- Require a computer literacy course for all students.
- Include algebra in the program of all capable students, delaying it until grade 11 or 12 for some.
- Reevaluate and possibly deemphasize the role of calculus in a differentiated mathematics curriculum.

The College Board's (1983) recommendations for college preparatory mathematics seem quite similar to those of the NCTM. The board recommends several goals for all college-bound students in each of the following areas: computing, statistics, algebra, geometry, and functions. Additional preparation in each of these areas is recommended for those preparing for majors in mathematics, science, and engineering.

Implementing these recommendations in a comprehensive K–12 program is a much more difficult matter than simply making recommendations about goals and the placement of subjects. Here Romberg (1983) provides some very useful guidance. He first recommends that the curriculum should be framed around these conceptual strands: whole-numbers arithmetic, spatial relations, measurement, fractions, coordinate geometry, algebra, and statistics. Next, he argues that every specific instructional activity should require students to use one or more mathematical processes, emphasizing these four as basic sets of processes: relation processes (classifying, ordering, comparing, etc.); representation processes (physical, pictorial, symbolic); symbolic-procedure processes (algorithms and transformations); and validation processes (by authority, by empirical testing, by logical-deductive reasoning).

The NCTM publications, along with the other resources listed, provide at least a framework for a contemporary mathematics curriculum.

SCIENCE

The recent history of science curricula provides perhaps a paradigmatic example of federal influence in curricular matters and therefore deserves perhaps a close examination.

The Past Three Decades in Science

Although it is customary to date the beginning of the movement to reform science curricula from the launching of Sputnik in 1957, Welch (1979) points out that more precise beginning points might be the creation of the National Science Foundation in 1950, the convening of an NSF-supported science curriculum conference in 1954, or the first award in 1956 to the Physical Science Curriculum Committee. At any rate, the launching of Sputnik provided further impetus for this developing interest in improving school science. The next year, the Chemical Bond Approach (CBA) group was funded, soon to be followed by the Biological Science Curriculum Study (BSCS) and the Chemical Education Material Study (CHEMS). By 1966, nineteen different science curriculum projects were receiving NSF support. And in most instances the curricular products were supported by teacher-training institutes: in 1965, some 420 summer institutes for science teachers were funded by NSF.

While these nineteen projects were quite different in many ways, they shared, Welch notes, three common characteristics. First, each project produced a variety of learning aids: student texts, films, laboratory apparatus, film loops, laboratory manuals, supplementary readers, overhead transparencies, tests, and teacher guides. Second, they all emphasized active learning—"doing science." Each curriculum project placed heavy emphasis on the science laboratory as a key component; laboratory experiments were presented as puzzles to be solved, not recipes to be followed. Finally, all the projects emphasized scientific concepts as the unifying themes, as a way of teaching the structure of science and counteracting the disjointed fragmentation of older science curricula.

By the mid-1960s, however, the forces that had given impetus to federal intervention seemed to wane in influence, Welch points out. Science manpower needs had been met. Soviet technology no longer seemed a threat, once the United States had landed a man on the moon. School enrollments were declining. Science and technology were attacked by the radical left as handmaidens of destruction. And problems that seemed more pressing than learning science—such as racial discrimination, sexism, and pollution—occupied the attention of legislators. Some science curriculum projects developed in the late 1960s attempted to respond to these societal issues by developing curricula that emphasized interdisciplinary themes and the social consequences of science; however, the reform movement seemed by 1970 to have reached its end.

The scope of that reform movement can perhaps be best understood by examining both the extent of funding and the number of projects supported. In the twenty-year period reviewed by Welch (1956–75), more than $695 million was appropriated by NSF for curriculum projects and teacher-training activities. And by 1977, the NSF along with other agencies was actively supporting more than five hundred different projects in science and mathematics. (See Lockard, 1977, for the complete list.)

What was the impact of such massive intervention? It first might be useful to examine the extent of implementation before analyzing the effects on achievement. A summary of Yager (1980) of several NSF-funded studies of the status of science education yields a somewhat discouraging picture of science education after two decades of federal intervention.

- The textbook still dominated curriculum and instruction: the textbook determined content, order, examples, and application of content. Relatively few textbooks dominated the field: three biology texts accounted for 80 percent of all sales. Ninety percent of the intermediate-grade teachers reported that they relied on a single textbook.
- Although the newer materials emphasized hands-on learning, teachers were still relying upon didactic instruction. There were few attempts to individualize learning; the teacher presented information to and quizzed the whole class.
- After reaching a peak in 1970, the use of newer national programs seemed to be declining. Teachers criticized the newer programs for not allowing for enough teacher autonomy, for overemphasizing pure content, for including material too difficult for their students, and for de-emphasizing practical science.
- While enrollments in science increased until 1973, there was a leveling off between the years 1973 and 1978; 50 percent of all students did not complete a high school science course after grade 10.

Welch (1979) is somewhat more positive in his assessment of the extent of implementation. He points out that "the goal of providing curricular alternatives has been achieved . . . " (p. 295), noting that more than five hundred curriculum projects have been developed and disseminated.

What were the effects on student achievement and attitude? A quantitative synthesis by Shymansky, Kyle, and Alport (1982) yielded a very positive picture. Achievement scores of students taking "new" science courses improved at all grade levels: female, urban, and low- and high-economic-status students showed the greatest increases. Student attitudes toward science were in general more positive, especially at the junior high level and in urban areas; and student performance in process skills, problem solving, and critical thinking was improved. Finally, there were some spin-off effects at the elementary level: students taking the new courses performed better in mathematics, reading, social studies, and communication.

Emerging Trends in Science

In analyzing emerging trends in science, three sources are especially useful for the curriculum leader. First, the National Science Teachers Association has adopted and promulgated a position statement which, while somewhat general in nature, does indicate some important curricular emphases. As the summary in Figure 13-4 indicates, this professional association places strong emphasis on laboratory and field experiences, on inquiry and problem solving, on a comprehensive concept-based curriculum, and on science-related societal issues.

How such a curriculum might be achieved is the focus of a second valuable study. The NSTA "Search for Excellence in Science Education" project identified fifty-four exemplary science programs throughout the nation and examined their common characteristics. (See Yager, Aldridge, and Penick, 1983.) The following features seemed to characterize all the exemplary programs: a considerable amount of time had been devoted to developing local curricula, many of which adapted content and materials from national curricula of the past; there was a single leader stimulating the active participation of other faculty members; the administration provided released time and other resources; there was extensive inservice education

---

FIGURE 13–4. Curriculum Recommendations:
National Science Teachers Association

The elementary science curriculum should . . .

1. Be an integral part of the elementary school program.
2. Provide daily opportunities for the sequential development of basic physical- and life-science concepts, along with the development of science-process and inquiry skills.
3. Provide opportunities for nurturing children's natural curiosity and for them to explore and investigate their world using a hands-on approach.
4. Focus on fostering in children an understanding of, an interest in, and an appreciation of the world in which they live.

The middle school science curriculum should . . .

1. Be designed to accommodate the needs and learning styles of the early adolescent, providing opportunities to explore science through reading, discussion, and learning experiences in classroom, laboratory, and field.
2. Contribute to the development of scientifically literate persons by providing a comprehensive program that emphasizes the physical and earth sciences, as well as the life sciences.
3. Continue to develop science-process skills and content, emphasizing the application of both skills and content to the students' personal life situations.

The high school science curriculum should . . .

1. Enable students to develop further their scientific and technological literacy, incorporating well-designed laboratory and field work.
2. Provide for one year of life science and one year of physical science for all students, both taught in a science-technology-society context.
3. Provide opportunities for interested students to take additional discipline-based courses in advanced biology, chemistry, physics, and earth sciences, with appropriate integration of advanced mathematics.

All science courses should . . .

1. Provide basic concepts for all students.
2. Use the laboratory to develop process and problem-solving skills.
3. Devote appropriate attention to science-related societal issues: a minimum of 5% of instruction in elementary schools, 15% in middle schools, and 20% in high schools.

Source: Paraphrased from *An NSTA Position Statement: Science–Technology–Society: Science Education for the 1980s.* National Science Teachers Association, Washington, DC, 1982.

for the teachers; the courses focused on process skills; textbooks played a secondary role as resources and references; and the community recognized the importance of and supported quality programs in science.

The final source is perhaps the most useful of all. By reviewing status studies of science education, by examining the results of national assessment tests, and by analyzing science education from multiple perspectives, Harms (Harms and Yager, 1981) was able to both identify the present status of science education and delineate a desired future. His suggestions for the future directions of science education begin by recommending that elementary science be considered as one of the "basics" and that school districts adopt one of the excellent elementary programs currently available. The middle school science program, from his perspective, should emphasize science issues related to personal, societal, and career-choice needs—and not be seen as preparation for high school science. In addition, the middle school science curriculum would emphasize decision making and problem solving. Although he would still offer biology in either grade 9 or grade 10, he recommends that this course as well shift to a general education emphasis, stressing topics in a personal and societal context. Chemistry, physics, and advanced biology would round out the high school curriculum; but again, these subjects would emphasize the relationship of developments in science and technology to life and problems in the twentieth century.

FOREIGN LANGUAGE

There seems to be a growing realization that we live in a "global village," where the price of oil from the Middle East affects employment levels in Texas. In such a global village, competence in a foreign language would seem be a vital necessity. Such was the obvious conclusion of several of the reform reports of the 1980s. However, recent studies indicate that only about one-fourth of the nation's students were studying a foreign language. The discussion that follows reviews some important developments in the recent history of language study and then examines some current trends.

The Past Three Decades in Language Study

For several decades students studied a foreign language by first mastering the grammar of that language and then applying that knowledge of grammar to the translation of classical texts. Then, in the 1960s, with the massive infusion of federal funds, the instructional approach changed radically. Spurred by the success of the army and the foreign services in using audiolingual methods to teach adults, schools all over the country installed language laboratories and developed curricula emphasizing the audiolingual method and sequencing objectives in a "natural" order—first listening, and then speaking, reading, and writing. Despite its bright promise, the audiolingual method never achieved what its advocates claimed it would achieve. As several cognitive psychologists pointed out, what was natural for the child learning a native language was not natural for adults learning a second language. (See Ausubel, 1968, for example.)

The sad state of foreign-language study in the United States led the nation's leaders to participate in the development of and sign the Helsinki Agreement of 1975, requiring signers to "encourage the study of foreign language and civilization as an important means of expanding communication among peoples." Stimulated by the signing of the Helsinki Agreement, Jimmy Carter appointed a President's Commission on Foreign Language and International Studies. The commission report, entitled *Strength through Wisdom: A Critique of U.S. Capability*, was released in 1979. As Phillips (1982) notes, the recommendations of the commission set the tone for the 1980s and to a great extent stimulated several of the current developments noted below.

Current Developments in Language Study

The current trends in foreign-language education can perhaps best be analyzed by dividing them into curricular approaches and instructional approaches, although such a division is in some ways misleading, especially with respect to foreign language.

Curricular Approaches   Several new approaches to the design and development of curricula have appeared in recent years. One is termed *"problem-posing education,"* a foreign-language curriculum with an existentialist emphasis. As Crawford-Lange (1982) notes, the problem-posing approach to curriculum has been largely influenced by the work of Paulo Freire and the theory of curricular reconceptualists. In her overview of this approach, Crawford-Lange notes its salient features: problems faced by the learners in their daily lives become the source of content; learners identify a problem and then relate it to other facets of their lives; they then discuss the broader problem as it manifests itself in their own culture and also in the culture of the target language. As they examine their problems in the broader cultural context, students teach each other the target-language vocabulary and use problem-focused activities to develop competence in the grammar of the language.

The second curricular approach gaining attention, at least from leaders in the profession, is the *functional-notional syllabus.* Influenced greatly by the theories of psycho- and sociolinguistics, the functional-notional syllabus is predicated on the importance of two closely related aspects of language: the functions of language (such as requesting information, giving instructions, clarifying the order of events); and the notions or semantic meanings (concepts such as time, quantification, possession, modality). Thus, a functional-notional syllabus stresses the purposes for which learners need the language and the notions or concepts involved with those purposes. Although Crawford-Lange believes that the complexity of the functional-notional syllabus may delay its utilization in the classroom for some time, leaders in the field, such as Albert Valdman (1982), have begun some excellent work in synthesizing more conventional structural approaches with the newer functional-notional ideas.

A third approach to curriculum development might be termed the *proficiency approach.* These are curricula developed around the proficiencies identified by the American Council on the Teaching of Foreign Languages (ACTFL, 1982). The ACTFL guidelines describe in very specific terms six proficiency levels in speaking, reading, listening, and writing: Level 0, no functional ability; Level 1, elementary survival-level proficiency; Level 2, limited working proficiency; Level 3, professional working proficiency; Level 4, full professional proficiency; Level 5, the proficiency of a native speaker. As Liskin-Gasparro (1984) notes, these specific proficiencies can become the basis of both curriculum work and language testing; she also demonstrates in general terms how a proficiency framework can accommodate functional-notional emphases. Keiser and Freed (1984) indicate how these proficiency guidelines can be used in developing materials for the German classroom; and Miller and Cole (1985) have developed a comprehensive proficiency-based French syllabus for the Walpole (Massachusetts) school system.

Instructional Approaches   Two quite different instructional approaches have attracted the attention of foreign-language specialists: immersion programs and "Suggestopedia."

Immersion programs, first developed in Canada in response to the concerns of English-speaking parents in Quebec, use the target language to teach regular school subjects: the second language is not another subject but is instead the medium of instruction. In early total-immersion programs, all instruction for the first three or four grades is presented in the target language; the native language is not introduced until second or third grade. By the end of elementary school, each language is used to teach about half of the curriculum. As Genesee (1985) notes, immersion programs have been used in the United States for three distinct purposes: as linguistic, cultural, and general educational enrichment; as magnet schools designed to effect a desired ethnolinguistic balance; and as a means of achieving some degree of two-way bilingualism in communities with large numbers of non-English-speaking residents. His review of several research studies on all types of immersion programs yields several positive findings: English-speaking students experience no long-term deficits in their English language development as a result of participation in immersion programs; students had no difficulty assimilating new academic knowledge and skills; and immersion students attained functional proficiency in the target languages.

Suggestopedia, first developed by Lozanov (1978), is an instructional method that attempts to involve both conscious and unconscious faculties by using intensive time periods (three- or four-hour sessions for five to six days a week), a secure group atmosphere (ideally, six males and six females with a highly skilled teacher), rhythmic breathing exercises, and baroque music. Its instructional procedure consists of three parts: a review of the previous day's work through conversation, games, and skits; new material introduced using dialogue in familiar situations; and a "seance," which aims at unconscious memorization using yogic breathing and baroque music. As Crawford-Lange notes, this method would seem to have only restricted classroom application, even though there have been several reports of its success.

Rather than searching for the one best curricula and instructional approach, it would seem to make more sense, as Phillips (1982) recommends, to examine more closely how individual learners best learn a foreign language and analyze the particular problems they are facing. Some good work along this line has already been started: Birckbichler and Omaggio (1978) have developed a guide to help teachers diagnose foreign-language learning problems and prescribe specific learning activities to deal with them.

EDUCATION IN THE ARTS

Over the years, the arts have had to struggle for a place in the school's curriculum. Ever since the Committee of Fifteen's report (National Education Association, 1895), they have usually been defined as "minor" subjects taught only an hour or two a week up to grade 8 and then offered as electives at the high school level. As the survey below notes, this situation seems unlikely to change in the near future.

The Recent History of Education in the Arts

During the 1950s and 1960s, art education was conceived rather narrowly as including only the visual arts and music. Children in the elementary grades were assisted by art and music specialists, who emphasized performance (drawing and singing, primarily) as a way of making those subjects interesting. At the junior high level, units and courses in art appreciation and music appreciation were introduced, usually emphasizing the study of the great masters as a means of teaching students some elementary aesthetic principles. At the high school level, students majoring in art spent five or more periods a week in art studies. The emphasis on performance continued: many suburban high schools offered courses called "band," "orchestra," and "chorus," in which students spent most of their time preparing for public performances.

This patchwork arts curriculum, which seemed to lack any organizing principle or governing theory, was the target of two major reform efforts during the 1970s, both supported with the federal funds that seemed so abundant in that decade. The first was launched by the Central Midwestern Regional Educational Laboratory (CEMREL). The CEMREL project began with the publication of *Guidelines: Curriculum Development in Aesthetic Education* (Barkan, Chapman, and Kern, 1970) and continued for a period of ten years. During that extensive period of development and dissemination, CEMREL produced several yearbooks focusing on aesthetic theory and a comprehensive set of curricular packages that translated the guidelines and principles into classroom materials. Initially, reviewers were highly enthusiastic about the CEMREL materials. Kaelin and Ecker (1977) summed up the prevailing view in this manner: "CEMREL is aesthetic education in this country, it has the field to itself" (p. 233). However, the materials failed to reach a significant number of schools. Administrators felt they were too expensive; teachers thought they were too complicated and demanded too much knowledge on their part.

Federal funding also was instrumental in Project IMPACT (Interdisciplinary Model Program in the Arts for Children and Teachers), which began in 1970 in five demonstration projects scattered throughout the nation. Most of the projects emphasized an interdisciplinary approach to the arts and used the arts as a vehicle of instruction for related disciplines. Williams (1977) notes that the projects reported positive results, although there was no rigorous evaluation of their effects. When federal funds were no longer available, the local districts found it possible to support these exemplary projects for only a few more years.

Current Trends in Education in the Arts

These disappointing results from the federally funded projects of the past decade have not deterred leaders in the field from their continued efforts to strengthen education in the arts and to reassert the importance of the arts at a time when the rest of the profession seemed obsessed with the academic curriculum.

Those efforts seemed to have found expression in three related developments. The first is an attempt to broaden the field. Rather than limiting the arts to the visual arts and music, current thinking stresses the multiple nature of aesthetic expression. A recent publication funded by the National Endowment for the Arts identified seven arts deserving of inclusion in the school curriculum: dance; design and architecture; literary arts; media arts (film, video, and sound media); music; theatre; and visual arts (Fowler, 1984). While such an expanded understanding of the nature of the arts seems theoretically desirable, practitioners have expressed reservations about the difficulties of finding the time, the money, and the staff to support such a diversified and comprehensive program.

The second development is an attempt to formulate and promulgate a new rationale for the arts. In previous years, those advocating the arts tended to speak in terms that connoted a subtle elitism: the arts refine the aesthetic sensibilities and help people appreciate the finer things in life. The tendency in the current period is to defend the arts as an essential and unique way of knowing—one that is basic for all students. Eisner expressed such a view quite cogently in his 1982 work when he noted several justifications for emphasizing the arts: they help the child receive and convey information in forms that capitalize on the use of different sensory systems; they give the child access to the apotheoses of human achievement; they are one of the primary ways through which humans construct and convey meaning.

Finally, there seems to be a resurgence of interest in interdisciplinary humanities courses in which the arts play a central role. Such courses enjoyed a period of brief popularity in the early 1960s; during that period, these courses tended to emphasize literature and history and gave only scant attention to the fine arts. At the present time there seems to be a concerted effort to position the arts more centrally in such interdisciplinary courses. Thus, a recent (1984) publication of the Pennsylvania Department of Education cites a course offered in a suburban high school entitled "The Life Cycle through the Arts," in which students examine various stages of life through literature, art, and music. The difficulties of developing and implementing such courses at a time of strong pressures to stress the academics and to standardize the curriculum were highlighted in a recent study (Witlin, 1985). This study documented how well-meaning teachers interested in developing arts-centered interdisciplinary courses reluctantly jettisoned their plans when faced with pacing schedules from the central office mandating the coverage of large amounts of social studies content in relatively short periods of time.

APPLICATIONS

1. An analysis of these trends suggests quite clearly that the ideal curriculum proposed by national commissions is always far ahead of the taught curriculum delivered in the classroom. In a well organized essay that draws from your own experience and your knowledge of the research, explain why it seems to difficult to change the taught curriculum.

2. Select one of the fields discussed. By analyzing how it has changed and is changing now, project what major changes might occur during the next ten years. Write a summary of your projections.

3. Based upon a close reading of this chapter and your own observations, determine which of the fields seems to have experienced the greatest changes. Write a brief essay in which you explain why this particular field seems to have changed most of all.

4. Select one of the fields not discussed in this chapter, such as home economics. Write a report in which you review the history of curriculum in that field of study, focusing on present trends.

REFERENCES

Adams, M. J., and Collins, A. M. (1979). A schema theoretic view of reading. In R. O. Freedle (ed.), *New Directions in Discourse Processing* (Vol. 2). Norwood, NJ: Ablex.

Allen, R. R., and Brown, K. L. (1976). *Developing communication competence in children.* Skokie, IL: National Textbook Company.

Althappilly, K., Smidchens, U., and Kofel, J. W. (1983). A computer-based meta-analysis of the effects of modern mathematics in comparison with traditional mathematics. *Educational Evaluation and Policy Analysis, 5,* 485–493.

American Council of Teachers of Foreign Languages. (1982). *ACTFL provisional proficiency guidelines.* Hastings-on-Hudson, NY: Author.

American Institute for Character Education. (n.d.). *Character-education curriculum.* San Antonio, TX: Author.

Ausubel, D. P. (1968). *Educational psychology: A cognitive view.* New York: Holt, Rinehart, and Winston.

Barkan, M., Chapman, L., and Kern, E. (1970). *Guidelines: Curriculum development in aesthetic education.* St. Louis: CEMREL.

Becker, W. C., and Carnine, D. W. (1980). Direct instruction as an effective approach to educational intervention with disadvantaged and low performers. In B. Lahey and A. Kazdin (eds.), *Advances in clinical child psychology* (Vol. 3). New York: Plenum Press.

Birckbichler, D. W., and Omaggio, A. C. (1978). Diagnosing and responding to individual learner needs. *Modern Language Journal, 62,* 336–345.

Bruner, J. S. (1960). *The process of education.* Cambridge, MA: Harvard University Press.

Calfee, R., and Drum, P. (1986). Research on testing reading. In M. C. Wittrock (ed.), *Handbook of research on teaching* (3rd ed.), pp. 804–849. New York: Macmillan.

Chall, J. S. (1967). *Learning to read: The great debate.* New York: McGraw-Hill.

_____. (1983). *Stages of reading development.* New York: McGraw-Hill.

Chall, J. S., and Stahl. S. A. (1982). Reading. In H. E. Mitzel (ed.), *Encyclopedia of educational research* (5th Ed.), pp. 1535–1559. New York: Macmillan.

College Board. (1983). *Academic preparation for college: What students need to know and be able to do.* New York: Author.

College Entrance Examination Board, Commission on English. (1965). *Freedom and discipline in English.* New York: Author.

Copperman, P. (1978). *The literacy hoax.* New York: William Morrow.

Crabtree, C. (1983). A common curriculum in the social studies. In G. D. Fenstermacher and J. I. Goodlad (eds.), *Individual differences and the common curriculum,* pp. 248–281. Chicago: University of Chicago Press.

Crawford-Lange, L. M. (1982). Curricular alternatives for second-language learning. In T. V. Higgs (ed.), *Curriculum, competence, and the foreign language teacher,* pp. 81–112. Skokie, IL: National Textbook.

Dixon, J. (1967). *Growth through English.* Reading, Great Britain: National Association for the Teaching of English.

Early, M. (1983). A common curriculum for language and literature. In G. D. Fenstermacher and J. I. Goodlad (eds.), *Individual differences and the common curriculum,* pp. 186–218. Chicago: University of Chicago Press.

Eisner, E. W. (1982). *Cognition and the curriculum: A basis for deciding what to teach.* New York: Longman.

EPIE Staff. (1976). Report on a national study of the nature and quality of instructional materials most used by teachers and learners. EPIE Report #71. New York: EPIE Institute.

Fowler, C. B. (ed.). (1984). *Arts in education: Education in arts.* Washington, DC: National Endowment for the Arts.

Genesee, F. (1985). Second language learning through immersion: A review of U.S. programs. *Review of Educational Research, 55,* 541–561.

Gibney, T., and Karns, E. (1979). Mathematics education–1955–1975: A summary of the findings. *Educational Leadership, 36,* 356–359.

Glatthorn, A. A. (1980). *A guide for developing an English curriculum for the eighties.* Urbana, IL: National Council of Teachers of English.

Goodman, Y. M. (1980). From a university faculty member. *Language Arts, 57,* 601–603.

Harms, N. C., and Yager, R. E. (eds.). (1981). *What research says to the science teacher* (Vol. 3). Washington, DC: National Science Teachers Association.

Hillocks, G., Jr. (1972). *Alternatives in English: A critical appraisal of elective programs.* Urbana, IL: National Council of Teachers of English.

Jarolimek, J. (1981). The social studies: An overview. In H. D. Mehlinger and O. L. Davis, Jr. (eds.), *The social studies,* pp. 3–18. Chicago: University of Chicago Press.

Kaelin, E. F., and Ecker, D. W. (1977). The institutional prospects of aesthetic education. In S. Madeja (ed.), *Arts and aesthetics: An agenda for the future,* pp. 229–241. St. Louis: CEMREL.

Keiser, B., and Freed, B. F. (Fall, 1984). The ACTFL proficiency guidelines and materials for the German class. *Die Unterrichts-Praxis, 2,* 279–298.

Kline, M. (1973). *Why Johnny can't add: The failure of the new math.* New York: St. Martin's Press.

Liskin-Gasparro, J. E. (1984). The ACTFL guidelines: Gateway to testing and curriculum. *Foreign Language Annals, 17,* 475–489.

Lockard, J. D. (ed.). (1977). The 10th report of the international clearinghouse on science and mathematics curricular developments. College Park, MD: University of Maryland.

Lockwood, A. L. (1978). The effects of values clarification and moral development curricula on school-age subjects: A critical review of recent research. *Review of Educational Research, 48,* 325–364.

Lozanov, G. (1978). *Suggestology and outlines of Suggestopedia.* New York: Gordon and Breach.

Mandel, B. J. (ed.). (1980). *Three language-arts curriculum models: Pre-kindergarten through college.* Urbana, IL: National Council of Teachers of English.

Miller, F., and Cole, C. (1985). Formulating a secondary proficiency-oriented curriculum. Walpole, MA: Walpole School District.

Moffett, J., and Wagner, B. J. (1976). *Student-centered language arts and reading, K-13: A handbook for teachers* (2nd Ed.). Boston: Houghton-Mifflin.

Mosher, R. L. (ed.). (1980). *Moral education: A first generation of research and development.* New York: Praeger.

Muller, H. J. (1967). *The uses of English.* New York: Holt, Rinehart, and Winston.

National Association of Secondary School Principals. (1980). *State mandated grad-*

uation requirements. Reston, VA: Author.

National Council for the Social Studies. (1984). In search of a scope and sequence for social studies. *Social Education, 48,* 249–262.

National Council for Teaching of English, Committee on National Interest. (1961). *The national interest and the teaching of English: A report on the status of the profession.* Urbana, IL: National Council of Teachers of English.

National Council of Teachers of English. (1983). Essentials of English: A document for reflection and dialogue. *College English, 45,* 184–189.

National Council of Teachers of Mathematics. (1980). *An agenda for action: Recommendations for school mathematics of the 1980s.* Reston, VA: Author.

_____. (1981). *Priorities in school mathematics: Executive summary of the PRISM Project.* Reston, VA: Author.

National Education Association. (1895, 1969). *Report of the Committee of Fifteen.* New York: Arno Press. (Originally published by New England Publishing.)

National Science Teachers Association. (1982). *An NSTA position statement: Science–technology–society: Science education for the 1980s.* Washington, DC: Author.

Palincsar, A. S., and Brown, A. L. (1984). Reciprocal teaching of comprehension-fostering and monitoring activities. *Cognition and Instruction, 1,* 117–175.

Pennsylvania Department of Education. (1984). *Arts and humanities.* Harrisburg, PA: Author.

Pflaum-Connor, S. (ed.). (1978). *Aspects of reading education.* Berkeley, CA: McCutchan.

Phillips, J. K. (1982). Foreign language education. In H. E. Mitzel (ed.), *Encyclopedia of Educational Research* (5th Ed.), pp. 702–711. New York: Macmillan.

Ponder, G. (1979). The more things change . . . : The status of social studies. *Educational Leadership, 36,* 515–518.

Resnick, D. P., and Resnick, L. B. (1977). The nature of literacy: An historical explanation. *Harvard Educational Review, 47,* 370–385.

Roberts, H. D., Kaulfers, W. V., and Kefaurer, G. N. (eds.). (1943). *English for social living.* New York: McGraw-Hill.

Romberg, T. A. (1983). A common curriculum in mathematics. In G. D. Fenstermacher and J. I. Goodlad (eds.), *Individual differences and the common curriculum,* pp. 121–159. Chicago: University of Chicago Press.

Shaver, J. P., Davis, O. L., Jr., and Helburn, S. W. (1979). The status of social studies education: Impressions from three NSF studies. *Social Education, 43,* 150–163.

Shuy, R. (1979). The mismatch of child language and school language: Implications for beginning reading instruction. In L. B. Resnick and P. A. Weaver (eds.), *Theory and practice of early reading* (Vol. 1). Hillsdale, NJ: Lawrence Earlbaum.

Shymansky, J. A., Kyle, W. C., Jr., and Alport, J. (1982). Research synthesis on the science curriculum projects of the sixties. *Educational Leadership, 40,* 63–66.

Simons, H. D. (1979). Black dialect, reading interference, and classroom interaction. In L. B. Resnick and P. A. Weaver (eds.), *Theory and practice of early reading* (Vol. 3). Hillsdale, NJ: Lawrence Earlbaum.

Spiro, R. J. (1977). Remembering information from text. In R. Anderson, R. Spiro, and W. Montague (eds.), *Theoretical issues in reading comprehension.* Hillsdale, NJ: Lawrence Earlbaum.

Squire, J. R., and Applebee, R. K. (1968). *High school English instruction today: The national study of high school English programs.* New York: Appleton Century Crofts.

Stake, R. E., and Easley, J. A. (1978). Case studies in science education: Findings I, Booklet XII. Washington, DC: National Science Foundation.

Staton, J. (1984). Thinking together: Interaction in children's reasoning. In C. J. Thaiss and C. Suhor (eds.), *Speaking and writing K-12,* pp. 144–187. Urbana, IL: National Council of Teachers of English.

Strength through wisdom: A critique of U.S. capability. (1979). Washington, DC: U.S. Government Printing Office.

Superka, D. P., Hawke, S., and Morrissett, I. (1980). The current and future status of the social studies. *Social Education, 44,* 362–369.

Valdman, A. (1982). Toward a modified structural syllabus. *Studies in Language Acquisition, 5* (1), 34–51.

Weiss, I. R. (1978). Report of the 1977 national survey of science, mathematics, and social studies education. Research Triangle Park, NC: Center for Educational Research and Evaluation.

Welch, W. W. (1979). Twenty years of science curriculum development: A look back. In D. C. Berliner (ed.), *Review of research in education* (Vol. I), pp. 282–308. Washington, DC: American Educational Research Association.

Williams, R. M. (September 3, 1977). Why children should draw: The surprising link between art and learning. *Saturday Review,* pp. 11–16.

Witlin, M. (1985). A case study of curriculum change in an urban school district. Doctoral dissertation, University of Pennsylvania, Philadelphia.

Yager, R. E. (ed.) (1980). *Crisis in science education.* Science Education Center Technical Report #21. Iowa City: University of Iowa.

Yager, R. E., Aldridge, B. G., and Penick, J. E. (1983). Current practice: School science today. In F. K. Brown and D. P. Butts (eds.), *Science teaching: A profession speaks.* Washington, DC: National Science Teachers Association.

14

Current Developments Across the Curriculum

Ordinarily, most curricular change takes place within a given discipline, since the discipline tends to be the beginning point of curriculum work. In recent years, however, curriculum workers have become concerned with three changes that transcend a single discipline: using writing to learn; improving thinking skills; and the place of the computer in the curriculum. Such changes require both a different perspective about curriculum change and different processes for planning and implementation.

USING WRITING TO LEARN

The interest in using writing as a way of learning, sometimes called "writing across the curriculum," stemmed initially from two intersecting research thrusts. One such thrust was research into the composing process, derived from several detailed studies of how skilled and unskilled students write. Building upon a seminal study by Janet Emig (1971), numerous researchers have determined that skilled writers in general work through a process that includes several interactive and recursive stages:

1. Prewriting: the writer searches for a subject, gathers information, considers audience, reflects about purpose, and makes a tentative plan.
2. Drafting: the writer begins to write, using a word processor, typewriter, pen, or pencil.
3. Revising: almost as soon as the drafting process has started, the writer begins to evaluate what has been written and makes changes

in the larger elements of content, order, paragraphing, and sentence structure.

4. Editing: at the end of a generally successful draft, the writer polishes, paying close attention to matters of form.

5. Publishing: the writer shares what has been written with the intended audience.

Unskilled writers, however, tend to short-cut the process. They give little attention to prewriting; they begin instead by drafting without thinking. As they write, they worry compulsively about matters of form and consider revision an onerous burden: "Do I have to write it over in ink?" (See Glatthorn, 1981, for a more detailed review of the research.) The cumulative effect of this composing-process research was to give teachers a usable model for teaching writing, even though some seemed to have applied the model too inflexibly.

The second area of research included investigations of the uses of writing in the classroom. Britton and his colleagues (1975), in examining the uses of writing in a variety of subject areas in British secondary schools, discovered that almost all the writing was addressed to the teacher and most of that was to the teacher as an examiner. Applebee's (1981) study of writing in schools in the United States yielded findings at least as discouraging as those of the British study. Writing activities most often involved calculations, short-answer responses, and "fill-in-the-blank" exercises. Almost all writing reflected the informational uses of writing; very little required students to use their imaginations. Almost all writing was addressed to the teacher as an examiner; students rarely played a role as audiences for their classmates' writing. Teachers allowed an average of three minutes for prewriting, and only 29 percent of the teachers surveyed required students to revise. The Britton and the Applebee studies provided evidence that writing was not being used extensively as a means of learning.

Should writing be used as a way of learning all disciplines? Perhaps the most cogent arguments for using writing in this manner have been advanced by Yinger and Clark (1981). By reviewing the work of such scholars as Jerome Bruner, L. S. Vygotsky, A. R. Luria, and Michael Polanyi, they are able to adduce several persuasive reasons for using writing as a way of learning. First, writing is integrative, involving one's total intellectual capacities. Second, when one writes, the lexical, syntactical, and rhetorical constraints of language demand explicit and systematic symbol manipulation, which in turn facilitates learning. Next, writing serves an epistemic function: representations of human knowledge are modified in the process of being written down. Also, writing is a unique mode of learning, involving the enactive, the iconic, and the symbolic modes. Further, the act of writing provides both immediate and long-term self-provided feedback. And writing is active and personal, providing access to one's tacit knowledge.

Finally, writing is a self-paced mode of learning; the pace of writing seems to match better the pace of learning.

There are, however, two cautions to be noted about the extensive use of writing as a way of learning. First, there is the danger that excessive use of writing in all classes will penalize the nonverbal student; such a student needs diverse learning activities that provide opportunities to use talents other than writing ability. Second, writing does not seem to be an essential means of learning such subjects as mathematics and art, and too much attention to writing in such disciplines would inevitably take time away from other productive approaches.

As yet, unfortunately, there is not a great deal of empirical evidence to guide curriculum workers here. Although there have been several anecdotal accounts of how a given department used writing to improve learning, well-designed research studies have been lacking. In fact, Newell (1984), in reporting his own positive findings, commented, "At this time there is virtually no empirical evidence that writing contributes to the learning of subject-area content" (p. 266).

Given cogent theoretical reasons but little empirical evidence here, what response should local curriculum leaders make? Glatthorn (1984) recommends a teacher-centered process that he has found useful in several staff-development workshops. This process asks teachers in each department to develop their own "writing-to-learn" framework. They first identify what Glatthorn calls the "continuing" uses of writing in their discipline. These continuing uses are ways that teachers use writing in an ongoing manner, without making special assignments or giving special instructions; they include such uses as taking notes from lectures, taking notes from the text, writing essay answers, doing written exercises at home or in class, keeping a journal for that subject, and writing responses in class to clarify and fix learning.

Glatthorn next turns to what he calls "special" uses—writing tasks in that discipline that require special assignments and focused instruction. These special uses include the following: writing a report from several sources; reporting on one's own investigations; describing one's problem-solving processes; translating from one symbol system to another; writing a creative paper based on that subject; writing about one's response to a work; explaining how that subject relates to one's personal life; explaining to other students how to do some process related to that subject; persuading students about some issue relating to that subject; and doing an exercise that teaches a thinking skill important in that subject.

Through discussion and analysis, therefore, each department identifies the special and continuing uses of writing that teachers consider appropriate for that subject. The final task in developing the framework is for the teachers in each department to identify the essential qualities they want evidenced in all longer pieces of writing in that discipline. Thus, science teachers might note the importance of objectivity and accuracy in reporting experiments; social studies teachers, the careful use of historical evidence in supporting conclusions; English teachers, the value of creative personal responses in interpreting literature; and mathematics teachers, the need for precision in writing verbal translations of mathematical equations.

A sample framework summarizing all three types of information is shown in Figure 14–1.

FIGURE 14–1.   Framework for "Writing-to-Learn" Project

DEPARTMENT: Home Economics

The following "continuing uses" of writing are important in home economics:

1. Taking notes from lectures and class discussions
2. Taking notes from texts and other resources
3. Keeping a home economics journal

The following "special uses" of writing are important in home economics:

1. Writing recipes
2. Writing directions for craft and decorating projects

The following qualities are considered essential to writing in home economics:

1. Precision in measurements and quantities
2. Clarity in giving directions

With that framework established, each department would then develop instructional materials to support both the special and continuing uses. These instructional materials would typically include the following resources:

- A description of the composing process and a summary of the pertinent research.
- A reproduction of the framework.
- Suggestions for implementing the "continuing uses" effectively.
- Suggestions for making the "special-uses" assignments more productive.
- Sample assignment sheets for the "special uses" assignments.
- Suggestions to the teachers on responding to and grading student writing.
- Handouts for the students, clarifying matters of format and style and explaining the special qualities desired.

Obviously, all this curriculum work would be supported by continuing staff development. Each set of departmental "writing-to-learn" materials would then be reviewed by curriculum leaders. In reviewing and refining the materials, the leaders would use the following criteria:

1. Do the special uses reported seem appropriate for this subject?
2. Do the continuing uses identified seem sufficiently comprehensive without requiring inordinate amounts of time?
3. Are the materials for teacher and student use clear in their writing and sound in their pedagogy?

This departmental approach would obviously be modified somewhat for elementary teachers working in self-contained classrooms. Each teacher would be asked to consider each subject area for which he or she is responsible and then determine for each subject area both the special and continuing uses. Elementary teachers thus have a simpler task, since they have a view of the total curriculum.

The instructional leaders of the school would then examine all the frameworks together, to be sure that the total school "writing-to-learn" program seemed comprehensive, balanced, and likely to be effective.

IMPROVING THINKING SKILLS

The second major movement to effect improvements across the curriculum is the concerted effort to improve thinking. As Cuban (1984) notes, there have been previous and somewhat unsuccessful efforts to accomplish this goal. He points out that, as early as 1924, progressive educators influenced by John Dewey's writings attempted to teach thinking skills through the Project Method. In the Project Method, teachers and students would cooperatively identify a problem and then work through Dewey's five steps of problem solving: identify a perplexing situation; define what has been experienced into a problem; generate hypotheses and collect data; reason to further develop a hypothesis; and test the hypothesis. And then again in the early 1960s, the short-lived attention given to the education of the gifted seemed to spark renewed interest in the teaching of thinking.

Undoubtedly, the widespread use of the computer and allied technology stimulated the present resurgence of interest. As a report from the Education Commission of the States (1982) noted, the "new basics" in an information age are essentially information-processing and thinking skills. After reviewing economic and societal trends, ECS identified the following skills as essential: evaluation and analysis skills; critical thinking; problem-solving strategies; organizational and reference skills; synthesis; application; creativity; decision making given incomplete information; communication skills through a variety of modes.

One could, of course, fault ECS for its own lack of critical thinking, for its list represents a confusing mix of levels of generality. In fact, one of the troubling problems that seems to beset those interested in improving critical thinking is agreeing on what the concept means. Cuban calls this area a "conceptual swamp" (p. 676) and does not even attempt a definition in his own critique. One formulation that seems especially useful to curriculum workers is a three-level hierarchy offered by Presseisen (1984). At the first level are five basic processes: causation; transformations; relationships; classification; and qualification. The second level includes four complex processes that integrate the basic processes: problem solving; decision making; critical thinking; and creative thinking. The highest level is metacognition—monitoring one's own task performance and selecting and understanding the appropriate strategy.

A second question that seems to divide the profession is whether thinking skills (whatever they might happen to be) are more usefully perceived as a set of general processes that transcend the disciplines or as content-specific skills that should be anchored in a discipline. Cuban calls this issue a "continuing unresolved debate among psychologists" (p. 671) and cautions district policy makers about the dangers of making an unexamined decision in the face of such controversy. Yet district policy makers must resolve the issue, for the way that question is answered has obvious curricular implications. If thinking is a set of general processes, then these processes can best be taught in separate "thinking" courses; if thinking is subject-specific, then it is best taught within the context of a discipline.

After reviewing the evidence from artificial-intelligence programs that perform professional-level tasks and from human-transfer experiments, Simon (1980) reaches this conclusion: " . . . powerful general methods do exist and . . . they can be taught in such a way that they can be used in new domains where they are relevant . . . . effective professional education calls for attention to both subject-matter knowledge and general skills" (p. 86). Or, as he puts it, the scissors has two blades: both approaches seem needed. Frederiksen (1984) seems to reach the same conclusion. He points out reasonably enough that if we wish to teach problem solving in such areas as automobile repair, then we should teach specific rules and procedures; however, if we wish to help students deal with the unknown ill-structured problems of the future, then generality will be essential.

Given this controversy, then it has perhaps predictable that both general and subject-specific approaches would be developed. Among the general approaches that seem to be widely accepted by the schools, two seem especially important. Matthew Lipman's "Philosophy for Children" program is based on six novels that use fiction to teach philosophical concepts and skills. (Johnson's 1984 Phi Delta Kappa "Fastback" is a convenient introduction to the Lipman materials.) Teachers' manuals accompanying each novel provide explicit guidance for using the materials. Thus, *Pixie*, intended for children in the third and fourth grades, has a main character who tells a story about making up a story for class; philosophical puzzles are used to stimulate class discussions about logical, social, familial, and aesthetic relationships. After reviewing several studies on the effectiveness of the Lipman materials, Johnson concludes that "empirical evidence suggests that the philosophy for children program significantly enhances the thinking skills of children" (p. 29).

The other widely disseminated program is Edward de Bono's CoRT (Cognitive Research Trust) materials. (He summarizes his program in the 1984 *Educational Leadership* article; a detailed teacher's handbook is available from Pergamon Press.) The CoRT thinking lessons focus on six broad processes, each presented in a separate set of materials: breadth; organization; interaction; creativity; information and feeling; and action. Although de Bono's promotional materials cite several very positive testimonials from satisfied users, several scholars have observed that de Bono does not provide empirical evidence to support his claims. And several have questioned the quality of the materials. After closely analyzing the strategies taught in the CoRT materials, McPeck (1981) concludes, "the CoRT operations, when abstracted from subject content, are empty and superficial to the context of discovery and would be absolutely useless as methods of justification" (p. 118).

Among those who advocate a subject-anchored approach, Beyer (1984) is perhaps the most persuasive in recommending "sequential instruction in thinking skills across all subject areas and throughout all grades" (p. 559). He recommends that such a subject-based thinking curriculum should exhibit five important features: it should introduce a limited number of skills (perhaps three to five) at each grade level; clearly describe for teachers the key components of each skill; provide for the teaching of the same skill across all appropriate content areas; provide instruction in a variety of media and contexts; and provide sequenced development of each skill from the primary through the secondary grades.

He also offers specific recommendations about such sequential development. In early elementary grades, the curriculum would include simplified versions of the skills of recall, comprehension, classifying, comparing, and contrasting. At the middle school level, the curriculum would introduce additional analytical skills, judging, and simple decision making. Then "critical thinking skills and conceptualizing" would be introduced in grades 8 to 10. There would, of course, be appropriate review and reinforcement throughout the grades of skills taught previously.

One of the most comprehensive attempts to develop a subject-centered program is Project IMPACT from Orange County, California. Project IMPACT, a program certified by the National Diffusion Network as effective, uses the secondary mathematics and English language arts curricula to teach the following thinking skills: classifying and categorizing information; ordering, sequencing, and prioritizing ideas; recognizing patterns and relationships; recognizing fact and opinion; identifying relevant and irrelevant information; identifying reliable sources of information; effective questioning; understanding the meaning of statements; seeing cause-and-effect relationships; making generalizations; forming predictions; making assumptions; identifying point-of-view; and logical reasoning. (Further information about the project can be secured from the Orange County Department of Education, Costa Mesa, California.)

Both the general approaches and the subject-anchored materials suffer perhaps from the same weakness: they attempt to change the curriculum through a "top-down" process, asking teachers to use materials developed in some central office. Others in the field, therefore, are placing more emphasis on staff-development programs that teach teachers how to think critically and how to use their own curriculum as a means for improving student thinking.

Glatthorn (1985) has had some success in using such an approach. After reviewing current theory and research on thinking, teachers in each secondary department are first asked to select one of the following units of study as being most appropriate for each grade level they teach: controlled problem solving (using algorithms and heuristic strategies for solving convergent problems with one right answer); open-ended problem solving (using systematic strategies to find the optimal solution to an open-ended problem; information processing (storing, retrieving, and evaluating information); reasoning (the systematic application of logic); evaluating (using critical-thinking processes to evaluate products and individuals); analyzing persuasive messages (including critical analysis of the mass media); mastering disciplinary inquiry (learning the special inquiry processes and truth tests used in a discipline); making moral choices (making ethical judgments); and using thinking in making other life choices (especially college and careers). These particular unit topics, focusing as they do on more general processes that are relatively simple to link to a given discipline, seem to appeal to most teachers as both important and subject-relevant. After each departmental team reaches a consensus on the units to be developed, the team then works together to develop discipline-based instructional materials focusing on the general processes identified. They are thus able to produce a graded series of units that, while lacking professional sophistication, are likely to be used.

With that phase of the project accomplished, they then turn their attention to specific thinking skills that were not incorporated into the units. They review a comprehensive list of such specific skills as classifying and making inferences and identify those that they think should be taught. In teams they then decide whether each skill so identified would be better taught in an "integrated" or a "focused" lesson. (See Figure 14–2 for a form that can be used to assist teachers in making these decisions.) In an "integrated" lesson, as the term is used here, a content objective (such as being able to describe Cortez's first meeting with Native Americans) is the focus of the lesson; the thinking skill (in this case, perhaps, contrasting) is taught as part of that lesson. In a "focused" lesson, a thinking skill, such as evaluating sources for bias, is the focus of the lesson; subject content is merely the carrier. Teachers are then helped in developing both integrated and focused lessons.

THE COMPUTER AND THE CURRICULUM

Before turning to the focal issue of this section—the impact of the computer on the curriculum—it might be useful to begin with a brief assessment of the current status of the computer in education. The general picture is one of

FIGURE 14–2. Identifying Specific Thinking Skills

The following critical-thinking skills are often taught in school subjects. Consider that skill and its importance in the subject and grade level you teach. Indicate your preference for teaching that subject by putting an X in the appropriate column. A "focused lesson" is one in which the thinking skill represents the main objective of that lesson. An "integrated lesson" is one in which a subject-matter concept or skill represents the main objective; the thinking skill is taught in the process of teaching that concept or skill. "Not Appropriate" means that you do not think that particular skill is appropriate for your subject or grade level.

Skill	Focused	Integrated	Not Appropriate
1. Finding and defining problems	———	———	———
2. Representing problems in an appropriate symbol system	———	———	———
3. Organizing facts and concepts in a systematic way	———	———	———
4. Inferring a conclusion from what is stated	———	———	———
5. Locating and evaluating sources	———	———	———
6. Synthesizing information to reach a conclusion	———	———	———
7. Distinguishing between observations, assumptions, and inferences	———	———	———
8. Classifying logically	———	———	———
9. Making predictions	———	———	———
10. Interpreting nonliteral material	———	———	———
11. Identifying persuasive messages and techniques	———	———	———
12. Applying logical operations of negation, disjunction, and conjunction	———	———	———
13. Making and using analogies	———	———	———
14. Determining likely causes	———	———	———
15. Explaining cause-and-effect relationships	———	———	———
16. Avoiding misleading use of language	———	———	———
17. Avoiding statistical fallacies	———	———	———
18. Other _____	———	———	———

widespread and successful use. Recent reports (Valdez, 1986; Becker, 1986) indicate that there are more than one million computers in use in elementary and secondary schools, used by one-fourth of the nation's teachers; half of the secondary schools have fifteen or more computers; and even somewhat conservative projections estimate that there will be three million in the schools by 1990. And a recent review of all the research on computer-based instruction (O'Neil, Anderson, and Freeman, 1986) indicates that student achievement in computer-based education is either the same as or superior to that in conventional instruction, that the computer effects a 32-percent savings in time, and that student attitudes are generally positive.

In examining the impact of the computer on the curriculum, it seems useful to examine the issue from four quite different perspectives: the computer as manager of the curriculum; the computer as deliverer of the curriculum; the computer as an integral tool in the curriculum; and the computer as the curriculum. In the discussions that follow, there are brief reviews of current developments, followed by analyses of their impacts.

The Computer as Manager of the Curriculum

In many ways the computer can play a key role in managing the curriculum. The term *manage*, as used here, includes four major functions, as noted in Figure 14–3. First, the computer can be a useful tool in developing the curriculum. It can store needs-assessment data in a way that such data would be easily retrieved and analyzed. It can also aid in locating and retrieving exemplary scope-and-sequence charts, objectives, and learning activities and materials for those districts that feel the need to draw from existing curricula when they develop their own. For example, one computer-software firm offers to provide "2500+ goals and objectives in mathematics for the Apple or IBM computer."

FIGURE 14–3. The Computer as Manager of the Curriculum

Developing the Curriculum

1. Store and provide data on student achievement and interests.
2. Locate and retrieve exemplary scope-and-sequence charts.
3. Locate and retrieve objectives from objectives banks.
4. Locate and retrieve exemplary learning activities.
5. Locate and retrieve appropriate learning materials.

Facilitating and Monitoring the Learned Curriculum

1. Using student achievement and interest data to identify appropriate objectives.
2. Recording and storing student performance with individual learning objectives.
3. Using performance data to suggest remediation, further exploration, or next new objective.

Aligning the Curriculum

1. Storing written curriculum in retrievable form.
2. Storing teacher reports of objectives taught, matching written and taught.
3. Storing test items, matching test items with written and taught.
4. Storing test scores, providing achievement data in usable form to teachers and administrators.
5. Analyzing congruencies and discrepancies between two or more of the above.

Evaluating the Curriculum

1. Storing, analyzing data on student and teacher perceptions.
2. Storing, analyzing achievement data relevant to specific units, objectives.

The computer can also be useful in facilitating and monitoring the learned curriculum. These functions are usually subsumed under the term *computer-managed instruction* (CMI). Mitzel (1974) identified three levels of CMI. In Level I, the teacher provides data to the computer in a batch-processing mode, usually through optical scanning of tests or teacher evaluation of student progress. The computer sorts, tabulates, and provides summary reports on student progress. In Level II, besides providing reports on student progress, the computer provides instructional prescriptions for remediating deficiencies. In Level III, the student and the computer work interactively; the computer diagnoses learning problems based upon the learner's responses to materials stored in the system and makes appropriate prescriptions.

In describing what he believes CMI software should look like, Kohl (1985) offers some intriguing possibilities for the future. As he envisions it, such software would be interactive, designed to facilitate, not control, teacher planning. The program would first include a "Criteria Generator," which would encourage the teacher to define and modify his or her philosophy of education; the program in this mode would help the teacher organize ideas and generate a structure for implementing those ideas. The second part of the menu, "Learning Goals," would ask the teacher to specify general goals for student learning, based upon the criteria generated. "Lesson Plans and Editor," the third part, would help the teacher develop lesson plans to suit those objectives. The rest of the program would do the usual tasks of evaluating individual and group progress and generating reports. And Halff (1986), in analyzing the potential of work in artificial intelligence, envisions a time in the near future when computers would learn how we construct exercises, would imitate that process in developing exercises for the target material, and would analyze draft materials to de-bug them.

Next, the computer can be very useful in helping administrators and supervisors align the written, taught, and tested curricula. In using the computer to facilitate alignment, four types of information would be stored in the computer: the mastery objectives of the written curriculum; teacher reports on objectives taught; items in curriculum-referenced tests; and student-achievement data. The computer could then readily analyze the congruence between two or more of these information sets and identify significant discrepancies.

Finally, of course, the computer can play a key role in evaluating the curriculum by storing and analyzing two types of information: student and teacher perceptions of and responses to the curriculum; and individual and group achievement data relative to each objective and each cluster of objectives.

How shall we assess the potential of the computer as a manager of the curriculum? There is some risk, obviously, that the inappropriate use of the computer as a manager of the curriculum can lead to some serious problems. First, the reliance upon computerized banks of objectives can significantly impact upon the deliberative process that should be used in developing curricula. Most curriculum leaders would agree with Schwab (1978), who sees curriculum making as a deliberative and dialogic process involving scholars, administrators, and classroom teachers, who interact creatively and imaginatively in shaping curriculum units.

Second, there is a likelihood that the use of the computer as the manager of the curriculum can lead to centralization of the curriculum-development process. And with centralization inevitably comes standardization; in general, decentralization and diversity seem more desirable.

A final concern here is that inappropriate use of the computer in the curriculum-alignment process can reduce teacher initiative and creativity in the classroom. While there is obviously a need for administrators to work with teachers to ensure that there is not too much of a gap between the written, the taught, and the tested curricula, a heavy-handed implementation of computerized alignment processes can so control teachers that they will be reluctant to enrich the curriculum, to improvise instructional activities, and to respond spontaneously and creatively to the unpredictable elements of classroom life.

The Computer as Deliverer of the Curriculum

The computer can also be used to deliver the written curriculum. In this process, usually identified as computer-assisted instruction (CAI), the computer is used as the primary delivery system for the predetermined content. Three types of CAI have been frequently identified in the growing literature on computer education: tutorial, in which the computer is used to present new lessons; drill and practice, in which the computer is used for remediation; and simulations, which involve the learner in solving complex problems. In most simulations, the computer program describes a model situation that imitates some aspect of reality and then asks the learner to solve a problem based upon that model by analyzing, integrating, and synthesizing information.

Despite problems with the quality of software, the research on CAI has been generally highly positive. In his review of all the pertinent research, Kulik (1983) concludes that the average effect of CAI on student achievement, when compared with traditional instruction, is to increase test scores from the 50th to the 63rd percentile. And student attitudes toward the subject are slightly more positive. Beyond this general conclusion, Forman (1982) provides some more specific and useful gleanings from the research: tutorial and drill modes are more effective for low-ability students than for middle- or high-ability groups; most of the studies showing a positive effect of CAI have used the computer as an adjunct, with a teacher readily available; foreign language and science are two areas in which CAI seems to have been especially effective; and retention rates are somewhat lower with CAI then with conventional instruction. And a recent study (Arkansas Department of Education, 1986) suggests that twelve to twenty minutes a day per subject is an optimal time allocation for CAI; much less time decreases instructional effectiveness, and much more time leads to boredom and the neglect of other subjects.

Finally, there are some encouraging trends in the types of software being produced. The Educational Products Information Exchange in a recent publication (1986) reports that logic and problem-solving programs have increased by 90 percent, and fine-arts programs by 46 percent.

In a sense, we should be past the point of asking whether the computer is an effective instructional medium. We need instead to increase our efforts to determine how it can best be used. The first caution, obviously, is to avoid excessive use of the computer as the instructional medium, especially by younger pupils. Several problems have been noted here by learning researchers. The first is that excessive use of the computer may limit the use of experiential learning, especially for younger children. As Cuffaro (1985) notes, "At the young child's level of capability, the world of microcomputers lacks the permeability and flexibility to accommodate the kinds of problems that children spontaneously deal with . . . the questions that arise from daily encounters with people and things" (p. 26).

The second concern, as Sloan (1985) notes, is that excessive use of the computer as an instructional tool may sharply limit the role of the emotions in learning. Despite the attempts of some to separate the affective from the cognitive, most psychologists would agree with the philosopher John Macmurray (1935), who spoke of the connection in this manner: "It is not that our feelings have a secondary and subordinate capacity for being rational or irrational. It is that reason is primarily an affair of emotion, and that the rationality of thought is the derivative and secondary one" (p. 26).

Third, excessive use of the computer as an instructional medium may sharply narrow the image-making capacities of all learners. A great deal of our thinking is guided by images—visual, auditory, and verbal pictures of reality. And the most creative thinkers are those who can use a variety of images in conceptualizing problems and solutions. Despite its sophistication, the computer tends to suggest a mechanistic and linear image of what are often intuitive and recursive processes. In her analysis of software, Trumbull (1986) concludes that most of the software programs that she examined in her study reified knowledge as objective, determinate, and finite, and convinced the children using that software that answers are either right or wrong and that the reward of learning is getting a better score than one's peers.

Finally, some observations should be noted here about the use of the computer for drill and practice. The conventional wisdom in the profession disparages the use of the computer for this aspect of learning, and current school practice seems to reflect the same view. Whereas 64 percent of the high schools in the "National Survey of School Uses of Microcomputers" reported that they used the computer for programming, only 11 percent reported using it for drill and practice (Becker, 1984). Obviously, it would be foolhardy to make excessive use of the computer for drill-and-practice work. However, some arguments can be made for its appropriate use. There is, to begin with, no doubt in anyone's mind that a certain amount of drill and practice is essential for most kinds of learning. If this is the case, we do not now have any technology better than the computer for administering, assessing, and analyzing drill-and-practice material. Mevarech and Rich (1985) point out that the computer is the optimal medium for drill and practice and refer to their own three-year study of its positive effects on disadvantaged children in Israel.

In addition to these pedagogical problems, there are also some technical problems in making effective use of the computer as a delivery system. In her review of the literature on implementation and effectiveness of CAI, Forman (1982) identifies five crucial problems: insufficient funding; the confusing diversity of languages and hardware systems; lack of knowledge among educators about the possible uses of CAI; teacher attitudes; and "CAI materials that are poorly constructed, largely undocumented, and able to run only on equipment for which they were written" (p. 43).

Several organizations and publications are attempting to deal with the problem of software quality by performing and publishing evaluations of educational software. For example, Project SEED, from the Southeastern Educational Improvement Laboratory, collects and disseminates software evaluations from states and other agencies. By 1985 the project had assembled for dissemination evaluations of close to one thousand programs. Molek and Switzer (1984) describe a systematic process which local districts can use in evaluating software, applying sixty-one criteria grouped into the following categories: documentation; introductory part of lesson; presentation of information; program questioning technique; feedback; sequence; motivation; content; student control; and overall.

The Computer as an Integral Tool in the Curriculum

In this third mode, the computer is essentially used as an important tool in the curriculum. Rather than delivering a predetermined curriculum, the computer is used instead as a tool which the student uses in accomplishing curricular goals. This tool typically takes the form of a word processor, a spread sheet, a graphics generator, and a data base—usually designated as "utilities" by computer specialists.

The computer has been used successfully as a tool in several of the disciplines. In English, its primary use is as a word processor, a basic tool for writing. Watt (1982) is among several who claim that word processors enable children's writing ability to match their verbal ability, since the word-processing program eliminates many of the psychomotor tasks involved in writing. Watt also argues that the word processor facilitates the revision process. However, the research here is somewhat inconclusive. Daiute (1985), in summarizing five years of her research with word processors, concludes that students using such programs do not reread or expand their drafts; any revision they do is simply adding restatements or new details at the ends of their texts. Some programs go beyond word processing in trying to facilitate the composing process. For example, *Bank Street StoryBook* enables the user to create illustrations and text, place them anywhere on the screen, and revise them as needed.

In social studies, the computer has been used very effectively to enable students to understand and attempt to replicate the methods social scientists use in their inquiry processes. Hunter (1983) describes several software programs that give students first-hand experience in collecting, organizing, storing, interpreting, and communicating data. For example, the program *TeloFacts* (produced by Dilithium Software) assists in creating and editing questionnaires and surveys, organizes and protects data, assists in the collection of data, performs several statistical tests, analyzes individual items, prints results in a report format, and performs complex subanalyses. And Copeland (1984) describes a program called *Historian*, created by a group of high school teachers, historians, and programmers, which takes students, as they examine nine historical problems, through the four stages of problem solving: problem presentation; hypothesis generation; hypothesis testing; and hypothesis publication.

In addition to the usual tutorial and drill-and-practice programs, science educators have found three special uses of the computer as a tool, according to Nakhleh (1983). It first can be used to simulate laboratory experiments of industrial processes; one program, for example, allows the student to practice titrations and determine the ionization constant of a weak acid. Second, it can provide models and case studies of scientific inquiry. Finally, it can be used in hands-on laboratory experiments, enabling the student to collect, record, analyze, and print out laboratory data.

Finally, of course, Papert's LOGO is a special example of the use of the computer as a tool. LOGO is the name of the programming language, but it also designates the teaching program which uses that language to teach several things. As Papert (1980) describes it, it uses "syntonic" learning (learning that is coherent, related, and associative) to develop "child epistemologists" as it develops the skills and understandings of such related fields as programming, geometry, physics, and poetry. Although the initial reaction to LOGO was highly positive and the early research quite promising, several critics now question its effectiveness. Davy (1985), in a rather critical article, faults it on three grounds: its tendency to impoverish the experiential learning of children; its uncritical "headstart" philosophy of overemphasizing the cognitive development of young children; and its idolatry of computer thinking. As he notes, there are several ways of knowing, but the computer models only one way: "If we are scientifically honest, the real mysteries of human consciousness are still shrouded in darkness. They do not cease to exist because we learn to operate brilliantly in a confined and tightly defined cognitive mode" (p. 19).

A balanced appraisal of LOGO as computer-based learning is offered by Siegel and Davis (1986). In their objective review of its strengths and weaknesses, they note these strengths: it effectively uses visual analogs to teach programming; it uses an inductive approach that makes effective use of the computer's unique capacities; it uses syntonic learning to concretize formal concepts; it de-emphasizes abstract formal treatment in favor of building generalizations from known facts; and it teaches general concepts or "powerful ideas," instead of specific facts and skills. However, they also note some serious drawbacks: it overemphasizes programming; there is no evidence of transfer of learning; there is not a clear relationship between the programming aspects and the applications; and it requires too much teacher training and teacher involvement in the classroom.

If we take a broader look at the impact of these utility programs, they do seem to have a great potential for changing the way students learn. They give both teachers and students powerful tools they did not have before. They use the unique capabilities of the computer, rather than using it as an expensive and sophisticated book. And they actively involve the student in the learning process, rather than simply having the student user sit passively, reading the monitor and punching keys.

The Computer as the Curriculum

In this mode the computer is the focus of the curriculum: the student studies *about* the computer. Usually presented under the rubric of *computer literacy*, such courses and units typically are conceptualized as a K–12 sequence of learning experiences offered to all students. One of the more comprehensive district-wide programs is that developed by the Alameda County (California) School District. As Fisher (1983) describes the program, it is organized into three levels, K–5; 6–8; and 9–12. At each level, there are five important goals which consitute the strands of the program: learning to use computers; programming; instructional uses; computer parts and functions; and careers in computers and their impact on society. The levels vary, of course, in the degree of complexity with which goals are presented and accomplished.

Several leaders in the field have questioned the value of such courses, however. In a report on such criticisms, Shaffer (1983) notes the following arguments from the experts: the hardware is changing so rapidly that it is foolish to focus on it; learning to program is an unnecessary skill for almost all users; and such courses raise false career hopes. In this regard, several have compared using the computer with driving a car: you can learn how to drive without studying the history and the parts of the automobile.

However, a strong case can be made for a reconceptualized computer literacy in the classroom. First, a new term is needed, since "computer literacy" seems misleading. A broader and more accurate term is needed, perhaps something like "information technology education," although that term is too cumbersome. This broader term suggests a more comprehensive curriculum—one that would examine the nature, impact, and related issues of cable television, the video cassette, compact audio disks, interactive video disks, and the computer. This curriculum would perhaps best encompass the middle school and high school years only, since there seem to be no cogent reasons for elementary pupils to study about this new technology.

One possible version of this reconceptualized curriculum is shown in Figure 14–4. Perhaps three features are worth noting here. First, it reflects an integrated technology curriculum: rather than separate courses, it proposes special units in English, social studies, and science—the three disciplines that seem most appropriate. Second, it reflects the realities of the way those curricula are structured in schools: social studies is usually not offered in tenth grade, and high school science is so discipline-centered that it would be difficult to introduce integrated units.

Third, it attempts to reflect what we know about the developmental capabilities of children and adolescents. The science units in the middle grades respond to the curiosity of these young adolescents about how things work. The eighth-grade science unit uses the new technology to help students understand the way discoveries actually are made, not how they are supposed to happen in an ideal world. The seventh-grade social studies unit stresses right actions as it deals with the ethical questions involved with the new technology; these youngsters tend to be at a stage of moral development when they want to know what is right and what is wrong. In contrast, the twelfth-grade unit emphasizes ethical choices, helping these older students weigh the complexities of these moral issues.

FIGURE 14–4. Proposed Scope and Sequence:
Information Technology Education

Subjects

Grade	English	Social Studies	Science
5	Talking with computers; Programs as languages		How it works: broadcast and cassette video
6		Computers in our community	How it works: lasers; sound and sight
7		Doing what's right with computers and video cassettes	How it works: the computer
8	Using, not being used by, the new technology		Scientific discovery in the new technology
9	The computer as a communications medium	The new technology and politics	
10	The new technology as art		
11	Careers in the new technology	The new technology shapes our society	
12	The new technology and the future	Ethical choices and the new technology	

Facilitating the Use of the Computer in the Classroom

What can be done to make even more effective use of the computer in the classroom? On the one hand, there are many who espouse a top-down change process. One distinguished professor of computer science (Bork, 1986) proposes a six-year trial project to develop twenty exemplary courses using interactive technology, courses which he hopes would be "highly competitive with conventional instruction" (p. 37). There are two somewhat surprising elements here. One is his naive belief that the centralized development and dissemination of exemplary courses is the appropriate change strategy. The massive failure of the federally funded curriculum projects of the 1960s clearly suggests the folly of such a course. The other surprising element is his suggestion that the goal is to make these exemplary courses competitive with conventional instruction. The computer is a unique learning medium, and the most forward-looking leaders in the field are suggesting that we abandon the "horse-race" mentality of trying to prove that it is better than conventional instruction.

A more enlightened view of the change process is expressed by Turkle (Rhodes, 1986), one of the leading experts in the field. Turkle suggests quite seriously that schools should issue a computer and a printer to every teacher, along with four pieces of software: a good data-base program, a good spreadsheet program, a word-processing program, and LOGO. Let teachers take the hardware and the software home to play with and to use as they see fit. Then give teachers extensive staff development, and let them use it as they wish. Although such an approach would involve a great deal of expense, it represents a much more effective way of changing the way teachers teach. It begins by giving them the tools and helping them become users.

APPLICATIONS

1. Develop the outlines of a "writing-to-learn" project which could be used in a subject or discipline you know well. Use the framework suggested in Figure 14–1 to describe the major components of the program.

2. If you were charged with the responsibility of developing a district curriculum in critical thinking, would you recommend developing separate courses, integrating critical thinking into existing courses, or using both approaches? Provide a rationale for your recommendation.

3. Consider the four uses of the computer in relation to the curriculum: the computer as developer, the computer as deliverer, the computer as a tool, and the computer as the curriculum. As you assess the needs of a school system with which you are familiar, how would you prioritize these four approaches? What processes would you use in making such a determination systematically?

4. As reported in Chapter 2, the reform report *A Nation at Risk* identified "computer literacy" as one of the "Five New Basics" and recommended that a one-semester course in computer literacy be required for each high school student. How do you assess the wisdom of such a suggestion?

5. One of the issues dividing specialists in early childhood education is how much use should be made of the computer as an instructional tool for the early elementary grades. Based upon your knowledge and your values, explain the position you would take on this issue and the reasons you would advance in support of your position.

REFERENCES

Applebee, A. N. (1981). *Writing in the secondary school: English and the content areas.* Urbana, IL: National Council of Teachers of English.

Arkansas Department of Education. (1986). *Basic skills achievement through technology.* Little Rock, AR: Author.

Becker, H. J. (1984). School uses of microcomputers: Report #3 from a national survey. *Journal of Computers in Mathematics and Science Teaching, 3* (3), 26–32.

————. (January 1986). Our national report card: Preliminary results from the new Johns Hopkins survey. *Classroom Computer Learning, 7,* 30–33.

Beyer, B. K. (1984). Improving thinking skills: Practical approaches. *Phi Delta Kappan, 65,* 556–560.

Bork, A. (1986). Let's test the power of interactive technology. *Educational Leadership, 43* (6), 36–37.

Britton, J., Burgess, T., Martin, N., McLeod, A., and Rosen, R. (1975). *The development of writing abilities (11–18).* London: Macmillan.

Copeland, W. D. (1984). Creating a historian's microworld. *Classroom Computer Learning, 5* (3), 49–53.

Cuban, L. (1984). Policy and research dilemmas in the teaching of reasoning: Unplanned designs. *Review of Educational Research, 54,* 655–681.

Cuffaro, H. K. (1985). Microcomputers in education: Why is earlier better? In D. Sloan (ed.), *The computer in education: A critical perspective,* pp. 21–30. New York: Teachers College Press.

Daiute, C. (August 1985). Effects of word processing on the writing process. *Harvard Education Letter,* p. 3.

Davy, J. (1985). Mindstorms in the lamplight. In D. Sloan (ed.), *The computer in education: A critical perspective,* pp. 11–20. New York: Teachers College Press.

de Bono, E. (1984). Critical thinking is not enough. *Educational Leadership, 42,* 16–17.

Education Commission of the States. (1982). *The information society: Are high school graduates ready?* Denver, CO: Author.

Educational Products Information Exchange. (February 1986). TESS tables tally trends. *Educational Software Selector,* 3–4.

Emig, J. (1971). *The composing processes of twelfth graders.* Urbana, IL: National Council of Teachers of English.

Fisher, G. (1983). Developing a district-wide computer-use plan. *The Computing Teacher, 11* (5), 52–59.

Forman, D. (1982). Search of the literature. *The Computing Teacher, 10* (5), 37–51.

Frederiksen, N. (1984). Implications of cognitive theory for instruction in problem solving. *Review of Educational Research, 54,* 363–407.

Glatthorn, A. A. (1981). *Writing in the schools: Improvement through effective leadership.* Reston, VA: National Association of Secondary School Principals.

————. (1984). *Writing to learn.* Unpublished manuscript, University of Pennsylvania, Philadelphia.

————. (1985). *Teaching critical thinking: A teacher-centered process.* Unpublished manuscript, University of Pennsylvania, Philadelphia.

Halff, H. M. (1986). Instructional applications of artificial intelligence. *Educational Leadership, 43* (6), 24–31.

Hunter, B. (1983). Powerful tools for your social studies classroom. *Classroom Computer Learning, 4* (3), 50–57.

Johnson, T. W. (1984). *Philosophy for children: An approach to critical thinking.* Bloomington, IN: Phi Delta Kappa Educational Fastbacks.

Kohl, H. (1985). Classroom management software: Beware the hidden agenda. *Classroom Computer Learning, 5* (8), 19–21.

Kulik, J. A. (1983). Synthesis of research on computer-based instruction. *Educational Leadership, 41,* 19–21.

Macmurray, J. (1935). *Reason and emotion.* London: Faber and Faber.

McPeck, J. E. (1981). *Critical thinking and education.* Oxford, England: Martin Robertson.

Mevarech, Z., and Rich, Y. (September-October 1985). *Journal of Educational Research, 79* (1), 5–11.

Mitzel, H. E. (1974). Mobile computer-assisted instruction for inservice teacher education. *Journal of Educational Technology Systems, 2,* 305–313.

Molek, R., and Switzer, D. (1984). Educational software: An evaluation process. *The Executive Review, 4* (4), 1–4.

Nakhleh, M. B. (1983). An overview of microcomputers in the secondary science curriculum. *Journal of Computers in Mathematics and Science Teaching, 3* (1), 13–21.

Newell, G. E. (1984). Learning from writing in two content areas: A case study/protocol analysis. *Research in the Teaching of English, 18,* 265–287.

O'Neil, H. F., Anderson, C. C., and Freeman, J. A. (1986). Research on teaching in the armed forces. In M. C. Wittrock (ed.), *Handbook of research on teaching* (3rd Ed.), pp. 971–987. New York: Macmillan.

Papert, S. (1980). *Mindstorms: Children, computers, and powerful ideas.* New York: Basic Books.

Presseisen, B. Z. (1984). *Thinking skills: Meanings, models, and materials.* Philadelphia: Research on Better Schools.

Rhodes, L. (1986). On computers, personal styles, and being human: a conversation with Sherry Turkle. *Educational Leadership, 43* (6), 12–17.

Schwab, J. T. (1978). *Science, curriculum, and liberal education.* Chicago: University of Chicago Press.

Shaffer, R. A. (September 16, 1983). Courses in computer literacy beginning to draw bad marks. *Wall Street Journal,* p. 37.

Siegel, M. A., and Davis, D. M. (1986). *Understanding computer-based education.* New York: Random House.

Simon, H. A. (1980). Problem-solving and education. In D. T. Tuma and F. Reif (eds.), *Problem solving and education: Issues in teaching and research*, pp. 81–96. Hillsdale, NJ: Erlbaum.

Sloan, D. (1985). Introduction: On raising critical questions about the computer in education. In D. Sloan (ed.), *The computer in education: A critical perspective*, pp. 1–10. New York: Teachers College Press.

Trumbull, D. J. (1986). Games children play: A cautionary tale. *Educational Leadership, 43* (6), 18–21.

Valdez, G. (1986). Realizing the potential of educational technology. *Educational Leadership, 43* (6), 4–6.

Watt, D. (June 1982). Word processors and writing. *Popular Computing,* 124–126.

Yinger, R. J., and Clark, C. M. (1981). *Reflective journal writing: Theory and practice.* East Lansing, MI: Institute for Research in Teaching, Michigan State University.

15

Individualizing the Curriculum

Plato may have been one of the first writers to recommend individualization through tracking. In his *Republic* he made clear his belief that children should be directed toward roles of philosopher, guardian, or artisan based upon their talents. While contemporary educators reject such a deterministic differentiation, the search for curricula that respond to individual differences continues. This chapter will analyze the types of individualized programs, review previous attempts to respond to individual differences, and assess current models. The chapter concludes by examining the challenging problems inherent in providing for very special student populations.

TYPES OF INDIVIDUALIZED PROGRAMS

It would be useful to begin the analysis by clarifying the concept. Here it seems wise to substitute the clearer term *adaptive* for the more ambiguous *individualized*. Largely because of the vague and conflicting connotations associated with the latter term, specialists in the field now are referring to *adaptive* curricula and *adaptive* instructional practices. These two closely related constructs might be defined in this manner:

> Adaptive curricula and instructional practices are educational processes that arrange the conditions and materials of learning so that they fit learner individual differences.

Corno and Snow (1986) note the complexity of the process. In their model of the relationship between aptitude and performance, they identify several complex sets of relationships. A learner, in their analysis, has an aptitiude complex for performance in a particular educational situation. (Note that the aptitude complex is particularistic, not general.) This aptitude complex comprises three related elements: intellectual abilities and prior knowledge; cognitive and learning styles; and academic motivation and other personality complexes. That aptitude complex produces a level of purposive striving and control of learning. The aptitude complex and the striving and control in turn influence and are mediated by the quantity and quality of the learning act. All these factors affect the level and nature of learner engagement, which in turn affect the nature of educational performance.

The complexity of the task and the diversity of human aptitudes have predictably resulted in numerous models of adaptive education. Perhaps the clearest delineation of the salient features of adaptive instruction is that provided by Waxman et al. (1984). In their comprehensive review of the research on adaptive instruction, they were able to identify these seven features: instruction based on the assessed capabilities of each student; materials and procedures that permit each student to make progress at a pace suited to his or her abilities; periodic evaluation of student progress to inform the student about mastery; student assumption of responsibility for diagnosing present needs and for planning individual learning activities; alternative activities and materials for aiding student learning; student choice in selecting goals, outcomes, and activities; and students' assistance of one another in pursuing individual goals and cooperation in achieving group goals.

PREVIOUS ATTEMPTS TO INDIVIDUALIZE

As Grinder and Nelsen (1985) note, attempts to individualize education in the United States go back to Colonial times, a period they characterize as "individualized instruction by default." One hundred youngsters would be seated in a large ungraded classroom, working on exercises, while one teacher monitored their work. However, the need to educate large numbers of children in a more systematic manner led nineteenth-century educational reformers to institute graded classrooms, each with a teacher in charge presenting a standard program. While this self-contained graded classroom has persisted as the norm for at least one hundred years, there have been during this time numerous attempts to break out of the constraints imposed by standardized education. Rather than presenting a comprehensive historical review of such attempts, the discussion that follows concentrates on those approaches that persist to the present. (For a fuller discussion of the history of individualized instruction, consult the Grinder and Nelsen work.)

Providing Elective Courses

During the first century of American education, educators seemed concerned solely with identifying the common curriculum for all students; electives as such were not even considered. Even though Charles Eliot was chairman of the Committee of Ten, he was not able to persuade the committee that electives were desirable; the only option provided in their (1893) recommendations was that bookkeeping and commercial arithmetic could be substituted for algebra. The first official statement recommending elective courses was the *Cardinal Principles of Secondary Education,* published by the Commission on the Reorganization of Secondary Education in 1918. In their formulation of the ideal program, the commission recommended a balance between the *constants* (those courses to help all students achieve essential goals), *curriculum variables* (special courses determined by the student's specific educational and career goals), and *free electives* (courses chosen in response to special interests).

For the past seventy years the debate over what constitutes the best balance of these three components has continued unabated. The debate unfortunately has not been informed by rational analysis and too often has produced prescriptions that reflect only the participants' bias about the need to control the education of the young. Thus, the recommendations published during a given period usually were consonant with the prevailing mood of the times. During the period termed in this work *privatistic conservatism,* the tendency was to increase requirements and decrease electives because of the general perception that students needed more rigorous programs. For example, Goodlad (1984) proposed that the student should have from 9 to 20 percent of the time available for electives to develop special talents or interests. He seemed to arrive at this figure by default: it is the time not required for the common curriculum that he recommends. Boyer's (1983) report took a slightly more positive view of the importance of electives: his ideal program of studies would provide as much as one-third of the time for elective courses over the four-year high school period.

Curriculum Tracking

Curriculum tracking, sorting students into somewhat rigid tracks based upon career and educational goals, was probably first formally recognized as a desirable practice by the Committee of Ten. Their report recommended four tracks, differentiated chiefly by the language studied: Classical; Latin Scientific; Modern Languages; and English. And they were quite explicit about the relative qualities of those four: "The programs called respectively Modern Languages and English must in practice be distinctly inferior to the other two" (p. 48). Thus the practice of tracking and the status accorded to certain tracks have continued for almost one hundred years; all that changes are the number of tracks and their names. Most high schools that track now provide for three tracks, determined primarily by educational and career goals: college preparatory; general; and vocational/technical.

How desirable is tracking from an educational standpoint? Here Rosenbaum's (1980) review of the research is most enlightening. He first notes that there is no clear finding from the research as to whether ability or social class is the primary determiner of track placement. The key individual in determining track placement, he finds, is the guidance counselor. Two of his findings seem especially troubling: many students are in curricular tracks inconsistent with career choices; and curricular tracking is relatively stable, with more movement from college preparatory to general or vocational than the other way around. The more serious problem, of course, is the differences in curricular and instructional quality. Several researchers, most notably Goodlad (1984), have observed these problems with "general" courses: the content is boring and unchallenging; the classroom climate is unstimulating; teachers convey low expectations; and teachers spend more time in enforcing the rules.

The data would seem to suggest rather clearly, then, that curriculum tracking is not a useful way of responding to individual differences.

Offering "Minicourses"

As noted in Chapter 2, many school districts attempted to give students content options within a field of study by developing minicourses lasting from six to eighteen weeks. Thus, rather than taking English II, students could choose from an array of offerings with titles such as *Women in Literature, The Mass Media,* and *The Search for Wisdom.* While such minicourses were more often developed in the fields of English and social studies, they could also be found in science and mathematics; in fact, many schools prided themselves on offering more than two hundred courses.

The minicourse approach was highly popular with teachers, since it enabled them to develop and teach courses relating to their special interests and knowledge. Most schools using a minicourse curriculum reported high levels of student satisfaction. However, most of these courses seemed poorly designed. They seemed not to have been produced with some overall conceptualization of that field and gave scant attention to important skills and concepts. Thus, the claim that this "smorgasbord curriculum" contributed to the decline in academic achievement seems warranted, even though there was no persuasive empirical evidence on this point. However, as Glatthorn (1980) points out, the problems associated with the minicourses can be avoided by careful design.

Open Classrooms

The open classroom popular during the late 1960s and early 1970s attempted to respond to individual differences in several ways. First, open classroom teachers felt less constrained by district curriculum guides and fashioned curricula that they believed responded to the special needs and interests of their pupils. Thus, while elementary teachers in open classrooms all taught language arts, social studies, mathematics, and science, they chose content that they believed would be most meaningful to their pupils, and that content typically involved the integration of several subject fields. Second, pupils had some options about their use of time: they could work in special learning centers any time during the day, unlimited by bells and artificial distinctions between subjects; and they could spend as much time as they needed. Also, they had some choice about activities and materials; the learning centers were usually provisioned with a rich assortment of materials for learning. Finally, there was an atmosphere of informality, which advocates believed was truly individualized: pupils could talk together and move about the room as necessary.

The open classroom movement was short-lived, of course, succumbing to conservative pressures for more teacher control and higher achievement in the basics. Its rapid demise was probably unfortunate. Walberg's (1986) review of all the research on open classes reached this conclusion: "Students in open classes do slightly or no worse in standardized achievement and slightly to substantially better on several outcomes that educators, parents, and students hold to be of great value" (p. 226).

Self-Paced Instruction

During the 1960s and 1970s there was also much interest in several varieties of self-paced instruction, usually called "individualized learning." While these programs varied in their details, there were several common elements:

1. The curriculum is analyzed into several components, arranged in a tightly controlled sequence.
2. The learner is assessed and placed appropriately along that sequence.
3. The learner works on self-instructional packets or lessons, usually in isolation, in order to achieve clearly specified objectives.
4. The learner gets feedback about progress and remediates where necessary.

In most such programs, only the pace of learning (and, concomitantly, the time spent on learning a particular set of objectives) is adapted to learner needs; every other important element is controlled and standardized. How effective are such programs? A comprehensive and systematic review of all soundly designed studies on the issue concluded that secondary school students in such programs, when compared with students taught by conventional methods, did not gain more on achievement measures, did not gain more in critical thinking, and did not improve in self-esteem or in attitudes toward the subject (Bangert, Kulik, and Kulik, 1983). However, the same reviewers note that studies of such systems in higher education produced strikingly different results: college students using individualized systems made significant gains in achievement and rated their courses more highly. They conclude that elementary and secondary students may need more stimulation, guidance, support, and constraint than individualized systems seem to provide.

CURRENT ADAPTIVE APPROACHES

At the present there are five major adaptive approaches that seem to have promise: the Adaptive Learning Environments Model (ALEM); cooperative learning models; learning-styles models; mastery learning models; and computer-based models. Since computer-based models were reviewed in the previous chapter, this section examines the other four models. In each case, the discussion below describes the model and reviews the research on its effectiveness.

Adaptive Learning Environments Model

The Adaptive Learning Environments Model (ALEM) was developed at the Learning Research and Development Center of the University of Pittsburgh. It is, in the views of its developers, an attempt to combine prescriptive or direct instruction with those aspects of open education that have been found to be effective. ALEM is a rather ambitious model that attempts to restructure the school environment, not simply alter the instructional system. As Wang and Walberg (1983) point out, it has five major components: a basic-skills curriculum consisting of highly structured and hierarchically organized prescriptive learning activities, as well as more open-ended exploratory learning activities; an instructional-management system designed to maximize the use of time and materials; a family-involvement component; a flexible-grouping and instructional-team system; and a data-based staff-development program.

According to researchers from the University of Pittsburgh (Wang, Gennari, and Waxman, 1985), the results of four studies indicate that ALEM can be implemented with a relatively high degree of fidelity, that trained teachers can use the processes required by the program, and that the model seems to facilitate student achievement, having an especially positive effect on the achievement of mainstreamed handicapped students. However, in a critique of this research, Corno and Snow (1986) point out that the researchers did not examine relationships among student aptitudes, the ALEM program, and achievement across school sites.

Cooperative Learning Models

Perhaps the most promising of current models are those that involve cooperative learning. As Johnson and Johnson (1985) note, cooperative learning models should have four key attributes: positive interdependence, achieved through mutual goals, divisions of labor, dividing resources or information among members, assigning students, and giving joint rewards; face-to-face interaction among students; individual accountability for mastering the assigned materials; and appropriate use of interpersonal and small-group skills.

Their review of twenty separate studies they have conducted yields very positive results. Cooperative learning experiences, compared with competitive and individualistic ones, result in higher achievement, promote greater competencies in critical thinking, develop more positive attitudes toward the subject, and lead students to believe that the grading system is fairer.

They conclude their review with six useful guidelines for teachers interested in using cooperative learning:

1. Cooperative procedures may be used with any type of academic task—but the greater the conceptual learning required, the greater will be the efficacy of cooperation.
2. Cooperative groups should be structured so that controversy is possible and managed constructively.
3. Students should be encouraged to keep each other on task and discuss the material in ways that will ensure the use of higher-level learning strategies.
4. Students should be encouraged to support each other's efforts to achieve, regulate each other's task-related efforts, provide each other with feedback, and ensure that all are involved.
5. Cooperative groups should be heterogeneous in ability.
6. Positive relationships among members should be encouraged.

The Team-Assisted Individualized program (TAI) combines group and individual work for the teaching of mathematics. Students are assigned to four- and five-member heterogeneous teams and are given a placement test to determine placement. During the individualized portion of the program, they work on prepared curriculum materials that include an instruction sheet, several problem sheets, a practice test, and a final test. Students work on their units in teams, helping each other and assisting with the practice tests. The teams receive scores, with special recognition for high performance. The teacher works each day with groups of students who are at about the same point in the curriculum. Slavin (1985) reports that in five of six studies, TAI students significantly exceeded control students in mathematics achievement.

Learning-Styles Models

Learning-styles models are built upon the assumptions that learners differ significantly in their styles of learning, that those styles can be assessed, and that knowledge of styles can help both teachers and learners. In a very useful analysis, Keefe (1979) conceives of learning style as having three dimensions. The first dimension is cognitive styles—the individual's typical modes of perceiving, thinking, problem solving, and remembering. In his view, cognitive style itself has two broad divisions: reception styles (such as field independence versus field dependence) and concept-formation and retention styles (such as cognitive complexity versus cognitive simplicity). The second dimension is affective styles—those dimensions of personality involving attention, emotion, and valuing. This dimension he divides into two categories: attention styles (such as conceptual level) and expectancy and incentive styles (such as locus of control). Finally there are physiological styles involving such aspects as time rhythms, need for mobility, and environmental elements.

Predictably, there are numerous instruments designed to test one or more of the dimensions noted by Keefe. For example, Gregorc's (1982) "Style Delineator" asks the adult to respond to twenty sets of behavioral descriptors indicating the most- and least-preferred descriptor; the results are used to categorize the adult as predominantly concrete sequential, concrete random, abstract sequential, or abstract random. On the other hand, the Dunn, Dunn, and Price (1978) Learning Style Inventory asks the student to express preferences about learning conditions; the student is asked to respond to more than one hundred items, such as "I like to study in bed" and "I study best when the lights are low."

What should educators do once a student's learning style has been identified? Most of the learning-style advocates recommend a matching strategy: find the student's preferred learning style and then provide learning experiences that match that style. For example, teachers in the Shoreham-Wading River Schools (New York) are taught how to assess students' conceptual levels and then how to modify their curricula so that their instruction matches students' cognitive abilities (see Brooks, 1986). On the other hand, McCarthy (1981) recommends restructuring the curriculum so that every unit of study provides some dissonance and some consonance for every learning style. In her formulation there are four main types of learners: innovative learners; analytic learners; common-sense learners; and dynamic learners. Her "4Mat System" provides for four general types of sequential learning experiences: integrating experience with the self; concept formulation; practice and personlization; and integrating application and experience. In turn, each of these four types is divided into two kinds of learning: those that rely mainly upon right-brain activity and those that use primarily the left brain. Thus, she claims that her "curricular progression" includes all four learning styles and uses right- and left-mode techniques.

What does the research say about the usefulness of the learning-styles models? First, there is a considerable body of evidence that aspects of cognitive style especially play an important role in learning. Here the dimension of field independence/field dependence is perhaps the most studied. The field-dependent person in perceiving phenomena is less able than the field-independent person to keep an item separate from its context. In reviewing the research on this key dimension, Good and Stipek (1983) note several findings of importance to educators. Field-dependent students usually prefer to work in groups with frequent teacher interaction; field-independent students may work better in independent study. Field-dependent students work to please the teacher and are more motivated by teacher praise. Field-independent students prefer to structure their own learning tasks; field-dependent students need more explicit teacher instruction.

Whether schools can constructively respond to such differences is another issue. Despite the claims of learning-styles advocates that their approaches produce excellent results, more dispassionate researchers are less sanguine. After reviewing the research, Good and Stipek reach this conclusion: "We conclude . . . that the research evidence for adapting instruction for students solely on the basis of students' cognitive styles is not compelling . . . . there is only weak support for the claim that instructional treatment should always be consistent with students' learning styles" (p. 35).

Mastery Learning Models

As explained in Chapter 2, mastery learning principles were first enunciated by Benjamin Bloom; they have since been adapted in several different approaches. As Anderson (1985) analyzes all these mastery learning approaches, they have six features in common: clearly specified learning objectives; short, valid assessment procedures; present mastery standards; a sequence of learning units; provision of feedback of learning progress to students; and provision of additional time and help to correct specified errors of students failing to meet the mastery standard. In his review of all the research on mastery learning, Anderson concludes that learning-for-mastery students have outperformed students in conventional classrooms on measures of achievement, retention, learning rate, attitudes, and self-esteem.

He also calls attention to some important findings about the application of the mastery model. First, the research evidence suggests that standards between 85 and 95 percent correct are most appropriate; setting lower performance standards seems to result in no substantial improvement. Second, the effective use of corrective procedures is critical; in fact, he concludes that corrective instruction targeted to the needs of particular learners and their learning problems is more important than the clarity of the original instruction.

ADAPTIVE PROGRAMS FOR THE GIFTED

Obviously, all the adaptive models described above can be used in educating the gifted and talented. There have been, however, several programs especially designed to adapt to the special needs of this population. Before reviewing specific programs it would be useful to identify some general guidelines for developing and evaluating programs for the gifted. Those that seem to be most widely used by educators in the field are the ones proposed by the Leadership Training Institute (cited in VanTassel-Baska, 1985):

1. The content of curricula for the gifted and talented (G/T) should focus on and be organized to include more elaborate, complex, and in-depth study of major ideas, problems, and themes that integrate knowledge within and across systems of thought.
2. Curricula for the G/T should allow for the development and application of productive thinking skills to enable students to reconceptualize existing knowledge and/or generate new knowledge.
3. Curricula for the G/T should enable them to explore constantly changing knowledge and information and develop the attitude that knowledge is worth pursuing in an open world.
4. Curricula for the G/T should encourage exposure to, selection of, and use of specialized and appropriate resources.
5. Curricula for the G/T should promote self-initiated and self-directed learning and growth.
6. Curricula for the G/T should provide for the development of self-understanding and the understanding of one's relationship to persons, societal institutions, nature, and culture.
7. Evaluations of curricula for the G/T should be conducted in accordance with prior stated principles, stressing higher-level thinking skills, creativity, and excellence in performance and products.

In addition to these general guidelines, VanTassel-Baska (1985) argues that curricula for the gifted should be distinguished from regular programs by placing more emphasis on the following: the principle of economy (delete from the program content or skills previously mastered); concentration on higher-level thinking skills; concentration on the interrelationships between and among bodies of knowledge; exposure to nontraditional school subjects (such as logic, law, and philosophy); self-directed learning; and commitment to future learning. Observe that both the Leadership Training Institute guidelines and the VanTassel-Baska differentiating characteristics are rather similar.

In fact, a critical review of both sets leaves one with the feeling that they are simply describing high-quality programs that might be offered to all students, not just the gifted. This observation, of course, touches on the basic controversy among educators about programs for the gifted: do they really need special programs? Those who believe that they do have in general offered programs that could be characterized in one of three ways: special pace; special curricula; or special resources.

Special Pace: Acceleration

Acceleration as an adaptive strategy helps gifted students advance through the grades and master advanced academic content at a rapidly accelerated rate. Thus, a highly gifted ten-year-old might be placed in a ninth-grade science class, or a very intelligent elementary school pupil might be studying the mathematics normally taught in high school. Also, high school students preparing for and taking the Advanced Placement examinations of the College Entrance Examination Board are experiencing a type of acceleration.

Many educators have expressed reservations about rapid acceleration, citing the problems of the gifted pupil who is separated from age-mates and exposed to too much academic pressure. Such fears do not seem to be warranted. In a review of two hundred studies covering a fifty-year time span, Daurio (1979) could not find one study that indicated negative effects of acceleration; two-thirds of the studies yielded positive results for the pupils on nonacademic measures.

There is no longer any doubt at all that acceleration pays off academically. For several years, Julian Stanley and his colleagues at Johns Hopkins University have gotten excellent results with radical acceleration of mathematically precocious youth. (See, for example, Stanley, 1978.) The program has been expanded to include the verbally gifted as well. And in a meta-analysis of twenty-six studies of acceleration, Kulik and Kulik (1984) conclude that talented students who were accelerated into higher grades performed as well as the talented older students already in those grades and showed almost a year's advancement in subject achievement over talented youngsters of the same age who had not been accelerated. They also note that the findings on affective outcomes were "sketchy and inconclusive" (p. 422).

Special Curricula

Curricular modifications for the gifted have in general taken two forms: offering special subjects and providing for enrichment activities. In many school districts, gifted students can study subjects ordinarily not included in the curriculum by following independent study programs or by receiving group instruction in a special program. The "Philosophy for Children" program described in Chapter 14 has been used by many school districts for such purposes, with generally successful results. In one study of fifth- and sixth-grade students, the researcher discovered that the philosophy students made significant gains on several measures of thinking and expressed highly positive attitudes about the program; parents of these children were also quite positive about their perceptions of the value of the program (Cinquino, 1980).

Several enrichment models have been used in programs for the gifted. Two of those that seem in widest use are Renzulli's "Triad/RDIM" model and Meeker's SOI model.

Triad/RDIM Model The Triad/RDIM model combines the *Enrichment Triad Model* originally proposed by Renzulli (1977) with a relatively recent approach to selection, the Revolving Door Identification Model (Renzulli, Reis, and Smith, 1981). The Enrichment Triad Model is based upon three types of enrichment activites for the gifted. Type I activities are "general exploratory activities," in which learners explore areas of personal interest. Type II activities are "group training activities," consisting of materials and instructional techniques designed to develop critical and creative thinking skills. Type III activities are "individual or small group investigations," in which students have an opportunity to investigate real problems through research and inquiry.

The Revolving Door Identification Model begins by identifying a pool of the top 15 to 20 percent of the student population. All these students are exposed to Type I and Type II activities on a regular basis. As these students work on these enriching activities, teachers remain alert for students who demonstrate signs of interest, creativity, task commitment, and advanced ability. As a student is so identified, the teacher encourages the student to move into a Type III activity, using either the resources of the regular classroom or attending the special "resource room" until the project is completed.

On the basis of implementation studies in thirty Connecticut schools, Reis and Renzulli (1984) have been able to identify several key features that account for successful programs: thorough orientation of teachers, parents, and administrators; extensive planning by the local school team; inservice and administrative support; school-wide enrichment teams, composed of the principal, the resource teacher, classroom teachers, parents, and in some cases a student; developing in the entire staff a sense of ownership of the program; detailed orientation of the students; communication with prime interest groups; program flexibility; and evaluation and program monitoring.

The Triad/RDIM model seems to be a very productive means for providing interesting learning experiences. The obvious question arises again, however: why for only the top 20 percent?

Meeker's Structure of the Intellect Model Over the course of several decades, J. P. Guilford (1977) has been conducting research on and refining his "Structure of the Intellect" model of intelligence, represented by a three-dimensional cube. The three dimensions are the five *operations* of the intellect, the four *contents* of the intellect, and the six *classes*. Of these 120 possible intellectual abilities that result from the intersection of these three dimensions, ninety-six have been substantiated through testing. Mary Meeker and her associates (1985) have been able to validate twenty-six of those factored abilities as necessary for successful learning. Those twenty-six intellectual abilities have been used to develop several tests that have been very useful in identifying potentially gifted students, especially minority students. Meeker has found in her own work that Blacks, Hispanics, and

Native Americans score higher on some SOI measures than do white students. The SOI model has also been useful in diagnosing and prescribing for the developmental needs of the gifted.

Also, as Meeker (1985) notes, the SOI model can be used to develop curricula and instructional strategies. Through further analysis of the intellectual abilities, she has been able to identify some ninety specific thinking skills and suggest how they can be linked with school subjects in a developmental sequence. Her own analysis, for example, identifies four basic reasoning skills essential for language arts/reading: concept formation, differentiating concepts; comprehending verbal relations; and comprehending verbal systems. Eight enrichment reasoning skills are also identified: memory for implied meanings; judging verbal implications; problem solving; interpreting verbal meanings; using analogical ideas; creative writing; creative interpretations; and creative grammatics. Special workbooks have also been developed with individual and group tasks designed to improve cognition, memory, convergent production, divergent production, and evaluation.

Special Resources

The third general approach is to provide special resources—that is, special schools (such as the Bronx High School of Science), special summer programs, or special mentors for the gifted. Of these, mentoring perhaps deserves a more detailed examination here. The mentoring approach involves associating a gifted student with an adult mentor, who can serve as a role model, provide support and encouragement, and give the necessary direction on a one-to-one basis. As VanTassel-Baska notes, some mentoring programs are more highly structured, requiring a contract between mentor and student that stipulates the tasks to be accomplished, the types of supports provided, and a schedule for completion.

In a twenty-two-year longitudinal study of mentoring, Torrance (1984) found several results of mentorships: having a mentor makes a significant difference in creative achievement; more than half of the mentor relationships persisted for a number of years; many gifted students, especially the economically disadvantaged, will need help in identifying and affiliating with a mentor; and many mentors were able to help the student receive academic credit for self-directed learning by validating the student's competence and performance.

PROVIDING FOR MILDLY
HANDICAPPED LEARNERS

One of the recurring issues among those concerned with the education of the handicapped is how to categorize and label such learners. While earlier experts in the field seemed concerned with dividing the group into numerous categories, each with a special label, special teacher, and special program, the current trend seems to minimize such distinctions. In current practice, the group of handicapped individuals who can be educated in regular schools are usually identified as *mildly handicapped learners* and include children commonly categorized as educable mentally retarded, learning disabled, behavior disordered, mildly emotionally disturbed, and those with minimal brain dysfunction.

As explained in Chapter 4, Public Law 94–142 was landmark legislation that radically changed how the schools were to provide for these special students. Four basic rights and protections are specified in PL 94–142, as Macmillan (1982) analyzed the law: the right to due process in the classification and placement of learners; protection against discriminatory testing during assessment; placement in the least restrictive educational setting; and individualized educational programs. Programmatic responses to PL 94–142 in general have been of three types: early intervention programs; mainstreaming; and special curricula.

Early Intervention

Since the relationships between poverty environments and developmental learning problems have been clearly established, most early-intervention programs have focused on the children of the poor. Increasingly, such programs have attempted to reach infant children and their parents, on the theory that "the earlier, the better." A careful assessment of four such experimental projects for children who had not reached the age of twelve months indicated that by the age of three years, children in all the experimental programs surpassed all control groups on mean IQ scores (Ramey and Bryant, 1982). The greatest gains in IQ were achieved in the Milwaukee Project, which provided educational daycare, home visits, vocational training for parents, and periodic assessments: children from this project were thirty IQ points ahead of children in the control group.

One of the early childhood programs that seemed to achieve the greatest success was the Perry Preschool Program, which used the High/Scope Cognitively Oriented Curriculum (Hohman, Banet, and Weikart, 1979). In a survey of the research on a longitudinal study of children enrolled in the Perry Program, Schweinhart and his colleagues (1985) note several positive results when comparing members of this preschool group with a nonpreschool group: they stayed in school longer; scored better on tests of social competence; were less often classified as mentally retarded; spent fewer years in special education classes; were arrested less often; had higher levels of employment; had lower levels of welfare support; and (females) had fewer pregnancies as teenagers. In an interesting cost-benefit analysis of the program, the authors conclude that the return on initial investment was seven times the cost of one year of preschool education.

Their analysis of several preschool programs led them to identify these hallmarks of quality in preschool education for "at-risk" children: parent involvement; programmatic leadership by supervisors and directors; competent and enthusiastic teachers; an articulated curriculum of proven effectiveness; sound inservice training; and program evaluation.

Mainstreaming

Mainstreaming in general is the educational practice of integrating mildly handicapped learners into regular classrooms; one commonly used standard is that such integration should account for at least half of the learner's program if it is to count as mainstreaming. In addition to such integration, mainstreaming is often accompanied by the specification of Individualized Educational Programs (IEP) and the support of a multidisciplinary team.

How effective is mainstreaming? One of the most comprehensive of all the sound research on the issue available at the time (Semmel, Gottleib, and Robinson, 1979) yielded somewhat discouraging findings. The authors first of all found little evidence that mainstreaming practices resulted in superior academic performance, although they note that special education in general seems to have little effect regardless of how those services are delivered. Second, their review indicated that mainstreaming was not rectifying the racial imbalance that existed in self-contained "special" classes. Third, they discovered that regular teachers did not modify their teaching styles and strategies to accommodate the added diversity resulting from the placement of handicapped children. Finally there was no conclusive evidence that mainstreaming increased the social acceptance of mildly retarded pupils. A more recent review by Macmillan, Keogh, and Jones (1986) reached the same conclusion: simply placing mildly handicapped children into regular grades without special treatment is likely to result in low peer acceptance for most of those children.

All experts in the field seem to reach the same conclusion: simply placing the mildly handicapped in regular classrooms does not accomplish very much. But neither do special classes.

Special Curricula

The hope is that curricular modifications will make an impact. In general, most curricula for the mildly handicapped have emphasized the development of the basic skills, along with a broader concern for improving social skills, helping handicapped learners manage their own behavior, and improving their cognitive skills.

This last emphasis on the cognitive skills of the mildly handicapped seems especially promising, since recent research has provided some productive insights into the special learning problems of the learning handicapped. A review of such research suggests that the following specific cognitive deficiencies are prevalent among this group: they are deficient in attention; have poor short-term memory; make inadequate use of memory strategies; have slower perceptual speed; are less efficient at categorizing incoming data into chunks; fail to organize input efficiently; use memory rehearsal strategies inefficiently; and cannot plan, select, sequence, and evaluate the use of such strategies.

As a consequence, several leaders in the field have been developing and implementing special instructional programs aimed at such deficiencies. For example, Douglas and her colleagues at McGill have developed a program designed for the cognitive training of hyperactive children emphasizing the role of "executive operations"—analysis, reflection, planning, and monitoring. Their research indicates that the program has a very positive impact on such children (see Douglas, 1980). After reviewing all the pertinent research on cognitive training, Macmillan, Keogh, and Jones (1986) reach this conclusion: "From a number of perspectives, then, there is evidence that cognitive training approaches are useful and effective interventions for many mildly impaired learners" (p. 697).

BILINGUAL EDUCATION

Perhaps no area of the school's curriculum has been the subject of such vehement controversy as bilingual education. As indicated in Chapter 4, bilingual educational programs were institutionalized in the law primarily as a result of political forces. The political controversies surrounding bilingual education continue, with partisans unable to agree about several issues. The ongoing controversy has revolved around four issues: What is bilingual education? How extensive is the need for special education for those with limited English proficiency (LEP)? To what extent should local districts have flexibility in responding to those needs? Is bilingual education effective for such students? These four issues seem to provide a useful framework for the following discussion.

What Is Bilingual Education?

Central to understanding all the controversy is having some clear understanding of several complex and somewhat ambiguous terms. As noted below, much of the controversy focuses on matters of definition. In order to be as objective as possible, the following definitions have been drawn from a current review of the literature (chiefly from Fillmore and Valadez, 1986).

Submersion Programs. These are "sink-or-swim" approaches—essentially nonprograms that make no effort to accommodate the special needs of LEP students.

English as a Second Language (ESL) Programs. These are formal courses that teach English as a foreign language to non-native speakers. In the strictest sense of the term, such courses should not be categorized as "bilingual education."

Bilingual Education. The two significant characteristics of bilingual education, as Fillmore and Valadez (1986) define the term, are these: instruction is given in two languages—English (in the United States) and the home language of the LEP student; and instruction in English is given in a way that permits students to learn it as a second language. As will be noted below, the definition of the term has become a matter of much controversy.

Bilingual Transition Programs. There are several types of transitional programs, whose chief goal is to enable LEP students to move as quickly as possible into an all-English program of studies; dual language in-instruction is offered only until LEP students have acquired enough English to deal with instruction in English.

Bilingual Maintenance Programs. In maintenance programs, the goal is to develop proficiency in both languages; students remain in these programs even after they have achieved proficiency in English.

How Extensive Is the Need?

Partisans in the debate about bilingual education cannot even agree about the extent of the need. In a report to Congress in April, 1986, the Department of Education reported that between 1.2 million and 1.7 million students in the United States were likely to benefit from bilingual education, in contrast with its 1982 estimate of 2.4 million. Several leaders in the field of bilingual education considered that estimate much too low, with some putting the figure as high as five million students. (See the April 9, 1986 issue of *Education Week* for a summary of the "battle of the numbers.") One of the basic problems, obviously, is how to determine which students should be counted. While the Department of Education used a cut-off score of the 20th percentile on English-proficiency tests (in addition to ten other criteria), critics maintained that higher cut-off scores should be used.

How Much Flexibility Should Local Districts Have?

Intense argument also rages about the issue of local autonomy: to what extent should the federal government limit the types of programs offered by local school districts? Certain constraints were imposed on local districts in the 1974 version of the Bilingual Education Act (Title VII of the Elementary and Secondary Education Act). Its key elements are expressed in this portion of the law:

> . . . there is instruction given in, and study of, English and, to the extent necessary to allow a child to progress effectively through the educational system, the native language of the children of limited English-speaking ability, and such instruction is given with appreciation of the cultural heritage of such children, and with respect to elementary school instruction, such instruction shall to the extent necessary be in all courses or subjects of study which will allow a child to progress effectively through the educational system. [Sec. 703, (a) (4) (A)]

However, the 1984 Bilingual Education Act was even more specific about the limitations of "transitional" programs, specifically requiring "instruction in the child's native language" sufficient to achieve competence in the English language.

This definition, in the eyes of Secretary of Education William J. Bennett, was too restrictive for local school districts; he believed they needed more flexibility since, in his view, there was not sufficient evidence to support specific bilingual approaches. He first attempted unilaterally to change the definition, until legal advisers pointed out that he had no such power. He then decided that a change in definition was not needed, since the 1984 act empowered him to grant up to 4 percent of allocated funds to "special alternative-instructional programs." At the time of publication of this work, he had proposed new legislation which would eliminate the 4 percent cap and make Title VII programs available, within the limits of the law, for any type of instructional approach which a local educational agency considered appropriate. Several applauded his stand as an attempt to increase local autonomy; many of those supporting "flexibility" were also quite open in their objective to maintain English as an official language of the country. Others attacked his stand as an ill-disguised attempt to undermine bilingual education; some went so far as to accuse him of bias against non-English-speaking minorities.

Is Bilingual Education Effective?

Even though Secretary Bennett and several of his supporters seemed to believe that there was not sufficient research evidence to support bilingual education, a careful review of the evidence would suggest otherwise. One of the special problems in resolving this issue is the quality of the research: after reviewing three hundred studies in bilingual education, Baker and De Kanter (1981) were able to identify only twenty-eight that met their standards for methodological adequacy. Willig (1985) puts the matter this way:

> A major result of the current synthesis has been the revelation that bilingual education has been badly served by a predominance of research that is inadequate in design and that makes inappropriate comparisons of children in bilingual programs to children who are dissimilar in many crucial respects. (p. 312)

What do methodologically sound studies reveal about the issue? After performing a meta-analysis of the twenty-eight studies previously identified by Baker and De Kanter, Willig found that students in bilingual programs, when compared with students in "submersion" programs, achieved significantly better results in the following areas: reading in English; language in English; mathematics in English; and total English. For tests not administered in English, significant gains were found in listening comprehension, reading, writing, total language, mathematics, social studies, and attitudes toward school or self.

Insights into specific instructional approaches were yielded by two major studies (Fisher and Guthrie, 1984; Tikunoff, 1983). In general, these two studies identified three "significant instructional features." First, the effective teachers in bilingual programs used many of the same skills identified as effective in regular classes; maintained a strong academic focus; allocated most of class time to academic work; and communicated clear intentions and high expectations. Second, the effective bilingual teachers used the students' native language extensively for instruction; they did not use it only occasionally or only for trivial matters. Finally, they made extensive use of the students' culture in interpreting student behavior and in modifying instruction.

APPLICATIONS

1. Some have argued that all learning is individualized: the learner makes individual meaning out of what is learned. They continue by disparaging the need for any type of individualized or adaptive instruction, contending that group-paced learning can be just as effective. How would you respond to such an argument?

2. Identify a subject or grade level you know best. Which of the adaptive approaches do you think would work best? Explain your choice and the reasons supporting it.

3. Some have suggested that the knowledge about learning styles will produce an "educational revolution." Others are much less sanguine about the possibilities, pointing out that the research so far has not yielded significant gains for learning-styles adaptations. As you review the models described and analyze the research findings, what position do you take regarding this issue?

4. Several in the field have criticized the Dunns' "Learning Style Inventory" and other similar instruments that place too much emphasis on environmental considerations. They argue that such matters are trivial. As you analyze your own learning style, do you find that such considerations are important? Do you think it would be useful for educators to assess these matters?

5. Suppose you were not limited by laws such as PL 94–142 that mandate mainstreaming. As an educational leader, would you use mainstreaming in your school? On what grounds would you justify your position?

REFERENCES

Anderson, L. W. (1985). A retrospective and prospective view of Bloom's "Learning for Mastery." In M. C. Wang and H. J. Walberg (eds.), *Adapting instruction to individual differences*, pp. 254–268. Berkeley, CA: McCutchan.

Baker, K. A., and De Kanter, A. A. (1981). *Effectiveness of bilingual education: A review of the literature.* Washington, DC: U.S. Department of Education.

Bangert, R. L., Kulik, J. A., and Kulik, C. C. (1983). Individualized systems of instruction in secondary schools. *Review of Educational Research, 53,* 143–158.

Bilingual Education Act. (August 21, 1974). (Title VII, ESEA). Public Law 93–380, 20 U.S.C. 800b.

Boyer, E. L. (1983). *High school: A report on secondary education in America.* New York: Harper & Row.

Brooks, M. (April 1986). Curriculum development from a constructivist perspective. Paper presented at annual conference of the American Educational Research Association, San Francisco.

Cinquino, D. (1980). An evaluation of a philosophy program with 5th and 6th grade academically talented students. *Thinking, 2* (3, 4), 79–83.

Commission on the Reorganization of Secondary Education. (1918). *Cardinal principles of secondary education.* Washington, DC: U.S. Government Printing Office.

Committee of Ten. (1893). *Report of the Committee of Ten on Secondary School Students.* Washington, DC: National Education Association.

Corno, L., and Snow, R. E. (1986). Adapting teaching to individual differences among learners. In M. C. Wittrock (ed.), *Handbook of research on teaching* (3rd Ed.), pp. 605–629. New York: Macmillan.

Daurio, S. P. (1979). Educational enrichment versus acceleration: A review of the literature. In W. C. George, S. J. Cohn, and J. C. Stanley (eds.), *Educating the gifted: Acceleration and enrichment.* Baltimore: Johns Hopkins University Press.

Douglas, V. I. (1980). Treatment and training approaches to hyperactivity: Establishing internal and external control. In C. V. Whalen and B. Henker (eds.), *Hyperactive children: The social ecology of identity and treatment.* New York: Academic Press.

Dunn, R., Dunn, K., and Price, G. E. (1978). *Learning Style Inventory.* Lawrence, KA: Price Systems.

Education Week. (April 9, 1986). Administration cuts estimate of bilingual need, p. 1.

Fillmore, L. W., and Valadez, C. (1986). Teaching bilingual learners. In M. C. Wittrock (ed.), *Handbook of research on teaching* (3rd Ed.), pp. 648–685. New York: Macmillan.

Fisher, C. W., and Guthrie, L. F. (1984). Significant bilingual instructional features study. San Francisco: Far West Laboratory.

Glatthorn, A. A. (1980). *A guide for developing an English curriculum for the eighties.* Urbana, IL: National Council of Teachers of English.

Good, T. L., and Stipek, D. J. (1983). Individual differences in the classroom: A psychological perspective. In G. D. Fenstermacher and J. I. Goodlad (eds.), *Individual differences and the common curriculum,* pp. 9–43. (82nd yearbook of the National Society for the Study of Education, Part 1.) Chicago: University of Chicago Press.

Goodlad, J. I. (1984). *A place called school: Prospects for the future.* New York: McGraw-Hill.

Gregorc, A. (1982). *Style delineator.* Maynard, MA: Gabriel Systems.

Grinder, R. E., and Nelsen, E. A. (1985). Individualized instruction in American pedagogy. In M. C. Wang and H. J. Walberg (eds.), *Adapting instruction to individual differences,* pp. 24–43. Berkeley, CA: McCutchan.

Guilford, J. P. (1977). *Way beyond the IQ.* Great Neck, NY: Creative Synergetic Associates.

Hohman, M., Banet, B., and Weikart, D. P. (1979). Young children in action: A manual for preschool educators. Ypsilanti, MI: High/Scope Press.

Johnson, D. W., and Johnson, R. T. (1985). Cooperative learning and adaptive education. In M. C. Wang and H. J. Walberg (eds.), *Adapting instruction to individual differences,* pp. 105–134. Berkeley, CA: McCutchan.

Keefe, J. W. (1979). Learning styles: An overview. In J. W. Keefe (ed.), *Student learning styles: Diagnosing and prescribing programs,* pp. 1–18. Reston, VA: National Association of Secondary School Principals.

Kulik, J. A., and Kulik, C. C. (1984). Effects of acceleration on instruction. *Review of Educational Research, 54,* 409–425.

Macmillan, D. L. (1982). *Mental retardation in school and society* (2nd Ed.). Boston: Little Brown.

Macmillan, D. L., Keogh, B. K., and Jones, R. L. (1986). Special educational research on mildly handicapped learners. In M. C. Wittrock (ed.), *Handbook of research on teaching* (3rd Ed.), pp. 686–726. New York: Macmillan.

McCarthy, B. (1981). *The 4Mat system: Teaching to learning styles with right/left mode techniques* (2nd Ed.). Oak Brook, IL: EXCEL.

Meeker, M. N. (1985). SOI. In A. L. Costa (ed.), *Developing minds: A resource book for teaching thinking,* pp. 187–192. Alexandria, VA: Association for Supervision and Curriculum Development.

Meeker, M. N., Meeker, R., and Roid, G. (1985). *The basic SOI manual.* Los Angeles: WPS.

Ramey, C. T., and Bryant, D. M. (1982). Evidence for prevention of developmental retardation during infancy. *Journal of the Division of Early Childhood, 5,* 73–78.

Reis, S. M., and Renzulli, J. S. (April 1984). Key features of successful programs for the gifted and talented. *Educational Leadership, 41,* 28–34.

Renzulli, J. S. (1977). *The enrichment triad model: A guide for developing defensible programs for the gifted.* Mansfield Center, CT: Creative Learning.

Renzulli, J. S., Reis, S. M., and Smith, L. H. (1981). *The revolving door identification model.* Mansfield Center, CT: Creative Learning.

Rosenbaum, J. E. (1980). Social implications of educational grouping. In D. C. Berliner (ed.), *Review of Research in Education* (Vol. 8), pp. 361–404. Washington, DC: American Educational Research Association.

Schweinhart, L. J., Berrueta-Clement, J. R., Barnett, W. S., Epstein, A. S., and Weikart, D. P. (1985). The promise of early childhood education. *Phi Delta Kappan, 66,* 548–551.

Semmel, M. I., Gottlieb, J., and Robinson, N. M. (1979). Mainstreaming: Perspectives on educating handicapped children in the public schools. In D. C. Berliner (ed.), *Review of Research in Education* (Vol. 7), pp. 223–281. Washington, DC: American Educational Research Association.

Slavin, R. E. (1985). Team-assisted individualization: A cooperative learning solution for adaptive instruction in mathematics. In M. C. Wang and H. J. Walberg (eds.), *Adapting instruction to individual differences,* pp. 236–253. Berkeley, CA: McCutchan.

Stanley, J. C. (1978). Radical acceleration: Recent educational innovation at Johns Hopkins University. *Gifted Child Quarterly, 27,* 129–132.

Tikunoff, W. J. (1983). Significant bilingual features descriptive study. San Francisco: Far West Laboratory.

Torrance, E. P. (1984). *Mentor relationships: How they aid creative achievement, endure, change, and die.* Buffalo, NY: Bearly Limited.

VanTassel-Baska, J. (1985). Appropriate curriculum for the gifted. In J. Feldhusen (ed.), *Toward excellence in gifted education*, pp. 45–67. Denver: Love Publishing.

Walberg, H. J. (1986). Syntheses of research on teaching. In M. C. Wittrock (ed.), *Handbook of research on teaching* (3rd Ed.), pp. 214–229. New York: Macmillan.

Wang, M. C., Gennari, P., and Waxman, H. C. (1985). The adaptive learning environments model: Design, implementation, and effects. In M. C. Wang and H. J. Walberg (eds.), *Adapting instruction to individual differences*, pp. 160–190. Berkeley, CA: McCutchan.

Wang, M. C., and Walberg, H. J. (1983). Adaptive instruction and classroom time. *American Educational Research Journal, 20,* 601–626.

Waxman, H. C., Wang, M. C., Anderson, V. A., and Walberg, H. J. (1984). *Adaptive education and student outcomes.* Pittsburgh: University of Pittsburgh Learning Research and Development.

Willig, A. C. (1985). A meta-analysis of selected studies on the effectiveness of bilingual education. *Review of Educational Research, 55,* 269–317.

Name Index

Subject Index